BY THE POWER
VESTED IN ME

BY THE POWER
VESTED IN ME

How Experts Shape
Same-Sex Marriage Debates

MICHAEL STAMBOLIS-RUHSTORFER

Columbia University Press
New York

Columbia University Press
Publishers Since 1893
New York   Chichester, West Sussex

Library of Congress Cataloging-in-Publication Data
Names: Stambolis-Ruhstorfer, Michael, author.
Title: By the power vested in me : how experts shape same-sex marriage
    debates / Michael Stambolis-Ruhstorfer.
Description: New York : Columbia University Press, [2025] |
    Includes bibliographical references and index.
Identifiers: LCCN 2024050276 | ISBN 9780231202220 (hardback) |
    ISBN 9780231202237 (trade paperback) | ISBN 9780231554459 (ebook)
Subjects: LCSH: Same-sex marriage—Law and legislation—United States. |
    Same-sex marriage—Law and legislation—France. | Sexual minorities—
    Legal status, laws, etc.—United States. | Sexual minorities—
    Legal status, laws, etc.—France. | Expertise.
Classification: LCC K698.5 .S73 2025 | DDC 346.4401/68—dc23/eng/20250306

Cover design: Elliott S. Cairns

GPSR Authorized Representative: Easy Access System Europe,
Mustamäe tee 50, 10621 Tallinn, Estonia, gpsr.requests@easproject.com

—To my family

CONTENTS

ACKNOWLEDGMENTS

I owe a debt of gratitude to so many people, individually and collectively, for making this, my first book, possible. I fear I will forget someone but thank them for their indulgence and hope they know that I am grateful for their support even if I did not name them. Importantly, I acknowledge that the labor of many people I've never met allowed me to conduct this research: the librarians who catalogued the databases, the archivists of previous generations, the clerk who gave advice to a judge behind the scenes that left a trace for me to analyze, and the people who kept the technology working, my working spaces clean, and the trains running on time.

This book is about experts, decision-makers, and the people they interact with. It's also a book about gay families. I would like to take this opportunity to thank them—the lovers, partners, parents, grandparents, siblings, and everyone else—for their bravery. I would also like to thank the extraordinary communities and the chosen families that supported them. Despite state repression, social stigma, and a host of other challenges, LGBTQ people forged their relationships anyway, carving out a space for themselves, changing the world in the process. There is still plenty of work to be done, and change is never unidirectional. May we never forget the lessons of our queer elders. I also thank the lawmakers, judges, lawyers, and their staff, as well as the activists and ordinary citizens who worked—and continue to work—tirelessly over many decades to make life better for LGBTQ people in the United States and France, doing so at immense cost. And, of course, thank you to the experts who contributed to that process.

Many thanks go to the people of all ideological and political stripes who responded to my request for interviews and who we were willing to share their stories with me. They generously offered me their time, and I hope that this book does justice to their experiences. Also, I appreciate the incredibly patient and helpful staff at the California State Archives who helped me understand the complicated catalogue and sift through hours of VHS recordings of legislative hearings to find what I was looking for. Thank you to Texas and France for putting many of the recordings of your legislative hearings online.

I was lucky to have met Abigail Saguy as a graduate student at UCLA. She was and continues to be an incredible mentor. She showed me the ropes, took me seriously, and offered some of the best advice I've ever received about what it means to be a sociologist. Her faith in my ability, especially when I didn't have faith in myself, helped me tackle the tricky and daunting work that went into this book. She is the kind of mentor I aspire to be. I am also deeply grateful to Eric Fassin whose guidance and access to the French field gave me insight into the role of experts there thanks, in part, to his personal experience in these debates.

Thank you to Daniel Sabbagh and Frédérique Matonti for writing thoughtful, incisive, and engaging evaluations of early drafts of this manuscript. Those perspectives gave me the feedback I needed to take my analysis to the next level. Ed Walker, Hannah Landecker, and Juliet Williams were so encouraging throughout the research and writing process. In many ways, they helped me understand the sociological question I was trying to analyze when I couldn't see it yet for myself.

Other faculty at UCLA whose teaching and mentorship helped me become the sociologist I am today include Gail Kligman, Megan Sweeney, Aaron Panofsky, Stefan Timmermans, Bill Roy, and Gabriel Rossman. Mignon Moore, whom I was very fortunate to work with there, was especially encouraging. By offering me the opportunity to co-author an article with her, she helped me understand what good research on queer families can look like. I am also indebted to UCLA sociology staff members, Wendy Fujinami and Allan Hill, whose patience and guidance through the bureaucracy was indispensable. Judith Ezekiel, who mentored my first MA in Toulouse, was the person who encouraged me to consider applying to UCLA and who nourished my desire to become a sociologist. She also offered me a copy of *Writing for Social Scientists*, by Howard Becker. That was a very good idea.

It is difficult to describe just how important the friends I made in graduate school were to making this book come to fruition: Laura Enriquez, William Rosales, and Lisa Kietzer. I never would have gotten through graduate school without them. I'm also immensely grateful to the emotional and intellectual support of Kjerstin Gruys, Diya Bose, Susila Gurusami, Rebecca DiBernardo, Zach Griffen,

Pamela Pricket, John O'Brien, Danielle Wondra, Lianna Hartmour, Anthony Ocampo, Elena Shih, Isaac Speer, Manuela Salcedo Robledo, Michal Raz, Josselin Tricou, and many others. A particular mention is deserved for Pauline Delage. We embarked on our sociological journeys together in Toulouse in 2006.

This research would not have been possible materially without the financial support of grants I received from institutions along the way, specifically the National Science Foundation (DDRI, Law and Social Sciences Division, Grant No. SES 1226663); the Chateaubriand Fellowship program organized by the French Ministry of Foreign Affairs and the Fulbright Foundation; the UCLA Center for European and Russian Studies; and the UCLA Graduate Division. The support from institutional homes while I was working was indispensable. In particular, the UCLA College of Letters and Science Division of Social Sciences, the Department of Sociology, the École des Hautes Études en Sciences Sociales, and the Institut de recherche interdisciplinaire sur les enjeux sociaux.

The fieldwork for this project was extensive and time-consuming. I would like to thank all of the people who hosted me while I was doing interviews and observations in Paris, Baltimore, Washinton, DC, Sacramento, Los Angeles, and elsewhere. Françoise Lacroix offered me her guest bedroom on many occasions.

Many people were crucial to the successful completion of this book. First among them are the three anonymous reviewers. Their comments were so constructive and precise that I was able to use them to make significant, and I hope satisfactory, changes. I'm convinced the argument is stronger. Thanks, of course, goes to my editor, Eric Schwartz, at Columbia University Press, as well as Lowell Frye and Alyssa Napier, for shepherding the manuscript along the way and for keeping me on task.

I have been very lucky to receive feedback and advice from other sociologists and social scientists over the more than a decade that went into this project at conferences, at seminars, and in informal meetings. Thank you to Mieke Verloo, Jan Willem Duyvendak, Erik Bleich, Kathy Hull, Hugo Bouvard, Christophe Bertossi, Mathieu Trachman, Wilfried Rault, Guillaume Marche, Massimo Prearo, Josselin Tricou, Roman Kuhar, Michèle Lamont, Graeme Hayes, Olivier Fillieule, Christophe Broqua, Stefan Vogler, Ghassan Moussawi, Salvador Vidal-Ortiz, Héctor Carrillo, Steven Epstein, Shai Dromi, Timothy O'Brien, Amy Steinbugler, Virginie Descoutures, Jérôme Courduriès, Martine Gross, Jennifer Merchant, Nancy Naples, Myra Marx Ferree, Iddo Tavory, and many others. I'm very fortunate to have had David Paternotte constantly telling me he was skeptical of my decision to compare the United States and France, pushing me to defend my choice.

Thank you as well to colleagues and friends at Université Toulouse—Jean Jaurès and Université Bordeaux Montaigne for their encouragement, including Eléana Sanchez, Étienne Février, Mathilde Bertrand, and Laurence Mullaly. I would also like to thank the many students who provided me with insights in seminars, classes, and meetings. Colleagues at the gender studies research network in Toulouse, Arpège, have also given me much needed support.

I am grateful to Melanie Heath, Tina Fetner, and Michelle Dion for inviting me to participate at the *Intersections: Social Policy and Sexuality Workshop* they organized at McMaster University in 2018. Over the course of three days, I had the opportunity to exchange about the book with colleagues whose work inspires me. In addition to the organizers, those colleagues include Mary Bernstein, Jyoti Puri, Ashley Currier, Régis Schlagdenhauffen, Jamie Budnick, Vrushali Patil, Jessica Fields, and Megan Carroll.

Some of the most helpful and vital feedback for this book came on versions of drafts and proposals and other parts of the manuscript. Thank you to Lisa Wade, Ashley Currier, Lucie Fremlova, Nicole Iturriaga, Marie Berry, and Léo Cerosky. There is not enough space in this section to say just how much I owe Koen Slootmaeckers. His kind encouragement, coupled with his absolutely ruthless eye for what makes a mediocre idea better, make him the best kind of friend one could ask for.

This book has also been a reflection on the people who taught me how to write, staring with my aunt Vicki Stambolis, a high school English teacher. My high school English teacher at the Baltimore School for the Arts, Mr. Gross, pushed me in ways I needed. My French teacher, Monsieur Tabegna, is the person who started it all. While an undergraduate at Dickinson College, I learned how to write thanks to Judy Gill, Neil Weissman, Nancy Mellerski, and Sharon Stockton.

And let me end by thanking those people to whom, in one way or another, this book belongs.

To the feline "research assistants" who show up in my yard and stare at me while I write.

To my aunties Liz and Sarah, who also raised me in many ways and nourished my curiosity and who trailblazed along with the rest of the Baltimore lesbians, making a space for queer families to thrive.

To the host family I lived with in Toulouse when I spent my junior year abroad. That experience sparked my sociological imagination, setting me on this particular career path. Our lives couldn't have been more different. When, a few days after I arrived, you told me that my family "could not exist in France," unbeknownst to both of us, you planted a seed.

To my dad, Tommy Ruhstorfer, the German auto mechanic who was happy to let me read books in the cars he was fixing when I was with him every other weekend. To Christi, Ryan, Angie, Thomas, and my Virginia family.

To my duchesse Sam Buker for letting me be "inspired" by her English homework in high school and who has been an ally ever since. Also, thank you for using your connections in DC so that I could have some interviews with experts who would have otherwise ignored my requests.

To Katie Lozier, who always believed in me.

To my French family and its international mix who has taught me their ways and opened their arms to me. To my nieces and nephews, all of whom do incredible things and let me feel like a cool uncle.

To Cameron, Auntie Lynn, Mimi and Papou, and Dominique.

To my parents, Lisa Stambolis and Lania D'Agostino. There are no words to express just how much I owe this book to you. I wouldn't have been interested in the question of gay family debates if it weren't for our very gay family. I wouldn't have been capable of writing it if you hadn't insisted I go to college, given me the means to get through, and then gently encouraged me not to drop out after the first semester and then gently persuaded me again, eight years later, not to drop out of graduate school.

To my sister, Anias Stambolis-D'Agostino, who keeps me real. She is a rock and an inspiration. Also, I would still like her to teach me how not to procrastinate. She has that gift. I do not. Thanks for letting me be your big brother.

And finally, to my husband, Nicolas Durand. This book would never have come out of my computer if it weren't for you. The talks, the meals, the long walks, the comfort, and the (much needed) teasing, I mean, "support," about my very slow writing progress. You've put up with me talking about how I'm "working on my book" for so long now that I was almost tempted not to turn this manuscript in. But don't worry. Thank you, mon amour.

BY THE POWER
VESTED IN ME

INTRODUCTION

On What Grounds? How Same-Sex Marriage Experts
Establish Power in Their Countries

I
n a tense room at the U.S. District Court in San Francisco, lawyers called
Edmund Eagan, chief economist for the City and County of San Francisco, to the stand. With precision, he explained to the court that legalizing same-sex marriage is good for local economies.[1] The wedding industry profits
and tax revenue increases. Progressive attorneys hoped his testimony would convince the judge presiding over this January 2010 trial that claims about the social
harms of same-sex marriage were wrong. Two years later, across the Atlantic in
Paris, a famous psychoanalyst, Jean-Pierre Winter, spoke to legislators about the
Oedipal complex and the complementarity of the sexes. To authorize gay and
lesbian couples to marry and raise children would constitute a "state lie" that
denies biological realities, he warned.[2] Attempting to convince French legislators
to scrap plans to legalize same-sex marriage and adoption, Winter claimed that
having a mother and father is crucial for a child's psychological well-being. In
both the United States and France, decision-makers grappled with the same divisive social issue—the marriage and parenting rights of same-sex couples—while
seeking information from "experts" to inform and justify their decisions. Yet,
despite dealing with the same legal questions, the kinds of people they relied on,
from economists and psychoanalysts to priests and ordinary community members, were remarkably different. This book traces these differences and explains
why some types of "experts" are ubiquitous in one context but absent in the other
and why some types of "expertise," such as empirical social science in the United
States and abstract theory in France, are predominant. This is the story of how
certain groups of people end up with an immense power to shape whether or not
gay families get equal rights.

Drawing back the curtain on the world of "experts," it asks a broader question about how, when, and why these people obtain the authority to influence democratic politics while others do not. Their role in our civic lives should not be taken for granted. Indeed, the quotation marks here signify that the meaning of "expert" and "expertise" is unsettled and itself the subject of controversy as people strongly disagree about whose voices should be uplifted and on what grounds. However, for ease of legibility in the remainder of the text, quotation marks are generally not used. Readers should keep them in mind, nevertheless, and not assume everyone shares the same definition of experts. A common misconception portrays them as a qualified group of neutral scientists cloistered away in universities that decision-makers call on when they need advice on complicated issues. We will see how politics, money, fame, emotions, and cultural taboos—and not just scientific or technical merit—determine who influences judges and lawmakers. This book analyzes the wide range of people, from ordinary citizens to renowned professors, and their testimony in major court cases and legislative proceedings. Drawing on seventy-two interviews with key people involved in expert testimony, over three hundred hours of ethnographic observation, and legal and media archives, it focuses on same-sex marriage debates from 1990 to 2015 in the United States and France.[3] The divergent paths to legalization in these countries make them ideal for thinking about the political role of experts.

In the United States, court cases, culminating in the Supreme Court's landmark *Obergefell v. Hodges* (2015), have been one of the most successful avenues to legalize same-sex marriage.[4] In these trials, empirical, peer-reviewed social science of all kinds, delivered by academics and professionals, was the most common type of expertise. For example, attorneys on one side sought out professors to present data on the economic benefits of same-sex marriage and the good outcomes of children raised by same-sex couples. Their rivals attempted to find academics who would claim that the research suggests legalizing same-sex marriage would cause social harms and hurt children. In addition to these battles over which side had the most scientific credibility, courts were also the venue for gay plaintiffs to tell moving stories about how their love merited legal recognition. Such accounts were even more prominent in American state legislatures where hearings became forums for storytelling.

In France, which ultimately legalized access to marriage and adoption for same-sex couples in 2013, more than a decade after civil partnerships, parliament was the prime venue for expertise. As impassioned anti-same-sex marriage protestors marched in Paris, lawmakers held months of nationally televised hearings with renowned academics and public intellectuals that riveted the media. Much of what they said was detached from the lived experiences of same-sex couples. For instance, instead of empirical social science or personal stories, these experts, many of whom were asked to testify because of their fame or personal connections to lawmakers, debated abstract theories about family and sexuality from the canonical French psychoanalyst Jacques Lacan and anthropologist Claude Lévi-Strauss. Even when leaders of religious groups were invited to testify, a rarity in a country that prides itself on strict secularism, they used the same psychoanalytic language to warn against the bill.

That American and French decision-makers draw on contrasting expertise is not the result of some national affinity for empirical science in the United States or passion for, say, psychoanalysis in France. Rather, this book argues that these patterns are caused by the way experts and decision-makers interact with one another as they navigate their respective fields whose shape and power dynamics are distinct in each country. First, courts, which dominate the U.S. debate, and legislatures, which dominate the French debate, use different metrics to weigh the value of expertise and who can legitimately deliver it. Second, the academic and professional fields where conservative and progressive experts compete for funding and prestige are not structured in the same way. This means, for example, that anti-same-sex marriage experts in France have wielded more power in key disciplines, such as law and anthropology, relative to their peers in the United States. Third, interactions between experts and decision-makers in the United States are mediated through think tanks, amplifying voices backed by organizational resources, while experts in France have intimate relationships with politicians who open their access to the debate. Finally, the large, American federal system generates both a demand for and capacity to produce detailed empirical information, while the smaller, centralized French system creates little opportunity for family law experts to invest in research beyond theory.

At a time marked by growing public distrust of experts—portrayed as out of touch and disconnected from democratic will—fueled by critiques from across the political spectrum, understanding why some people get to speak from a position of legitimacy is crucial. Rather than simply reflect the social class of experts on the one hand or an inherent value of their knowledge on the other, their presence in political and legal debates is the product of social interactions conditioned by institutions and culture. Experts produce a specific kind of currency, which I call *expert capital*, that lawmakers, judges, lawyers, journalists, activists, and other political actors covet. They use the credibility and aura of authority this special capital gives them to advance their particular agendas when lobbying, crafting law, shaping public opinion, and much more. Its value, availability, and form depend on the context and the issue at hand. This is why some experts, such as economists or psychoanalysts, might be highly sought after in one country but worthless in another. As we will see, looking at political debates in this way has implications for understanding the fraught role of experts in contemporary democracies more generally. It allows us to unpack a number of important questions, including, for example, the conditions under which ordinary citizens can provide expertise alongside elite, credential experts, or the unintended consequences for both science and politics that stem from sustained interaction between scientific experts and decision-makers.

EXPERTS MATTER

Experts have always provoked political and cultural ripples. In 2020, those ripples grew to the size of overwhelming waves as people across the globe scrambled to react to the threat of a deadly epidemic. Whether to ride those waves to new heights of popular appeal or swim against them, politicians and experts alike navigated very choppy water. For example, U.S. president Joseph Biden stated that under his administration, "we are letting science speak again."[5] Demonstrating this commitment, Biden elevated the White House Office of Science and Technology Policy to a cabinet-level position and publicly undid Trump-era directives restricting the public speech of scientists working for federal agencies. At the same time, other leaders, such as French president Emmanuel Macron, alternated between praising and bemoaning the advice of the scientific committees they themselves created to combat the epidemic. Their political rivals of all stripes walked a fine rhetorical line between denouncing a government of experts against the popular will on the one hand and the dangers of antiscientific conspiracy theories on the other. This book interrogates this uncomfortable, confusing, and consequential intersection of experts and politics, of which responses to the COVID-19 pandemic are only the latest dramatic example.

Decision-makers—and those who pressure them—confront technical, ethical, and political uncertainty when navigating controversial issues. They often seek information they hope will provide guidance or authority. But what kind of knowledge influences them to make a decision about questions whose very nature is a source of disagreement? Despite their classification as either primarily technical or purely moral, some social problems—especially those about the meaning, impact, or survival of human life and relationships—require policymakers to negotiate contested scientific and ethical terrain. Centering these questions, this book examines how and why experts, broadly defined, participate in the high-stakes issues of marriage and parenting for same-sex couples.

The interactions between experts, decision-makers, activists, and other political actors are important. Research shows that their relationships have consequences for a variety of contentious political decisions, of which same-sex marriage is only one example. These include the enacting of climate change mitigation efforts, the legalization of abortion, and vaccination programs.[6] However, this book does not claim that experts are only important because of their impact on legal outcomes per se. Instead, it argues that experts also matter for other reasons. Indeed, they have the more elusive effect of shaping public opinion because of the way political forums and the media amplify their voices. They shape how the public and policymakers perceive, say, the threat of climate change, the reproductive autonomy of women, or the safety of vaccines, as well as the value of the information that informs these debates.[7] In addition, experts create powerful indirect effects because civil society groups and the state develop "knowledge infrastructure"—in the shape of, for example, funding regimes, organizations, and formalized relationships—that lasts well beyond any legal changes.[8] In return, knowledge production itself is constituted by the inputs the political field feeds back into those places where experts work. It is therefore important to focus on this fraught intermingling of influence between expertise and politics because that relationship has spillover effects with broader social implications.[9]

Current research tends to analyze some contentious issues, such as climate change, from the angle of "politicized science."[10] Because of the technical aspect of these debates, the role of science is taken for granted while the moral dimensions—and the people who produce moral expertise—may be overlooked.[11] Contentious issues with obviously religious implications, such as abortion or same-sex marriage, are typically analyzed from the angle of "morality politics,"[12] which may underestimate the role of scientific or technical knowledge in shaping abortion policy. This book questions that dichotomy by looking at a range of experts in same-sex marriage and parenting debates. Indeed, while moral and religious arguments are clearly identified as important for gay family rights, research also finds that elite academic expertise is also relevant in gay rights debates.[13] Expertise, especially when grounded in peer-reviewed science and backed by recognized disciplinary or professional organizations, can be persuasive. For example, a variety of social science, such as that focusing on the demographics of same-sex couples, their parenting, the outcomes of their children, and the social effects of legalizing same-sex marriage, appears central in gay marriage debates globally.[14] Both supporters and opponents of gay family rights claim the science supports them, as this book will show.[15] These advocates thus behave like those in other social movements, such as climate change activism, who engage in what could be called "expertise work."[16]

Expertise plays a role in advancing—or hindering—the evolution of policy on contentious issues because it is a part of the toolkit that advocates on either side use when arguing their points as they attempt to change policy and culture.[17] It is thus an integral, but sometimes overlooked, component of social movement strategies. Most political science on morality politics issues acknowledges that experts play a role but focuses primarily on other parts of the puzzle. These approaches mostly center on explaining legal outcomes—why certain reforms, such the legalization of abortion or the implementation of antidiscrimination legislation, succeed or fail—across contexts and time.[18] They highlight the dynamics of contention, such as political and legal opportunity structures, including political parties and their religious or secular affiliations, as well as legal and political institutional contexts.[19] While building on that work, this book shifts our focus to explaining how people produce and share expertise that activists, decision-makers, and other political actors use to reach their political goals.

EXPERTS, SOCIAL PROBLEM CONSTRUCTION, AND SOCIAL MOVEMENTS

Experts matter not only because of their role in drafting specific policies but also, and perhaps more importantly, because of their unique capacity to change the very definition of social problems they are called on to help resolve. Social scientists have identified how previously ignored phenomena become urgent social problems that draw critical scrutiny from media, policymakers, and the public.[20] Across a wide range of issues, from sexual harassment to autism, activists create coalitions with political and academic elites to transform things that once seemed normal into problems deserving political attention.[21] Same-sex marriage and parenting are examples of such social problem construction. Once unthinkable, over the last fifty years, they have evolved into major, controversial issues on the political agenda. We know that once an issue is identified, advocates on either side continue to work with experts to produce information to convince policymakers.[22] Scientific information can be especially effective—particularly in courts—because it can better withstand critical scrutiny and exude legitimacy.[23] For this reason, social movements invest in academic allies.[24] For example, in the case of climate change, environmentalists have relied on climatologists to provide them with data they can use to push for restrictions on carbon emissions in Europe and the United States.[25] Similarly, abortion rights activists have relied on public health professionals and psychologists to provide research about the mortality rates and negative health outcomes associated with illicit abortion.[26] This book examines how this coalition work with experts plays out for gay family rights in the United States and France.

Research on the political role of science suggests that this triangular relationship between activists, experts, and policymakers creates "epistemic communities" among people with the same political or intellectual outlook.[27] These groups create spaces for the exchange of ideas, strategies, and resources to better organize against those they oppose. Thus, for instance, climatologists and environmentalists in favor of carbon restrictions must compete against scientists and their political allies who deny that humans cause climate change.[28] These epistemic communities' capacity to push their agendas depends both on the power they wield within academic and political fields and on public perceptions of their credibility.[29] Some have suggested that if experts dominate their professional or academic fields, they can share their high status with their political and social movement allies.[30] Specifically, decision-makers may be more likely to believe experts whose claims represent the current consensus within their discipline. Revealing the significance of this effect, recent scholarship suggests that activists specifically try to influence the production of scientific knowledge so that they can claim that research supports their goals.[31]

In addition, the influence of well-financed nongovernmental organizations and think tanks allows epistemic communities to pool their resources despite marginalization they may face.[32] Indeed, perhaps because of such resources, although climate change doubters are a minority in the academic sphere, they continue to have an outsized voice in public debates.[33] This book will examine how scientific experts involved in gay family rights debates face marginalization—or not—within the academy and how they leverage relationships with state actors, professional organizations, activist groups, and think tanks to gain traction and shape policy. The sociologist Mieke Verloo suggests that more research needs to analyze this "epistemic dimension" of contentious politics.[34] This book therefore investigates how epistemic communities on both sides of controversial issues organize their efforts in distinct national and legal contexts.

The concept of epistemic communities emerges out of research on technical issues, finding ideological alliances of people within scientific communities and their links to activists and politicians in specific cultural contexts.[35] We can better understand these triangular relationships by considering how moral questions impact these interactions within epistemic communities, on the one hand, and how scientific questions shape the creation of knowledge on moral issues, on the other. This book aims to accomplish that goal by bringing research on gender and politics that suggests patterns of academic-activist "knowledge networks" in contentious policy debates that are similar to those identified by sociologists of politicized science.[36] Specifically, this work finds that feminist activists—and their opponents—engage in a variety of types of "knowledge work" to create information, including science, to gain legitimacy.[37] People within these networks not only share policy goals but, as the research on morality politics suggests, might also share worldviews that shape their involvement in politics.[38] Moreover, feminist scholarship shows how science itself—what counts as "scientific" knowledge, what groups have the power to produce it, whose assumptions it upholds—is socially constructed in ways that make it integral to social change and a target of mobilization.[39] When we analyze the role of experts in gay family debates, we should consider the way in which their fundamental values inform the way they produce their knowledge and collaborate with activists and policymakers. We also need a way of defining who, exactly, the experts are and conceptualizing what it is that makes their contribution unique.

EXPERT CAPITAL: AN INDUCTIVE, INTERACTIONAL, AND INSTITUTIONAL APPROACH TO THE SOCIOLOGY OF EXPERTS

To explain how and why specific categories of people and knowledge come to matter in contentious political debates, I develop here the concept of *expert capital.*[40] Drawing on field theory and Pierre Bourdieu's concepts of cultural and symbolic capital, I argue that expert capital is the unique power that imbues those who deploy it with a form of legitimacy, credibility, and authority that augments their claims within specific institutional contexts.[41] It is a scarce resource produced exclusively by particular kinds of people, called experts, whose profile and productive capacity—conditioned by their access to material resources (economic capital) and relationships (social capital)—varies systematically according to context. They can share it—or not—with people in other fields, including politicians, activists, journalists, and other groups. And they often do so through pipelines like think tanks and professional societies that specialize in collecting and distributing it. In this way, expert capital is a form of "objectified" cultural capital.[42] That is, it can be materialized physically. An expert's signature on an official report, a quote in a newspaper, and their presence in the hearing room are examples of this physical manifestation. Yet, because only experts can produce it, expert capital depends on their access to resources in their respective fields, their credentials, recognition from their peers, and a variety of other contingencies. That also makes it an "embodied cultural capital," indelibly attached to the experts themselves and their reputations.[43] Moreover, because of the way it has the potential to accrue legitimacy to those who deploy it, it is a type of symbolic capital, which sociologist David Swartz defines as "a power resource in the form of authority that persons carry and can accumulate but often is associated with the authority of positions."[44] As a result, it is a combination both of what experts contribute and who they are.

That expert capital is at once distinct from and always tied to the expert is both a key feature of how this specific kind of capital works and a cause of tension. As politicians or activists seek to take advantage of the expert capital of, say, researchers who publish in peer-reviewed journals, those experts must negotiate the risk that their participation in the political processes will undermine their academic credibility. As we will see, the value of expert capital derives in part from the reputations and statuses of experts and in particular on the specific perception that they are not doing politics.[45] Indeed, one of its strengths as a symbolic resource is that it can help the political or legal actors who use it to legitimate their decisions by claiming their stances are disinterested because they are supported by expertise.[46] Transferring expert capital is, therefore, a risky business because it brings experts into proximity with precisely the kinds of people and places that could damage its value. When thinking about just how tricky it is to share forms of embodied cultural capital, Bourdieu asks: "How can this capital, so closely linked to the person, be bought without buying the person and so losing the very effect of legitimation which presupposes the dissimulation of dependence?"[47] This book provides answers to that question by identifying these tensions and their consequences, along with their specificities in each country, both for experts and those who want their capital.

In order to make sense of the range of people I saw providing testimony and weighing in on same-sex marriage debates, I discovered it was necessary to use an inductive definition of experts and expertise. By defining all people heard by decision-making institutions as types of experts who bring specific forms of expert capital, my approach ensures that no one is overlooked or excluded from the analysis because they might not fit our assumptions of what experts look like. This perspective contrasts markedly with definitions that focus primarily on academics and professionals with technical knowledge whose intervention is presumed to be necessary and useful.[48] An exclusive focus on elite actors might miss how other people, such as ordinary citizens, activists, or religious representatives— whose knowledge is based on their lived experiences and other uncredentialed sources—are among the groups decision-makers solicit, elevating their voices in the process.[49] I borrow the sociologist Steven Epstein's notion of "lay experts" to categorize such groups and their role.[50] I do not presume that any of these experts are inherently qualified or valuable. Rather, building on the work of other sociologists who take a similar perspective, I conceptualize expertise as a form of intervention in an expert field organized by power dynamics that confer legitimacy and power unequally, giving some people—but not others—access to the debate.[51] I therefore consider all people heard by decision-makers as experts regardless of their qualifications or status and treat what they say as expertise.

It should be noted that Bourdieu was himself interested in a particular category of experts: scientists. He analyzed the shape and dynamics of the scientific field and developed rich understandings of the logics and power dynamics undergirding the work of scientists.[52] However, he did not systematically theorize the unique power that scientists—or other kinds of experts for that matter— produce for use in other fields, including politics or the law. In this regard, the concept of expert capital builds on these ideas but is specific. It focuses on the moments of interaction where people we call experts share their value with those who want it for their own—and in this case political and legal—purposes. In this way, it is a cross-field capital that allows experts and those who court them to leverage resources, status, and positions from one field into a useful capital in another, such as politics.

Whether it be because it can help them to win arguments in courts, boost the seriousness of an assertion, or bring emotional weight through storytelling, activists and politicians alike are interested in getting their hands on expert capital. But to do so, they must find ways to collaborate with experts who can produce it. Although activists can forge alliances with experts who share their ideological perspectives, sometimes through mediating groups like think tanks, experts are situated within their own fields that have their own dynamics.[53] For this reason, in addition to analyzing the institutions where people exchange expert capital, this book also studies the places where they produce it. Like political and scientific fields, I conceptualize the various fields where expertise on gay family rights is produced, such as the legal and mental health professional fields, as competitive and hierarchical. Within them, access to power, including symbolic and material resources, such as funding, disciplinary recognition, or professional promotion is unevenly distributed. Like other knowledge production fields on contentious subjects, political ideologies organize these hierarchies.[54] When experts of a particular stance dominate their field, they produce more research and prestige, potentially increasing the value of their expert capital relative to their ideological rivals, whose power is reduced.[55] This book thus looks at experts arguing for and against gay family rights and compares their relative power within their respective fields, which are best understood comparatively across national contexts.[56]

The exchange of expert capital takes place in an expert field. It is coterminous neither with the fields where different kinds of experts work and create their capital, such as the scientific or religious fields, nor with the fields where decision-makers make their decisions, such as the political and juridical fields.[57] Instead, the expert field is the space in which experts and political actors—which can include any people and entities working to shape the political process, such as elected officials, public officers, judges, lawyers, journalists, social movement organizations, and journalists—interact. Whether it be through briefs filed in courts or public administrations, articles in newspapers, testimony before lawmakers, or behind the scenes work with think tanks, it is in this arena that expert capital is at play. The boundaries and dynamics of the expert field are contingent on their specific national and historical contexts, just as are all the fields—political, juridical, scientific, and others—it intersects with. Because of these differences, the expert field and the value attributed to sorts of expert capital can look different in the United States and France even when lawmakers are dealing with the same legal questions.

In addition to being inductive, my theorization of expertise is also interactional. Expert capital is not inherently valuable but becomes so as the result of struggles between people who define it as such and do so within the constraints of their situations. Rather than assume that these experts and what they say are equally legitimate and audible, this book investigates how policymaking settings—such as courts and legislatures—and the particularities of national legal debates might confer different values and status on specific types of experts and expertise. It argues that the legitimacy, authority, and worthiness that undergird expert capital are contingent on the contexts in which different kinds of expertise are created and consumed.

This theorization builds on research growing out of Thomas Gieryn's idea that the value of expertise is rooted in the social environment rather than in its essential qualities.[58] Indeed, independent of the merits of different experts, certain kinds of information, such as economics or the physical sciences, might be perceived as more serious and worthy of following in certain policymaking contexts.[59] This approach allows us to see how experts interact with each other and negotiate the expert field without making a priori assumptions about their relative importance. In so doing, this book contributes to the call by Henri Bergeron—a sociologist of expertise, public policy, and health—for more research that looks empirically at how decision-makers perceive certain information as legitimate in specific contexts.[60]

Although they do not usually center on the specific role of experts, research in comparative politics shows that legal and political debates take nationally specific forms. We know that people staking claims in contentious political battles, from lawyers to lawmakers and activists, make arguments in order to justify their stances and processes.[61] To gain credibility, they draw on knowledge they hope will be convincing, relevant, and resonant in their "policy forums."[62] Specific cultural repertoires and frames, which vary systematically across locales, shape how people, including decision-makers and the public, process these issues.[63] This literature pays less attention to the specific mechanisms that shape both the value and availability of types of expertise across contexts. To overcome this gap, this book follows the idea of "civic epistemologies," developed by science and technology studies (STS) scholar Sheila Jasanoff, who finds that knowledge claims are deployed to make collective decisions in ways that follow nationally specific patterns.[64] In the United States, for example, an adversarial style of reasoning encourages competing parties to rally evidence against one other.[65]

Understanding these patterns requires that we look at the "institutional logics" of decision-making bodies—with more or less explicit rules about the role of expertise that constrain and enable how they can use evidence, testimony, and other information—within distinct national cultural contexts.[66] It also requires that we consider how authorities in different legal settings use specific ways of knowing, or what Stefan Vogler calls "civic logics," when making determinations in cases.[67] This book thus brings the insights on scholarship about the role of these institutional logics in policymaking processes across Europe and the United States to shed new light on the ways interest groups mobilize resources within the expert field.[68] More broadly, it looks at the social processes behind the production of knowledge claims where information based on, say, "objective" science and "subjective" experience or moral values compete and complement each other in decision-making institutions that endow them with specific kinds of value.

I am not the first to grapple with these questions. Indeed, understanding the nexus between experts and politics is a consistent line of inquiry in the sociology of science, knowledge, and technology and in the interdisciplinary field of STS. Several concepts tackle the political role of experts in fruitful ways, but they have limitations because they take a wide historical scope, focus exclusively on scientists and professionals, assume an inherent value of expertise, or do not fully engage with the notion of power. Looking at things from a broad level, with her concept of "coproduction," Jasanoff argues that science and policy are mutually constitutive.[69] Knowledge production practices enable ways of understanding reality that then frame political action, which in turn shapes how knowledge is produced by, for example, guiding the types of questions scientists ask. Focusing specifically on professions and professionals, such as doctors and lawyers, Andrew Abbott theorized that over time these groups compete with one another to create and defend the conditions that justify their exclusive right to make decisions and determine working conditions in particular social domains.[70] He calls this process "jurisdiction." One way to understand how a professional group holds onto or even expands its jurisdiction is by looking at how it establishes what Paul Starr calls "authority."[71] Mostly used to analyze the expanding social power of medical professionals, cultural "authority" describes the conditions that allow these professionals to frame problems in ways that make them best suited to solve them, leading the public to seek their advice and services.[72] While these concepts open the door for deeper critical analysis, by centering professional group dynamics, they tend to deal with only one part of the puzzle and do not enable us to capture the full picture.[73] Expert capital brings their insights together and pushes them forward by unpacking the processes that give experts—broadened to include people who are not just scientists and skilled professionals—their unique social power in particular political and cultural settings without essentializing them.

Another key building block of my theory that comes out of this area of research is an explanation for what makes experts feel reliable. Indeed, one of the main ways a group of experts—or people seeking to compete with them—comes to be taken seriously by the public and political actors is by gaining their trust. This notion, and the concepts related to it, are especially germane for understanding expert capital. Thinking about trust in the context of scientific knowledge production, Steven Shapin elaborated the idea of "credibility," which explains how scientists come to trust one another for the purposes of collaboration.[74] Unable to know everything themselves, they put faith in their peers. Exploring the political, cultural, and conflictual dimensions of this trust, Steven Epstein elaborated a theory of "credibility struggles" to describe how experts—with a specific focus on scientists, researchers, and people doing similar activities—work and compete to establish themselves and their claims as believable, legitimate, and authoritative.[75] As do I, he argues that this credibility can be established in many ways— from diplomas to " 'anointment' by the media"—depending on the situation. Similarly, whether a knowledge claim is perceived as credible can "depend on who advances it, how plausible it seems, or what sort of experimental evidence is invoked to support it."[76] The concept of credibility struggles, therefore, is an important part of understanding how expert capital works because it shows how credibility has multiple sources and depends on the status of the speaker.

Expert capital incorporates these ideas and builds on them in several ways. First, it foregrounds the fields in which experts and political actors interact, rather than looking at only one group or the other. It thus brings our attention to the way people working in media, politics, and the law evaluate what kinds of people and information might be deemed credible in the first place according to patterns of practice that follow particular logics embedded within institutions, such as courts and legislatures. In so doing, it shows how science and technical knowledge are not the only types of potentially credible information. Second, the currency of expert capital can be composed of credibility but is not reducible to it. Whether or not a claim or claimant is believable, supported by evidence, or backed by their peers might not be what gives expert capital its value in, say, a French parliamentary hearing where, as we will see, the ideological stance of the expert can be just as important. Finally, thinking about expert capital as a resource contingent on specific contexts allows us to more clearly examine the calculations that experts—and the people who want access to their capital—make to maximize the positive outcomes and minimize the negative consequences of their interactions.

This book takes the lens of expert capital in order to explain the contrasting and sometimes even surprising role of experts in same-sex marriage debates in two distinct national cases. Because they spark deep disagreements about normative values—what a society ought to allow—and raise many empirical questions—about family, parenting, intimacy, discrimination, and much more—these debates are especially well suited for thinking about the curious position of experts who are called upon to help resolve them.

WHY COMPARE EXPERTISE IN
THE UNITED STATES AND FRANCE?

Same-sex couples' access to partnership and parenting rights is one of the major, and contested, issues of our era. As countries across the globe have wrestled with the question, many observers have focused on the rapid pace of change, the uneven progress within regions, and the political and social movement dynamics that have made these evolutions possible.[77] Because they emphasize the "morality politics" aspect of gay rights, these analyses tend to overlook the role of experts and expertise. Most of this work has analyzed social movement organizations, religious groups, and other actors as they battle in public arenas to shape legal outcomes. Research on France, however, points out that other people, such as academics and intellectuals, have both helped and hindered the advance of gay rights there.[78] More recently, work by the sociologists Kathleen Hull and Michael Rosenfeld confirm the same trends for the United States.[79] This cross-national comparison suggests that different categories of people—from social movement groups and ordinary citizens to scientists and intellectuals—may therefore participate in the political and legal process in ways specific to their national contexts. Shifting the focus from legal outcomes to expertise, this book systematically examines the types of people and information decision-makers hear in contemporary gay family rights debates in each country.

Drawing on comparative political science showing the merits of focused international comparison for revealing mechanisms of social phenomena, such as the political role of experts in controversial legal debates, this book compares the United States and France.[80] These countries share characteristics that form a baseline for comparison.[81] They are both rich industrialized countries whose democracies formed after revolutions in the same era based on the Enlightenment principles of freedom and equality. In addition, they both have trajectories as colonial powers, which has been integral to their respective formations of sexualities and racialized heteronormativities, including, for example, social norms and legal regimes on gender, heterosexuality, marriage, parenting, and monogamy.[82] Yet, they also diverge in four key ways that may reveal how and why certain kinds of experts and expertise—as well as the systems that justify their participation in these debates—come to matter in one context and not the other.

First, they diverge in their political approaches to inequality and difference.[83] American policies tend to recognize and count people according to social characteristics based on the idea that overcoming discrimination requires acknowledging differences. In contrast, French traditions of republican universalism discourage the acknowledgement of race, religion, and sexuality because doing so would, from this perspective, engender discrimination.[84] As a result, social movement organizations in both countries, from feminist and antiracist groups to those dedicated to fighting for LGBTQ rights and HIV prevention, have taken different tacks as they respond to these contrasting ideologies about social differences, their causes, and solutions.[85] Furthermore, French academics researching racial minorities, for example, face more restrictions on studying people of color relative to their peers in the United States.[86] Experts studying research related to gay families may face similar limitations. More broadly, these differences shape how people involved in political debates—politicians, journalists, activists—frame inequality and discrimination, emphasizing group-based characteristics in the United States and universality in France.[87]

Second, they differ in political and legal systems. The United States has a federal, common law system, with significant legal variation across states. This decentralized, court-centered approach allowed early legalization of some gay family rights in some states, as described in further detail below.[88] Indeed, some organizations specifically targeted courts on the state and federal levels in the hopes that these venues would be more favorable toward gay family causes.[89] France's centralized, civil law legal system prevented any recognition of gay families until the legislature passed the Pacte civil de solidarité (Pacs) in 1999—a law recognizing same and different-sex civil unions but not gay parenting—and marriage and adoption in 2013. Unlike in the United States, the courts were not a viable avenue to pursue these changes. These political and legal differences have several consequences. In addition to creating specific rhythms, geographies, and intensities of gay family reforms, they determine the institutional spaces in which debates take place. Because courts, legislatures, and other decision-making forums process information differently, comparing across them is necessary for contextualizing and explaining the role of experts within them.

Third, the United States and France differ in their "knowledge regimes" that organize the production, dissemination, and purpose of expertise.[90] In the United States, with a large and decentralized knowledge regime, "structural fragmentation"—the federal system with many outlets for reform and separation of power between government branches—decreases the importance of state-sponsored experts relative to Europe.[91] While not necessarily leading to more democratic or representative interests and perspectives, expertise has moved beyond the strict confines of the academy, the professions, and scientific institutions.[92] The participation of multiple actors in the production of "usable knowledge" allows entities, such as think tanks, to generate information or repackage existing information that academics produce, which they then tailor to their policy goals.[93]

As this book will describe, in the United States, activist organizations and think tanks on both sides of LGBTQ rights, especially those involved in "cause lawyering," developed strong ties to researchers and academics.[94] Together they have worked to supply a policy context with a high demand for their information, highlighting how a country's laws and political institutions themselves can create interests leading to the production of specific kinds of information.[95] In contrast, the smaller, more centralized French knowledge regime favors bureaucracies where technocrats and elite intellectual experts exert direct influence on the policy process. France is a representative case of a technocracy where state institutions, generally in Paris, produce most influential knowledge.[96] For example, opponents of gay family rights found strong allies in the corps of high-ranking officials of the states' social services.[97] Further, French think tanks are relatively small and new. They are less able to counter state-produced knowledge or act as mediators between elite experts and decision-makers, as they do in the United States.[98] Given its small size relative to the United States and concentration in Paris, France is also especially marked by a close interrelationship between its academic, political, and media fields, favoring direct ties between elite experts and decision-makers.[99] That proximity may give certain elite experts, especially those with strong ties to political parties, the possibility to directly impact legal reforms. However, those close ties could also contribute to the exclusion of a more diverse group of people from decision-making institutions in France.

Fourth, broader cultural frames and political opinions about expertise, science, and intellectuals distinguish the two countries. Sociologists have shown how, across a wide range of contentious political debates, the media, politicians, and ordinary citizens discuss issues in ways that are both relatively consistent within each country and different across them. These overarching frameworks are called "cultural repertoires of evaluation."[100] Whether it be about environmental crises, sexual harassment, or racist discrimination, in the United States, an economic cultural repertoire dominates. People think about the costs of social problems and wonder whether the benefits of political intervention are worth the financial investment. Beginning in the 1970s, this "economic style of reasoning" began to replace the value of equality, first impacting federal public policy and eventually spreading to journalism and other public conversations.[101] Today, market logics, and the economists who talk about them, are seen by many as the best and most legitimate way to think about major issues.[102] In France, dominant cultural repertoires of evaluation emphasize the idea of solidarity, across social groups and generations, as well as universal values of the French Republic. Given these divergent cultural repertoires of evaluation, it would not be surprising to find economic expertise in arguments about same-sex marriage in the United States—supporters arguing that it would boost the economy and detractors that it would cost the state or employers too much, for example—and arguments about solidarity and expertise grounded in broader universal principles, such as philosophy, in France. Added to these broad cultural differences, these countries diverge in public perceptions of the legitimacy of science and intellectuals. While anti-intellectualism is present in both countries, some research suggests that, in the United States, there is a specific and conservative political resistance to the idea that highly educated elites and scientists should have a special role in developing public policy.[103] In contrast, France has a long tradition of lauding intellectuals as well as promoting an educated class with training in math and engineering, but also in the humanities and social sciences, as its political elite.[104] These differences suggest that academics and intellectuals may be perceived differently in each country when it comes to their interventions in policy debates around same-sex marriage.

PARTNERSHIP AND PARENTING RIGHTS IN
THE UNITED STATES AND FRANCE: A BRIEF HISTORY

Since 2015, after the U.S. Supreme Court ruling in *Obergefell v. Hodges* in June of that year and a French legislative bill from May 2013, both countries have recognized same-sex marriage on the national level.[105] This two-year difference to national legalization makes these countries relatively similar to one another but masks important differences.[106] Indeed, the legal recognition of same-sex couples' relationships, such as civil unions, domestic partnerships, and full marriage, has followed a long and complicated trajectory over the last twenty-five years in ways that reveal distinct national patterns.[107] Moreover, the access of same-sex couples to forms of parenting via joint adoption, second-parent adoption, and medically assisted reproduction, such as donor insemination for lesbian couples or surrogacy for gay male couples, is not equal in each country. As of 2025, in the United States, parenting rights vary significantly by state and by type of access, whereas in France, joint and second-parent adoption were completely illegal until the 2013 marriage bill. Surrogacy is banned there for all people, and access to artificial insemination and other reproductive technologies was strictly limited to medically infertile long-term heterosexual couples until 2021.[108] These differences in partnership and parenting rights reflect both legal structural configurations across these countries, such as federalism in the United States and centralization in France, as well as other factors, including their approaches to new reproductive technologies, public opinion, and social movement organizing. These circumstances help explain the availability and utility of certain kinds of experts and expertise in each country, as this book will show.

   In the United States, laws relating to marriage and parenting have traditionally been the jurisdiction of individual states and, for more limited family policy questions, to counties and municipalities. As a result, since as early as the late 1970s, certain locales have offered same-sex couples some partial partnership rights, such as protection against eviction in the case of the death of one of the partners. Mobilization around these issues continued to grow as LGBTQ rights organizations sought increased protections through state and local governments, especially as the AIDS crisis revealed just how vicious families, landlords, hospitals, and other groups could be in disregarding gay couples.[109] Courts also became a prime venue for change. In the early 1990s, a same-sex couple seeking full marriage rights filed a suit in Hawaii where the Supreme Court there eventually ruled that the state constitution required same-sex marriage.[110] However, in a referendum, voters there modified their state constitution, effectively overturning the court's decision. That initial ruling sparked a wave of antigay backlash, which propelled same-sex marriage to the federal level. For the first time, Congress enacted legislation outside of its traditional jurisdiction in the form of the Defense of Marriage Act (DOMA). Signed by President Bill Clinton in 1996, the law prohibited the federal government from recognizing same-sex marriage and permitted states to refuse to recognize them within their borders even if they were legally contracted elsewhere.[111]

After that, states across the country followed divergent and multiple paths. Some, such as Texas, enacted their own versions of DOMA and prohibited civil unions or other marriage-like contracts. Others, such as California, created domestic partnerships but banned same-sex marriage.[112] A period of increased recognition began in 2004 after Massachusetts's Supreme Court legalized same-sex marriage, followed by other states, such as Vermont. In 2008, after voters passed Proposition 8, which overturned California's Supreme Court decision legalizing same-sex marriage, attorneys began new litigation in federal courts. The U.S. Supreme Court ruled in 2013 on two cases, *Hollingsworth v. Perry* (originally known as *Perry v. Schwarzenegger*), which invalidated Proposition 8, and *U.S. v. Windsor*, which invalidated DOMA.[113] Those successes sparked litigation in federal courts that struck down state-level marriage bans and eventually led to *Obergefell*, consolidated from several cases originating in Michigan, Ohio, Kentucky, and Tennessee, ultimately leading to the legalization of same-sex marriage nationally.[114]

As legislation and case law evolved on same-sex partnerships, access to parenting for same-sex couples remained a relatively distinct issue. Only a few states had explicit bans on adoption by same-sex couples or, like Michigan, limited adoption to married couples, which created a de facto exclusion of same-sex couples. However, most other states explicitly allowed joint and second-parent adoption, or in the absence of legislation—which was the case in Texas, for example—courts created case law by allowing such adoptions on a case-by-case basis.[115] In addition, because of liberal policies and lack of any specific regulation, states never prohibited lesbian couples and single women from access to sperm banks that were willing to offer their services.[116] Similarly, only a few states have statutory law explicitly addressing surrogacy. Some states, such as Texas, have passed legislation recognizing gestational surrogacy contracts but limited them to married couples, creating a de facto exclusion of same-sex couples until 2015. In contrast, California has enforced surrogacy contracts without regard to sexual orientation. Most states, however, have no legislation on surrogacy, and judges have created conflicting case law. As a result of these policies, surrogacy agencies have been able to offer their services to gay male couples in some states.

The complexity of U.S. partnership and parenting law is represented in table 0.1, which shows states' stances on marriage, adoption, and surrogacy in 2014, before the *Obergefell* ruling. It shows the variety of state approaches to these issues, creating state-level "experimentation," as well as the strength of the judiciary, especially on the federal level. Both factors have given gay family rights momentum and propelled those issue forward in the United States.[117]

In France, legal reforms on marriage and parenting have followed a simpler, if not easier, path. France's policies apply nationally, so there is no room for significant lower-level jurisdictional experimentation as there is in the United States on issues related to gay family rights. The national level is thus the primary venue for reform. Furthermore, unlike the U.S. common law system, where courts can make broad case law that significantly modifies legislation, the French civil law system has limited the role of the courts. Decisions by France's *Conseil Constitutionnel, Cour de Cassation*, and *Conseil d'État*, as well as the European Court of Human Rights (ECtHR)—to which French citizens can appeal if they believe national law violates their rights under the European Convention on Human Rights—have consistently ruled that France's legislature has the authority to determine its policy on same-sex marriage and parenting.[118] Furthermore, French law, unlike U.S. state law, has limited adoption either to married couples or single people, thus rendering it impossible for same-sex couples to openly adopt together until 2013. Unmarried single people could adopt, but gays and lesbians were frequently denied approval based on their sexual orientation if discovered by social workers. Although the ECtHR first upheld and then condemned such practices, in *Fretté v. France* (2002) and *E.B. v. France* (2008), respectively, French

TABLE 0.1 Legalization of Same-Sex Marriage, Adoption, and Surrogacy
Before *Obergefell v. Hodges*, 2015

State	Marriage	Joint adoption	Second-parent adoption	Surrogacy
Alabama				?
Alaska	2014 [J-F]	?	?	?
Arizona	2014 [J-F]	2014 [J]	2014 [J]	
Arkansas		2011 [J]		?
California	**2013 [J-F]**	**2003 [L]**	**Yes**	**1993 [J]**
Colorado	2014 [J-F]	Yes	Yes	?
Connecticut	2008 [J]	2008 [J]	2000 [L]	2008 [J]
Delaware	2013 [L]	2011 [L]	2011 [L]	
Florida	2014 [J]	2014 [J]	2010 [J]	2014 [J]
Georgia		?	?	?
Hawaii	2013 [L]	Yes	Yes	?
Idaho	2014 [J-F]	Yes	2013 [J]	?
Illinois	2013 [L]	Yes	Yes	Yes*
Indiana	2014 [J-F]	2006 [J]	Yes	
Iowa	2009 [J]	2009 [J]	Yes	Yes*
Kansas	2014 [J-F]	?	[2013]	
Kentucky		?		?
Louisiana		?	?	$
Maine	2012 [R]	2007 [J]	2007 [J]	?
Maryland	2013 [L/R]	Yes	Yes	?
Massachusetts	2004 [J]	1993 [J]	1993 [J]	yes*
Michigan			?	
Minnesota	2013 [L]	2013 [L]	2013 [L]	?
Mississippi				?
Missouri		Yes	Yes	?
Montana	2014 [J-F]	Yes	Yes	?
Nebraska		?		
Nevada	2014 [J-F]	Yes	Yes	2014 [J]
New Hampshire	2010 [L]	2010 [L]	2010 [L]	Yes*
New Jersey	2013 [J]	1997 [L]	Yes	$
New Mexico	2013 [J-F]	Yes	2012 [J]	$
New York	2011 [L]	Yes	Yes	
North Carolina	2014 [J-F]	2014 [J]	2014 [J]	?
North Dakota		?	?	Yes*
Ohio		?		?
Oklahoma	2014 [J-F]	2007 [J]	Yes	?
Oregon	2014 [J-F]	Yes	Yes	$
Pennsylvania	2014 [J-F]	Yes	2002 [J]	?
Rhode Island	2013 [L]	Yes	Yes	?
South Carolina	2014 [J-F]	Yes	Yes	?
South Dakota		?	?	?
Tennessee		?	?	

Texas		?	?	2003 [L]
Utah	2014 [J-F]	2014 [J]	Yes	2014 [J]
Vermont	2009 [L]	Yes	1993 [J]	?
Virginia	2014 [J-F]	Yes	Yes	$
Washington	2012 [L/R]	2012 [L/R]	2012 [L/R]	$
Washington (DC)	2010 [L]	Yes	Yes	
West Virginia	2014 [J-F]	2014 [J]	?	?
Wisconsin	2014 [J-F]	2014 [J]	2014 [J]	?
Wyoming	2014 [J-F]	Yes	Yes	?

Legend:
[J] State judicial decision; [J-F] Federal judicial decision; [L] Legislative decision; [R] Referendum
?: No clear statutory law; contradictory or nonexistent jurisprudence in state lower-level courts
Yes: Trial courts have authorized adoptions on a case-by-case basis. However, no law explicitly formalizes a right to same-sex couple adoption, and no cases have been appealed to the state's highest court, which would instantiate a formal right.
Yes*: Authorizes surrogacy but no jurisprudence on the sexual orientation of future parents.
$: Authorizes surrogacy but without payment to the surrogate. No jurisprudence on the sexual orientation of the future parents.

Sources:
The Human Rights Campaign, "Human Rights Campaign State Maps," http://www.selectsurrogate.com /surrogacy-laws-by-state.html; Gay and Lesbian Advocates and Defenders, "GLAD Know Your Rights Information by State," http://www.glad.org/rights/states; Select Surrogacy Agency, "The Select Surrogate Surrogacy Laws by State," http://www.glad.org/rights/states; consulted January 21, 2015.

adoption authorities have been slow to implement that decision.[119] The ECtHR further ruled in 2012 in the case *Gas and Dubois v. France* that barring access to second-parent adoption for unmarried couples did not violate the convention.[120]

Before 1999, when the French Parliament passed the Pacs—a contract granting same-sex and different-sex couples some partnership rights but excluding any access to adoption—there was no recognition of same-sex couples.[121] Much like the situation for gay couples across the Atlantic, the tragedy of the AIDS epidemic made clear the scale of discrimination faced by gay people as partners were kicked out of their homes, refused entry into hospitals, and stripped out of wills. The Pacs, therefore, represented a major advance and success of LGBTQ and AIDS organizations who fought for its implementation, putting France ahead of the United States in terms of nationally authorizing legal unions for same-sex couples.[122] But it only went so far and left many marriage advocates dissatisfied, notably for its lack of parental rights.[123] After 1999, faced with refusal by the Conseil Constitutionnel or the Cour de Cassation to rule, same-sex marriage and adoption remained off the legislative agenda until the Socialist Party, which had integrated those issues in their platform, won a parliamentary majority in 2012 in the same year that François Hollande, also a Socialist, was elected president. Though they had originally planned to legalize access to artificial insemination, they limited themselves to marriage and adoption in the face of strong public and political opposition.

France has also taken the opposite approach of the United States in terms of medically assisted procreation. It instituted a ban on surrogacy and prohibited donor insemination (DI) for lesbians and single women almost as soon as these technologies were developed, enshrining the idea that only heterosexual couples were worthy of help with their fertility.[124] As a result, French lesbian couples never had legal access to DI within their country and have typically traveled to sperm banks in Belgium and Spain.[125] It took almost ten years after the legalization of same-sex marriage and adoption before the legislature would finally take that issue up again in 2021.

These differences in legal history, jurisdictional structures, and avenues of reform have several concrete implications for experts and expertise in both countries. In the United States, legal variety created by federalism and differences in laws on parenting allowed same-sex couples and their children to achieve legal recognition and public visibility. Researchers recruited these families for studies about gay couples and their children while advocacy groups encouraged them to make public testimony and speak to journalists. Variation across states also created legal contexts within the country that decision-makers, such as lawmakers and judges, could compare or that experts, such as leaders in activist organizations and think tanks, could bring to the discussion. Furthermore, by developing political strategies that took advantage of the plethora of "legal opportunity structures" in state and federal courts on gay family rights issues, LGBTQ activists created a high demand for knowledge adapted to these settings.[126]

In France, anticipatory bans on reproductive technologies and restrictions on adoption limited the visibility and presence of gay families, making information about them more difficult to gather. The homogeneity of the French legal terrain also reduced the ability of activists, social scientists, and other knowledge producers to generate information locally—that is, about gay people living in France rather than in other places—or to compare circumstances within the country. Finally, French experts have dealt primarily with legislatures—rather than courts—and have had far fewer opportunities to participate in changing the law. On the whole, this has inhibited the demand for expertise relative to the

United States, leading to all kinds of secondary effects in a general economy for expertise. Moreover, the parliamentary avenue of reform also channels experts and expertise into a political institution whose rules about the validity of different types of knowledge are not as explicit as they are in courts. This gives French experts, and the politicians who rely on them, a different set of circumstances to negotiate as they go about producing, sharing, and evaluating expert capital.

DIVERGENT MARRIAGE AND PARENTING CULTURES

American and French people react in different and culturally specific ways to gay families and their demands for recognition. Just as the laws have followed unique paths in these countries, public opinion polls suggest that what might seem perfectly acceptable in one place is much more controversial in the other. Americans have expressed more opposition, anxiety, and hesitation around same-sex marriage but, on average, have been more open to same-sex couples parenting and raising children than the French. In other words, the politically contentious issues are flipped in these countries.

Figure 0.1 shows, for example, how French respondents have consistently had more favorable views of same-sex marriage than Americans in major public opinion polls. French support flagged during the lead up to the Pacs debates in 1996 and then again during the marriage debates. U.S. support fluctuated and did not become majority in favor until May 2011. In contrast, figure 0.2 shows that Americans have generally been more favorable to adoption by same-sex couples than the French. As gay and lesbian families grew increasingly visible in American public debates, support for adoption increased and remained almost always ahead of same-sex marriage. For example, in May 2009, only 40 percent of U.S. respondents supported same-sex marriage even as 54 percent supported adoption. In the meantime, French respondents have been much less favorable to same-sex adoption, and their support waned in the early 2010s as the possibility that legal access to it became more likely. Indeed, throughout the 2012–2013 parliamentary debates on marriage and adoption, support dropped below 50 percent.

These reactions to same-sex couples and their children, whether in law or public opinion, reflect broader differences over the social organization of families.[127] Relative to other countries, sociologists describe a lasting and exceptional "culture of marriage" in the United States, where a variety of practices,

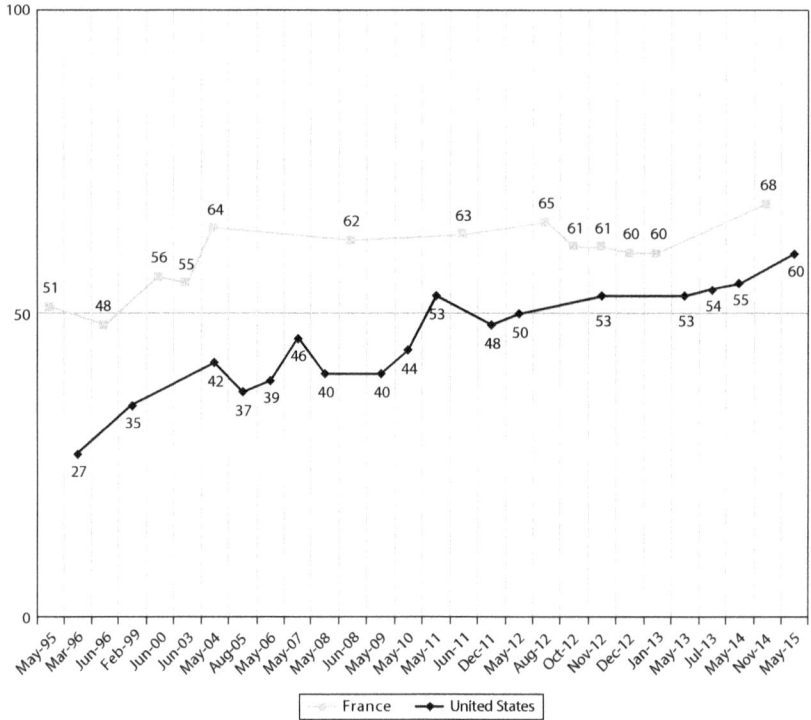

0.1 Favorable opinions on marriage for same-sex couples in the United States and France from 1995 to 2015

Sources: Gallup http://www.gallup.com/poll/183272/record-high-americans-support-sex-marriage.aspx?utm _source=marriage&utm_medium=search&utm_campaign=tiles; Ifop http://www.ifop.com/?option=com _publication&type=poll&id=2839

norms, and institutions center marriage as a keystone of American life.[128] Marriage appears to have less sway for French people, who, despite having about as many children on average as their American counterparts, tend to get married less.[129] Indeed, having children before marriage—or not getting married at all—is much more common for heterosexual couples in France than it is in the United States.[130] American culture and politics are awash in marriage discourse and direct social pressure to get married. Religious and community groups, schools, and other organizations—some of which receive public funding—run programs to prepare people for heterosexual marriage, framing divorce, single parenthood, and unmarried cohabiting couples as the sources of social problems to which marriage is the best solution.[131] The cultural salience of marriage is also evident in the way American policymakers have long blamed the effects

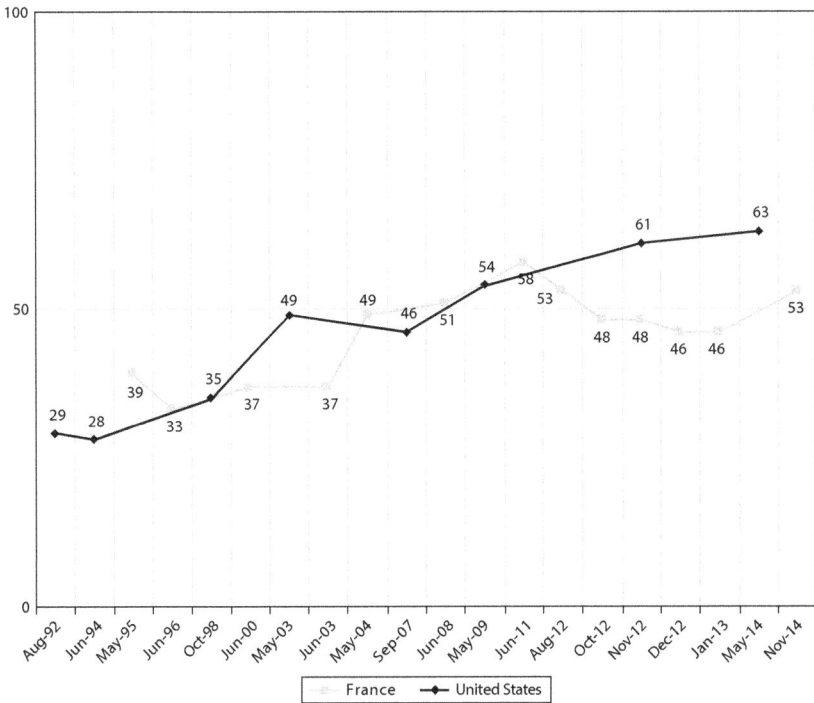

0.2 Favorable opinions on adoption by same-sex couples in the United States and France from 1992 to 2014

Sources: Gallup http://www.gallup.com/poll/170801/americans-say-sex-couples-entitled-adopt.aspx?utm_source=marriage&utm_medium=search&utm_campaign=tiles; Ifop http://www.ifop.com/?option=com_publication&type=poll&id=2839

of inequality on a supposed failure to adhere to the values of marriage among poor and racialized groups, particularly among working-class Black communities.[132] Rather than provide benefits directly to individual parents and children, as is the case in France, many federal and state-level policies are geared toward incentivizing couples to get married.[133] In contrast, the French state today provides much more generous family leave and early childhood education policies regardless of the marital status of parents, highlighting the centrality of childrearing in French culture relative to marriage.[134] Whether or not gay romantic and familial relationships can or should be included within the range of nationally authorized families, either to marry in the United States or raise children in France, is one of the central questions structuring debates on all sides.[135]

These cultural and legal differences around marriage and parenting help us understand the contexts that experts, policymakers, activists, journalists, and gay families themselves confront and create. Demands for same-sex marriage, with all the symbols that go along with it, could illicit the ire of Americans who see any change in that institution as a major upheaval even as they happily recognize that same-sex couples should be allowed to raise their children. Many French people, however, might find it odd that Americans are so invested in marriage on one side or the other. That all couples should have the same rights and obligations to one another does not seem to bother a majority of them. Children, on the other hand, are another matter entirely. When contemplating the possibility that a child could have two mothers or two fathers in the eyes of the law, the French public has been more skeptical. Anyone engaging in these debates, whether it be a French anthropologist called to testify to parliament about gay relationships or an American attorney looking for the perfect, sympathetic lay witness to illustrate the cruelty of a same-sex marriage ban, these cultural contexts will inform their decisions. At the same time, they are also contributing in their own ways to changing them. Norms and opinions, just like laws, are, of course, not static. Indeed, polls show that both French and American people have only grown more favorable toward gay families since legalization.[136] Romantic relationships and family life are some of the main areas of social life that have changed the most in the last century, thanks in no small part to feminist and queer movements that have nevertheless had to contend with well-organized conservative groups whose power has recently increased, especially in the United States. Family law will undoubtedly continue to evolve in ways that may be difficult to predict. This book unpacks the key role of experts in shaping such changes.

THE DATA AND METHODS

I mobilize archival, interview, and ethnographic data in both countries, focusing on legal debates that took place between 1990 and 2015.[137] My cases include France, European Union institutions affecting France, U.S. federal institutions, and two comparable U.S. states: California and Texas. This time frame is wide enough to capture most major reforms in France and the United States on gay family rights, including marriage legalization in both countries, while also being manageable analytically.

I conducted content analysis to identify "experts" and "expertise" in over 5,000 pages of expert testimony; 9,000 pages of congressional and courtroom proceedings, including debate transcripts, amicus briefs, legislative reports, and committee hearings; and news coverage in 2,335 articles in *The New York Times* and *Le Monde*. From the entire set of archives, I specifically analyzed and tracked who provided which kinds of expertise in these settings to identify patterns in variation across time, institution, and country. To understand how and why they became involved in these debates, I conducted seventy-two in-depth interviews with people who provided expertise—in major court cases, legislative processes, and other reforms—as well as with key lawmakers and lawyers responsible for organizing expert testimony.[138] This sample includes people identified from the archival data and represents the range of profiles of experts, stances on the issue, and degree of implication in the debates over time. I also observed and participated in think tank and policy institute seminars and presentations—identifying those most frequently involved or cited by the interviewees as influential—to look at the conditions of knowledge production. The methodological appendix at the end of this book details how I gathered and analyzed the data and lists the names of interviewees. I also explain how my position as an American sociologist constrained and enabled my access to interviewees who were sometimes wary of me in a politically sensitive and cross-national context.

BOOK OUTLINE

To provide readers with a picture of the way expertise circulates broadly, chapter 1, "According to Authorities: Expertise in the Media," analyzes press coverage of gay family debates between 1990 and 2013 in *The New York Times* and *Le Monde*, the newspapers of record in each country. It identifies both the types of people that journalists cite and what they say. This distinction—overlooked in the media analysis literature—matters because it reveals how certain kinds of knowledge, such as personal experience, are shared across categories of experts. U.S. reporting elevates everyday lived experiences, especially those of same-sex couples and their families, while French reporting takes a detached, top-down view. Indeed, in contrast to U.S. coverage, which usually cites ordinary citizens and advocacy organizations, French journalists and op-ed pieces feature abstract academic and intellectual arguments from professors and mental health professionals. There is thus a clear national distinction between dominance of lay expertise in the U.S. and elite expertise in France. Moreover, experts of all sorts within each country use these prevailing types of knowledge, suggesting they act as a shared national language for justifying claims.

Chapter 2, "The Floor Is Yours: Expertise in Courts and Legislatures," focuses on the things that experts say when they speak directly to judges and lawmakers as they determine the fate of gay and lesbian families. The institutional records nuance the patterns of national differences found in the media. In these high-stakes public environments, American and French decision-makers are presented with contrasting evidence about same-sex couples and their needs. U.S. legislatures, especially on the state level, are forums for ordinary citizens to describe how potential bills affect their families and friends. U.S. courts create more opportunities for elite voices because lawyers call on "expert witnesses," specifically professors and law professionals, to complement plaintiffs' experiences. French legislatures resemble extreme versions of U.S. courts but with more anti-same-sex marriage voices. French lawmakers call elite experts—but almost never ordinary citizens—to speak in the abstract about gay and lesbian relationships and parenting. Drawing on archival data, this chapter details these patterns over time and across countries, suggesting that expertise is a function of how legal institutions process available knowledge in a given context. The next chapter provides evidence to support that hypothesis.

Chapter 3, "For the Record: Becoming and Creating Experts," explores how experts having been called to give testimony navigate their political interventions and make sense of their place in the debates. It also examines how lawmakers and lawyers think about and organize experts and expertise as they plan and carry out their legal reforms. This analysis reveals that U.S. and French media, legislatures, and courts draw on different kinds of information because of embedded institutional logics that shape how people interact with and understand information. Specifically, open legislatures, such as those in U.S. states, allow anyone to speak before committees so any interested citizen can testify. U.S. courts, however, put high demands on the quality of knowledge because judges must determine whether what experts say is credible. This favors scientific and empirical evidence that can validate specific legal claims. In France, legislators in the majority decide who gets to testify. Because of the political risks involved and their desire to appear legitimate to their peers and the public, they invite famous, elite experts and other people they believe will make their hearings seem balanced. In this context, contrary to U.S. courts, the content of information is less important. Rather, in formal French hearings, experts serve a political function to undermine opponents and buttress a legal reform that has largely already been decided. Taken together, the accounts told both by people testifying and the decision-makers soliciting them belies the idea of the inherent value of experts. Rather, these stories bring to light how the meaning and value of experts and their knowledge is produced in interaction with institutions and the people who run them.

Chapter 4, "From Scratch: Experts Work with What They've Got," follows some elite experts from the previous chapter back to their professional and academic fields. It examines the conditions under which they generate the knowledge, prestige, and authority that make them attractive to decision-makers. In particular, it contextualizes the relative power of such experts in each country according to their support for or opposition to same-sex marriage and parenting. U.S. progressives studying sexual minorities and their families have entered the mainstreams of their fields and enjoy strong institutionalized resources to produce high-quality, empirical research. At the same time, conservatives have been marginalized in the United States and operate outside the academic and professional mainstream. In contrast, French progressives are stigmatized because of their research interests and face a chronic lack of institutional support in a social context where gay families have been invisible. Moreover, their field is small, interpersonal, and marked by longstanding conflict, which limits their ability to work effectively. French conservatives, on the other hand, though increasingly decentered, still occupy relatively strong institutional positions. These challenges explain in part why expertise in French political debates lacks empirical grounding and leans conservatively. This chapter thus argues that experts' work environments directly condition their capacity to shape gay family law.

The channels experts use to bring their information to the political field also shape the value of their expert capital. Chapter 5, "Ties That Bind: How Experts Connect with Lawmakers," explores the links experts make to decision-makers in each country. Interviews and ethnography reveal that elite U.S. experts face a highly professionalized field in which advocacy and professional organizations centralize knowledge, which they then distribute to courts and legislatures. In contrast, elite French experts have direct personal ties with lawmakers and political parties in ways that suggest they work as political advisors. Indeed, unlike their American peers, whose academic and professional fields overlap less with those of judges and politicians, some French experts are friends with elected officials. In this context, the line between the politician and the expert becomes blurred. In the United States, most experts provide information from a distance, leaving advocacy work to organizations, though some engage in activism from behind the scenes. Many French experts, in contrast, intervene much as politicians or other political actors would to directly shape and influence the debate even as they claim to be above the fray.

Chapter 6, "To Have and to Hold: Expert Capital as a Scarce Resource," draws on the explanations from the previous chapters to flesh out the concept of expert capital and provide illustrations of how it works. Readers will have learned at this point that political institutions in each country favor certain kinds of information and that experts are dealing with cultural, professional, and academic circumstances that favor or hinder their capacity to create that information. From there, this chapter explores examples from each country that detail how decision-makers, activists, and experts on both sides of gay family battles strive to generate expert capital to further their cause. It also lays out the strategies that experts, activists, and lawmakers use to undermine the value of the expert capital of their opponents. These tactics include ad hominem attacks on experts' sexual orientation, religious affiliation, discipline, publication record, and other factors. In sum, this chapter shows how expert capital is a cultural resource that requires cultivation, safeguarding, and curating that can only be accomplished through coordinated work between experts and those who want to use their power.

The conclusion, "Authoritative Knowledge, Authorizing Families," invites readers to think about the influence of experts on the trajectory of gay family rights as well as on contentious social and scientific issues more broadly. Though they took different paths to get there, the United States and France both legalized same-sex marriage nationally within the same three-year period between 2013 and 2015. At first glance, this seems to suggest that differences in expertise do not matter for legal outcomes. Indeed, experts are just one of many figures in the web of causal factors that explain the success or failure of gay rights law. Yet, as this book shows, they are especially important because their voices—amplified and elevated by the spotlight legal institutions give them—shape cultural and scientific perceptions of gay and lesbian families in the long term. Furthermore, in their drive to generate and use expert capital to win their causes, activists and lawmakers on both sides of the debate create lasting feedback loops between

academic and social movement fields. The infrastructure to support these interactions, the discredit or praise that winning or losing the debate brings, and
the attendant shifts in power across disciplines and discourses this creates will
reverberate for some time.

Emphasizing the unique role played by experts in the democratic process and
its implications for politics, science, and democratic representation, the conclusion gives readers three takeaways. First, elite, credentialed experts, such as
scientists, are sometimes rightly critiqued for usurping democratic will, preventing less powerful people, whose lives are directly impacted by these reforms,
from being heard. What we learn is that ordinary citizens are not systematically excluded. Indeed, they can and do find a place in these political debates,
drawing on their personal experience or other forms of lay expertise to change
the minds of lawmakers in ways that other experts cannot. However, the value
of their expert capital will depend on the context. Second, I warn against the
risk of relying on and lauding science as the answer to political questions. For
example, psychological evidence on children raised by same-sex couples was an
asset to gay rights supporters because it supported their cause. Yet, if research
were to suggest that children suffer psychologically because of gay parenting,
advocates would have to either admit defeat or claim expertise is irrelevant. This
quandary puts into focus the problematic role science can play in human rights
debates more broadly. Third, I generalize from my findings on gay family law to
speculate about how the concept of *expert capital* can be useful for making sense
of other contentious political debates at the intersection of rights and expertise,
including anti-vaccine activism, climate change denial, and abortion restrictions.

CHAPTER 1

ACCORDING TO AUTHORITIES

Expertise in the Media

I n 2010, *Le Monde*, France's daily newspaper of record, published an op-ed piece entitled, "Let's Not Be the Sorcerer's Apprentice," by Jean-Pierre Winter, a psychoanalyst and author of the book *Homoparenté* [*Gay Parenting*].[1] In his piece, he argues against the notion that same-sex couples should be allowed to raise children together, finding it both preposterous and dangerous. He says:

> This leads us to question the fantastical thoughts that may be going on in the minds of two women or two men who decide, with the best of intentions, to bring up children, depriving them, a priori, not only of a father or a mother, but, through them, of the whole ancestral chain. The fantastical belief that no man has penetrated our mother, that we are not the offspring of a coitus of which we only have a representation insofar as we are excluded from it, that our little brother is the fruit of our desire for our parent of the same sex as us, are unconscious imaginings long since catalogued under the heading of "primal fantasies."[2]

Drawing on basic concepts from psychoanalysis, Winter accuses same-sex couples of indulging in the immature fantasy that they can raise children. Winter offers *Le Monde* readers his opposition to same-sex marriage, whose legalization was not yet officially on the table, in terms of expertise derived from his interpretation of knowledge specific to his profession but provides no concrete examples. In his telling, same-sex couples raising children are an abstract threat that should be prevented from becoming a reality for the sake of the kids.

In a 2012 article entitled, "Illinois Clergy Members Support Same-Sex Marriage in Letter Signed by 260," Maggie Astor of *The New York Times* describes the decision of Reverend Kevin E. Tindell, a United Church of Christ minister at the church New Dimensions Chicago, to sign a petition in favor of same-sex marriage.[3] He is quoted as saying, "It's a matter of justice, and so as a Christian, as a citizen, I feel that it's my duty." The article goes on to describe the life of the clergyman: "Mr. Tindell, who is gay, is raising three children with his partner of 17 years." The minister draws on his moral beliefs as a Christian to describe why he supports same-sex marriage, and we learn that the issue concerns him personally as a father and partnered gay man. In the article, journalists present readers with a religious representative who draws on religion and his own experience to explain his support for gay family rights. The article seems to take for granted the idea that gay men—pastors even—raise children together. The controversy is about his demand for marriage.

These quotes present several key contrasts: (1) the issues prioritized; (2) the kinds of information readers of these newspapers encounter; and (3) the categories of people presenting that information. In the first case, a mental health professional uses psychoanalysis to denounce gay parenting reforms, and in the second, a religious representative uses religious expertise and personal experience to support gay marriage. Several questions emerge from these examples. In the area of gay family rights, from partnerships to access to parenting, which issues garner more attention? To what degree is expertise like this representative of broader media discussions of same-sex couples in France and the United States? How often are psychoanalysis, religion, and other types of information used to support or critique the legal recognition of same-sex families? What kinds of people speak out in the press, and what do they say? Have the categories of experts and type of knowledge they use changed over time?

To answer these questions, this chapter analyzes how news media reporting covers gay family rights focusing specifically on how experts and their knowledge play a role through editorials and quotes from journalists. It sheds light on the people and information that dominate what the French and American public read about the romantic and family lives of same-sex couples. By choosing to highlight some facts, themes, or ideas over others, media sources create a specific narrative—sometimes called a frame—telling readers what an issue is about. These frames can vary in systematically different ways by country and show up in the press. This is true in the case of France and the United States.[4] Specifically, over a range of widely different issues, from sexual harassment to environmental policy and the art world, the French often frame social problems in terms of "civic solidarity," while Americans draw on "market performance."[5] The former evoke justifications grounded in the idea of the common good, while the latter analyze a problem through its financial consequences. Because journalists are embedded within their cultures, media discussions on gay families in each country are likely to resonate to some degree with these broader systems of justification.[6] We can expect, therefore, to find arguments evoking collective well-being in France and economic consequences in the United States and a recourse to experts that buttress such ideas.

Specific cultural differences on sexuality also indicate which kinds of information might be more or less common in either country. Because they generally have opposing views on the distinction between the public and private sphere, French and American journalists, politicians, and social movements have historically reacted to sexuality, gender, and family issues differently.[7] In France, they tend to support the idea that one's sexuality and family life should be protected from public scrutiny, while in the United States, they are tools of public self-identification and interaction. Both customs also favor heterosexuality in specific ways. In France, heterosexual privilege is upheld because it serves as the universal unmarked category in a sphere where all sexuality is "private." In the United States, heterosexuality is reinforced through its public visibility and display. More broadly, these differences impact the way politics and journalism deal with the "private lives" of politicians. For example, unlike the reaction to President Bill Clinton's affair with Monica Lewinsky, the public acknowledgement of President François Mitterrand's second family did not lead to political outcry.[8] These differences also constrain and enable the degree to which politicians, journalists, and activists involved in political debates can legitimately evoke their families, friends, or sexuality as the basis for claims-making.[9] Relatedly, judgments about sexuality are more tightly linked with moral and religious arguments in the United States than they are in France, which reflects larger traditions about the status of religion in the public sphere in either country and higher degrees of religiosity and church attendance in the United States relative to France.[10] Given these trends, media coverage of gay family debates is likely to treat "private" and religious information differently. Specifically, people who intervene in the French press may be less likely to talk about their own experiences with sexual minorities and their families or draw on religiously grounded arguments.

Descriptions of frames alone are not sufficient to understand the power and weight behind arguments that people mobilize in political and media debates.[11] Drawing on the idea of expert capital, it is possible to identify which kinds of people use which kinds of arguments to justify their claims in the media. That some categories of experts are more prominent in coverage of same-sex marriage debates, such as professors in France or ordinary citizens in the United States, as we will see, tells us about the people journalists and newspaper contributors consider worthwhile to highlight. Perhaps they do so because they seek balance or credibility or simply draw on a pre-established list of people who will answer their phone calls. Regardless of how they get there, understanding what these experts say and whether their information is drawn from, say, social science, mental health, or personal experience, tells us about the terms through which readers see gay families. Because the news media's wide reach shapes public opinion and perceptions, including that of policymakers, the expertise and experts the news uses can impact the politics and mobilization around these issues. Moreover, as we will see in later chapters, speaking out in the media is a viable way for experts in France, in particular, to gain notoriety, attract solicitations from lawmakers, and criticize their opponents.

This chapter provides a picture of discourse easily accessible outside of governmental institutions, such as legislative hearings, complementing the other chapters' analysis of how different types of experts participate in those settings. It does not aim to describe the breadth of civil society debates on gay family and parenting issues in both countries; that is beyond the scope of what is possible here. Instead, it focuses on *Le Monde* and the *Times*, which offer a fruitful comparison because they are both newspapers of record, share generally center-left editorial viewpoints, and have similar proportions of readership in their respective countries.[12] Their credibility and status among journalists and the public also give their reporting an outsized level of political influence, especially in the years before the rise of social media.[13] Thus, it is reasonable to assume that the kind of experts and expertise discussed in these newspapers between 1990 and 2013, though not necessarily representative of all knowledge present in the media, reverberates in national discourse more broadly. Understanding the patterns of expertise in *Le Monde* and the *Times* therefore provides a useful sketch of public discourse about same-sex marriage and parenting over the historical period covered in this book. The methodological appendix provides a detailed description of how I collected, categorized, coded, and statistically analyzed types of expertise and categories of experts in 2,335 articles published between 1990 and 2013 in both newspapers, which I present in the next sections.

TRACKING THE COVERAGE OVER TIME

Having a picture of the way coverage maps onto the chronology of political events in each country provides a context for understanding the trends in experts and expertise discussed below. Figure 1.1 shows the number of articles published each year from 1990 to July 30, 2013, in both newspapers. There are several notable trends. First, the *Times* coverage began earlier. *Le Monde* did not publish its first articles until 1992, and then in small numbers, reflecting the relative lack of legal and media attention paid to same-sex couples and families in France. Coverage in both newspapers, not surprisingly, is driven primarily by major political and legal battles with peaks in articles corresponding to major events.

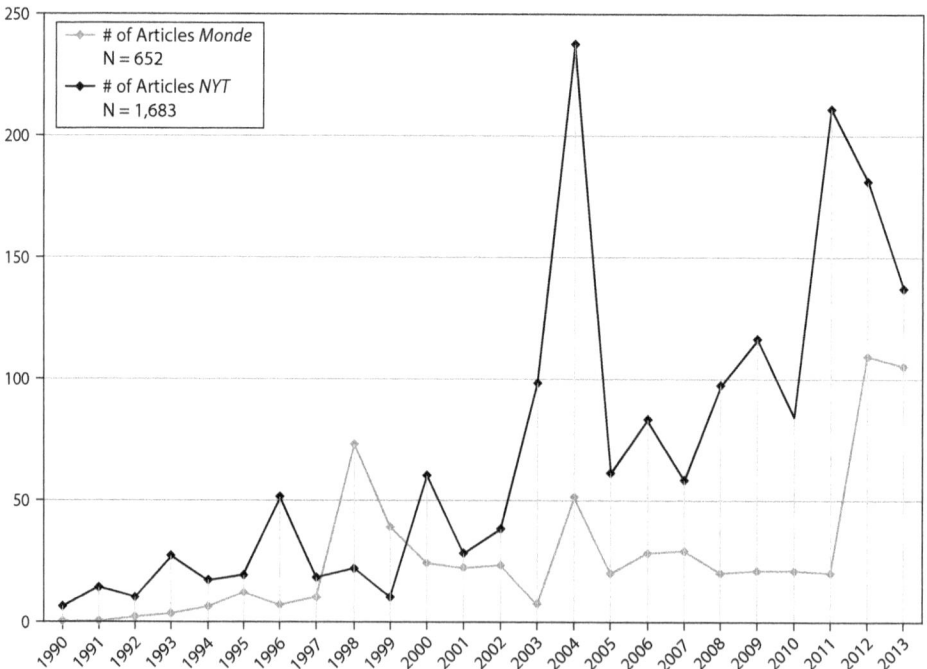

1.1 History of coverage of expertise in *Le Monde* and *The New York Times*, 1990–2013

In the *Times*, the spike in coverage in 1993 is related to a ruling in favor of same-sex marriage by Hawaii's supreme court, which sparked anti–same-sex marriage referenda and the passage of the Defense of Marriage Act (DOMA) in 1996. Coverage increased again in the 2000s, peaking in 2004 because of the legalization of same-sex marriage in Massachusetts, the first state to do so, and a backlash of state voter and legislative initiatives to ban it. Gay family rights, and same-sex marriage in particular, became an increasingly integral part of electoral politics during this period, in which the Republican party made opposition a major part of its strategy to mobilize its base beginning with the 2004 presidential elections.[14] Articles were steadily published in the late 2000s and early 2010s as legislative and judicial efforts to either prohibit or establish same-sex marriage spread through state and federal institutions. The higher number of articles in the *Times* likely reflects the quantity of legal and political battles on gay family rights in the United States occurring in multiple state-level jurisdictions relative to France's single national jurisdiction.

In *Le Monde*, the first spike occurred in 1998 before and after the passage of the Pacte civil de solidarité (Pacs). Reporting increased again in 2004, at the moment of a highly publicized same-sex wedding celebrated in the city of Bègles by its mayor Noël Mamère, an MP for the Green Party.[15] Knowing that the marriage would likely be invalidated by the courts, which it ultimately was, this was Mamère's attempt, coordinated with activist groups and a few gay and lesbian lawyers, to force the issue into the national conversation and create a test case for judicial action. Coverage in *Le Monde* then ticked up again in the years preceding the legalization of same-sex marriage in 2012.

INSTITUTIONAL DOMAINS AND ISSUES: COURTS, LEGISLATURES, KIDS, AND COUPLES

In addition to following the chronology of legal reforms, news reporting also reflects the specific importance of courts and legislatures as well as the types of gay partnerships and parenting reforms that matter most in each country. Table 1.1 shows the institutional domains of reforms as well as the proportion of specific parenting and family issues journalists in each newspaper cover.

The legislature dominates French discussion (62 percent), while a range of institutions, such as courts, legislatures, and referenda (29, 21, and 6 percent,

TABLE 1.1 Proportion of Occurrences by Institutional Domain and Issue Covered in *Le Monde* and *The New York Times (NYT)*

Legal domain	Monde	NYT	Monde–NYT
Courts	0.13	0.29	−0.17
Legislature	0.62	0.21	0.41
Multiple	0.09	0.26	−0.17
None	0.12	0.17	−0.05
Other	0.04	0.03	0.00
Private sector	0.01	0.01	0.00
Referendum	0.00	0.03	−0.03
N	738	1,951	

$\chi^2 = 515.6306$ (df 6), $p < .001$

Issue covered	Monde	NYT	Monde–NYT
Adoption	0.06	0.04	0.02
Assisted reproduction	0.04	0.01	0.03
Custody	0.00	0.02	−0.02
Multiple	0.26	0.04	0.22
Parenting	0.29	0.04	0.25
Partnerships	0.35	0.85	−0.50
N	1,299	1,734	

$\chi^2 = 919.9558$ (df 5), $p < .001$

respectively), or multiple combinations of these appear in American articles. This disparity in avenues of reform is consistent with my overarching argument that institutions, because of the way people interact with them, shape the kinds of knowledge and experts required in each country. For example, in the U.S. case, lawyers and judges are necessary for navigating judicial reform just as activists and members of the public work to convince voters in a referendum. And, as is discussed below, all of these actors are cited more frequently in the *Times* than in *Le Monde*. These institutional differences, however, do not suggest that courts fill media debates at the expense of legislatures in the U.S. coverage. Rather, these avenues of reform are additive; they increase the opportunity for expert discourse. Thus, the dominant presence of legislatures in *Le Monde* coverage as compared to that in the *Times* reflects the absence of the judiciary as a powerful avenue of reform in France rather than a weakness of legislatures in the United States.

As we saw in the introduction of this book, in public opinion polls, Americans have historically expressed more opposition to gay marriage than have the French but are, on average, more accepting of gay adoption and parenting. These stances also parallel the legal landscape in each country; same-sex couples have been able to raise children, without access to legal partnerships, in some parts of the United States much earlier than they could in France. Related to this, 85 percent of coverage in the *Times* is about partnerships (civil unions, marriage, domestic partnerships, and other issues related to gay couples). Indeed, the fact that gay men and lesbians raise children is taken for granted and used as an argument to justify legalizing marriage. For example, in a 2013 article covering the Supreme Court trial against Proposition 8, Justice Anthony Kennedy is quoted as saying, "There are some 40,000 children in California . . . [who] . . . live with same-sex parents, and they want their parents to have full recognition and full status. The voice of those children is important in this case."[16] Kennedy's affirmation that the voices of those people most affected by these laws should be heard is an unintentional but accurate reflection of precisely the kinds of knowledge that would appear most commonly in coverage of these issues.

The French preoccupation with parenting over marriage, as expressed in public opinion polls, is reflected in reporting. Correspondingly, 65 percent of articles in *Le Monde* deal with legal issues related to having and raising children, but only 15 percent do in the *Times*. In many instances, French articles about legal reforms strictly affecting same-sex couples, such as the Pacs, which has no implications for access to parenting through adoption, involve opponents expressing concern that if same-sex relationships are recognized to any degree, it may inevitably lead to gay parenting. French articles treat gay parenting as a contentious legal and social controversy, not a simple matter of fact. That gays and lesbians can and do raise children is hypothetical, marginal, or, in the eyes of its opponents, a grave danger to be prevented. A 2013 op-ed by Maurice Berger, a well-known psychiatrist, psychoanalyst, and then head of child psychiatry at the University Hospital of Saint-Etienne, is exemplary. Arguing against the legalization of adoption by same-sex couples, he argues that only the "complementarity" of a man and woman can bring a child psychological stability: "The heterosexual parental couple, even divorced, is therefore the best way to ensure that sexuality, conception and parental tenderness are inseparably linked. And how can a little girl understand that two men who do not want to have a wife could have wanted a daughter?"[17] His comments illustrate how French news debates contain more expertise that casts doubt on the moral legitimacy and demographic reality of gay families than those in the United States.

FRENCH AND AMERICAN READERS SEE GAY FAMILIES FROM CONTRASTING PERSPECTIVES

Beyond their focus on legal issues and decision-making institutions specific to their national contexts, contributors to *Le Monde* and the *Times* draw on different kinds of knowledge when discussing gay family rights. Although each type of expertise—from social science and mental health to religious knowledge and personal experience—has at least a few occurrences in either newspaper, their proportions are significantly different. Furthermore, the quantity and distribution of knowledge that is favorable or opposed to these reforms are distinct. Table 1.2 shows these proportions for the twenty-three-year period, the differences between them, and whether they express a stance for or against same-sex family issues.

Legal expertise—information about laws, legal code, and processes of reform—is the single most common type of knowledge for both newspapers, at 21 percent

TABLE 1.2 Proportion of Expertise Occurrences by Type and Stance in *Le Monde* and *The New York Times (NYT)* Between 1990 and 2013

	All			For			Against		
	Monde	NYT	Monde–NYT	Monde	NYT	Monde–NYT	Monde	NYT	Monde–NYT
Social science	0.12	0.09	0.03	0.06	0.05	0.01	0.05	0.02	0.02
Religion	0.05	0.08	−0.03	0.01	0.02	−0.01	0.03	0.06	−0.03
Personal experience	0.10	0.17	−0.07	0.08	0.16	−0.08	0.01	0.01	0.00
Mental health	0.17	0.07	0.10	0.07	0.03	0.03	0.10	0.03	0.07
Law	0.21	0.29	−0.08	0.09	0.14	−0.04	0.06	0.07	−0.01
General	0.12	0.14	−0.02	0.04	0.08	−0.04	0.07	0.06	0.01
All other	0.24	0.16	0.08	0.12	0.09	0.03	0.05	0.04	0.01
Total	1	1		0.47	0.57	−0.09	0.36	0.28	0.08
N	1,318	4,243							

$\chi^2 = 248.8223$ (df 6), $p < .001$ $\chi^2 = 108.8476$ (df 6), $p < .001$ $\chi^2 = 112.771$ (df 6), $p < .001$

Note: Neutral stance not shown.

in *Le Monde* and at a larger and statistically significant proportion of 29 percent in the *Times*. Both newspapers also include similar quantities of "general" expertise—justifications couched in unspecific terms—tied at 12 percent for third place with social science in *Le Monde* and also in third place with 14 percent in the *Times*. Proponents of gay parenting rights often use legal arguments, and as a result, legal information is more supportive than critical in both newspapers, though more so in the *Times*. The paper regularly quotes lawyers, such as Jennifer Pizer, chief legal officer at Lambda Legal, one of the largest and oldest LGBTQ legal organizations in the United States, who speak about the judicial merits of gay marriage.[18] In addition, legal expertise makes up the largest fraction of neutral information in both publications because journalists quote legal experts, such as law professors, to either explain the stakes of a given reform but whose stance is unknown or to contextualize an article by describing the current status of gay rights. That legal expertise and general statements based on broad principles are some of the most common forms of knowledge in discussions of legal reforms on a contentious social issue is not surprising.

Beyond these kinds of knowledge that one would expect to find in such a debate, however, the knowledge patterns diverge. Specifically, elite knowledge grounded in academic disciplines and professional information occupies a higher proportion of expertise in *Le Monde*, while personal experience is more represented in the *Times*. Social sciences and mental health together make up 29 percent of expertise in the French coverage but only 16 percent in the U.S. coverage. In fact, after law, mental health is the second most important single type of expertise contributors to *Le Monde* use. Moreover, when they use it, they are more likely to use it to denounce rather than support gay family rights; mental health against gay family rights makes up 10 percent of all expertise occurrences in *Le Monde* and is the largest type of opposing expertise.

Even among social science and mental health expertise, there are significant differences among the specific disciplines—presented in table 1.3—that each newspaper references. Among social science expertise, anthropology and sociology are significantly more common in *Le Monde* than in the *Times*, where economy dominates. Among mental health fields, psychology is most common for both, but the significance of psychoanalysis in the French press (32 percent of mental health expertise generally) is remarkable when compared to its virtual absence in the United States. For example, Serge Lesourd, a psychoanalyst and professor of psychology, made statements in an article published during the height of

TABLE 1.3 Types of Social Science and Mental Health Expertise Occurrences in *Le Monde* and *The New York Times (NYT)*

Social science	Monde	NYT	Monde–NYT
Anthropology	0.36	0.04	0.31
Sociology	0.42	0.23	0.19
Economy	0.13	0.42	−0.28
Politics	0.09	0.31	−0.22
N	160	370	

$\chi^2 = 142.2940$ (df 3), $p < .001$

Mental health	Monde	NYT	Monde–NYT
Psychiatry	0.07	0.04	0.03
Psychoanalysis	0.32	0.03	0.29
Psychology	0.61	0.94	−0.33
N	227	284	

$\chi^2 = 87.7185$ (df 2), $p < .001$

the Pacs debates that uses this kind of expertise. Explaining his opposition to the hypothetical situation of gay adoption—a reform lawmakers did not take up during the Pacs debates but brandished by opponents of the new law as a slippery slope—he says, "[For homosexuals] there is often a psychic denial of sexual difference in adolescence. . . . It would be dangerous to give a child the impression that there are no limits, no prohibitions, by refusing to recognize the sterility that homosexuality implies. Frustration is the foundation of education."[19] These patterns confirm observations about the specific combination and importance of anthropology and psychoanalysis in historical French public policy debates and their contemporary influence, and as we will see in later chapters, they show up in French policymaking arenas as much as they do in the press.[20]

Opponents of same-sex families also draw on psychology or the concept of "psychological research" in the *Times* but virtually never in psychoanalytic terms. Moreover, unlike their French counterparts, U.S. opponents privilege the importance of marriage, rather than biological relatedness, for children's psychological well-being. For example, people like Jim Daly, then president of Focus on the Family, the influential fundamentalist Christian activist organization founded in 1977, make claims that children "fare best with a married mother and father."[21] This stance reflects the importance of marriage culture in the United States and the wider place marriage, rather than parenting, occupies as a controversial issue in the American political field.

The relative weight of economic expertise in the *Times* (28 percent more than in *Le Monde* and 41 percent of all social science knowledge) also distinguishes U.S. reporting. Exemplifying economic expertise is an article published in 2009 in which the journalists calculated the extra financial burdens, such as taxes, health insurance, and retirement accounts, accrued to a hypothetical same-sex couple because they could not marry.[22] Creating such economic knowledge is available and usable in the United States—and not in France—because state variation in marriage laws creates the possibility for comparison. The presence of economic expertise is also evidence of how human rights issues, such as same-sex marriage, fit within the cultural repertoire of markets and intrastate competition that shapes discourse on a variety of unrelated issues in American policy debates.[23] Nevertheless, this kind of elite expertise proffered by highly credentialed people, which is characteristic of reporting in *Le Monde*, is less present in the *Times*.

Instead, in the *Times*, the conversation on gay family rights is predominantly one that focuses on the lived experiences of different people, such as same-sex couples, their children, and people with gay family members who talk about how the law affects them. Indeed, as shown in table 1.2, at 17 percent of all expertise occurrences, personal experience is the second most common form of knowledge after law. Almost all of this expertise is favorable to extending relationship and parenting rights to same-sex couples. The *Times* has a much higher proportion of personal experience because its articles consistently include a vignette of a member of the general public talking about how the law affects them. Often, these include statements by same-sex couples raising children. As a result of this journalistic convention, unlike in *Le Monde*, gay family debates are dependably personified. *New York Times* readers have a direct sense of how legal reforms affect people concretely, whereas *Le Monde* readers are more likely to be presented with information, such as academic discourse, that views gay families from a distance, only occasionally giving readers a glimpse of what these fights mean for ordinary people.

COVERAGE OVER TIME: HOW EXPERTISE EVOLVES (OR NOT)

The overall patterns described above help us understand the kinds of expertise readers of these newspapers saw on average. Breaking down coverage by year between 1990 and 2013, we see that expertise in the coverage of gay family debates is also dynamic. While some types of knowledge remained relatively constant, such as legal expertise, other kinds of information have either dwindled or grown even more prominent. Moreover, the degree to which that expertise supports arguments for or against same-sex marriage and parenting has also evolved over the twenty-three-year period analyzed. The changes matter because they reveal how the public is informed in the long term and whether or not they are exposed to novel kinds of expertise, on the one hand, or familiar expertise but with a new ideological orientation, on the other.

For *Le Monde*, figure 1.2 details the relative annual proportions of major forms of expertise. Figure 1.3 depicts annual proportions of several major types of

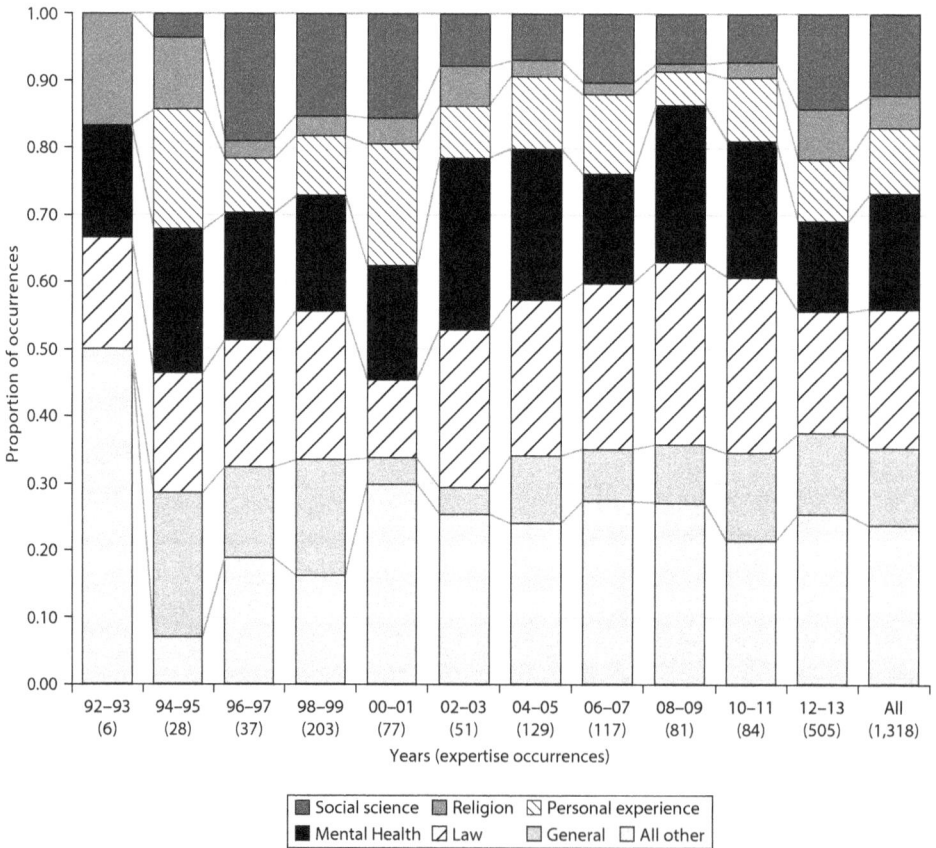

1.2 Types of expertise in *Le Monde*, 1990–2013

Note: No articles published in 1990–1991

expertise according to their favorable or unfavorable stances on gay family rights. Several observations jump out from these data. First, counter to the general impression that the news media represent sexual minorities more frequently now than they did in the past, the proportion of personal experience in Le Monde has not significantly increased. In fact, the proportion of personal experience was higher—about 18 percent of all expertise—in 1994–1995 and in 2000–2001, immediately following the passage of the Pacs, than the twenty-three-year average (10 percent). Second, typical of Le Monde coverage, mental health expertise has constituted a significant proportion of knowledge throughout the last two decades, averaging 17 precent and never dipping below 10 percent. Furthermore, on average, a majority (56 percent) of this expertise has criticized same-sex families. Analysis of the annual breakdown shows, however, that these stances have fluctuated. Negative stances were even stronger in the early 1990s and remained dominant (54 percent) during the Pacs debate years. Then, in the intervening years until the marriage and adoption debates of 2012–2013,

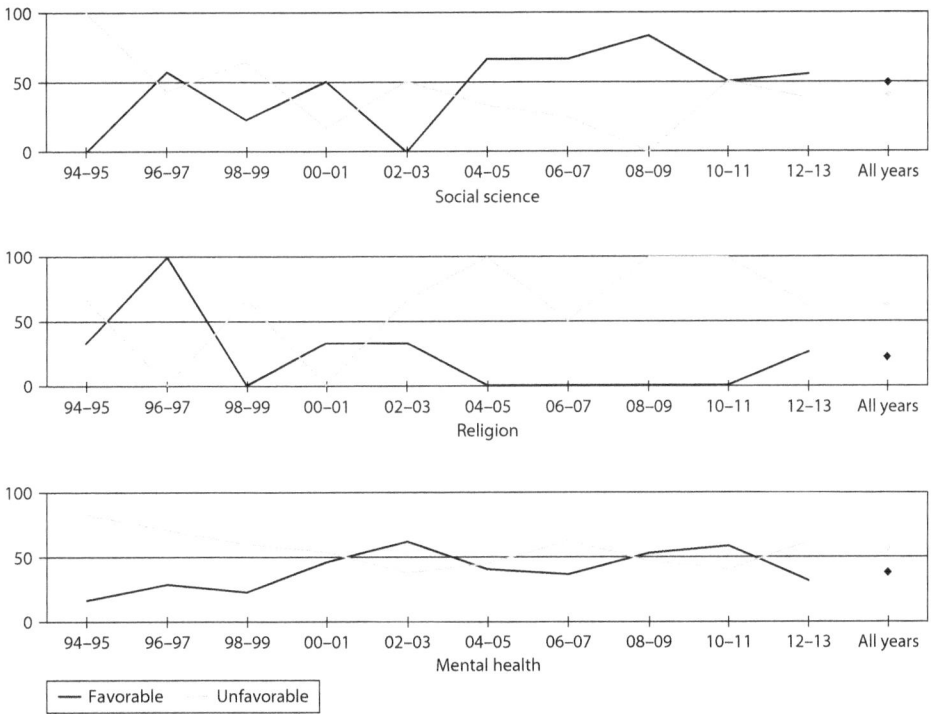

1.3 Percentage of favorable and unfavorable expertise in Le Monde, 1994–2013

favorable mental health expertise was more common. This pattern suggests that when legislative activity is low, the media creates more space for dissident stances. In other words, the closer same-sex couples are to gaining rights, the more likely it is that conservative mental health professionals and other opponents who mobilize psychology and psychoanalysis will make themselves heard.

Social science expertise has also been a constant feature of coverage in *Le Monde*. Its proportion increases in years of peak political debates, during and around the Pacs debates and during the marriage debates of 2012–2013. Most striking is the flip in its stance between 1990 and 2013. While almost half of such knowledge is favorable to gay families on average, during the Pacs debates, 65 percent of social science expertise opposed the reforms. Since the 2000s, social science expertise has generally been more favorable, suggesting a more durable change. One likely explanation is that prominent figures within French sociology and anthropology, the two most-cited social science disciplines, changed their stances during this period. Examples of these figures include the renowned anthropologist and member of the Collège de France, Françoise Héritier, and the influential sociologist Irène Théry, a professor at the prestigious École des Hautes Études en Sciences Sociales [School of Advanced Studies in the Social Sciences]. Both were openly opposed to the Pacs and adoption for same-sex couples before becoming outspoken supporters in the 2000s. Because they changed their minds, they drove the flip in ideology of social science expertise in *Le Monde* both directly and indirectly. First, because they are frequently quoted themselves, their new views shifted the balance in favor of gay families. Second, once these influential academics were no longer opposed, it became no doubt easier for social scientists supportive of gay families to speak to the press without fear that it could hurt their scholarly reputations and careers.

Defining peak years of political debate, on which to map changes over time, is less obvious in the United States because of the way reforms have progressed more continuously and less discretely than they have in France. Nevertheless, there are some clear patterns that show gradual changes over time, as depicted in figure 1.4. Coverage in the *Times* is dominated by a combination of elite and lay expertise: law and personal experience. Both of these types of expertise have increased over time. Compared to *Le Monde*, the contrast between personal experience and mental health is striking. As the proportion of psychology decreased to a low of only 4 percent in 2012–2013, stories about same-sex couples, politicians, and others talking about their gay family members, or being gay themselves, increased markedly, never falling under 18 percent after 2004. In another

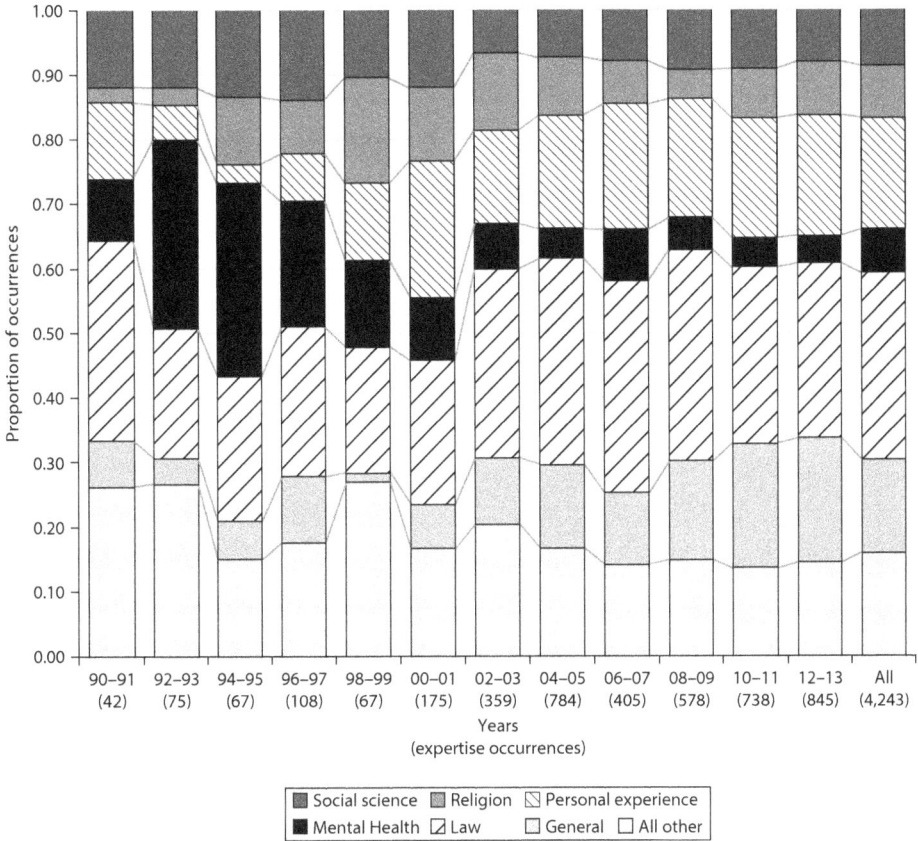

1.4 Types of expertise in *The New York Times*, 1990–2013

difference with *Le Monde*, social science has almost always been in favor of gay family rights in the *Times*, as seen in figure 1.5. In fact, the proportion of unfavorable social science expertise has generally trended downward since 2004.

Religious expertise is relatively minor overall in both newspapers, although statistically greater in the *Times* (8 percent) than in *Le Monde* (5 percent). The patterns in proportional change of such knowledge, though, are similar. Religious expertise was higher during the Pacs years in *Le Monde*, decreased during the 2000s, but then expanded noticeably in 2012–2013. Similarly, in the *Times*, quotes from people making scriptural arguments decreased from a peak in 1998–1999 throughout the 2000s, only to increase again between 2010 and 2013. One noticeable difference, however, is that religious discourse in support of gay family rights,

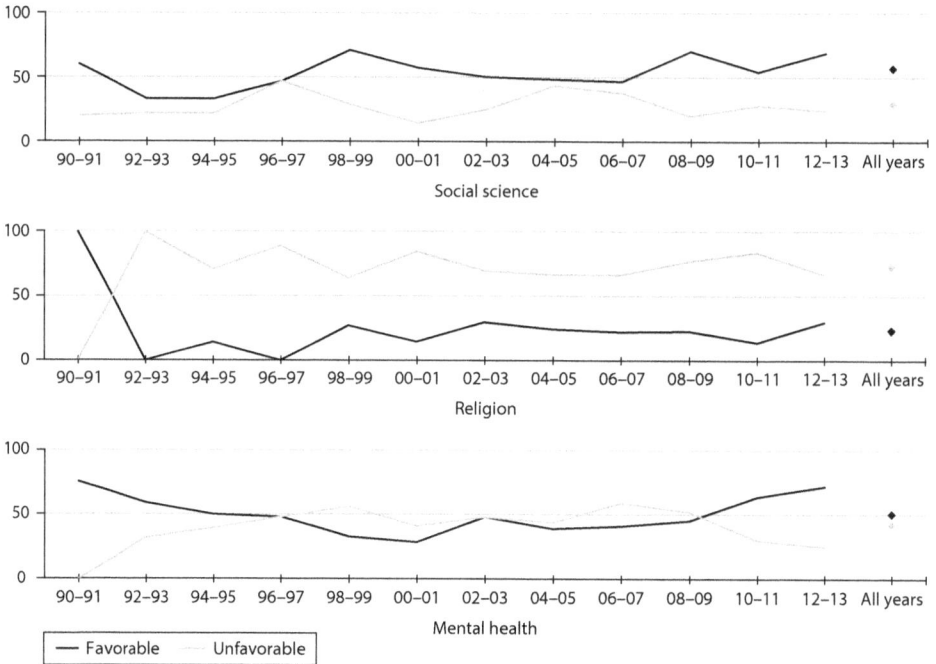

Social science

Religion

Mental health

- Favorable   ⋯⋯ Unfavorable

1.5 Percentage of favorable and unfavorable expertise in *The New York Times*, 1990–2013

though still in the minority in both newspapers, is more common in the *Times* and has been a consistent presence each year. Such gay-supportive religious expertise has been inconsistent or absent in many of the twenty-three years in *Le Monde*.

EXPERTS: MESSENGERS, THEIR MESSAGES, AND THEIR POWER

Having discussed the kinds of information *Le Monde* and the *Times* readers encounter, we now turn our attention to the people who provide it. Identifying which kinds of people deliver the messages, as well as the kinds of information they use, gives insight into the particular strength—or weakness—of specific forms of expert capital. For instance, knowing that mental health expertise is prevalent in French coverage only provides part of the picture. Psychoanalytic information will mean something different if it is quoted from, say, a Catholic

TABLE I.4 Proportion of Articles Citing Different Categories of Experts in *Le Monde* and *The New York Times (NYT)* Between 1990 and 2013

	Monde			NYT		Monde–NYT	
	Rank	Proportion		Rank	Proportion		
Activist	1	0.22	Average person	1	0.34	Activist	−0.11
Organization	2	0.21	Activist	2	0.33	Artist/public figure	−0.01
Politician	2	0.21	Organization	3	0.32	Author/ intellectual	−0.01
Professor	4	0.20	Politician	4	0.25	Average person	−0.17
Average person	5	0.17	Lawyer	5	0.18	Government agency	0.02
Health professional	6	0.14	Professor	6	0.14	Health professional	0.09
Religious representative	7	0.12	Judge	7	0.13	Industry	−0.05
Judge	8	0.07	Religious representative	8	0.11	Judge	−0.06
Lawyer	8	0.07	Think tank	9	0.06	Lawyer	−0.11
Government agency	10	0.06	Industry	10	0.05	Organization	−0.11
Philosopher	10	0.06	Health professional	10	0.05	Philosopher	0.06
Author/ intellectual	12	0.02	Government agency	12	0.04	Politician	−0.04
Artist/public figure	13	0.01	Author/ intellectual	13	0.03	Professor	0.06
Think tank	14	0.00	Artist/public figure	14	0.02	Religious representative	0.01
Industry	14	0.00	Philosopher	15	0.00	Think tank	−0.06
N		652			1,683		

$\chi^2 = 333.7734$ (df 14), $p < .001$

bishop. A person sharing intimate details about their lesbian granddaughter will resonate differently if that person is a prominent Republican politician. Furthermore, tracking the categories of people most often cited can give clues about who journalists and editors have access to and which voices they want to amplify at the expense of others. Table 1.4 ranks the principal experts—who I categorized based on journalists' descriptions, bylines, and public records—by the proportion of total articles over the sample period that cite them, as well as the differences in these proportions across newspapers.

The categories of experts who are cited most often in each newspaper confirm the disparity between elite discourse from the top down in French coverage and experience from the ground up in American reporting. Looking at the rightmost column, displaying differences in proportions across newspapers, reveals that experts across most categories have higher proportions in the *Times*. Tellingly, however, health professionals, professors, government agencies, and philosophers are the only experts who are cited in higher proportions in *Le Monde*. These kinds of experts represent a particularly elite group. The rankings of the most often cited experts in each newspaper show similar patterns. People of a higher institutional and social status are among the top categories of experts in *Le Monde*. While citations involving activists, politicians, and members of organizations are among the four most common types of experts across both newspapers, professors and health professionals—which includes medical and mental health professionals—are more highly ranked in *Le Monde*. Note also the relatively similar proportions of media space given to activists and professors. In contrast to the credentialed groups in French reporting, average people are the most commonly cited kind of expert in the *Times* (34 percent of all articles), outranking professionals and academics, but only ranking fifth in *Le Monde* (17 percent). Readers of U.S. coverage are thus more likely to directly encounter the people whose lives the law affects more often than their French peers who, instead, hear arguments about gay families via professionals and activists, two unequally regarded groups—the former seen as neutral observers and the latter as biased partisans—that are often presented as facing off. One smaller particularity of *New York Times* coverage is the higher proportion of lawyers and judges who are cited relative to *Le Monde*, which is likely explained by the importance of courts of gay rights in the United States.

This dichotomy between types of experts has grown over time in news coverage between the two papers. Table 1.5 shows that between the first and second half of the twenty-three-year period, in the *Times*, the proportion of articles citing average people doubled. At the same time, the proportion of articles citing health professionals and professors decreased. Think tanks, which gained ground in the American policy field, also saw their proportions increase. In contrast, there was no significant difference in the proportion of articles citing average

TABLE 1.5 Experts Whose Proportion of Citations Changed Significantly Over Sample Period in *Le Monde* and *The New York Times (NYT)*

Monde	1990–2001	2002–2013	Change
Author/intellectual	0.01	0.03	+0.02
Government agency	0.02	0.08	+0.06
Judge	0.04	0.09	+0.05
Organization	0.26	0.19	−0.07
N	198	454	

$\chi^2 = 22.2797$ (df 3), $p < .001$

NYT	1990–2001	2002–2013	Change
Average person	0.18	0.37	+0.19
Health professional	0.13	0.03	−0.10
Politician	0.11	0.28	+0.18
Professor	0.20	0.13	−0.07
Think tank	0.01	0.06	+0.05
N	282	1,401	

$\chi^2 = 131.8030$ (df 4), $p < .001$

people in *Le Monde* between the first and second halves of the period studied. Thus, unlike their American peers, readers of French coverage did not encounter more members of gay families telling stories about their lives in a country that refuses to recognize them. Not only does this silence their voices, but it can also leave the impression that they do not constitute a growing social group making legitimate demands deserving of political attention. Instead, in *Le Monde*, top-down viewpoints, specifically those from government agencies, judges, and intellectuals, have increased.

As described earlier, religious expertise—arguments grounded in scripture—makes up a smaller proportion of knowledge in *Le Monde* than in the *Times*. On its own, this observation gives the impression that French *laïcité* and American religiosity are echoed in media reporting, as one might expect. However, as table 1.4 reveals, there is, surprisingly, no statistically significant difference between the number of articles in these newspapers citing religious representatives (12 and 11 percent, respectively). In other words, clergy are present in equal quantities in both, defying the common idea of clear-cut French and American differences about the degree of secularization of public discourse. Looking more closely at what these religious representatives actually say, however, as well as how other kinds of experts use, or not, religious discourse brings another pattern to light.

Figures 1.6 and 1.7 depict the most commonly cited categories of people in each newspaper and the types of information they provide to these newspapers. They show that religious representatives use different kinds of expertise in France and the United States. Specifically, of all the kinds of expertise clergy bring to the debate in each newspaper, actual claims based on religion account for 50 percent in the *Times* but only 33 percent in *Le Monde*. American clergy also use personal experience (10 percent) more than their French peers (1 percent). In contrast, French priests, bishops, imams, and other religious representatives use significantly higher quantities of social science (16 percent) and mental health expertise (18 percent) than those in the United States (6 and 4 percent, respectively). Tony Anatrella, the French priest, psychoanalyst, outspoken opponent to gender and sexual equality, and driving force behind the Vatican's demonization of "gender ideology," exemplifies this strategy.[24] In an editorial entitled "An Anxious Rush" published in *Le Monde* during the Pacs debates, he declared that same-sex couples should not be given any legal recognition. Such unions are unworthy

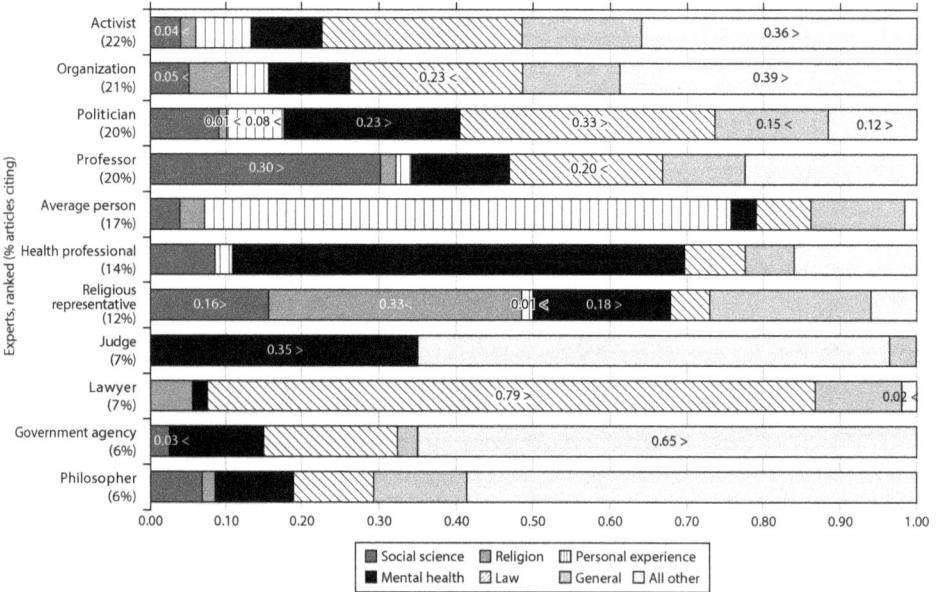

1.6 Proportion and type of expertise used by experts in *Le Monde*

Note: < or > signifies proportion of expert citations is greater/less than that for the same expert in *The New York Times*. All instances p-value <0.05 (Chi-square test).

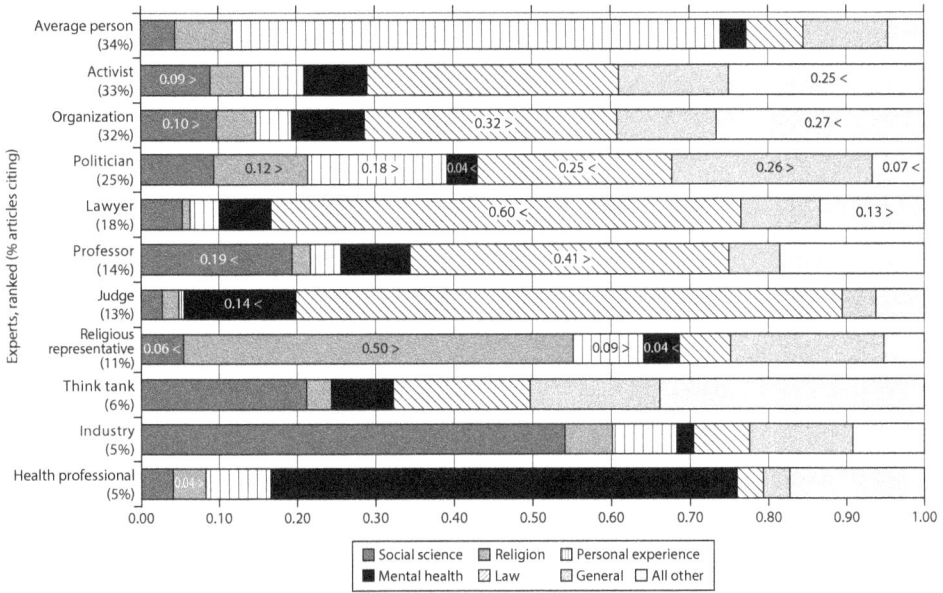

1.7 Proportion and type of expertise used by experts in *The New York Times*

Note: < or > signifies proportion of expert citations is greater/less than that for the same expert in *Le Monde*. All instances p-value <0.05 (Chi-square test).

of institutionalization, he writes, not because homosexuality is a sin but because it is a "pre-oedipal" sexual fantasy, a theory he would develop in a series of books warning against the dangers of homosexuality.[25]

When speaking to a broad public in France's most celebrated newspaper, French religious representatives, like Anatrella, foreground secular expertise to a higher degree than their American peers. Only about 33 percent of what clergy in *Le Monde* say is related to religion, whereas 18 percent is mental health expertise. In contrast, roughly half of what religious representatives say in the *Times* is religious and 4 percent related to mental health. These patterns show how these experts are likely responding to different cultural and institutional pressures. Expectations that political discussions on important public issues should be free from obviously religious discourse may be driving French religious representatives to use a kind of expert capital they think will make them more audible and credible. In this instance, French secularism does not appear to limit the appearance of clergy in political debates altogether. Rather, that they draw on social science and mental health suggests that French clergy tap into popular forms of expertise in their context, which is shared across many types of actors, to be taken more seriously. In contrast, American clergy may mobilize such quantities of religious discourse precisely because other actors, especially those with more institutional power, such as politicians, use scripture as well.

Because of their desire to appeal to the public and convince their colleagues, politicians provide good insight into the kinds of discourse that have power and currency in a given context. The example of religious expertise is telling. As shown in figures 1.6 and 1.7, French politicians use almost no religious expertise (1 percent), but their American peers use more (12 percent) and on both sides of the issue. For example, in 2008, then-president Barack Obama, who initially argued that "marriage is a sacred union, a blessing from God, and one that is intended for a man and a woman exclusively," later changed his stance.[26] Explaining his reversal, he states, "The thing at root that we think about is, not only Christ sacrificing himself on our behalf, but it's also the golden rule—you know, treat others the way you would want to be treated."[27] Politicians also use more personal experience in American coverage (18 percent) than their peers in French reporting (8 percent). American politicians of all sexual orientations talk about how gay family rights impact themselves as well as their friends and family. For example, in support of same-sex marriage, Hilary Clinton, who in 2013 was then a Democratic senator representing New York, used the feelings she had as a mother attending her daughter's wedding to affirm, "I wish every parent that same joy," alluding to parents of gays and lesbians.[28] Some French politicians use their own experiences, but this remains much less present than in American reporting. Jean-Luc Romero, an operative of the conservative Union for a Popular Movement (UMP) party and former council member in the city and region of Paris, was one of the rare openly gay French politicians—and was also open about being HIV positive, which was even less common—in the early 2000s. His interventions are a good example. In articles about gay rights that cited him, he describes his life with his partner, which was rather novel.[29]

If French politicians are evidently loath to talk about their lives, they are much happier to bring up mental health expertise. It accounts for 23 percent of what French politicians say, compared to only 4 percent among Americans. An example of this comes from a *Le Monde* article that cites the lawmaker, Jean Raquin, explaining why he refused to grant an adoption authorization to a lesbian, using his authority as president of the Département in which she lived. In the early 2000s, Emmanuelle B., a special education teacher living with her partner, applied for the authorization as a single woman—same-sex couples being excluded from adoption—and was denied multiple times. Despite a ruling from the European Court of Human Rights judging the refusal discriminatory, Raquin declined to change his decision. Justifying his stance, he says, "your request does not currently present the necessary guaranties to preserve the best interest of the child you would welcome into your home . . . [because your partner would] occupy a third party to the mother-child relationship."[30] Mobilizing similar knowledge to oppose the 2012 marriage and adoption bill, Éric Woerth—who held various political positions including mayor, assembly member, and minister of the budget under conservative president Nicolas Sarkozy—states, "inscribing into the law that one can become a parent without being a man and woman runs the risk of dismantling the structure of society. . . . We do not know what the consequences will be on children; we're playing with fire."[31] In both examples, politicians wield basic notions in psychology—the idea that having two mothers will interfere with maternal bonding or that same-sex parenting will have unpredictable consequences on children's outcomes—to express their opposition. This demonstrates how mental health concepts become a politically powerful argument to delegitimize the rights' claims of gay families in France. What makes them so effective is their repetition and circulation across and between many categories of experts, giving them legitimacy along the way.

To get a sense of how widely types of expertise are shared, we can zoom out to look at all of the categories of experts. Figures 1.6 and 1.7 depict the kinds of expertise the eleven most highly ranked experts in both newspapers employ. It reveals that the differences in type of knowledge religious representatives and politicians in each country use also hold up for the other experts. For instance, the most highly ranked actors in Le Monde use large proportions of mental health expertise in their press interventions, while those in the Times have less mental health and more personal experience. Indeed, in Le Monde, only seven of the top-ranked categories of experts use religion and personal experience, whereas all in the Times draw on religion, and only one, think tank staff, does not use personal experience. Not surprisingly, in the Times, average people, the largest conveyors of personal experience, are the highest ranked experts, whereas health professionals, who use the biggest proportion of mental health expertise, rank in eleventh place. The same institutional experts in both countries, such as judges, also reflect these trends in reporting; French and American judges use similar proportions of legal expertise, which is logical given their roles, but the former use no personal experience and 35 percent of mental health, while the latter use some personal experience and only 14 percent of mental health.

Other smaller trends are also noteworthy. Activists and organizations in the *Times* use more social science (9 and 10 percent, respectively)—which, as described earlier, is primarily economic expertise—than their French equivalents (4 and 5 percent, respectively). Activists and members of organizations use a range of knowledge in both newspapers, but only those in the United States present neoliberal arguments about the economic benefit of same-sex marriage as one of them. Organizations and professors in the *Times* use more law (32 and 41 percent, respectively) than their peers in *Le Monde* (23 and 20 percent, respectively). This dichotomy reflects differences between the French and American political spheres more broadly and on gay rights issues in particular. Many organizations advocating for or against gay family reforms, such as Lambda Legal or the Thomas More Center for Law and Justice, fill the demand for legal expertise generated by judicial reforms in the American context. Similarly, because most professors cited in the *Times* are law professors, legal expertise is significantly more common among American professors as a group relative to their French peers, who hail from more disciplines. These two groups of experts provide *New York Times* journalists with analyses of court rulings, reform strategies, and predictions of future judgments. In contrast, in *Le Monde*, 30 percent of the knowledge professors use is social science—compared to only 19 percent in the *Times*—reflecting the weight of anthropologists and sociologists who produce this popular form of knowledge for decision-makers and the press.

CONCLUSION

In 1990, same-sex couples had little, if any, legal recognition in most parts of the United States, whereas in France, some organizations, particularly those focused on AIDS activism, were pushing the state to recognize gay couples but had not yet made much headway. Between those early years and 2013, *Le Monde* and the *Times* reported on the contentious debates pitting gay families seeking formal rights against those striving to thwart them. Their readers, who included politicians and other elites, learned about the merits of same-sex marriage and parenting from a diverse group of people, cited by journalists and published by editorialists. But the parliamentary staffer reading the pages of *Le Monde* in an office near the Seine would not be informed with the same sorts of analyses as the teacher skimming the *Times* on her lunch break. Despite dealing with the same set of controversial issues, people who read these newspapers would have been exposed to particular and nationally specific kinds of experts and expertise, potentially leading them to think about gay families in different ways.

The distinction between these national patterns in expertise manifests in several ways. By relying heavily on knowledge grounded in social science and mental health, and in particular anthropology and psychoanalysis, French reporting emphasizes information that speaks to notions of the "universal" rather than "particular." Indeed, *Le Monde* reporting is characterized by a top-down view of gay families read abstractly through the lens of theory that sidelines the lived experiences of people, who are, in contrast, a significant feature in the *Times*. Indeed, one of the most salient features of American reporting is the dominant presence of average people, who constitute the most often cited group, and the widespread use of personal experience across most categories of experts. Even French gay politicians and activists, who we might expect to bring something intimate to the debate, are less likely to be quoted about their personal experiences than their American peers. By speaking to journalists in the idiom of academic knowledge, French supporters and opponents of gay family rights can appear detached from the issue personally, making it easier to appeal to universal values. Contrasts in coverage are thus consistent with the dominant cultural repertoires of civic solidarity in France and markets in the United States that scholars have identified for many other issues. Furthermore, the significant differences in proportions of economic expertise in the *Times* and *Le Monde* seem to support the resonance of market logics within American systems of justification.

The news media can be a platform for experts to engage the public and each other. It is not a unidirectional communication, meant only to spread information. It can also serve to develop alliances and shape the trajectories of knowledge production, creating a feedback loop between the media and experts. News coverage is thus an important tool for cultivating—and not simply distributing—expert capital. This is particularly remarkable in *Le Monde*, where professionals and academics have an important presence relative to the *Times*. As we will see in chapter 3, the higher proportion of these groups in French coverage is directly related to the incentive elite French experts have to speak out in the press. French newspapers, *Le Monde* foremost among them, are not just forums for informing the public and selling advertisements. They are a battleground where opposing clans of experts guard their territory and score political points through editorial salvos. Information they share through journalists' quotations and op-eds creates a platform around which their allies among politicians and activists can rally and against which adversaries will almost inevitably react. Furthermore, this struggle between experts is transposed directly into the political field because lawmakers pay attention to the people quoted in the papers, using that information to decide who they should be reaching out to as they write laws. Elite French experts thus have strong professional and political motives to answer journalists' phone calls and write opinion pieces. Of course, the media landscape in both countries has changed significantly over time. Perhaps the significance of newspapers has diminished, especially since 2013. However, throughout most of the period studied here, they were a key component of these debates, and their importance for French academic and professional experts comes through in their high proportions among those cited in the pages of Le Monde.

The patterns of experts and expertise in Le Monde and the Times also give us a sense of which discourse is likely to seem acceptable in a given cultural context. Indeed, aside from the common types of expertise between them, such as legal information, the patterns of their contrasts are sharp and enduring. Furthermore, results show that very different categories of people—from think tank researchers to ordinary citizens—deploy similar kinds of expertise specific to their cultural context. By drawing on the same repertoires, such as mental health in France and personal experience in the United States, they are more audible in their respective political and media fields. These forms of expert capital become a kind of shared language that may give those who use it more credibility and easier access to the debate. Some groups may use it to overcome what might be barriers to their participation. For example, religious representatives in France can counteract pressures against overtly religious discourse by arguing in terms of mental health, a form of expertise that politicians, activists, professors, and healthcare professionals also use. This strategy helps explain the equal numbers of religious representatives in media coverage but much lower quantities of religious discourse in Le Monde. These results show that much analytical leverage is gained by distinguishing experts from their expertise. By precisely determining who says what and in which quantities, we get a rich picture of the types of discourse at play, but also, and more importantly, the power of specific kinds of knowledge.

While these common kinds of expertise open opportunities for those who use them, they also lead to a lack of informational diversity and structure how members of the public, including lawmakers, judges, lawyers, and activists, perceive gay family rights. On a broader level, the dichotomy between top-down elite knowledge in *Le Monde* and bottom-up lay expertise in the *Times* means that the public and decision-makers are exposed to profoundly different representations of gay families in France and the United States. Readers of the *Times* have gotten to know same-sex couples and their children much earlier than readers of *Le Monde* and in much higher numbers. Indeed, if popular television series like *Modern Family* or talk shows like *Ellen* are any indication, gay families—at least privileged white ones conforming to bourgeois models of "normal" coupledom—entered the American mainstream much earlier than in France. Relative gay family invisibility, especially in the 1990s and 2000s, may help explain why gay parenting faced higher popular and political opposition in France. French advocates of gay parenting rights have faced obstacles to representing the lives of families affected by the lack of state recognition. Indeed, it may be that academic and professional discourse about gay families has wielded power in the French news media because it is relatively unchecked by the voices of average people, even when that discourse supports them. In the future, as more same-sex couples raise children with the authorization of the state, their visibility may increase in French media. Representation of such families—and that of other experts and expertise—in political and legal institutional debates in both countries, such as hearings and trials, is the focus of the next chapter.

CHAPTER 2

THE FLOOR IS YOURS

Expertise in Courts and Legislatures

On April 4, 2005, Steve Creasy, a self-described "father, tax payer, and concerned citizen," stood at a podium before the members of the State Affairs Committee of the Texas House of Representatives. The lawmakers peered down at him from their elevated seats in a crowded hearing room at the capitol complex in Austin. Accompanied by his wife and other family members, who would also testify, he pleaded with the lawmakers to reject House Joint Resolution 6 (HJR 6), a bill that would trigger a referendum giving Texans the opportunity to amend their state constitution to ban both same-sex marriage and civil unions. Speaking determinedly into the microphone, Mr. Creasy told them that the future of his gay son to live a full life would be jeopardized by the bill that had "shocked and saddened" them all. During the course of daylong hearings, a line of representatives of fifteen advocacy organizations—including the CEO and chief counsel of the First Liberty Institute, a conservative "religious freedom" organization—and seventy-five ordinary citizens, such as Mr. Creasy, presented a variety of testimony, some of it very personal and some of it dry and academic. In the end, the committee approved the bill that would become Proposition 2, and on November 8, 2005, 76.5 percent of voters agreed to modify the Constitution of the State of Texas to ensure that same-sex couples would be excluded from any and all recognition in the Lone Star State.

On the other side of the Atlantic, in the fall of 2012, the Judiciary Committee of the Assemblée Nationale held hearings about a proposed bill to allow same-sex couples to marry and adopt. As protests began to brew under the slogan that children need "*un père et une mère* [a father and mother]" and Catholic groups held candlelit prayer sessions outside the Assemblée, lawmakers organized over six weeks' worth of expert hearings. Though safely held deep within the chambers, what was said in this austere forum was projected out to a surprisingly wide audience: The hearings were livestreamed and excerpted in magazines, on the radio, and in the evening news. Featuring over 127 people, they included forty-three academics and professionals and representatives of twenty-nine organizations and agencies, but only fourteen ordinary citizens. Much of this testimony was technical and academic. Observers learned about the intricate theories of family formation as developed by the famous French structural anthropologist Claude Lévi-Strauss, as well as the minutiae of the Civil Code and the potential knock-on effects created by removing a reference to sex in the legal establishment of parenthood. In an exceptional and highly uncharacteristic session, the lawmakers—as well as those watching at home—heard adult children raised by same-sex couples talk about what the law would mean to them.

With gay families' lives on the line and the pressure of decades of activism leading up to these moments, decision-makers carved out time to hear people speak before them in the codified and formal settings of the institutions where they presided. These two examples showcase the ritualized encounter between lawmakers and the groups of people speaking into the literal and metaphorical public microphone. Whether they represent themselves, an ideological current, or a scientific consensus, their discourse enters the record, giving us clues about the disputed meanings of same-sex couples and the battle for their legal recognition. The contrasts between the two cases above lead to a series of questions: What kinds of things are lawmakers hearing and from whom? Are there systematic differences between the United States and France? If so, what are they? To answer these questions, this chapter analyzes the archival records of a sample of major legislative and judicial reforms between 1990 and 2013 in both countries.[1] Observing the differences in each context, it argues that cultural norms, rules in decision-making institutions, and the legality of certain gay family rights in the United States and France constrain and enable the specific categories of experts and the kinds of information they provide to lawmakers and judges in each country. More broadly, these patterns give us clues about the value of different kinds of expert capital and the people who deliver it in legal institutions. By not presupposing that one form of expertise is necessarily better than another, we get a clearer picture of the range of people weaving stories before lawmakers and the kinds of information they use to do so. The first half of the chapter examines legislatures in the United States before moving on to the courts. The second half briefly touches on courts in France, which are relatively less important, before unpacking the work of the French legislature.

U.S. LEGISLATURES: EMOTIONS, SCRIPTURE, AND MONEY

As described in the introduction, most major U.S. legislative efforts on marriage and parenting laws have occurred on the state, not federal, levels. State-level hearings have therefore been the primary legislative outlet for expertise. Over the years, lawmakers have considered bills expanding and contracting partnership rights, adoption and fostering regulations, and other laws that would fundamentally alter the everyday lives of same-sex couples and their children. Understanding the expertise they heard as they made these decisions requires paying attention to the norms and rules governing hearings. California and Texas, the two states this chapter analyzes, generally allow any interested party to register to testify at hearings and provide their views within an allotted time for opponents and supporters of proposed legislation. In addition, bill authors can bring several witnesses with them as they present their legislation to their colleagues, and in the case of California, opposing witnesses are given equal time. Examination of hearings held on major reforms since the 1990s in these states reveals that ordinary citizens, advocacy organizations, and religious representatives outnumbered all other categories of experts. Their interventions have grounded U.S. legislative debates in ways that connect lived experiences of people with moral values and technical knowledge, such as legal history and economic side effects of reforms. This particular combination is enabled by open legislative rules that create spaces for anyone to speak out, as well as by legal and social circumstances that allow these people to generate technical and lay expertise in the first place.

As depicted in table 2.1, across hearings for California bills, leaders from advocacy organizations, ordinary citizens, and religious representatives provided 48, 23, and 13 percent of all instances of testimony, respectively. Although other types of experts have also provided information, such as representatives of professional organizations or professors, their testimony is less present. California legislators have also heard more testimony favorable to legal recognition for same-sex couples, but given the mechanism guaranteeing time for both sides, opponents are still represented, even when the majority of the legislators in committees and full chambers are in favor of such rights.

TABLE 2.1 Proportion of Categories of Experts in California Hearings by Stance

Category of expert	For	Against	Neutral	Total
Advocacy organizations	0.33	0.15	0.00	0.48
Average people	0.09	0.13	0.00	0.23
Religious Representatives	0.06	0.06	0.00	0.13
Elected Officials/politicians	0.07	0.01	0.01	0.09
Professional organizations	0.04	0.00	0.00	0.04
Professors	0.02	0.01	0.01	0.03
Lawyers	0.00	0.00	0.01	0.01
Mental/health professionals	0.01	0.00	0.00	0.01
Total instances (N = 190)	0.62	0.36	0.02	1.00

Note: Sum of instances at hearings for AB 1982, AB 43, AB 205, and Prop 8. Stance is for or against gay family rights.

In Texas legislatures, ordinary citizens provide almost all of the testimony at hearings. As shown in table 2.2, they make up 82 percent of all instances of people providing information to legislators during hearings for major reforms, followed by advocacy organizations and religious representatives. Overall, Texas legislators have heard more from people who favor legal recognition for same-sex couples (86 percent of testimony).[2] This balance in favor, which may seem surprising given Texas's conservative political makeup relative to California, is likely the result of the content of the bills heard there. Between 1990 and 2015, Texas lawmakers did not consider legislation to legalize same-sex couples' rights. Rather, they considered and passed a statutory law and then language for a constitutional amendment—later approved by voters—to ban same-sex marriage and any other legal status, such as civil unions, that afford rights similar to marriage. Therefore,

TABLE 2.2 Proportion of Categories of Experts in Texas Hearings by Stance

Category of expert	For	Against	Total
Average people	0.76	0.06	0.82
Advocacy organizations	0.08	0.04	0.12
Religious representatives	0.02	0.03	0.05
Elected officials/politicians	0.00	0.00	0.00
Lawyers	0.00	0.00	0.00
Total instances (N = 251)	0.86	0.14	1.00

Note: Sum of instances at hearings for SB 7 and HJR 6. Stance is for or against gay family rights.

the people presenting testimony at these hearings, most of whom were ordinary Texans, were speaking out in order to prevent the state from making it even more difficult for themselves and their families, friends, or acquaintances to one day have their same-sex unions legally recognized.

Unsurprisingly, given the high proportion of ordinary citizens at California and Texas hearings, legislators hear people's personal experiences, stories, and backgrounds. Indeed, much like coverage in *The New York Times*, these legal institutions provided a forum for extended "storytelling."[3] The testimony was emotional and intimate. The video recordings of these hearings, which render the emotions of the speakers more fully than transcripts, show people hoping to elicit sympathy, spark outrage, and even shame lawmakers into agreeing with them. There are many examples of this kind of personal knowledge, much of it coming from those whose lives or those of their families would be most impacted by the legislation. For instance, at a California Senate Judiciary Committee hearing during debates over Assembly Bill (AB) 1982 in 1996—a failed bill that would have prevented the state from recognizing same-sex marriages performed outside the state—Cynthia Asperdidies came with her partner and their daughter to testify about how the proposed law, by specifically targeting same-sex couples, would single their family out, stigmatizing them as different from others and making future legal recognition even more difficult. Seven years later, at a hearing before the California Assembly Judiciary Committee over AB 205, "The California Domestic Partner Rights and Responsibilities Act of 2003," the bill's author, Assemblywoman Jackie Goldberg, brought a guest witness to demonstrate why the law was necessary. Lydia Ramos testified about losing her partner of fourteen years, Linda, whose death was made even more traumatic by the heavy financial and logistic burdens she faced—including Linda's relatives who took their youngest daughter upon finding out that Lydia had no legal rights as a spouse—because the state refused to fully recognize their relationship. Lydia Ramos's daughter, who was a minor at the time and one of the Ramos's three children, sat next to her mother and said she supported the bill. Meanwhile, in Texas in 2005, at hearings on the constitutional ban against same-sex marriage HJR 6, a middle-aged man described his family life with his partner and their adopted son, who was a former ward of the state of Texas, and described the measure as an attack on their dignity and human rights. At the same hearing, a father described his long marriage to his wife and his sadness that his daughters, one of whom was a lesbian and the other who was straight, would not have the same opportunity to experience the happiness he had.

Elite experts also drew on personal experience when testifying. Many advocate organization representatives, politicians, and even the few professionals and academics present drew on personal narratives in addition to other types of expertise. Straight witnesses in favor of same-sex couples talked about their own marriages and their desires for their gay and lesbian family and friends to have the same experiences. Those in opposition attempted to personalize their testimony. For example, Janine Bedley of the California Federation of Republican Women, who spoke out in opposition to AB 205, began her testimony by saying, "Let me make it clear to every one of you and every member of the audience that I do have friends who are homosexual. I do not have anything against homosexuals. I am personally straight." These intimate claims situated her stance within the register of personal experience, giving it the appearance of an equal stake in the debate. Academics and professionals who were openly gay described their families. Testifying in 2006 in favor of California domestic partnerships, for example, Kate O'Hanlon, a gynecological oncologist, described the research on the outcomes of children raised by same-sex couples, the endorsements of same-sex marriage by the U.S. major medical and mental health organizations, and the meaning of marriage to her as a lesbian raising children in a committed relationship.

The breadth of personal experience brought by a variety of types of experts in state legislative hearings shows that these institutional outlets are especially well suited for "lay expertise." One's life can serve as evidence of the potential harm from or need for legal changes, a justification for speaking out, a tactic to demonstrate concern and empathy, a way to humanize more technical expertise, and a means of making the situation tangible for lawmakers. Such personification of the law resembles U.S. press coverage where concrete portrayals of people's lives and emotions are more common than abstractions. Personal experience also creates a unique set of obstacles and opportunities for activists on both sides of American debates.

Had access to parenting for gays and lesbians been completely illegal in the United States, as it was in France, heart-wrenching stories of familial trauma would have been more difficult to present to lawmakers. The range of these stories and the presence of same-sex family narratives since at least the mid-1990s, including those people who had adopted or raised children through reproductive technology, were only possible in a broader U.S. legal and social context where same-sex parenting—but not marriage or civil unions—was legal in many jurisdictions. These circumstances permitted same-sex couples to lawfully parent in some otherwise conservative states, such as Texas, even as they were denied partnership rights.[4] Legal access to parenting also facilitated another type of expertise deployed by American advocates: empirical research about same-sex couples and the outcomes of their children. Indeed, as I document in chapter 4, researchers were able to study them in part because relatively liberal laws made it possible for same-sex couples to create families in the first place. Scholars and organizations benefitted from that situation to generate data that could be brought before lawmakers. For instance, at these hearings, advocacy groups described the numbers of same-sex couples raising children based on the 2000 Census as well as the research on childhood outcomes and literature reviews by mental health and medical professional organizations.

The physical presence of gay families at hearings, along with personal experience about them, constituted what could be called a self-evidence, an undeniable social group that American opponents of same-sex marriage and parenting could not easily ignore. Even as they argued that heterosexual married households were ideal environments for children, they had to concede that many same-sex couples—and single gay, lesbian, bisexual, and trans people—do raise children with explicit state approval. They also had to recognize that these adoptive parents filled a need in places with a critical shortage of people willing to adopt and high numbers of children in the foster system.[5] This was evident during a large public hearing on Proposition 8 organized by the California Senate and Assembly Judiciary Committees in Los Angeles a month before the ballot initiative would eventually pass, overturning the California Supreme Court's decision that had legalized same-sex marriage. Jennifer Roback Morse, a formerly tenured economics professor and founder of the conservative religious think tank, the Ruth Institute, argued against same-sex marriage on the grounds that children should be raised by their married biological mother and father. In response to legislators' questions, however, she had to acknowledge that she did not, in fact, advocate the removal of same-sex couples from adoption rosters or for placing limitations on lesbians' access to artificial insemination. At the hearing and during the debates around Proposition 8 more broadly, opponents had to find other arguments to justify their stances. For example, witnesses opposing same-sex couples frequently described their frustration that their own children would be taught in public school that two men or two women can marry and that homosexuality is a normal sexual orientation.

Religious expertise, such as claims about scripture, was also a common kind of knowledge people presented in state hearings. Representatives of churches and religious organizations as well as ordinary citizens opposing sexual minority families frequently spoke in such terms. They described, for example, how marriage was a sacred union, enshrined in their holy texts, and that same-sex couples, if granted entry to the institution, would undermine its sanctity. Yet, religious knowledge was not limited to opponents. In fact, as seen in tables 2.1 and 2.2, supportive religious representatives in Texas and California testified almost as much as opponents. They described their church's embrace of same-sex couples and their children as well as their views of how scripture viewed them as equal members of their communities. Illustrating such knowledge is the testimony of Kathleen Thomas at the Texas House State Affairs committee hearing on HJR 6. She first described herself as a straight adoptive mother and "mediocre Christian" because she has trouble "praying for people [she] doesn't consider to be really nice," joking that "my pastor's here and he can attest to that." Thomas then told the lawmakers that she is the service elder and member of the worship committee at her Presbyterian church that is "deliberately diverse and intentionally inclusive," where "all are welcome as God's family." She stated that the proposed bill would infringe on her church's religious liberty by forcing them to treat their gay and lesbian members as unequal and undeserving. Thomas's testimony typifies the everydayness of religious language that often underscores public speech in the United States more broadly. Archival analysis of state-level debates confirms that people bring that discourse into the legislative context, mobilizing religion to ground their claims in favor of or against gay people and their families.

Economics, including knowledge about the costs and benefits of partnership legalization, is another form of expertise unique to the U.S. context. Proponents and opponents of same-sex marriage, especially representatives from advocacy organizations and think tanks, drew on this kind of information to support their positions. Examples go back as early as 1995 during hearings over California's AB 1982, a bill proposed by Republican Assemblyman William J. Knight that aimed to specify marriage as a union between a man and woman in the state's Civil Code. Knight and the organizations that supported him, such as Concerned Women for America and the Committee on Moral Concerns, were reacting to the potential legalization of same-sex marriage in Hawaii, then under consideration by that state's supreme court, worried that interstate marital recognition would allow California gay and lesbian couples to marry there and demand recognition at home. During the hearings, Randy Thomason of the Capital Resource Institute, a California-based conservative "traditional family values" activist group, told the Senate Judiciary Committee that preventing same-sex marriage was necessary to preserve the health of California businesses and the state's budget. Same-sex marriage would be too expensive, he argued:

> [There is] a legitimate interest to protect California persons and consumers from the sizable cost and government mandates that would accompany same-sex marriage. There are hidden costs here and those costs hit taxpayers and business people in the pocket book. For businesses that have to pay attention to the bottom line, the prospect of same-sex marriage is a negative one. If same-sex marriage happens to be legalized, businesses that already provide healthcare benefits for spouses of employees, will also provide to what would now be called gay spouses of employees. . . . That potential cost could range into the hundreds of millions of dollars for businesses and potentially above one billion dollars a year. This is no exaggeration. . . . On the issue of what taxpayers would be subsidizing, taxpayers would have to foot the bill for . . . hundreds of millions of dollars for state supplied marriage benefits for same-sex marriage and there are many, many kinds: social security disability payments, retirement pensions, subsidized married student housing, capital gains tax deferment, workman's comp, transfer of death benefits and IRAs by surviving spouses, the state and transfer taxes. Many other tax breaks and government benefits that are currently only limited to married couples, a man and a woman.

Thomason attempted to make the case that fighting against same-sex marriage could be justified on purely economic grounds, a logic designed to undermine accusations of antigay bigotry and garner the support of the business community.

This economic style of reasoning has the appearance of apolitical neutrality even as it subordinates fundamental rights to imperatives of efficiency.[6] Although LGBTQ advocates defended same-sex marriage as a matter of equality and justice, organizations evidently felt compelled to make counter economic arguments about AB 1982 that would demonstrate not only the feasibility but even the financial advantages of same-sex marriage. Before the Assembly Judiciary Committee, Laurie McBride, the executive director of the Lobby for Individual Freedom and

Equality (LIFE), explained to those in the hearing room that changing California's marriage laws would be detrimental for companies. Emphasizing the importance of consistency, she stated: "The real harm to business will be the renewal of distinctions in marriage law. Many third-party vendors, employers, lenders, and businesses already recognize same-gender unions and treat them with the same regard as any other marriage. AB 1982 will force these companies to reconsider those policies or risk suit from the marriage police." Because some private sector actors in California had already begun to accord the same benefits to same-sex couples as those afforded to different-sex couples in a bid to recruit the best talent, a change to the legal definition of marriage could hurt those efforts.

These examples of competing economic testimony from 1995 would only grow in frequency and intricacy in the following years as organizations and scholars, especially those on the side of same-sex couples, developed increasingly sophisticated ways to measure the economic stakes. Those fighting in favor of same-sex marriage would draw on data generated by states and locales that had already recognized same-sex partnerships or generated by employers who had already provided spousal healthcare coverage to their employees to show that such measures are economically beneficial.[7] Organizations such as the Williams Institute—a think tank affiliated with the UCLA School of Law focused on advances in LGBTQ rights—were founded in part to publish and compile precisely this kind of economic evidence. Much like the visibility of gay and lesbian families, debates about the economic stakes and the resulting mobilization of economic expertise—which is virtually absent in France—would not have been possible without state-level legal variations. Indeed, the combination of U.S. federalism, allowing same-sex marriage rights in some place and not others, along with the privatized employer-based healthcare system, which allows companies to extend insurance to their employees' spouses, made it possible to generate economic expertise in the first place.

While almost all legislative action on same-sex marriage and parenting in the United States took place on the state level, Congress did weigh in on the question. First, after the so-called Republican Revolution in 1994 when Republican lawmakers won majorities in both the House of Representatives and the Senate, they, along with their conservative Democratic allies, aimed to thwart any national attempts at legalizing same-sex marriage by passing the Defense of Marriage Act (DOMA) in 1996. Then, in 2004, under support from George W. Bush, Congress attempted but failed to pass a Federal Marriage Amendment. Finally, federal lawmakers took up the question again in 2011, when they discussed the possibility of repealing DOMA. While far fewer than state-level hearings, the experts called to participate in these few federal debates merit our attention because DOMA shaped the political context on same-sex marriage mobilizations more generally.

Testifying in a congressional hearing is a closed and restricted process. Unlike state legislatures, which are open to the public and where generally anyone can register to express a stance on a bill, congresspeople have exclusive control over who they invite to speak before them. Interested parties can, however, contribute written statements for later inclusion in the record. The number of people who have actually testified in person in Congress is much smaller compared to the state-level marriage and parenting hearings. Their decisions about what kinds of people to invite resulted in a slate of witnesses that contrasted with the states. Indeed, most testimony was provided by a more elite category of experts. Specifically, of all instances of testimony at congressional hearings between 1994 and 2011, representatives of advocacy organizations provided 33 percent, elected officials provided 30 percent, and professors—all of whom had jobs in law schools—provided 12 percent. Ordinary citizens provided less than 1 percent of oral testimony and were mostly present in the written statements. Furthermore, because of the system of committees, which includes representatives from both parties, the oral testimony was relatively ideologically balanced: 46 percent was in favor of federal restrictions on same-sex marriage, 52 percent was opposed, and the remainder was neutral.

This more elite configuration of categories of expertise is likely due to the higher barriers to participation as a result of elected officials' control over the hearings who focused primarily on the contentious nature of Congress determining marriage law on the federal level. Lawmakers invited professors and advocates who spoke primarily about the legal grounding—or lack thereof—in their efforts to intervene on a question heretofore outside Congress's jurisdiction. Unsurprisingly, most of the knowledge heard in this setting, especially during the 1996 and 2004 hearings, focused on technical legal aspects of the legislation and the federal mechanisms through which same-sex marriage would or would not spread to different states if it were legalized in one state. For example, during the July 11, 1996, Senate Judiciary Committee hearings on DOMA, law professors Lynn Wardle (Brigham Young University) and Cass Sunstein (University of Chicago) offered diametrically opposed views about whether Congress was within its historical tradition and constitutional purview to legislate on marriage, the former defending DOMA and the latter opposing it. In addition to this technical expertise and despite the elite profile of the witnesses, many of the participants in the hearings, including professors, representatives of advocacy organizations, and elected officials, also drew on personal experience and their private lives to justify their stances. During the July 20, 2011, Senate Judiciary Committee hearings on the Respect for Marriage Act—a bill that would have overturned DOMA—Joe Solmonese, then the president of the Human Rights Campaign, the major mainstream U.S. LGBTQ lobbying organization, described his own marriage in a speech where he also told the stories of same-sex couples whose lives were negatively impacted by marriage restrictions. During an exchange, Senator Sheldon Whitehouse of Rhode Island told the stories of gay and lesbian constituents who shared with him about what same-sex relationships are like in a country that refuses to recognize them. Such knowledge illustrates the enduring importance of personal experience in U.S. debates, reaching even the apex of political decision-making institutions.

FEDERAL COURTS: ELITE EXPERTS TO THE FORE

Unlike in France, the judiciary has been a particularly fruitful avenue toward the legalization of same-sex marriage in the United States on the state and federal levels.[8] Courts have also built case law on adoption, second parent adoption, and surrogacy in states on a case-by-case level in the absence of clear legislation on those issues.[9] As far as mobilizing experts and expertise, courts put into place a specific set of expectations and routines that create a distinct profile compared to legislatures. Whereas lawmakers offer hearings as a space for people to air their views—among other kinds of expertise—courts put knowledge gatekeeping squarely in the hands of judges, lawyers, and interested parties. Like their peers in legislatures, they engage in ongoing patterns of practice within the norms of their institutions to find the available expert capital that fits their purposes. Furthermore, that information is explicitly mobilized when judges render their opinion, even if it is difficult to measure if or how expertise actually weighed on their decisions. Advocates on either side spend a great deal of time and considerable sums of money strategizing to curate and package expertise in order to attempt to sway them. Given the power of U.S. courts to produce case law and the particular status they accord to knowledge, understanding who provides what kind of information is especially relevant here.

An analysis of categories of experts and expertise presented in friend of the court briefs, or amici curiae briefs, in major federal cases provides an overview of the kinds of knowledge judges encounter in the juridical field. Similar to written statements in legislatures, any interested person can file an amicus brief on behalf of either party in the case in hopes that the court will take their statements into account when making their decisions. Moreover, there is no formal mechanism for guaranteeing the reliability or credibility of the information contained within them, leading some scholars to worry that briefs can distort or misrepresent facts or the state of scientific understanding of certain phenomena.[10] Although it is unclear how exactly judges use amicus briefs in their decision-making, research suggests they are important for a few reasons.[11] First, if there are many briefs supporting one of the parties or a set of arguments, they can give the impression of broad-based support or, in the case of learned societies and professional groups, that technical and scientific communities in general have a preferred outcome in the case, one that is grounded in reason and consensus. Second, judges can and have reproduced the specific wording and lines of reasoning in some briefs, suggesting that they look to them for inspiration.

Amicus briefs present the lowest bar for expert participation in judicial proceedings. As a result, their authors are the broadest possible spectrum of people who formally give their views to judges. However, given the complex submission process and legal jargon required to understand how to submit these briefs, the categories of people submitting them tend to be more certified by professional and academic organizations than the ordinary citizens who show up to state capitals to speak in public hearings. For example, as shown in table 2.3, briefs submitted to the U.S. Supreme Court as it considered the appeal in *Hollingsworth v. Perry* showed higher proportions of professors and professional organizations (20 and 10 percent, respectively) than ordinary citizens (5 percent). Because many of the same groups and individuals habitually submit briefs in gay rights cases, especially in the decade leading up to *Obergefell v. Hodges*, this pattern of elite knowledge is common across major federal and state cases where briefs are submitted.

The breakdown by stance of brief submitters in table 2.3 shows an equal number of briefs submitted on either side. The balance, however, is only superficial. When accounting for the types of brief authors, it becomes clear that categories of experts with more social prestige and credibility weigh more heavily on the

TABLE 2.3 Proportion of Categories of Experts in Appeals Briefs to U.S. Supreme
Court in *Hollingsworth v. Perry*

Category	For	Against	Total
Advocacy organizations	0.17	0.25	0.43
Professors	0.12	0.09	0.20
Religious organizations	0.04	0.13	0.16
Politicians	0.05	0.05	0.10
Professional organizations	0.10	0.00	0.10
Average people	0.03	0.02	0.05
Lawyers	0.03	0.01	0.05
Total briefs (N = 104)	0.50	0.49	1.00

side of same-sex marriage. Professors, including those in law, mental health, and
the social sciences, as well as professional organizations, such as the American
Psychological Association, the American Medical Association, the American
Bar Association, and most other major professional organizations submitted
briefs in favor. In contrast, religious organizations and conservative advocacy
groups, such as the National Organization for Marriage, the Eagle Forum, and
the American College of Pediatricians—an activist group founded by conservative healthcare professionals to promote reactionary policies, especially against
abortion and reproductive health, and intentionally named to create confusion
among the public about their political motives—submitted more briefs against
same-sex marriage. These patterns have several implications. Scholars, doctors,
lawyers, and other elite experts opposed to same-sex family rights seem to have
held less sway within their respective mainstream academic and professional
organizations relative to their peers. This may reflect both their smaller numbers
and their absence within decision-making processes, such as the committees and
spaces where these briefs were drafted. They mobilize instead the considerable
financial and networking resources of conservative groups to have their voices
heard but cannot rally the same kinds of prestigious, peer-recognized experts as
their rivals.

Amicus briefs are formulaic and grounded in legal information because, as the
next chapter describes, they must respond to specific legal questions in a given
case and make a concrete legal argument relative to things like constitutional
principles, statutory law, and jurisprudence.[12] Beyond legal knowledge, which

almost all briefs cited because of this format, they also drew on other kinds of knowledge, such as social science, mental health, history, and economics. Thanks to the visibility of LGBTQ people and same-sex couples in the United States and researchers who worked for decades, initially in difficult conditions, to study them, empirical research about the psychological and social experiences of sexual minorities and gay families was common among briefs of marriage supporters. However, unlike in legislatures, where much of this information is presented by advocacy organizations, academics and their respective professional organizations provided the information themselves to courts, making it seem less motivated by activism and supported by science. This was also true for economic expertise, which was not only offered by economics professors but also by labor unions and major business leaders, including executives of U.S. corporations and commerce associations, who submitted briefs describing the economic advantages of recognizing same-sex marriage for businesses and states. The so-called "business brief," co-signed by over eighty major American companies including Apple, Alaska Airlines, Morgan Stanley, Nike, and Office Depot, is a good example.[13] Among other things, they argue that laws banning same-sex marriage impede efficiency and reduce productivity, causing harm to their bottom line.

The central role of empirical social science in the courts is especially clear on the issue of parenting. Brief authors opposing same-sex marriage in the United States took a two-pronged approach to the issue of children raised by gays and lesbians. They acknowledged that same-sex couples raise children as a matter of established fact—something they could not deny given the demographic reality of these families in the United States—but argued that heterosexual married parents are ideal. For example, in a brief submitted in *Hollingsworth v. Perry* by the attorneys general of nineteen conservative states, even as they argued that sex differences justify excluding same-sex couples from marriage because they cannot procreate together, they admitted the "capacity of same-sex parents to raise their children in a loving and supporting environment."[14] They grounded their arguments in ideas of history, tradition, and religious liberty, but without the support of major academic and professional organizations specializing in children's welfare, their claims of the superiority of heterosexual families lacked the formal scientific backing of their opponents. To overcome this barrier, anti-marriage groups sought to provide information that had at least the imprimatur of scientific rigor, probably assuming that their audience would be looking for something to latch onto.

Scientifically sound information is especially important in courts that, at least in theory, place a premium on evidence that can pass as credible. Because of this particular value of scientific evidence in this context, many conservative briefs drew heavily on the few peer-reviewed studies claiming to show children raised by same-sex couples fare poorly, such as that by the sociologist Mark Regnerus, which later chapters will describe in more detail.[15] Other antimarriage briefs criticized the social scientific and mental health literature as biased, inconclusive, and unrepresentative of the scientific consensus in order to attempt to counter the institutional and scholarly weight on the side of same-sex marriage proponents. They aimed to undermine the expert capital of their adversaries and shore up their own.

These patterns of elite knowledge are even more pronounced in the proceedings of several major federal District Court cases: *Perry v. Schwarzenegger*, which was appealed to the Supreme Court as *Hollingsworth v. Perry*, and *DeBoer v. Snyder*, which was consolidated with other cases on appeal to the Supreme Court to form *Obergefell v. Hodges*. In these cases, the judges called for full trials featuring presentation of evidence and the possibility to hear plaintiffs and witnesses. Unlike hearings in U.S. legislatures or amici briefs, which are comparatively accessible forums, trials are closed and rigidly guarded. Litigators on either side have full control over whom they call to testify before the judge. This gives us a valuable perspective on the kinds of experts and knowledge that attorneys expect will help their case the most. In other words, these trials are a showcase for expert capital and its relationship to institutional logics. The attorneys aim to provide information they believe responds to precise legal questions set out by the case, such as whether or not sexual minorities constitute a historically subjugated class or whether states have a demonstrably rational interest in excluding them from marriage. The explicit constraints of the trial setting and the higher standards applied to information in courts, which I analyze in the next chapter, favor higher representation of elite experts relative to U.S. legislatures.

In these two trials, twenty out of the twenty-nine individuals providing testimony were among the sorts that might typically come to mind when we think of qualified people: professors and those with distinguished academic or professional credentials and impressive resumés. Of these, five were professors and researchers in psychology, five in economy, four in sociology or social studies, two in history, two in political science, one in law, and one in demography. Their respective disciplines highlight the kind of information—knowledge about the demography and social circumstances of same-sex couples and families, the history of their discrimination, their relative political power, their fitness to raise children, and the causes and nature of their sexual orientation—at the core of the legal arguments in the trials.

Litigators arguing in favor of same-sex marriage were more successful at rallying these prestigious experts to their cause. Indeed, out of the twenty academic experts, fourteen were on the side of same-sex marriage proponents and only six testified on behalf of the team arguing against them. This striking imbalance has several implications. First, it suggests that when faced with academic and professional subfields that could provide the information they wanted—from political science about the voting power of sexual minorities to the psychological research about the academic outcomes and emotional well-being of children raised by same-sex couples or the legal history of the criminalization of homosexuality in the United States—attorneys found that most of the evidence, and the scholars willing to talk about it, supported same-sex marriage. Second, the lack of experts on the conservative side means that lawyers making that argument were dealing with fields that could not provide them with the kinds of information they wanted. Most of the research did not support their stance, and academic and professional experts who agreed with them were reluctant to go on the stand.[16] As a result of this imbalance, when faced with the task of deciding the relative weight of evidence, judges in these trials heard far more expertise—backed by specifically accredited people—in favor of same-sex marriage. These trials thus give the impression that science is overwhelmingly on the side of same-sex couples and their families. As we will see shortly, that impression would not translate to the French context, where lawmakers and the public would see the evidence as more divided and inconclusive.

Despite their much higher barrier to access and premium on qualifications, U.S. courts still offer a decision-making forum grounded in personal experience and the testimony of ordinary people. Like legislatures, emotional and personal storytelling is key. Indeed, even in these specific trials with days of testimony from expert witnesses, the cases are fundamentally about specific people—the litigants—and the circumstances of their lives that led them to demand the state to recognize their relationships. In *Perry v. Schwarzenegger* and *DeBoer v. Snyder*, the plaintiffs, who were suing their respective states in federal courts in order to access full marriage rights, presented their testimony to the judges. They described their relationships, their children—if they were parents—as well as their experiences of discrimination and stigmatization as a result of their sexual identities.

Attorneys in *Perry* also augmented the testimony of the plaintiffs by having lay witnesses, a lesbian woman and two gay men who were not party to the trial, outline in rich detail how their lives illuminated specific legal points the attorneys were trying to argue. For example, Helen Zia, an author and activist for Asian American civil rights, described how getting married to her wife in 2008 changed the way her family perceived their relationship, underlying the importance of marriage as a civil right. She also described the importance of being a visible lesbian in the Chinese American community, countering a set of ideas mobilized by antigay groups that same-sex marriage only concerns white people and that racial and ethnic minority groups adhere to "traditional" values. Ryan Kendall told the judge about his traumatic and unsuccessful experience undergoing "conversion therapy," supporting with personal testimony the scientific evidence that sexual orientation is immutable and thus deserving of heightened legal protections. Even in cases without full trials, such as *U.S. v. Windsor*, judges considered the facts of the lives of the people bringing suit, which personalized and grounded their ruling. As LGBTQ rights activists argued in the streets that same-sex marriage was about love, lawyers in courts were debating before judges about the lives of gay couples and their families through the lens of social science. Through their institutional logics, federal courts favor a rhetorical environment where elite scientific expertise provided by credentialed experts comes to weigh directly on the particular circumstances of the litigants and, by extension, on the potential legal rights of all sexual minorities.

FRENCH AND EUROPEAN COURTS: A DEAD END FOR SAME-SEX COUPLES

Courts in France have not provided an especially fruitful avenue for reforms on same-sex marriage and parenting rights. Unlike the United States, which offers many states in which same-sex couples can attempt to build case law, relative legal homogeny on the national level and the civil law system, which does not lend itself to creating case law through precedent and jurisprudence, have limited these opportunities in France. As a result, these institutional outlets for expertise are relatively absent in the French case. This is not for lack of trying. In my interview with Caroline Mécary, one of the first and best-known out lesbian lawyers in France, she explained how attempts to pursue an avenue through the French courts failed. In 2004, the Cour de cassation annulled the same-sex marriage performed by the mayor of Bègles that she and others were defending and that had been started as a bid to force the courts to expand the definition of marriage in the years following the legalization of the Pacte civil de solidarité (Pacs).[17] Those efforts were thwarted when the court not only declared the marriage invalid but also unequivocally stated that modifying marriage law was the domain of the legislature. Importantly, that trial presented little, if any, expertise that made it into the record that could be analyzed here.

The few cases originating in France that were appealed to the European Court of Human Rights, including several relating to adoption as well as the Bègles marriage itself, have not featured friend of the court briefs or full trials that could have created the opportunity for expertise as they have in the United States. Several third parties, two European gay rights groups and two gay family organizations, were allowed to submit statements in support for the record.[18] These cases also involved the stories of the men and women seeking adoption rights as couples and individuals as well as the unfavorable reports submitted by state-mandated psychoanalysts and child psychiatrists to French adoption administrators, which were at the origin of the trials and appeals process.

What little expertise that can be gleaned from this relative dearth of judicial scrutiny shows a strikingly different portrayal of gay parenting relative to the United States. Even marriage opponents in the United States could not deny the reality of same-sex couples raising children, going so far as to describe it in neutral or even positive terms. Here, gay parenting is a threat, but not a reality. The information cited in these French adoption reports discussed gay families as a negative hypothetical rather than empirical fact, as something to be avoided and prevented. The French mental health professionals who authored these statements said that children have a vital need to be adopted by a man and a woman or to at least to have a maternal or paternal figure in the case of adoption by a single person. This kind of expertise, which treats same-sex couples raising children from a critical and often alarmist distance, is typical of conservative knowledge in French gay family debates, which, as we will see, have primarily occurred in the legislature.

FRENCH LEGISLATURES: THEORY OVER FACT

Given the sheer number of ordinary citizens in U.S. legislative testimony, particularly on the state level, one could reasonably assume that French parliamentary hearings would also feature people speaking in favor of or against same-sex
marriage and parenting on the basis of their lived experiences. After all, because
they are directly concerned with the question, it would be logical to expect gay
families to have a prominent place, as they often did in California and Texas.
Yet, analysis of major French legislative debates on same-sex partnership and
parenting rights, particularly committee hearings, reveals stark differences in
the categories of people legislators called on and the kinds of information they
provided. The Assemblée Nationale, ensconced in buildings along the Seine, and
the Sénat, with its view over the Jardins du Luxembourg, were rarely a space for
ordinary folks to talk about their lives. Rather, these institutions appear to favor
knowledge in the shape of grand principles and abstract theory, looking at same-
sex marriage less as an issue of people's lives and more as a civilizational question
about the meaning of family and *filiation*. To that end, in contrast to U.S. legislative debates, elite knowledge provided by academics, favoring abstract discussions and what Éric Fassin calls "a priori" expertise about whether same-sex
couples and families should exist, is common in French hearings.[19]

The Pacs legislation—which had several competing versions before lawmakers
settled on its final form—was hotly contested in the streets by bible-brandishing
protestors, including the conservative Catholic MP Christine Boutin, some of
whom even called for gay people to be burned at the stake.[20] Many gay and lesbian activist organizations worked in public and behind the scenes to push the
Socialist majority, elected in 1997, to make the Pacs come to fruition despite this
resistance that included not only protest but also hostility expressed in the media
by public intellectuals and the opposition parties. Yet the hearings themselves
where notably devoid of testimony of everyday gay and lesbian people talking
about their lives.

As shown in table 2.4, during the Pacs debates in the late 1990s, ordinary
citizens were completely absent from hearings. As a result, the rich personalized storytelling that characterized American legislative hearings was rare in
France. The experiences of ordinary citizens were also mostly elided in the two
reports that the sociologist Irène Théry and law professor Françoise Dekeuwer-

TABLE 2.4 Proportion of Categories of Experts Heard by Assemblée Nationale and Sénat Judiciary Committees by Stance, PACS Hearings, 1998

Category of expert	For	Against	Neutral/unknown	Total
Advocacy organizations	0.38	0.15	0.02	0.55
Professional organizations	0.00	0.00	0.13	0.13
Professors	0.02	0.07	0.00	0.09
Elected officials/politicians	0.05	0.00	0.02	0.07
Religious representatives	0.00	0.07	0.00	0.07
Mental health professionals	0.02	0.02	0.00	0.04
State/quasi-state agencies	0.00	0.04	0.00	0.04
Judges	0.00	0.02	0.00	0.02
Average people	0.00	0.00	0.00	0.00
Total instances (N = 55)	0.47	0.36	0.16	1.00

Note: Assemblée Nationale hearings were not public. Stances were determined by media expression. Otherwise, stance is unknown.

Défossez submitted to lawmakers on the evolution of family law.[21] Instead, these hearings primarily concerned advocacy organizations (55 percent of instances of expertise), including gay rights and HIV prevention groups on the side of proponents and conservative family groups, such as Familles de France, on the side of opponents. Legislators also heard 13 percent of testimony from legal professional organizations, such the Parisian Bar Association, which unlike their U.S. equivalents in many states over the years, did not make a statement either in support of or against the proposed legislation. Finally, taken together, professors and mental health professionals represented 13 percent of testimony at these hearings.

Fifteen years after the passage of the Pacs, as the French parliament once again debated the state recognition of same-sex couples and their families, some things had changed but much stayed the same. The hearings before the passage of same-sex marriage and adoption, which also took place in a tense context of protest and resistance in the media, show similar patterns and confirm the dominance of elite expertise relative to lay expertise in the French institutional context. As table 2.5 highlights, the representation of ordinary citizens appeared for the first time and constituted 10 percent of testimony. However, the representation of professors (16 percent) and mental health professionals (10 percent) also increased and still outweighed the voices of gays and lesbians and their children. Indeed, during the marriage hearings at the Assemblée Nationale and the

TABLE 2.5 Proportion of Categories of Experts Heard by Assemblée Nationale and Sénat Judiciary Committees by Stance, Marriage and Adoption Hearings, 2012–2013

Category of expert	For	Against	Neutral	Total
Advocacy organizations	0.15	0.02	0.06	0.22
Professors	0.10	0.06	0.00	0.16
Average people	0.10	0.00	0.00	0.10
Mental health professionals	0.04	0.06	0.00	0.10
Religious representatives	0.00	0.08	0.01	0.09
State/quasi-state agencies	0.01	0.01	0.06	0.08
Elected officials/politicians	0.05	0.00	0.03	0.08
Medical professionals	0.00	0.00	0.07	0.07
Professional organizations	0.00	0.02	0.03	0.06
Judges	0.01	0.00	0.01	0.02
Lawyers	0.01	0.01	0.00	0.02
Total instances (N = 143)	0.47	0.26	0.27	1.00

Sénat, only one of the sixteen panels held over a period of several weeks featured ordinary citizens speaking from their personal experience to the Judiciary Committee. Of the fourteen people on that panel, there were same-sex couples raising children, several adult children having been raised by same-sex couples, and same-sex couples hoping to adopt. This exceptional panel only seems to confirm that French lawmakers consider laws about same-sex couples at a remove from the people who are most concerned by them. Moreover, that this kind of knowledge was not heard in the French legislature until 2012 and in relatively small quantities tracks with the relative invisibility of gay families in French culture more broadly.

In terms of ideological breakdown, unlike in the United States where most academic and mental health experts have supported gay family rights in legislatures and courts, in French hearings, these categories of elite experts have taken stances on both sides. As the tables show, during the Pacs hearings, two-thirds of professors, primarily sociologists, anthropologists, and philosophers, and half of the mental health professionals, all of whom were psychoanalysts, provided oral testimony against the reforms. During the marriage hearings, the professors, many of whom had first testified during the Pacs debates, were more in favor (62 percent) than against. This change reflects the shift in stance between the two periods of several key—and famous—social scientists, including the anthropologists Maurice Godelier and Françoise Héritier, as well as the sociologist

Irène Théry. Initially opposed to the Pacs, as their own stances changed, so did the orientation of the expert testimony overall; their presence at the hearings and impact on the field influenced the dominant orientation of the social science. Nevertheless, relative to their U.S. counterparts, these categories of experts remained more divided. Similarly, during the marriage hearings, legislators heard mental health professionals who also remained divided, with a majority still in opposition at 60 percent. This left observers, whether legislators or the journalists who cover them, with the impression that qualified experts were split about the merits of same-sex marriage and parenting.

Testimony by ordinary citizens and expressions of knowledge about lived experiences are constrained in France because of its closed legislative decision-making sphere. Indeed, unlike U.S. legislatures, where any interested party can contribute information, lawmakers in the parliamentary majority control access to French hearings. It is reasonable to assume that if hearings were open to all people interested in providing testimony, like in many U.S. state legislatures, more ordinary citizens might have participated. Ordinary citizens in U.S. debates brought knowledge—personal experience—to the hearings that other experts and lawmakers shared with them in the U.S. context. This common mode of discussing legal reform in personal terms, however, was relatively absent in the French institutional context more generally.

Unlike their U.S. counterparts, French experts and lawmakers debating the bills on the floor or in their lines of questioning in committee rarely drew on personal experience to justify their claims or clarify their stances. While U.S. witnesses and legislators frequently discussed their children, spouses, friends, and families in concrete and direct ways, their French counterparts spoke about them in the abstract, not referring to their own lives but to notions and concepts of family and children. For example, during the 2012 marriage debates on the parliamentary floor, French legislators talked in terms of "our gay friends," "our neighbors," and "our families," speaking to a universal subject rather than a particular instance.

This lack of personal experience in the French legislature suggests cultural barriers that go beyond institutional rules barring the participation of ordinary citizens. Indeed, no formal rules prevent French lawmakers from talking about their lives or highlighting those of others. Rather, French lawmakers seem to interpret the meaning and traditions of the role of law in a common law system as a universal to be applied the same way in all cases. The theory of the law and how it is made, as we will see in the next chapter, puts pressure on lawmakers to look at expertise through a lens of the universal versus the particular, with a clear preference for the former over the latter. As a result, personal experience becomes irrelevant or illegitimate because it is grounded in the individual and cannot be generalized to the abstract scale legal debates require, according to this perspective. This lens is consistent with the cultural repertoires of universalism and the common good that characterize French public discourse more broadly.[22] Some lawmakers may not have even considered bringing up their lives during the debates because it was outside of the scope of what they perceived as legitimate discourse in that setting. That personal experience was not shared across experts and legislators in France meant that the people who did bring that kind of knowledge—some ordinary citizens in 2012 and advocacy organizations during both the Pacs and marriage debates—were drawing on a marginalized form of expertise. That makes their knowledge less powerful or at least more open to criticism. The French legislative discursive environment also lends itself well to the abstract knowledge, rather than practical knowledge, that characterizes psychoanalysis and structural anthropology, which are common in the French media and legislative debates more generally.[23] Indeed, abstract theory disconnected from the particularity of experiences from the field was clear among elite experts.

One could assume that the academic and professional experts who make up a significant proportion of French legislative hearings, especially those in favor, would provide empirical evidence about same-sex couples and their children—such as the decades of psychological and sociological studies on gay families—or other knowledge that similar categories of experts provide in U.S. courts. After all, if major American professional organizations were supplying that information to judges and if lawyers could put the researchers themselves on the stand, it is possible that French advocates and lawmakers could have brought at least some of this expertise across the Atlantic. Yet, this information was relatively absent from French hearings. This was especially evident during the Pacs hearings. Even as legislatures and courts in the United States were hearing knowledge from researchers and professional organizations about the outcomes of children raised by same-sex couples and statistics of gay families, French lawmakers treated gay parenting as a strange, almost unthinkable issue and same-sex couples as an important but difficult to measure phenomenon.[24] For example, after conducting the Pacs hearings at the Sénat, the rapporteur for the Judiciary Committee, the right-leaning senator, Patrice Gélard, wrote in his final report that it was difficult to evaluate the number of same-sex couples who would be interested in a civil union.[25] This perceived lack of data gave credence to the idea that legal recognition might not be as urgent as some activists were arguing.

The French legal context hindered the capacity of academic experts and organizations supporting gay family rights to produce much meaningful research to counter claims of epistemological uncertainty. Laws severely restricting same-sex couples' access to parenting through adoption and reproductive technologies made it difficult for scholars to produce a reliable and undeniable scientific portrait of gay families in France. This situation constituted a clear advantage for French experts and groups first opposing the Pacs and later same-sex marriage. Unlike opponents of gay family rights in the United States, who could not deny that same-sex couples were raising children together as a matter of fact, French law barring same-sex couples from raising children legally before 2013 made them easy to discount. Indeed, those gays and lesbians who did raise children in the 1990s and 2000s were at the limits—both of the law and popular representations—and tended to keep a relatively low profile, some important organizing efforts notwithstanding.[26] Expert opponents and their movement allies could describe these families as if they did not exist, shed doubt on the size of the phenomenon, and deny their needs. Moreover, they could argue that while some gay families may exist, their access to joint parenting is fraudulent, because illegal, and a denial of essential sex differences. During legal debates over the Pacs—as others have also noted—and same-sex marriage, these experts grounded their arguments in psychoanalysis, structural anthropology, and social theory.[27]

For instance, during the Pacs hearings in the Sénat's Judiciary Committee, the psychoanalyst Samuel Lepastier argued that while some single lesbians may be raising children after a separation from the child's father or might have adopted as an individual, allowing two women to raise children together as joint mothers would be the symbolic and psychological "denial of everything that makes us human."[28] "We are constantly constructing ourselves in relation to an anatomical reality of sexually different parents. To be instituted as a child of same-sex parents (rather than to be raised by two parents of the same-sex) is to deny this corporeal representation," Pastier went on to explain. Rather than draw on any examples of actual same-sex couples, he discussed these families in the abstract, as a concept, exemplifying "a priori" normative knowledge.[29] This kind of psychoanalytic expertise, which appeared rarely in the United States, was especially important in a French context lacking in empirical knowledge or personal narratives of same-sex couples to counter them. In essence, such expertise ungirds the belief that we need no information about gay families because theory already tells us they are dangerous and the law, thus, should reflect that.

Empirical knowledge about same-sex couples and families was not entirely absent from hearings, especially the later ones. During the marriage hearings in 2012, several sociologists in favor of same-sex marriage and adoption, such as Martine Gross and Virginie Descoutures, who testified before the Assemblée Nationale's Judiciary Committee, discussed the limited French research on same-sex couples and the strong body of evidence from abroad showing that children raised by same-sex couples fare as well as their peers.[30] Nevertheless, relative to their U.S. counterparts, particularly those in courts, French lawmakers saw little of such information. The lack of empirical knowledge on same-sex couples and their children in France is partly the result of legal structural conditions that have hindered same-sex couples from legally creating families via joint adoption, second-parent adoption, or assisted reproductive technology within France. As I describe in further detail in chapter 4, these barriers have made it more difficult for French advocacy organizations and scholars to work on these issues and study sexual minority families in France relative to their American peers.

The increase in favorable empirical social science evidence in later French debates was not enough to fully offset elite experts opposing same-sex marriage, especially conservative mental health professionals who continued to draw on psychoanalysis to justify their stances. For example, Pierre Lévy-Soussan, like his other conservative colleagues testifying, explained during the marriage debates to the Judiciary Committee "that every child, even one who is adopted, must be able to recreate the 'primal scene' in his imagination, and, even if one can get beyond the inconsistencies related to differences in skin color in the cases of children adopted from abroad, for example, it is impossible to make conception between two men or two women credible [in the eyes of an adopted child]."[31] From Lévy-Soussan's perspective, and that of his colleagues, research on the actual outcomes of children raised by same-sex couples is irrelevant and should be discounted. The psychoanalytic theory, as they interpret it, requires that a child literally be able to picture his adoptive parents credibly having conceived him through heterosexual sex—even if he and his parents are of different racial backgrounds—because that fantasy is important for healthy psychological development. Same-sex couples, by virtue of their inability to conceive children together, are unable to offer this important mental and social structure to children they might raise, these experts argued.

Such French opponents could continue to make these claims for several reasons. First, unlike courts, legislative hearings do not deal with claims in a formal adversarial way, making it easier for unsubstantiated claims to go unchallenged. Therefore, experts can provide hypothetical information about same-sex couples and their children without having to demonstrate the facts on which they base their arguments as they would have if faced with cross-examination and clearly defined rules about what counts as expertise. Second, unlike in the United States, where same-sex couples already had the right to found families, French same-sex couples were always excluded from adoption until the passage of the 2012 bill. Therefore, no domestic couples having jointly adopted could be brought in as examples to counter their claims. Moreover, whereas in the United States, there were more children in need of adoptive parents than people willing to adopt them, which led some U.S. adoption and fostering service providers to valorize same-sex couples, in France, the circumstances were reversed.[32] In France, there was—and still is—a waiting list of potential adoptive parents and few children in French social services eligible for adoption.[33] As a result, French same-sex marriage and adoption proponents do not have the opportunity to evoke the merits of gay parenting to overcome a fostering crisis. Instead, opponents can continue to argue, from an abstract psychoanalytic perspective, that different-sex married couples are the ideal adoptive parents in a social context where the state can choose from among people on a long waiting list. Of course, these arguments are likely to evolve as circumstances change.

U.S. and French institutions share a category of experts that may seem surprising: religious representatives. As seen in tables 2.4 and 2.5, religious representatives of major faiths in France—Catholicism, Protestantism, Islam, Judaism, Orthodox Christianity, and Buddhism—accounted for 7 percent and 9 percent of all expertise in oral hearings during the Pacs and marriage debates, respectively. Although these numbers are somewhat lower than those in U.S. hearings, their presence at all seems paradoxical given French political rhetorical attachment to *laïcité*. However, just as they did in the French media, and in contrast to their American peers, these clergy were more likely to accompany their religious expertise with secular kinds of information or even downplay the religious aspect altogether. This was especially true in the hearings leading up to the legalization of marriage where they often spoke through the abstract language of legal principles, anthropology, psychoanalysis, and ethics. And, with the exception of the representative of Buddhists, who took a neutral stance, all were hostile to the legislation. They used the same kinds of concepts as their ideological allies in the mental health professions. For example, André Vingt-Trois, Cardinal and Archbishop of Paris, declared to the Sénat Judiciary Committee in 2012: "The anthropological and social stakes and the protection of children's rights have been silenced by egalitarian discourse that has chosen to ignore differences between homosexual and heterosexual people in their relation to procreation; they want us to believe that the relationship between conjugality and procreation is not pertinent for life in society."[34] Evoking the "anthropological" dimension of the reforms and the supposed necessity of biological sex differences for procreation, the cardinal channeled the same secular language as his conservative social scientist and psychoanalytic colleagues.

In the same hearing, when Gilles Bernheim, the Grand Rabbi of France, drew on similar kinds of knowledge, one of the legislators asked him why he did not use his point of view as a religious representative. "Why use my past and present as a philosopher rather than as a rabbi? The reason is simple," Bernheim answered. "When I want to talk to society, I use its language and not that of my community, with its references. It was therefore normal to develop a way of thinking that could be heard by everyone, so as not to suggest that the other [way of thinking] is wrong but, to give food for thought, including to those who don't think the way I do."[35] In this statement, Bernheim makes explicit his decision to speak in the idiom of philosophy, a kind of knowledge that he believed would resonate in the French political context. That expertise would fit into the expected framework of universality and secularism in contrast to the particularness that Bernheim presumably prescribed to Jewish religious traditions.

CONCLUSION

What are gay families and what rights, if any, should they be accorded? Since 1990, courts and legislatures in the United State and France have processed information through hearings, reports, briefs, and other sources in an attempt to answer that question. They did so because activists seized these institutions as part of decades-long efforts to shield themselves from the injustice of a state unwilling to recognize their familial bonds. Their opponents resisted them at every turn. Knowing that decision-makers' perceptions are key—whether they see gay and lesbian couples and their children as genuine, marginalized, and deserving of equality or fraudulent, powerful, and criminal—both sides tried to craft a narrative that would favor their side. To do so, they mobilized expertise, some of it from their own lives and those of their communities and some of it from professionals, scholars, or church leaders who they had to support or otherwise convince to work with them. Because of the constraints they faced related to availability of expertise and the rules around what kinds of information are admissible, the portrait of gay families that was ultimately presented before decision-makers looks different on either side of the Atlantic.

This chapter has revealed stark contrasts between the categories of experts and kinds of knowledge legislators and judges hear in the United States and France. On a broad level, U.S. institutions heard the stories and experiences of ordinary citizens who grounded the debates in the concrete realities of the people most concerned by the reforms. This is especially true in state-level legislatures where open testimony systems allow any interested party to contribute information, creating opportunities for lay witnesses to express their views. Religious expertise was also a common and shared kind of information on both sides. Courts, which significantly advanced gay family rights in the United States in the decades analyzed, combined the lived experiences of the litigants in a given case with empirical historical, psychological, and sociological information that expert witnesses or brief authors provided.

In contrast, these elite experts, especially academics, intellectuals, and mental health practitioners, along with advocacy organizations, dominated in the Assemblée Nationale and the Sénat. In the absence of any testimony from ordinary citizens until the 2012 marriage and adoption proposals, these experts provided testimony in legislatures—the primary venue for reform on gay family rights in France—that emphasized abstract knowledge. In an institution guided by a theory of law that frames legislation in universal rather than particular terms, French lawmakers seem to have an inclination for expertise articulated as general law of human behavior. Experts advocating same-sex marriage were at a disadvantage in this setting. They faced a lack of French-produced empirical knowledge on which to base their claims, especially during the Pacs debates. Opponents could therefore discount the realities or even existence of gay families and evoke a priori principles and theories about sexual difference to discount them. Religious representatives, who also had access to hearings, provided testimony that was consistent with the abstract psychoanalytic and anthropological knowledge of their fellow French opponents.

These differences are partly the result of the institutional contexts that hear this information and how they control who has access to the debate. For example, because U.S. state legislators do not have as much control as their French counterparts to determine access to hearings, ordinary citizens have more opportunities to speak out in the United States. In institutions with more control, such as Congress, U.S. courts, and the French Parliament, legislators and judges appear to rely more heavily on organizations, academics, and professionals. The more closed an institution, the more likely we are to find elite actors with the kinds of credentialed expert capital that projects confidence and legitimacy. That legitimacy depends on what makes experts appear credible in a given cultural context, which is conditioned by both formal and informal institutional logics. Indeed, as we saw in the previous chapter, many of these patterns also appear in U.S. and French news coverage, suggesting that popular categories of experts and expertise are part of broader cultural repertoires that can transcend specific institutions. And, in the case of France, it also shows how the media themselves play an important role in boosting the notoriety of certain intellectuals. In a context where fame—at least on the relative scale of public intellectuals—opens doors, such coverage is key.

The differences in categories of experts and types of expertise are also the result of larger macro-structural conditions and legal circumstances in each country that favor certain kinds of information. State-level differences in laws on partnership and parenting for same-sex couples created by federalism, coupled with laissez-faire policies on artificial insemination and surrogacy, helped gays and lesbians create families earlier in the United States than in France. This contributed to their visibility, capacity to speak out, and availability for empirical research. Policy variety on the state level also helped produce and create the demand for economic expertise. In France, the longstanding restriction against adoption by same-sex couples and access to assisted reproduction for lesbian couples across the country has limited the visibility of, and thus research on, gay families. Given this relative absence, knowledge based on principles and theories rather than facts makes it all the easier for people hesitant or hostile toward gay families to hold the upper hand. French policy, especially related to adoption and access to reproductive techniques, is rife with the "principle of precaution" claiming that outcomes of children raised by same-sex couples are uncertain.[36]

According to this logic, when faced with a lack of information, decision-makers should err on the side of restriction until things are proven safe. Nevertheless, despite this rhetoric about the scientific doubt over gay parenting, French lawmakers from leftist parties legalized gay family rights, taking it on faith that their decision was made in citizens' best interests and their right to equality.

Looking at the relative balance of elite experts, such as academics, intellectuals, and professional organizations, in terms of ideological stance in both countries shows that they are more in favor of same-sex marriage and parenting in the United States than France. These differences are partly a reflection of the institutions in the expert field—courts in the United States and legislatures in France—that hear their knowledge. The weight of expertise on one side or the other is not a simple reflection of the state of the art of the science or of opinions among professionals. Rather, the weight of arguments in the expert field is the result of the way people bringing expertise into it navigate the dynamics they encounter there, including institutional logics, the political context, the arguments of their opponents, and the availability of expertise produced by different kinds of experts in the first place. Both the access to decision-making institutions and the expectations about what experts are supposed to accomplish within them are different. The structure of debate and demands of evidence in courts appear to expose the lack of empirical evidence on the side of U.S. marriage opponents. In contrast, as we will see in the next chapter, French legislators set up hearings to justify their process and claim they heard all sides, which can favor more balance or even unfavorable stances. Yet, the ideological dichotomy across the United States and France also suggests that these differences may reflect circumstances within the fields where these groups work in each country. Specifically, U.S. academics and professional organizations supporting same-sex marriage may have been able to more fruitfully carry out their work—because of legal circumstances favoring the visibility of gay families and support for research in their fields—relative to their French peers. The following chapters provide these explanations.

CHAPTER 3

FOR THE RECORD

Becoming and Creating Experts

F rench mental health professionals and priests talking about Freud and sex differences do not end up in hearings because French lawmakers have a devotion for psychoanalysis. Peer-reviewed research about the outcomes of kids raised by same-sex couples is not at the heart of federal trials in the United States just because there is so much of that data available. These patterns have structural explanations. The previous two chapters showed that media, legislatures, and courts in the United States and France have drawn on different types of expertise and categories of experts when dealing with the partnership and parenting rights of same-sex couples. This chapter examines their causes and their effects on experts and decision-makers alike.

This chapter argues that some of the differences in expertise are due, in part, to the ways in which U.S. and French experts—focusing particularly on academics, professionals, and activists—interact with and negotiate the expectations about the role of information in their respective national expert fields. Indeed, institutional settings act like filters and boosters, promoting certain kinds of expert capital while devaluing others. Specifically, while courts play an important role in U.S. reforms, the legislature dominates the debate almost exclusively in France. These decision-making institutions, as this chapter will explain, create particular expert fields that constrain and enable expertise and the people who provide it in ways that reflect specific embedded institutional logics, such as political calculations in legislatures and the adversarial system in courts. They drive how people who interact within them make decisions about the kinds of expertise they value and the challenges they face when acquiring and using it.

Those in the United States have had more exposure to the courts than their French counterparts, who, in contrast, have had extensive interaction with legislatures and lawmakers more generally. Moreover, because of the close relationship between the French media and politicians, French elite experts, as this chapter will show, have had more dealings with the press relative to their American academic and professional peers. In short, experts interact with gatekeepers, such as judges, legislators, and journalists, through these institutions to bring information to the public sphere. Those interactions train experts to think about their roles and incentivize them to work in ways that help them accomplish their goals of informing the public and, sometimes, shaping legal outcomes.

This chapter draws on seventy-two in-depth interviews of U.S. and French academics, professionals, and advocates—all of whom I selected because they testified or provided information to legal and political institutions in either country—as well as interviews with key lawmakers and lawyers who brought experts' knowledge to decision-making institutions. It is also based on ethnographic observation of these elite experts—whom I identified through the analysis of the media, court, and legislative archival data—at university seminars, think tank events, and professional gatherings.[1] It explores how these experts ended up on the telephone with journalists, taking the stand in front of judges, testifying before elected officials, and sometimes working behind the scenes with lawmakers, lawyers, and activist organizations.

Not just anyone can be in the position to have their voices heard by powerful people. And just because an expert might be asked to speak into the microphone in a court does not mean they will be called to a hearing. In this chapter, I examine the mechanisms that guide journalists, decision-makers, lawyers, and other go-betweens to select certain experts. At the same time, I look at how experts themselves feel about their role in these debates. Although ordinary citizens and religious representatives are notable categories of lay experts, especially in the United States, I do not focus on them in detail here but do mention them where appropriate.[2]

EXPERTS AND INSTITUTIONAL LOGICS

This chapter focuses on the public institutions where the people I interviewed put expertise into action, including in the media, in public and behind the scenes work in legislatures, and in courts. This focus on how people navigate particular institutions within the expert field has two goals. First, it reflects the premise that experts, however defined, intervene in ways specific to the rules and power dynamics of a given context.[3] Legislatures and courts have their own "institutional logics," such as rules defining how hearings take place or how evidence is admitted, that shape how people bring and deliver knowledge to them.[4] And, in those contexts, interactions between experts and people using their expertise, such as lawmakers, lawyers, and judges, imbue knowledge with specific kinds of value whose worth depends on an economy of information.[5] Second, analyzing interactions within legal and political institutions helps account for differences across the United States and France. Indeed, because these institutions have historically played different roles on gay family rights in each country, we can expect those configurations to help account for the different experiences of experts. Put differently, cross-national comparison shows how specific policy environments in the United States and France condition what kinds of issues matter to advocates and decision-makers, on the one hand, and shape the demand for specific kinds of expert capital that experts can produce to discuss them, on the other.[6]

Unlike informal meetings—a common form of expert-lawmaker interaction in France but not the United States—where experts get access to lawmakers because of their personal relationships or status and where the rules of engagement are tacit, legislative hearings are more formal kinds of interaction. They require lawmakers to negotiate the political context and the specific rules of their chamber when deciding who to invite.[7] In open systems, such as in many U.S. state legislatures, anyone can testify at most hearings. For example, California and Texas legislatures allow any interested party to express their views at most hearings. In addition, bill sponsors and their opponents can bring several witnesses with them. This system takes much of the control out of the legislators' hands and, as seen in chapter 2, creates a space for average citizens and advocacy organizations to "tell stories" to lawmakers as they consider bills.[8]

In contrast, in closed systems, such as the French Parliament, lawmakers in the majority control hearings. They must therefore manage multiple political logics, including legitimizing their process and preventing backlash or resistance from their political opponents, in deciding whom to invite. In these cases, lawmakers act as knowledge gatekeepers who coordinate precise political objectives with their ideas of what hearings should look like. Understanding how lawmakers navigate these concerns and draw on their own subjective ideas about what the public ought to hear sheds light on why certain people or groups—but not others—are invited to French hearings on gay family rights.

Of all legal and political settings, U.S. courts lay out the most formal rules about who counts as an expert and how their information should be used. In other words, these institutions define problems and the solutions to those problems according to a "hermetic logic" specific to courts.[9] First, arguments lawyers make in courts must respond to precise legal questions, such as whether prohibiting same-sex couples from marrying is legal under specific articles of constitutions or other legal codes. Court cases are by their nature about specific people or events, whereas legislation is more abstract, especially in France. Second, unlike the media or legislatures, courts create mechanisms that strictly control both the content of what an expert says as well as the basis on which the expert makes that claim.[10] To provide testimony to the court as an "expert witness," a person must present qualifications that justify their presence and claims.[11] Opposing litigators have the opportunity to discredit those qualifications and the knowledge the witness provides. Ultimately, the judge makes a determination about the scientific, historical, or social validity and accuracy about those claims. This chapter explores how lawyers and expert witnesses navigate the institutional logics of courts as well as the effects those logics have on the meaning of knowledge they hear. It concludes with a reflection on how academic and intellectual experts integrate the logics and expectations of the expert field into their own research practices as a result of their interactions with decision-makers and other people who want their expert capital.

NEGOTIATING INSTITUTIONAL LOGICS IN THE UNITED STATES

Media: A Low-Stakes Environment for U.S. Academics and Professionals

Media is an important outlet for expertise in both countries. However, as chapter 1 showed, whereas U.S. reporting consists of higher representations of ordinary citizens and activists, in French news coverage, intellectuals, academics, and professionals occupy a significantly larger place. Editors and journalists in each country appear to prioritize different categories of people to interview or give places to on their op-ed pages. The showcasing of lived experiences in the U.S. press and elite discourse from above in the French press creates different circumstances for the kinds of people I interviewed, who were primarily academics, professionals, and advocates. Their decisions about engagement with the media reflected how they understood what their role in debates should be. Academics who thought of themselves as neutral did not say they particularly valued engaging with the press, whereas activists and academics working in think tanks and organizations geared toward policymaking did value engagement.

Regardless of their stance on gay family rights, most American experts did not describe the media as a high-stakes forum that they prioritize. Only a third said they had published in or been solicited by the press and other media outlets. Academics were the least invested in the media; they primarily participated by responding to journalists seeking quotes. These scholars did not specifically seek to express themselves individually in the media but said they were happy to respond when asked. They seemed to respond to academic incentive structures that put a premium on publishing in peer-reviewed journals, leading them to prioritize their academic research over engagement with the press. Moreover, lawyers and policymakers valued academic experts precisely because their work was validated by scientific processes and not for public recognition in the media. The value of their expert capital was not connected to their popularity in the press but to their academic affiliations and peer approval. American organizations, whether professional, like the American Psychological Association, or activist, like the Heritage Foundation, have taken up the task of disseminating research, which reduces the necessity for academics to do it directly.

Indeed, most scholarship entered the U.S. media through organizations, such as advocacy groups and think tanks, who gathered and distributed it via press releases and communications strategies. Reflecting this, activists and think tank affiliates were the group who spoke most frequently about their media interventions. Their missions included packaging and creating expertise with the express purpose of informing policy debates. Ilya Shapiro, a senior fellow at the Cato Institute, a libertarian think tank that drafted an amicus brief in favor of same-sex marriage, described organizations like his as knowledge "moderators" who, in addition to producing their own information, interface between academics and the broader public sphere.[12] Most American academics did not need to get directly involved with media outreach because organizations were already doing that work.

A few U.S. academics, both progressive and conservative, said they intentionally reached out to the media. They were among the most involved in mobilizing for or against same-sex families. These scholars were especially committed to shaping legal outcomes, and they emphasized the importance of media for their cause. Not coincidentally, they were also involved in advocacy organizations and think tanks and were especially committed to shaping policy outcomes. Lynn Wardle, a law professor at Brigham Young University, a Mormon institution known for producing socially conservative scholarship, is a good example. In addition to his involvement with conservative "traditional family" marriage organizations, such as the Marriage Law Project at the Catholic University of America, he explained that speaking out in the media is "a very important part of a scholar's responsibility." Similarly, Lee Badgett, a professor of economy at the University of Massachusetts Amherst who helped found the Institute for Gay and Lesbian Strategic Studies, which eventually merged with the Williams Institute, said she has written op-ed pieces and responded to media interviews because "that's how people get a lot of their information." She argued that speaking in the media can help "educate the general public about what I think are the best facts, figures, ways of thinking about . . . what the situation is for LGBTQ [people] in the U.S. today." Researchers like Badgett hoped bringing their scholarship to the media could shape public perceptions and legal outcomes on issues in which they were invested.

Similarly, activists, who seek to favorably shape media narratives to meet their policy goals, sought to speak out in the press. For example, Jennifer Roback Morse, a founder of a conservative religious think tank, the Ruth Institute, and formerly tenured professor, said she perceived a bias in the press—particularly *The New York Times*—obscuring negative consequences to people who establish families outside of heterosexual marriage. To combat this, she wrote articles and op-eds "to try to refute . . . puff pieces that show up in the press" as part of a strategy to discredit mainstream journalism that she claimed was favorable to same-sex marriage legalization. On the other side, the well-known lawyers Jennifer Pizer, director of law and policy at Lambda Legal, and Mary Bonauto, the Civil Rights Project Director of GLAD (GLBTQ Legal Advocates and Defenders), shared the stories and needs of sexual minorities in the media. For Pizer, part of her job included acting as "an amplifier of other people's voices [in order to convey] human stories that people haven't heard and that can help people adjust their understanding." To Bonauto, sharing the lived experiences of same-sex couples in the media helped raise awareness about the objectives and necessity of federal court cases to repeal the Defense of Marriage Act (DOMA). Her organization's lawsuits and media interventions both sought to illustrate "how damaging and harmful DOMA was to real married people." These activists, unlike the majority of their American academic colleagues, sought media exposure to influence the debate in their favor. The significant presence of lay experts in *New York Times* reporting, as chapter 1 described, suggests that this strategy pays off by ensuring that American readers learn about the everyday lives of gay families seeking legal recognition. Relative to academics and professionals, these leaders in activist organizations were also more invested in working with legislators.

U.S. Legislatures: Limited Participation for Academics and Professionals

Behind the Scenes Work Lawmakers solicit the input of experts in a variety of ways. The least public facing of these involves informal discussions. Some interviewees in both countries described working privately with legislators, political appointees, or public administrations. This work is not necessarily secret; lawmakers' public agendas sometimes noted appointments, but these exchanges were not always clearly on the record. Only a few U.S. interviewees, most of whom worked for advocacy organizations or think tanks, described this kind of work. For example, according to Jennifer Pizer, much of Lambda Legal's legislative work involves helping specific state and federal lawmakers draft legislation. However, this classic kind of lobbying has more often dealt with LGBTQ rights issues other than couples and families, such as workplace discrimination and hate crimes legislation.

The few U.S. academics and intellectuals I interviewed who did have personal interactions with lawmakers described these kinds of exchanges as unusual. Lynn Wardle, for example, who described his acquaintanceship with Orrin Hatch—who was a Republican senator from Utah, Wardle's home state—said instances of lawmakers "asking for [his] advice . . . [were] quite rare" outside of formal hearings. Most U.S. academic experts appeared to have had little, if any, personal proximity to legislators. They were not in the habit of attending legislators' dinner parties or attending social gatherings with them. Rather, the connections they did have to the political field in general, and lawmakers in particular, were often mediated by advocacy organizations and think tanks. As I will describe in chapter 5, organizations work as pipelines between lawmakers and academic and professional experts because they are better able to navigate across the abundance of policy outlets in the United States, which far outnumber those in France. These organizations help ensure a minimal direct overlap between academic fields on the one hand and the political field on the other, doing all kinds of translation work in the process to make expert capital usable for decision-makers.

Hearings: Whose Story Represents More People? As described in chapter 2, most legislative hearings in the United States, at least on the state level, do not often involve the direct participation of academics and intellectuals. Rather, local elected officials, average citizens, and representatives of local and national advocacy organizations occupy these spaces to tell their personal stories or explain their stances for or against proposed legislation. Because most hearings in the state legislative committees I examined are open to any witnesses who register to speak outside of the equal time allotted to the bill's sponsors and rivals, legislators do not always control who appears overall. As leaders at activist groups on both sides explained to me, lawmakers can and do coordinate with organizations that support their stances to encourage them to appear or, when possible, to invite them as witnesses. Jennifer Pizer, for example, described mobilizing social movement organization volunteers and concerned citizens in tandem with allied lawmakers to testify at California legislative hearings over gay family rights during her time at Lambda Legal. They did so to create an impression of political and social force. Their goal is to get lay experts, people who can tell enthralling stories about their lives, in front of the committees to make the stakes real for them. Also, in both state and federal legislatures, all members of the public are also permitted to contribute written statements in lieu of physical presence at hearings, which movement organizations also often encourage and coordinate. This can give an impression of spontaneous public reaction to a bill even when larger, and sometimes professionalized, groups are behind the action.

In some situations in U.S. states, such as when California voters gathered enough signatures to force a ballot measure amending the constitution to prohibit same-sex marriage in 2008, legislative committees may hold a hearing where lawmakers are responsible for controlling and inviting specific witnesses. This is also the case for U.S. congressional hearings. In these situations, as chapter 2 illustrated, legislators often reach out to local legislators, advocacy organizations, and law professors or professionals who support their stances. Examples of this include Jennifer Roback Morse's participation at California Proposition 8 hearings while she was on staff for the National Organization for Marriage and Professor Lynn Wardle's participation in U.S. congressional hearings in 1996 for DOMA. Because lawmakers on both sides are permitted to invite a certain number of witnesses, hearings have some ideological balance, reflecting the political makeup of the committee.

U.S. interviewees on both sides either experienced or observed legislative hearings as political forums where lawmakers, who have already made up their minds ahead of time, rally their supporters and disregard information with which they disagree. Because these settings have "no constraints," in the words of Terry Stewart—who was a chief deputy city attorney at the San Francisco City Attorney's office and affiliated with the team litigating in favor of same-sex marriage in *Perry v. Schwarzenegger*—the witnesses in hearings "can talk about whatever they want or whatever you want them to." The scope of information is broad, and the lines of questioning do not have to follow precise patterns of legal reasoning. Other interviewees described legislators as "posturing" and not "taking information seriously." The institutional logics of hearings on human rights issues favor emotions and storytelling.[13] For this reason, most academic interviewees, even if they had contributed information to hearings directly or through organizations, such as the Williams Institute or the Society for the Psychological Study of Social Issues, doubted whether legislators cared about scientific content. Indeed, in the words of one well-known psychologist involved in gay family debates for decades but who asked to remain anonymous, "it's about anecdotes, not data." Nevertheless, many also recognized that it was important to provide all information, regardless of whether lawmakers paid attention, because it would be included in the official record, which could be used to establish legislative intent in future court cases where the stakes around the content of their statements might be more important.

Those interviewees who had participated in both types of settings came to understand that legislative hearings, unlike court procedures, did not involve deliberate weighing of the quality and quantity of evidence. Rather, they saw hearings as "parades" and "varieties of theatre" in which lawmakers and advocates seek to display their force through the numbers of witnesses and contributions. The power of expert capital from academics in these settings is not so much about the veracity of their statements as it is the allure that their credentials can bring to the broader process. Precisely because the content of science is less relevant, such experts seem disinclined to get involved in hearings. These views should not lead us to conclude that courts do, in fact, have a knowledgeable and responsible relationship to scientific evidence. Indeed, as we will see, factors related to appearance, such as the personal lives and social backgrounds of experts, are important there and belie the idea that the facts are all that matter. Nevertheless, experts rightly perceived that the meaning of their information changes depending on the institution they are speaking to and took take steps to get involved or not based on their own priorities, whether professional or ideological.

U.S. Courts: Where Judges Weigh the Knowledge

Courtrooms are easy for us to imagine because we see them in popular culture all the time. Most of us can imagine the scene of a lawyer questioning a witness under the watchful eye of a judge. U.S. cases on same-sex marriage have themselves been dramatized. In reaction to the Supreme Court's ruling that the district court trial of *Perry v. Schwarzenegger* could not be filmed and live cast, gay playwright and filmmaker, Dustin Lance Black, adapted the trial transcript as a play, entitled *8*. In 2012, Hollywood stars, including George Clooney, Brad Pitt, and Jamie Lee Curtis, performed a staged reading.[14] The script even included scenes involving the testimony of experts. The trial was also reenacted in other formats. The stakes around these trials are elevated, both because their outcomes can significantly change the legal landscape through case law and because the expertise that goes into them becomes part of the public conversation. Emphasizing the cases as new iterations of America's civil rights history, the media and social movement organizations publicized the stories of those involved, such as plaintiff couples seeking legal recognition, as well as those of the lawyers and expert witnesses participating. Because of this attention, it is also safe to say that many people are familiar with some of the basic institutional logics of the judiciary, at least on a superficial level.

The logics governing the structure of debate and the role of expertise in courts create different circumstances than legislatures for expertise producers, wielders, and organizers as they interact with decision-makers. Unlike lawmakers, judges are meant to evaluate the validity of the arguments of two parties—or groupings of parties on one side or the other—vis-à-vis precise legal questions in a specific case. For example, lawyers representing the plaintiffs in *Perry v. Schwarzenegger*, two California same-sex couples who were denied marriage licenses, argued that the heterosexual definition of marriage in their state's constitution violated their clients' rights under the Constitution of the United States. Defenders of California's constitutional language, which was put into place by Proposition 8,

were then required to convincingly demonstrate a state interest justifying dif-
ferential treatment. This adversarial setup requires that parties on either side
defend their arguments with facts. If anti-same-sex marriage advocates contend,
for instance, that legalizing same-sex marriage would undermine or discourage
different-sex marriage, as they did in *Perry*, both sides would provide evidence—
sometimes delivered by "expert witnesses" called to the stand—such as heterosexual divorce rates in jurisdictions having legalized same-sex marriage. Both sides
would also have the opportunity to question the information presented by their
opponents—in the form of cross-examination of witnesses, for example—and
attempt to undermine its validity. Finally, the judge would then determine if
the evidence was sound and sufficiently supported the legal argument. As Judge
Walker put it himself in his opinion, "Proposition 8 raised significant disputed
factual questions" that justified his decision to set the matter for trial with a
discovery phase rather than make a summary judgement.[15] Thus, unlike in legislatures where lawmakers use knowledge politically to justify, legitimate, or inform
their process, in courts, lawyers are supposed to use knowledge in order to convince judges they have a substantiated legal argument.

In addition to arbitrating between different arguments and evaluating the
quality and quantity of knowledge on both sides, judges can also determine
which legal questions the trial will address before it even begins. For example, in
the federal district court trial *DeBoer v. Snyder*, April DeBoer and Jayne Rowse, a
lesbian couple, originally sued the state of Michigan for the right to jointly adopt
their children; the state only allowed married couples, limited to heterosexuals, to adopt. The judge, Bernard A. Friedman, however, had them amend their
suit to sue for the right to marry, which he determined was the underlying cause
of their grievance.

People interested in sharing their information with the courts, such as organizations, average citizens, professionals, academics, or other concerned parties,
must deal with the rules, barriers, and institutional logics of the judicial field.
Information enters the court through two main channels: amici curiae briefs and
testimony or evidence presented at trial. People hoping to convince the courts
in either of these avenues aim to give their statements a sheen of credibility. To
do so, they solicit the kinds of experts who can give it to them. Unsurprisingly,
thus, American interviewees had significant interactions with and understandings of courts and their demands on expertise, having experienced either or both
of these outlets.

Amicus Briefs: My Expert Is More Credible Than Yours Any party not formally affiliated with either side in a trial, but who believes they have information the court should consider as it weighs its decision, can submit an amicus curiae brief.[16] However, would-be amicus authors face high barriers that limit participation by untrained people because, unlike written statements for legislative hearings, they require specialized knowledge about formatting and submission. They must organize their briefs according to a precise configuration, use technical legal language, state why they believe they have a justified reason for submitting, and provide information that contributes to a specific argument pertinent to the trial. For these reasons, amicus authors generally work with advocacy lawyers or law firms who help them format their information and submit it on their behalf. Many U.S. professional groups, advocacy organizations, and think tanks have in-house or contracted legal service providers to perform these tasks, which I explain in further detail in chapter 5.

Although the attorneys for litigants in a given case do not officially solicit, assist, or prevent people from submitting amicus briefs, many amicus authors and trial attorneys, most of whom work in legal advocacy organizations, communicate with each other thanks to relationships they have built over years of collaboration. Mary Bonauto of GLAD, Leslie Cooper, the Deputy Director of the American Civil Liberties Union (ACLU) LGBTQ & HIV Project, and interviewees at think tanks and other advocacy and professional organizations on both sides talked about this planning. Many of the same attorneys organize trials, and the same people and groups submit briefs. They discuss strategies with each other about who should submit briefs and what they should say.

One of these strategies consists of mobilizing experts and expertise to write briefs that will bolster the credibility of legal arguments in the case. Over the years through these routine interactions over amicus briefs, attorneys and their staff develop lists of which experts are the most reliable and can respond to specific kinds of legal arguments. In general, the legal teams want to have the most prestigious and recognized names—top scientists, national professional organizations, well-regarded legal scholars whose names will be familiar to judges—submitting briefs in support of their side. And, for brief authors, the opportunity to publicly align oneself with a side in a case about human rights, as many major organizations and groups did on behalf of same-sex couples, is itself a source of possible renown, and also risk, depending on the outcome, public opinion, or divisions within the fields in which these experts work. The composition of the body of briefs in these trials, which chapter 2 described, reflects in part these negotiations between brief authors and attorneys running the trials and their respective objectives and interests.

If organizing written and oral testimony in legislatures is about giving the impression of mass mobilization presenting popular sentiment, briefs are best understood as a way to overwhelm the court with a breadth of interrelated, but not repeating, arguments and evidence. All parties I spoke to wanted to avoid what they called "me too" or "copycat" briefs that repeat the same information and arguments as others. Brief authors and attorneys described how specific briefs should speak to precise legal questions as well as also potentially send political or social messages. Attorneys and staff in advocacy organizations working with brief authors and coordinating the groups of briefs for their side in a given case wanted to ensure that briefs spoke to legal questions they prioritized or presented information they wanted the court to hear. They aimed for a web of data and arguments from different kinds of experts building in chorus to support the case in the courtroom. For example, Mary Bonauto described working with groups of jurists for different arguments in relation to challenges against DOMA. Her side wanted a brief from "constitutional litigators" with strong academic reputations and experience making constitutional arguments before federal courts who could talk about the violation of federalism aspects of DOMA. She wanted authors who would appear credible and, hopefully, command the attention of the justices. She also wanted family law scholars and local attorneys, who, thanks to their experience on the ground in everyday cases, could demonstrate that states already recognized same-sex parental relationships despite congressional legislators' claims to the contrary when they passed DOMA.

Attorneys and their allies also strove for briefs that would send a variety of political messages that, according to William Eskridge, the well-known Yale law professor, might appeal to the sensibility of specific judges. He was thinking in particular of Supreme Court Justice Anthony Kennedy—appointed by Ronald Reagan in 1987—who was the occasional "swing vote" on an otherwise ideologically split court at the time the same-sex marriage cases were heard. Bonauto described, for example, the centrist appeal of a brief co-signed by hundreds of private-sector employers discussing the economic downside of DOMA that sent the political message, "business is standing with us."[17] Similarly, Eskridge described how joint briefs between organizations that usually oppose one another give the impression that one's legal case has mainstream and consensual appeal.

He mentioned the brief supporting same-sex marriage filed jointly by the Cato Institute, a libertarian thank tank often aligned with conservative causes, such as deregulation, and the Constitutional Accountability Center, a progressive think tank.[18] In terms of the mobilization of expertise, these examples demonstrate how advocates involved in these cases are attuned to the leveraging of two distinct dimensions, the reputations of experts, including their ideological stances, and the content of what they say, in order to send targeted messages to the court.

While the primary aim of a brief is to shore up the arguments of one of the parties, professional organizations also use them to police their disciplines, augment their reputations, and signal their alliances. In other words, the briefs are not just products for a legal purpose. Their writing creates relationships, clarifies public stances, and creates habits within organizations that will go on to inform how experts think about their role and the relationship of their professional and scientific fields to politics. The American Sociological Association (ASA) and the American Psychological Association (APA) are good examples. According to Sally Hillsman, executive officer of the ASA from 2002 to 2016, the association began submitting briefs in major same-sex marriage trials to counter claims by anti-gay-marriage social scientists—especially those by Mark Regnerus, professor of sociology at the University of Texas at Austin, and those using his research—that the social science evidence is divided and inconclusive about the outcomes of children raised by same-sex couples. The ASA wanted to ensure that "people who speak on behalf of social science . . . are really presenting as accurate as is possible an understanding of what the social science says," she explained. The brief thus made a legal point about the evidence, which the ASA argued supported allowing same-sex couples to marry, buttressed the reputation of sociology, and aimed to undermine the scientific authority of conservative sociologists.

In another example, a variety of important national professional organizations, including the American Medical Association, the American Academy of Pediatrics, and the American Psychiatric Association, joined a brief drafted by the APA, which summarizes the social science evidence on the nature of sexual orientation, the children of same-sex couples, and the stigmatizing effects of marriage bans on same-sex couples.[19] According to Clinton Anderson, the APA's associate executive director of public interest and director of the APA's LGBT Concerns Office, the brief's symbolic value was all the stronger thanks to the collective weight of its prestigious institutional signatories. They sent the message that medical and mental health researchers support same-sex marriage as a group, casting opponents as unscientific and outside the bounds of their disciplines.

Brief authors on the side against same-sex marriage could also address specific legal questions while sending a broader message they hoped would generate more public support for their stance by giving the impression that it was grounded in objective arguments supported by data and motivated by constitutionally justifiable opinions. For example, William Duncan, a former visiting professor at Brigham Young University, former acting director of the Marriage Law Project at the Catholic University of America, and executive director of the Utah-based Marriage Law Foundation, explained his reasoning behind the brief he authored in *Perry v. Schwarzenegger* for the Ethics and Religious Liberty Commission of the Southern Baptist Convention. It dealt with whether opponents of same-sex marriage in Proposition 8 were motivated by animus against gays and lesbians, which would have constituted a constitutionally unjustifiable reason for denying equal treatment.[20] Their brief cited moral and religious reasons, specifically scriptural quotes condemning homosexual behavior, rather than outright hostility for homosexuals, for their opposition to same-sex marriage in an attempt to shield their party against the legally disqualifying claim of antigay hatred.

Witnesses: Finding the Best Person for the Job   The spotlight on same-sex marriage experts shines brightest when they take the stand in a trial. That intense scrutiny occurs when the judge overhearing the case decides to call a full "bench trial" as opposed to issuing a judgment based on the written and oral arguments of the attorneys on both sides. Most trials on the constitutionality of same-sex marriage have not gone to full trial. Nevertheless, the few that have, including *Baehr v. Miike* in the Hawaii Supreme Court in the 1990s as well as *Hollingsworth v. Perry* and *DeBoer v. Snyder*, both in federal district courts, had significant legal and political reverberations.[21] Baehr was the first trial of its kind on same-sex marriage and triggered major backlash against same-sex marriage in the form of DOMA and state bans, shaping gay national and local gay rights politics at the turn of the twenty-first century. *Hollingsworth*, the case against Proposition 8, was the first serious federal same-sex marriage trial and the first to reach the U.S. Supreme Court. It helped spark other trials like *DeBoer*, which would eventually be consolidated on appeal with *Obergefell v. Hodges* to ultimately legalize same-sex marriage nationwide.[22] Given their role in the history of changing same-sex marriage rights and the public attention they garnered, the information generated in these cases resonated beyond their original context.

In these cases, in addition to the plaintiffs, such as same-sex couples, who testify about their motivations to marry and the negative effects of its denial, attorneys can call "expert witnesses" to the stand. These witnesses must demonstrate to the court specific qualifications set by law and jurisprudence that make them particularly well suited to speak to the legal arguments of the case. Among the people I interviewed in the United States, eleven had testified in this context and seven worked either as litigators drawing on expert witnesses or helped to coordinate with attorneys who did. Another interviewee, Helen Zia, was heard as a "lay witness" in the *Hollingsworth* trial, where she shared her personal experience about what it felt like to be legally married—versus in a domestic partnership— to her wife. Lay witnesses provide opinions based on their experience but, unlike "expert witnesses," on whom I focus here because of their numerical superiority in these trials, do not need to meet any specific qualifications.

Only the Best Witnesses Will Do French legislators and U.S. attorneys, as well as the staff who work for them, face a similar task picking witnesses. They have to ask themselves which kinds of people will say the things they hope will make them most likely to meet their objectives. Yet, while the former juggle political calculations facing the committees and public reactions to the hearings, the latter contend with strict conditions on expertise as enshrined in the Federal Rules of Evidence governing expert testimony and defined by jurisprudence known as the Daubert standard.[23] Within these standards, attorneys must convince judges that their "expert witnesses" have the diplomas, training, scientific peer recognition, and publication record to qualify as experts. Moreover, judges must also determine that the testimony is "based on sufficient facts or data; is . . . the product of reliable principles and methods; and . . . the expert has reliably applied the principles and methods to the facts of the case."[24] Several types of materials go into establishing the expert's requisite position. Before the trial begins, potential expert witnesses write lengthy formal reports demonstrating their mandate, qualifications, and research relevant to the disputed facts. They also undergo pretrial depositions. Because of the adversarial court setting, lawyers on either side can use these records, which can be admitted in trial, as well as in-trial cross-examination to question the expert witnesses of their opponents in order to undermine their qualifications or reveal that their application of the facts to the case is flawed. This system gives U.S. attorneys an explicit structure with relatively clear rules, affording them less leeway than French legislative committee conveners as they strategize about experts.

Seeing an expert witness wither under scrutiny and damage the case is a lawyer's worst nightmare. Avoiding this scenario is one of their priorities. The high standards of evidence and the unrelenting efforts of their adversaries to delegitimize their witnesses drive attorneys to thoroughly vet and carefully select their experts. Indeed, if their opponents can convincingly undermine the testimony or credibility of their witness by, say, demonstrating that the witness does not thoroughly know the scientific literature in question or has a disqualifying bias, it could seriously reduce the likelihood of winning. Several respondents on both sides described how, because of these high stakes, when lawyers initially contacted them, they forwarded them to other people they thought would be better qualified, whose testimony could withstand the trial, and whose profile would be difficult to attack. This suggests that these experts had a vested interest in seeing a particular side succeed. They saw how courts emphasized strong credentials, especially academic peer recognition and publication records. Other interviewees described being contacted but then eventually passed over for someone else who lawyers thought would be a better fit because of their education, personal life, or publicly known stances.

Attorneys find experts that meet these standards through legal advocacy and professional organizations that, as will be described in chapter 5, act as expert banks. These groups keep lists of potential experts, sometimes cultivating and training them for this purpose, making them available when the time comes. Many of the expert witnesses testifying on behalf of same-sex marriage advocates had either been employed by or collaborated with the Williams Institute. By cataloguing experts, these organizations play a vital networking role. Attorneys can reach out to their colleagues at advocacy organizations, such as the Williams Institute, Lambda Legal, GLAD, and the ACLU, who had previously vetted and worked with experts to compare notes. For gay rights advocates, decades of collaboration at the intersection between expertise and legal activism proved particularly important. For example, Terry Stewart explained how the *Hollingsworth* trial litigators, Ted Olson and David Boies, who were famous and skilled in their own right, known for having represented opposite sides in the infamous 2000 Supreme Court case *Bush v. Gore*, had never litigated a gay rights trial. They delegated much of the expert witness work to her and her colleagues, whose accumulated knowledge and experience as gay rights litigators gave them access to the best lists of seasoned experts.

In addition to having excellent qualifications and backgrounds, the witnesses must provide testimony that speaks to specific legal issues of the trial. It is not about supporting or decrying same-sex marriage and parenting in general, as might be the case in a legislature, but tailoring expertise to fit within narrowly delimited questions as defined by judicial parameters. Working with the logic of the court, attorneys "siloed" experts, as several described it, to address those questions, some of which are not even specifically about same-sex marriage per se. For example, as Stewart described, litigators against Proposition 8 wanted to show that the voter-approved amendment to ban same-sex marriage in the California Constitution was unconstitutional according to the U.S. Constitution because it violated equal protection, was motivated by animus, and targeted a suspect class. Each of these questions called for specific kinds of experts who could address precise empirical questions that would lead the judge to a desired legal conclusion. For instance, to establish that sexual orientation constitutes a suspect class, like race or sex, litigators needed to convince the judge (1) that gays and lesbians are historically subjugated and stigmatized; (2) that the cause of their discrimination—their sexual orientation—is an immutable characteristic; and (3) that they are politically powerless. Judges in past cases have built a relatively consistent jurisprudential legacy setting out these three specific elements—a long history of discrimination, immutability, and relative political powerlessness—as necessary for establishing suspect classification.[25] To prove these points, lawyers decided to call several experts, including the groundbreaking historian of gay life in the United States, George Chauncey, then a professor at Yale, to describe the history of antigay discrimination; the University of California, Davis psychologist Gregory Herek to talk about the causes of homosexuality and failures to "cure" it; and the Stanford political scientist Gary Segura to talk about lack of political power of LGBTQ Americans.

Part of the vetting process, which several academics described as "grueling" and time consuming, involved lawyers thoroughly familiarizing themselves with everything they could find about potential witnesses in order to prepare themselves for the trial and best determine what legal questions the expert would address. It is as if the lawyers were both the most difficult hiring committee, aiming to find every flaw in a potential candidate, and the least indulgent reviewers, seeking to debunk and criticize every aspect of their research. Terry Stewart, who assisted in *Hollingsworth*, and Leslie Cooper of the ACLU, who assisted in *DeBoer*, described how they worked in teams of lawyers each assigned to prepare specific witnesses. They came to learn the literature intimately, like graduate students in a seminar whose research paper could determine the nuptial fates of gay couples across the country. Indeed, several academic respondents described how well the lawyers grasped the technical details of empirical social science, including differences between sampling methods, internal and external validity, and statistical significance and effect size. Experts also worked with the litigators to help guide them to the information they thought could be most helpful for their case. "[They] teach you what you need to know is scientifically . . . good evidence," Cooper explained. Working with the demographer Gary Gates and the Stanford sociologist Michael Rosenfeld, she learned, for example, that her team could demonstrate to the court "that there is a body of research that has developed over . . . the past several decades" on childhood outcomes. With their testimony, they could credibly establish—and withstand the cross-examination of the other side and testimony of opposing witnesses—that there is a scientific consensus that children raised by same-sex couples fare as well as those raised by different-sex couples, which was a key question in some of the major trials.

Seeing Science Through a Judicial Lens These negotiations between academic experts and lawyers illustrate how courts process knowledge with an eye toward accuracy as determined by the judge who is not themselves a trained scientist. Their institutional logics can be brought to bear on the claims supporters and opponents have made about same-sex marriage and parenting more broadly. Judge Vaughn Walker's decision to call for a full bench trial in the federal district suit against Proposition 8 created a unique opportunity to make public and thoroughly judge the factual claims of both sides in a controlled setting. In the judicial field, opponents, for example, could not simply make moralistic arguments, as they might in the press or on the streets, but had to defend their claims about the negative social consequences of same-sex marriage. Unlike legislative settings, which have no strict mechanism for evaluating claims beyond lawmakers' criticisms of each other and the witnesses at hearings, in the words of Nan Hunter, a distinguished professor of law, judges like Walker "forced" both sides to organize their defense and rally evidence to support their legal arguments in an "adversarial process." Illustrating this power, when attorneys on one side questioned the suitability of their opponent's expert witness during the trial, Walker explained, "I will permit the witness to testify, and make a final evaluation with respect to how much weight to give to that testimony and how to weigh it within the entire case, as we go along."[26] As other scholars and observers have noted, this situation puts expertise about gay rights "on trial."[27]

Progressive interviewees were satisfied with the way courts treated their arguments, which is unsurprising given the outcomes. The institutional logics of courts at the time these major trials took place were apparently more favorable to their stances. Many described judges as "vindicating" the science and upending the bothsidesism of the media and the political opportunity structures of the legislatures. In the eyes of pro-marriage experts and their allies, forcing the debate into the frame of empirical social science gave them the upper hand.

After assessing the facts and arguments in their respective trials, Judges Walker and Friedman wrote opinions that exposed the lack of evidence of same-sex marriage opponents and delegitimized much of their testimony. One point revolved around the quantity of expertise on both sides. In his ruling, Walker remarked that the "evidentiary presentation [of Proposition 8 supporters] was dwarfed by that of plaintiffs. Proponents presented two expert witnesses . . . but failed to build a credible factual record to support their claim that Proposition 8 served a legitimate government interest."[28] In addition to the lower number of experts against same-sex marriage, Walker explicitly disqualified one of them, David Blankenhorn, the founder of the Institute for American Values and author of several books about marriage and family. He determined that Blankenhorn's testimony should be "entitled to essentially no weight" because it failed to meet minimum standards for expertise: It was not "supported by reliable evidence or methodology," and Blankenhorn "failed to consider evidence contrary to his view."[29]

Another point centered on the quality of specific publications, particularly Mark Regnerus's same-sex parenting article, which the anti-marriage side had wielded during the trial as a smoking gun that was meant to definitively debunk the scientific consensus on the good outcomes of children with gay parents.[30] In his opinion striking down Michigan's same-sex marriage and adoption ban, Judge Friedman described the article as a "hastily concocted . . . 'study,' " and Regnerus's expert testimony as "entirely unbelievable and not worthy of serious consideration."[31] Friedman made this judgment based on an evaluation of the methods, data, and conclusions in Regnerus's article, which the plaintiff's witness, Michael Rosenfeld, unpacked in great detail during his testimony. Rosenfeld described how the paper was methodologically flawed. Drawing on data from his New Family Structures Study (NFSS), Regnerus compared the outcomes of adults who claimed that at least one of their parents was gay or lesbian when they were a child to those of adults who had only ever been raised by married heterosexual parents who were biologically related to them. Rosenfeld also demonstrated that this single publication was an outlier in the large body of LGBTQ parenting research that had been debated by many other sociologists.[32] Judge Friedman's severe assessment of Regnerus's testimony—literally putting the word study in quotation marks—effectively rendered Regnerus's expertise unusable for future trials. Conservative interviewees, who were disappointed with the outcome and believed that the facts were on their side, argued that the judges misunderstood the data, simply ignored it, or ruled ideologically. Some also suggested that few experts were willing to go on record as working with the anti-same-sex marriage side for fear that it could hurt their reputations.

While court demands on knowledge can appear to vindicate the science, their constraints can also distort it in significant ways both before and during the trial. Before the trial, the imperative that witnesses buttress a specific legal argument can lead lawyers to reject accurate scholarly information if they think it could undermine their case. For example, the facts of LGBTQ political dis-empowerment, essential for establishing that minority sexual orientation is a suspect classification, created difficulties. According to Terry Stewart and other interviewees, litigators arguing against Proposition 8 in *Hollingsworth* decided to ask Gary Segura—an esteemed political scientist working on minorities in politics but without much research on gay rights—to testify, rather than Hunter College professor of political science, Kenneth Sherrill, the leading U.S. expert on LGBTQ political power. While Sherrill's expertise was more germane than Segura's, he was excluded as a potential witness because he had published—accurately—that gays and lesbians had made significant gains through the political process. While this claim is true, lawyers had to emphasize the equally valid claim, which Segura could demonstrate, that despite their gains, historical lack of representation, as well as referenda, laws, and constitutional amendments targeting sexual minorities, demonstrate political powerlessness. If Sherrill had testified instead, Stewart and others knew the opposing attorneys would use his publications and statements to undermine their case.

Court logics also distort scientific information by limiting nuance, creating challenges for academics whose jobs are predicated on rejecting facile binaries.

For example, during the trial, this same legal question of suspect classification required George Chauncey to provide a more starkly contrasted—but not inaccurate—history of antigay persecution by downplaying episodes of LGBTQ social resilience than he otherwise would have in an academic forum. Indeed, while academic debate allows scholars to consider how scientific literature is graded, evolving, multifaceted, and, in the words of family demographer Wendy Manning, "knotty," court arguments favor definitive, unequivocal statements. Anticipating that their work might be used for policy purposes and knowing that nuance is lost in translation, especially in courts, some progressive scholars have downplayed parts of their research finding that some children raised by same-sex couples differ from their peers raised by different-sex couples. As early as 2001, sociologist Judith Stacey and others argued that this legitimate concern about misinterpretation or bad-faith weaponization in public debates created troubling distortions in the scientific literature.[33] However, more than ten years later, during the trials, this critical perspective was mostly mobilized by conservative lawyers and experts trying to delegitimize pro-marriage expertise. As a result, Stacey and other researchers decided to publicly state that their critiques of the impact of policy considerations on the scientific literature could not justify a refusal to legally recognize same-sex families.[34] It is unsurprising that Stacey was not invited to testify as an expert witness. Her queer critiques of marriage and her defense of the scientific nuance about childhood outcomes would have made her an easy target for anti-same-sex marriage litigants.[35]

Scientific information needs to be refined and repackaged before it can become expert capital suitable for the courtroom. Knowing that courts need definitive answers, legal teams trained their expert witnesses in these same-sex marriage cases to express themselves in the register of binaries. Unlike in a classroom or peer-reviewed article, where a professor might present a range of hypotheses and viewpoints about causal mechanisms on, say, the effect of family structure on children's mental health outcomes, in a court, the professor would have to present a firm, definite answer. Lee Badgett described learning these codes in preparation for the Proposition 8 trial: "Sometimes I was just sounding very professorial, like, well, 'some people say this, some people say that.' And, finally, somebody said, 'No. The point is you're the expert. What do you think?' . . . And I was like 'Oh, oh, right. I'm not teaching a class here, or I'm not trying to educate somebody. I'm trying to give my opinion that I have developed after studying this for a long time.'"

The vetting, training, and trial put witnesses in a position of explaining information in ways that were unfamiliar and sometimes frustrating. Several interviewees described having to unlearn saying, "It depends," when asked a specific question about the science. In a court setting, this answer suggests the speaker is either unqualified to respond or that the information is unclear. Training academics to speak in court-formatted language reveals how the patterns of practice in the courtroom transform scientific knowledge into usable expert capital that can buy credibility before judges, giving them appropriate justifications for their decisions.

In sum, the importance of these bench trials in the history of U.S. gay rights exposed experts and their handlers to specific courtroom demands: the adversarial system, close examination of facts, adjudication of accuracy, and tailoring of knowledge to legal arguments. Attorneys supporting same-sex marriage were probably successful in part because they were able to convince the judge that they had the weight of empirical science behind them. The incentive for strong empirical knowledge has also driven marriage opponents to try to produce more knowledge within the academy that can pass muster. These institutional logics introduced experts to ways of producing, negotiating, and presenting information that set them apart from the political imperatives of the media and legislatures, which dominate the French case.

NEGOTIATING INSTITUTIONAL LOGICS IN FRANCE

Courts: An Institution Most French Experts Do Not Encounter

Because of their limited implication in changing gay family rights, almost none of the people I interviewed in France had any direct experiences with courts and the institutional logics determining the value of expert capital that go with them. As described in the previous chapter, this reflects the broader lack of judicial avenues of reform for human rights issues in the last half century in France in general. The French law professors and legal professionals I interviewed contrasted the U.S. common law system with the French civil law system in which the judiciary has historically been weak on these issues. Indeed, the *Conseil Constitutionnel* and *Cour de Cassation*, two national courts of final appeal, have deferred to legislators on the questions of same-sex couples and their access to childrearing, suggesting it is not within the courts' domain.[36] Although the European Court of Human Rights (ECtHR) has been a venue for condemning France's refusal to allow single gays and lesbians and same-sex couples to adopt, because the court does not have enforcement capabilities, France was slow to implement policy changes in response to these rulings.[37]

The few law professors and lawyers who did engage with courts explained that they did not involve the recourse to expertise to the degree that their American peers did. There were no full bench trials that could create jurisprudence for sweeping change or frame the terms on which later debates might be held. Instances most resembling those in the United States were summary judgment trials in the ECtHR, at which attorneys provided written reports about the legal facts in addition to their oral arguments. For example, Robert Wintemute, a professor of human rights law at King's College London who litigated several of the ECtHR adoption cases with Caroline Mécary, worked with the lawyer and law professor Daniel Borrillo to examine whether French legal history and law required sexual difference to establish *filiation*. Their goal was to provide historical evidence that filial ties—the legal ties between parents and children in the French system—did not require that each of the two legal parents be of different sexes. Any expertise presented to the court was limited to legal arguments relative to the European Convention on Human Rights and the facts in the trial. There was little space for additional information, such as social or mental health science, that could have also spoken to the legal questions but from a broader angle.

Courts do intervene in individual family law cases in France, such as determinations around adoptions and child custody, as is common in the United States, and were one of the rare places where French tribunals heard expertise. However, these venues in France do not create jurisprudence that builds over time and are out of the public eye. Moreover, expertise here does not follow the same adversarial process as in the full bench trials described above. Mécary, who was one of the rare French lawyers representing gay and lesbian clients in such situations before the mid-2000s, explained how family law courts draw on a pre-established list of mental health professionals to provide expert assessments on cases. This is true even if those experts have made public statements criticizing gay parenting. The burden of proof to contest such expertise thus falls onto the lawyers representing gay clients. Mécary described how she must confront systematically negative reports by the psychiatrist and psychoanalyst Pierre Lévy-Soussan, who is an official expert to the Paris Court of Appeals and an expert I interviewed

because of his role in gay marriage legislation. She has ordered counter assessments from the progressive psychiatrist and psychoanalyst Serge Hefez, who is
well known to the public because of his popular books and TV appearances, but
the court is not required to make an adjudication about the relative weight or
scientific accuracy of their evaluations.

Because of this institutional setup, French same-sex marriage experts have had
little exposure to an expert field in which courts weigh the legitimacy of experts
and the credibility of their interventions. In the United States, trials, some with
implications for changing national law, created a series of expectations and conditions that made both empirical science and the lived experiences of gay families valuable kinds of expertise. Those structural conditions are mostly absent
in France. Moreover, the lack of court outlets also limits the demand for such
information and, as a consequence, reduces incentives among French academics
and professionals on both sides of the debate that could produce it. There is no
network of think tanks and organizations working with them to produce court-
ready expertise to fill a slate of jurisdictions with pressing cases. Instead, many
French interviewees were invested in directly engaging in the debate through the
media, which gave them public exposure and sometimes a pathway to influencing legislators who have the power to change family law.

Media: A Political Arena for French Experts

There has long been an idea that France is a country of public intellectuals where
politicians and the public take philosophers and other "thinkers" seriously.
Though it may be declining in recent years with the rise of social media and
twenty-four-hour TV news channels, the figure of the intellectual is indeed a
staple of public life in France.[38] In this environment, intellectuals can take advantage of policy controversies to develop strong reputations through their public
engagement, boosting their status within and outside the academy.[39] Some U.S.
experts I interviewed looked to France with envy, assuming they would enjoy
broader popular recognition. And in some ways, they are correct. Almost all
French respondents, unlike their American colleagues, were regularly involved
with the media, including the press, television, and radio. Through articles
and interviews, they shared their ideas and sparred with other experts, activists, politicians, and public figures with whom they disagreed. Many earned a
measure of celebrity, at least among elite audiences, including academic peers

and gatekeepers to decision-makers, that gave them influence in a context where the boundaries between the media and academic and political fields are porous. Although an afterthought to many American experts, their French counterparts, on the contrary, dedicated themselves to their media interventions and personas. They tracked columns, open letters, and interviews in newspapers and on popular radio shows. They developed a precise sense of the partisan and ideological orientations of national outlets and strategized with their colleagues and sympathetic journalists to outweigh their adversaries. It was not uncommon for interviewees to ask me if I had seen the latest guest editorial in *Le Monde* by a rival expert or heard the story of how they and other acquittances were preparing a rebuttal in a competing newspaper.

Media presence gave French experts credibility, public exposure, and potential political power because of the overlap between journalistic and legislative debates about same-sex marriage and parenting. First, both debates drew on the same pool of people, consisting of academics, professionals, activists, and other public figures, to represent different views. Second, they both systematically juxtaposed the same people on either side of the debate. For example, journalists often quoted the same pro- and anti-marriage experts, whose ideas were presented to create an impression of balance. Meanwhile, the same people would spar in confrontational op-eds published in newspapers affiliated with opposing political camps. Later they would find themselves in the same legislative hearings. The psychoanalyst Serge Hefez described how during the marriage debates he "always [faced] the same contradictors . . . on the radio, the television, and the benches of the Assemblée Nationale." Some experts gain access to the legislative arena by first attracting journalists' attention. For example, several conservative law professors said the media attention around an open letter against same-sex marriage they published put political pressure on Socialist lawmakers on the Assemblée Nationale Judiciary Committee to invite them to hearings in 2012.[40] Similarly, Virginie Descoutures, a sociologist studying lesbian mothers, said it was not a coincidence that she got a call from legislative staffers to appear for hearings a week after *Libération*, the best-known center-left newspaper, interviewed her about her research for an article on the pending same-sex marriage and adoption legislation.[41]

For some academics and professionals, these media interactions involved as much, if not more, attention as their scholarly work during the most intense periods of the debates in the 1990s and 2010s. For example, although she was retired in 2012, renowned anthropologist Françoise Héritier remained very busy and said she could not find time to finish the third volume of her series on sexual and gender difference because she had "radio shows to do [and] journalists to respond to."[42] Some also described these media interventions as an important responsibility. Illustrating this mindset, the equally famous anthropologist Maurice Godelier said, "To my eyes, as a scientist, if I have conclusions about a controversial or problematic social fact, I must give my position." Similarly, the anti-gay-parenting psychoanalyst Christian Flavigny explained, "I believe that I am very competent in the domain [and] I feel that I have a duty to give back to society information of which it is ignorant or unaware or that it neglects." Their sense of obligation to publicly position themselves on policy issues shows the degree of seriousness with which these French experts perceive the media field. Whether or not they effectively inform public debate is less important than the fact that they believe their involvement in same-sex marriage debates is indispensable and acknowledge the media as an effective vehicle. Moreover, in the case of Héritier and Godelier, speaking to journalists and writing op-eds gave them the opportunity to affirm their already dominant positions at the top of their scientific field.

French academics and activists alike wanted to speak out in the press to change people's minds, frame the debate, and influence the political process. Sociologist Éric Fassin said, "It's important for public opinion. It's important to advance an idea and important to support each other in a debate." For some activists committed to using social science and storytelling to advance their cause, like Alexandre Urwicz of the Association des Familles Homoparentales (ADFH) [Association of Gay Families], it was the best way to increase gay family visibility. He had developed working relationships with journalists and told them, "You have to do investigations and reports where you show the families." French advocates, academics, and public figures use the media to draw battlelines. Allies express solidarity and support for each other as they respond to their adversaries. For example, Urwicz described his satisfaction over co-signing an editorial with Élisabeth Badinter—a famed feminist philosopher with significant political connections through her husband Robert, who occupied major political positions including Minister of Justice (1981–1986) and president of the *Conseil Constitutionnel* (1986–1995)—as well as the sociologist Irène Théry in *Le Monde*.[43] Together they argued in favor of legalizing access to surrogacy. Such co-authorships are mutually beneficial for academics and activists; advocates like Urwicz share in the aura of legitimacy of famous academics and intellectuals, and the latter can claim to have the support of people on the ground. Unlike in U.S. debates, where activist organizations and think tanks gathered and distributed information in the absence of significant direct media participation by academics, French scholars intervened in the media independently of activist organizations or think tanks and—occasionally—agreed to offer their signatures or even spearhead collaborative editorials.

Because of the attention they garner, many French academics and intellectuals saw their media interventions as integral components in their personal strategies to influence political decisions and earn the attention of their peers. The audience is as much their fellow academics as it is policymakers and the broader public. Experts who do not engage in the press run the risk of seeing their adversaries—fellow intellectuals, politicians, or social movement spokespeople—dominate the discourse without any counternarrative. Many respondents described paying attention to what others wrote in the press and organizing their own reactions around them. This was true for interviewees on both sides of the issue. For example, the anthropologist Anne Cadoret and psychoanalyst Geneviève Delaisi de Parseval were motivated to debunk what they described as misinformation about parenting spread by anti-same-sex marriage and adoption advocates. During the height of the legislative debates over marriage, they wrote a special feature for the magazine *Marie Claire* in which they drew on anthropological and psychoanalytic theories to analyze children's drawings of their "two-mother households."[44] They argued that these drawings showed no evidence of psychological pathologies because of their upbringing. Conservatives reacted similarly. To respond to progressive criticism of anti-gay-marriage psychoanalysts, Christian Flavigny wrote editorials in *Le Monde*, some with other conservative colleagues, warning that same-sex marriage and adoption would erase sex differences between parents, which they argued are crucial for children's psychological development.[45]

Given the high political stakes around the media and experts' rush to occupy the terrain, complex and even arcane scientific debates that might otherwise remain within academic seminars and professional journals become public affairs. Respondents described many instances of drafting editorials in response to other pieces written by their rivals, characterizing articles against them as "shots fired in a battle." These interactions created an opportunity for ideologically aligned people to coordinate their efforts and develop connections. One example includes aggressive critiques against the publication of psychiatrist

Stéphane Nadaud's dissertation, among the first of its kind on the outcomes of children of same-sex couples, that other mental health professionals character-ized as a piece of activist propaganda.[46] Another is the series of back-and-forth editorials between Irène Théry and Éric Fassin, two sociologists who opposed each other during the Pacte civil de solidarité (Pacs) debates in the 1990s. In both examples—which I describe in further detail in later chapters—the media conflicts cemented alliances and defined intellectual and political fault lines that activists and policymakers, as well as the broader public, could see.

In many situations, these attacks concerned both advocates and academics. For example, Denis Quinqueton—long involved with promoting a gay rights platform within the Socialist Party through the organization Homosexualités et Socialisme (HES) [Homosexualities and Socialism]—described writing a response in 2013 to Sylviane Agacinski, the well-known and politically connected philosopher whose partner was the Socialist prime minister during the Pacs debates.[47] She wrote an opinion piece in *Le Monde* in which she claimed Quinqueton's organization contributed to the "commercialization of women's bodies" by advocating for sur-rogacy.[48] Irène Théry, also influential within the Socialist Party, defended HES and other gay family organizations against Agacinski's attacks in her own piece arguing that same-sex couples' demands for access to parenthood are legitimate and can be achieved ethically and democratically.[49] Mediated through oppos-ing op-eds, politically powerful experts used the language of their disciplines to defend opposing sides within an internal Socialist Party skirmish made public.

Journalists, editors, and other media actors maintain this battlefield of ideas by structuring "balance" into their reporting and editorial pages. This journalistic practice provides opportunities for minoritarian perspectives within academic disciplines or professions, both conservative and progressive, to get dispropor-tionate public exposure than they otherwise would based on their weight in their respective fields. For instance, the philosopher Thibaud Collin described his sat-isfaction when editors at *Le Monde*, who, despite supporting same-sex marriage, solicited an editorial from him to explain his philosophical opposition to the reform. Similarly, during the Pacs debates, at a time when many public figures and intellectuals were openly hostile to legal recognition for same-sex couples, journalists reached out to Daniel Borrillo, the lawyer and professor, to provide a counterpoint to such opposition.

As many media critics have demonstrated, this journalistic false balance fal-lacy can suggest to readers that all ideas carry the same weight or are equally representative of predominant views in a given area of research. Some experts I interviewed expressed frustration over journalists and television hosts who systematically juxtaposed their stances with those of contrarian experts. These artificially created binaries produce an idea of equivalences by treating all voices, regardless of their training or background, as equal, they argued. This media polarization, which French legislators also reproduce in hearings, as described below, also gives audiences the impression that academic and professional fields are divided over the evidence related to same-sex marriage and parenting even if they are not.

In sum, the experts I interviewed in France—but not the United States—talked about media interventions, particularly those in major newspapers, as essential for accessing and influencing the public debate. Indeed, publishing in *Le Monde* and other media outlets can be the reason why lawmakers invite experts to give their points of view in the legislative arena in the first place. Media debates are not merely reflections of the academic field, on the one hand, and the political field, on the other. Rather, media debates, while autonomous and responding to their own forces, are extensions of academics and politics. Disputes in the media between experts or between experts and politicians have ramifications both in the academic and political fields. Expert capital in the form of credibility and name recognition can be created and traded in the media. For this reason, French experts carefully attend to their relationships and interactions with journalists and editors, plotting their media interventions strategically.

Legislatures and Ministries: Where French Experts Play Political Roles

Behind the Scenes Work Beyond the view of cameras and off the official legislative record, there are many opportunities for French experts to shape policy. Resembling their American equivalents, interactions between French lawmakers and activists or staff at lobbying and nonprofit organizations, such as the Association des Parents et futurs parents Gays et Lesbiens (APGL), ADFH, and Aides, were common. Organizers could bring their needs and demands to the attention of politicians who could then use that information as they crafted laws. For example, Daniel Borrillo and Marianne Schulz worked in the mid to late 1990s as the law policy coordinators at Aides, France's premier AIDS organization founded by Daniel Defert after the death of his partner, Michel Foucault, in 1984.

During that time, they met regularly and privately with ministers and parliamentarians to inform them about the impact of the AIDS crisis on gay people who were facing devastating problems, such as evictions and lost inheritance after a partner's death, because the state did not formally recognize their relationships.

In contrast to their U.S. counterparts, most French academics had ongoing contact and sometimes regular meetings with legislators, their staff, and other politicians outside of formal hearings and reports. Almost all French respondents, on both sides, described meeting at least once individually with ministers or elected officials to discuss reforms. They generally worked with politicians who shared their values, at least to some extent. Some people who have been involved in these background settings for decades, such as Daniel Borrillo, Françoise Dekeuwer-Défossez, Geneviève Delaisi de Parseval, Éric Fassin, Maurice Godelier, or Irène Théry, took on roles akin to informal advisors. These academics and professionals in law, psychoanalysis, anthropology, and sociology—many of whom have led prestigious careers at elite French institutions—provided politicians with political strategies, inside knowledge about academic debates, technical suggestions, and arguments they could wield against their opponents. For example, during the 2012 marriage debates, several described invitations to eat lunch with President François Hollande and private meetings with the ministers of justice and of the family as well as with some members of parliament. In these settings, depending on their level of influence with lawmakers, it is possible that experts are able to directly help or hinder legal reforms.

French academics and professionals also met privately with political party groups both at the legislature and in their party headquarters. These meetings functioned like informal hearings to prepare lawmakers—especially those in the opposition parties who cannot control the formal parliamentary hearings—with arguments they could use to justify their stance in floor debates and in the media. The political groups generally invited people who agreed with their stance on the issues. For example, law professors Claire Neirinck and Françoise Dekeuwer-Défossez both said that a coalition of conservative politicians interviewed them because they wanted "weapons" to fight against progressive arguments in favor of same-sex marriage and parenting. These interpersonal and off-the-record interactions demonstrate how the shape of the expert field in France facilitates the proximity between experts and decision-makers, making it easier for both groups to have an influence on each other's affairs.

Governmental Reports Governmental reports are an official and publicly accessible—though not always widely publicized—example of expert-lawmaker interaction. In the decades leading up to the legalization of same-sex marriage and in its immediate aftermath, French parliamentarians and ministers commissioned several reports on the evolution of French couples and families directly from French academics, such as Irène Théry, a famous French sociologist with a history of working with Socialist administrations. Politicians used these reports—some of which involved recognizing same-sex couples or their parental rights—to inform legislation. Three stand out.

Irène Théry published the first just before the Pacs debates, followed by a kind of rebuttal coordinated by the law professor Françoise Dekeweur-Défossez.[50] A decade and half later, Théry led a team of experts who authored a third report the year after same-sex marriage was legalized.[51] Officially their remits included making suggestions to update French law to better account for the realities of families at the turn of the century. High divorce rates, remarriages, and children born out of wedlock all posed challenges for a legal regime born mostly out of the Napoleonic Code and designed around married heterosexual couples. Under ongoing pressure from gay and lesbian organizations and their allies who demanded their situations also be taken into account, these reports offered lawmakers an opportunity to show they were listening without necessarily taking legislative action. These reports were not simple fact-finding exercises about the needs of contemporary families. They are best understood as strategies to use expertise as a tool in political struggles within and between parties along ideological lines and across factions among experts with different views on gay and lesbian families.

The story of Irène Théry's first report is illustrative of the political dimension of these reports. About nine months after the socialist majority replaced a center-right coalition, the newly appointed minister of justice, Elisabeth Guigou, commissioned an "ambitious" report from Théry that, at least in the official request letter, should have "no taboos" in analyzing the realities of French families.[52] But behind the scenes, some subjects were off limits. According to Théry, Guigou demanded that she not write about homosexuality or discuss the Pacs legislation, an early version of which was already under discussion by select Socialist MPs at the time. Théry did not fully comply. Although it did not mention the Pacs directly, her report, which would be published as a full draft after the Pacs was already in committee, did talk about same-sex couples. In fact,

Théry explicitly wrote that same-sex couples should not be granted legal custody of children on par with heterosexual couples. Furthermore, in the press and public forums, she publicly opposed the Pacs and recommended instead that same-sex couples have access to *concubinage*.[53] The report ended up creating a political problem for the Socialist Party. Although the party opposed same-sex marriage and parenting at the time—and thus agreed with Théry on those issues—they faced stiff opposition to the Pacs from conservative politicians and part of the French public. As MPs who were trying to get the Pacs through the legislature attempted to downplay the implications of their reform for gays and lesbians— the Pacs would be open to all couples—Théry's report and public statements kept the spotlight on homosexuality and provided fodder for opponents. According to Théry, in the end, Guigou was "horrified" and did not publicly support the report. The minister ultimately commissioned a separate—one might say competing—report from Françoise Dekeuweur-Défossez, a professor of law opposed to same-sex marriage. This new report did not make any recommendations or references to same-sex couples or gay parenting, respecting the minister's command to steer clear of controversy.[54]

A decade and a half later, expert reports on family law continued to play a political role. The negotiations and outcome of Théry's second report on parenthood and procreation—co-authored with law professor Anne Marie-Leroyer and a team of social scientists and jurists Théry selected—were as much about partisan strategy as they were about scientific analysis.[55] Much like in the late 1990s, the Socialist Party was newly in power—in this case, under President François Hollande elected in 2012—and had plans to reform family law with the recognition of same-sex marriage and adoption. And, as in the previous era, the party was divided on just how far they were willing to go. The more conservative wing was unprepared to go as far as allowing lesbian couples and single women access to medically assisted procreation, such as artificial insemination, and refused any discussion of lifting the ban on surrogacy. Théry, who had reversed her stance against marriage and parenting for same-sex couples since the 1990s, would once again author a report that would displease the party officials who had commissioned it.

When the minister of family, Dominique Bertinotti, initially approached Théry to request the report after the same-sex marriage law was promulgated, the sociologist said she accepted the mission on the condition that she have a wide mandate. It was originally intended to focus on custody, parental authority, and removing anonymity for gamete donors and parents who had given their children up for adoption. Théry negotiated the specific terms of the mission, "line by line," to include broader analyses of kinship and parenting law. After these exchanges, Théry received her official, public commission reflecting these extended parameters. Nevertheless, as for her first report, the report's conclusions were politically untenable. Backlash against the recently passed same-sex marriage and adoption legislation led the Socialist majority to indefinitely postpone planned legislation to open-donor insemination for lesbians.[56] Unconcerned with this context, the report not only recommended access to assisted reproductive techniques for lesbian couples but also argued that despite bans on surrogacy, French immigration officials should cease putting up roadblocks that made it difficult for French parents to bring their children born through surrogacy abroad back to France. Because these recommendations no longer fit their revised political strategy, the ministry and other Socialist politicians refused to publicize Théry's report when it was completed.

The stories around these reports highlight that when it comes to public interventions, a few well-connected French academics become personally and directly involved in partisan and legislative negotiations around same-sex couples' family rights, unlike their U.S. peers whose participation is often mediated by think tanks and professional organizations. Even as these well-known French scholars preserve their status as academics, their official commissions give them political power that they can use to advance or hinder policy agendas.

Hearings: Expertise on the Political Stage French experts have a regular seat at the legislative table. On matters of family law reform, lawmakers in both chambers of parliament have frequently invited academics, professionals, and leaders of advocacy organizations to weigh in on proposed bills. All but one of the French experts I interviewed had been directly involved in at least one hearing over the last two and a half decades. That lawmakers in Paris are more inclined to invite such elite experts, as opposed to, say, average citizens, reveals the meaning of their process: a public consultation with a high tier of civil society representatives before changing a law whose scope concerns the everyday lives of a marginalized group. Because of their public exposure, these hearings have high stakes regardless of their potential to shape legal outcomes. They influence the quality and content of public debates even when large parliamentary majorities, whose platforms include planks supporting gay family rights, guarantee the bill will pass. This is especially true when they are broadcast or widely discussed by the news media, which was the case in 2012 and 2013 for same-sex marriage. The president of the Assemblée Nationale, Claude Bartolone, created a special parliamentary budget to record, livestream, and make the hearings available for download, partly in response to anti-same-sex marriage activism that grew quickly once the Socialist government officially introduced its bill in the summer of 2012. This public availability facilitated widespread public attention.

Understanding the role of expertise in these hearings requires an analysis of the mindset and calculations of politicians who were in charge of them. Called *rapporteurs*, they were responsible for drafting reports, based in part on the hearings, in the name of the legislative committees the bills were assigned to. Socialists Erwann Binet, Patrick Bloche, and Jean-Pierre Michel, who organized hearings in their respective chambers of the French Parliament for the Pacs, same-sex marriage, or other family reforms, had exclusive authority to decide which witnesses to invite.[57] That power gave them much leeway about which voices they thought their colleagues and, in some cases, the broader French public should hear. But it also came with risks: They could be held personally accountable if the hearings damaged their legislative goals, and the minority party, along with their civil society allies, could claim they were being shut out. The lawmakers I interviewed had to weigh political considerations, including solidifying support among those on their side, attempting to change the minds of reticent politicians and the public, and maintaining the legitimacy of their reforms in the face of strong opposition. In short, these hearings served a multipronged political strategy in which the ideologies, types of knowledge, and renown of experts played an important role.

Lawmakers in the majority, who have the authority to organize hearings as they see fit, can invite anyone they believe will best reflect the needs and purpose of the legislation, but they must do so within the constraints of their institutions and the pool of available experts. They can even specifically limit hearing experts they disagree with. For example, Alexandre Urwicz described how gay family organizations had a hard time making the needs of their members heard in the 2000s because conservative lawmakers, who held the majority, rarely invited them to hearings on family law issues. When the newly elected Socialist majority introduced its same-sex marriage bill in 2012, conservative lawmakers knew they had lost their ability to select which types of experts could be invited. They even campaigned for a special commission, which would have been bipartisan, in order to preempt Socialist control of the hearings but were ultimately unsuccessful.

Creating Balance but Distorting Perceptions of Professional and Academic Knowledge Because of these tensions and the risk of inciting resistance that could lead to diminished or even stalled legislation, lawmakers seem to have learned to seek, in the words of Erwann Binet, ideologically "balanced" hearings. Jean-Pierre Michel described that lawmakers feel "obliged" to invite experts who disagree with their bills because, if they do not, their political opponents attack them and delegitimize them on the floors of Parliament, in the press, and on the streets, claiming that the hearings are unfair. Those organizing hearings make the assumption that platforming experts opposed to their reform would quell the groups working against gay family rights.

These decisions to "balance" views and grant space to experts who have the institutional capacity to demand it leads French lawmakers to set up hearings that can inadvertently reproduce power imbalances and hierarchies within professional and academic fields. A series of hearings in 2012 and 2013 coordinated by Binet for the Judiciary Committee of the Assemblée Nationale is a good example of this. He opened himself up to loud critique from conservative lawmakers and well-known conservative law professors when he put together a panel for legal experts. The initial slate of witnesses only included jurists who had actually studied or worked with sexual minorities and their families, people who had an academic track record and specialized knowledge on the issue. They also all expressed support for same-sex marriage. Their progressive stance made them an ideological minority in their professional and academic fields where anti-same-sex marriage opinions dominated at the time. The conservative mobilization, through online posts and an open letter, led Binet to organize a second legal experts hearing where some of these outspoken conservative professors, such as Claire Neirinck, could express their views. Because of their power in their field, they had the clout to demand to be heard.

The imperative to maintain a perception of balanced hearings can also justify creating a space for progressive experts who are otherwise marginalized within certain professional fields. When revising laws that impact families, the French government is required to solicit the views of the Union Nationale des Associations Familiales (UNAF), a powerful quasi-state organization dealing with family and welfare issues. As a kind of umbrella organization, in theory, it is supposed to represent all family nonprofits and associations in France. In reality, the UNAF has been historically dominated by conservative religious and rural family associations and repeatedly refused to include LGBTQ family groups. The Socialist *rapporteurs* were aware of these dynamics at the UNAF and made a point of reserving hearing seats for organizations like the APGL and ADFH—France's main LGBTQ family groups—as well as secular and progressive associations within the UNAF to present their stances independently. Similarly, lawmakers felt obligated to invite official professional organizations representing the legal profession. But when those groups took public stances against same-sex couples rights, the hearing organizers also decided to invite lawyers working within pro-gay organizations, such as Aides, and, in so doing, amplified minority voices. Thus, the drive for balance can create access opportunities for progressive experts on the margins. But it can also create misrepresentations.

Indeed, ideologically balanced hearings distort the state of scientific knowledge on same-sex couples and their children. When considering who to invite to the hearings designed to get the perspective of social scientists on same-sex marriage, Erwann Binet was especially concerned with their public positions on gay family rights. He expressed frustration that the few who had empirically studied same-sex couples and their children "had all [publicly] spoken out in favor of the text." Their political stances were as important as the substance of their expertise. Because of their stances, he invited other experts, including psychoanalysts and child psychiatrists who had well-known anti-gay-family stances, such as Pierre-Lévy Soussan, despite the fact that they had conducted virtually no peer-reviewed research on the topic. In other words, because of political calculations and concerns about fairness, he was more worried about creating hearings that artificially presented an academic debate as if it had equally valid evidence on both sides than attempting to discern the weight of the evidence in a given discipline.

Making a Mark: Celebrities, Politics, and Breaking with Tradition The *rapporteurs* wanted their hearings to stick in people's minds. Experts unknown to the broader public could only get them so far. They were particularly interested in hearing from famous academics and intellectuals, such as the renowned anthropologist Maurice Godelier, as well as people who regularly appear in the media, such as the philosopher Thibaud Collin or the psychiatrist Christian Flavigny. They know these experts can shape public opinion through the legitimacy and exposure they have by already being in the public eye. Indeed, in our interviews, they all said it was crucial to invite experts who are "known" and "recognized." Thus, as highlighted earlier in the section on the media, fame and media exposure can open doors to spots at a legislative hearing. French lawmakers seek to capital-ize on the popularity of these marquee experts, probably in an attempt to share their spotlight, hoping that their process will seem more credible.

Famous French experts can be unpredictable. While the *rapporteurs* want them for their celebrity, their autonomy creates its own set of challenges, espe-cially when these experts change their stances on gay family rights. During the Pacs debates, many of these well-known invitees were a problem for advanc-ing the Socialist lawmakers' goals because they opposed same-sex marriage and parenting. For example, although it did not ultimately prevent the legislation from passing, Jean-Pierre Michel described feeling a sense of competition with the sociologist Irène Théry despite their ongoing friendship. Her voice, as well as that of other famous left-leaning intellectuals who opposed the Pacs in the 1990s, made it more challenging for him to create a credible scientific argument in favor of the bill, especially within his own political family. As they changed their stances on marriage and parenting in the intervening years, however, these famous intellectuals became assets to pro-gay-marriage lawmakers. Binet, for example, argued that hearing Maurice Godelier and Françoise Hériter—France's most famous anthropologists at the time—bear favorable witness in the name of their discipline helped undermine opponents who were claiming that same-sex marriage was an "anthropological aberration."[58] Rather than oppose their leg-islative efforts, as they had in earlier decades, these experts lent their powerful voices to the cause of gay and lesbian families.

Within these constraints, lawmakers also make assessments about which experts to invite depending on what they believed justified the purpose of their legislation to their fellow citizens. If they did not see a purpose for it, lawmakers in charge could reject potential experts that are common in other countries or in other forums, such as the media. For example, Binet specifically decided not to invite any demographers or statisticians to the hearings even though he knew they had data, which was published in the press, about the number of same-sex couples and same-sex couples raising children in France. For him, the bill was motivated by a "principle of equality" and not by the numbers of people the law would affect. Those numbers, he said, could be harmful to the debate. "Even if it only concerned 1 percent of the population," Binet explained in our inter-view, "we were not illegitimate to . . . defend [the bill]. I didn't want people to weigh heterosexuals against homosexuals to gauge, to judge, the legitimacy of the text." Another *rapporteur* might have made a different calculation about whether quantifying gay and lesbian families was a better tactic for the debate. Binet decided to take a different kind of risk.

He broke with long-standing parliamentary conventions and invited people who never appear at hearings. Binet's conviction that the public needed to hear average citizens directly concerned by the legislation—children of same-sex couples and same-sex couples themselves—overrode the tacit rule that Parliament "can't invite just anybody to a hearing," he stressed when he told me about his decision. The Assemblée Nationale never invites people who only "represent themselves," he said. Rather, "out of concern for equality and respect for the institution, we [only] hear representatives of [relevant] organizations." His colleagues resisted his decision, telling him there was no place for "personal experience [and] emotions" in the legislature. This stance helps explain the relative absence of ordinary citizens in French hearings relative to the United States. But it also shows how political calculations in extraordinary circumstances can lead French *rapporteurs* to take advantage of the institutional power they have to break norms and redefine what counts as expertise.

Out of a desire to counter the anti-gay-parenting messages of conservatives and protestors, Binet disregarded tradition and the warnings of his peers. He invited several adult children of gays and lesbians, as well as a few parents and couples, who had spoken out in the press, been interviewed by journalists, or written to him or whose names were given to him by gay family organizations. Pablo Seban, one of those who shared his testimony before the committee, told me that he had become somewhat of a public figure after having been featured in magazine and newspaper stories about adults who had grown up in gay households, which brought him to the attention of Binet.

In Binet's estimation, and that of most of the pro-same-sex-marriage experts I interviewed, this panel was the most successful and important. They told me stories of how friends and acquaintances, who saw the hearing on TV, told them it was moving and effective. For many, it was their first introduction to gay families. The chronic invisibility of gay families in formal hearings, outside of this important exception, illustrates how institutional logics, specifically tradition and a desire for "balance" and legitimacy, can limit specific kinds of knowledge, such as the personal experience of gay families. Yet, Binet's decision also reveals that under certain conditions, including political will and the availability of knowledge and the people to deliver it, lawmakers can sometimes overcome these constraints. Indeed, despite conventions against it, lay experts, it turned out, were exactly what Binet needed to help justify the marriage bill in that moment. His party's unilateral power to organize the hearings made that possible.

Political considerations also led Binet to break with cultural expectations around religious neutrality. For the marriage hearings in the 2010s, concerns over conservative backlash opened up an unusual space for representatives of major religious organizations to be heard despite French traditions of *laïcité*. In the late 1990s, Jean-Pierre Michel did not invite religious representatives to his Pacs hearings based on the idea that "they have nothing to do with the elaboration of a law . . . in a secular state." Yet, by the time the marriage hearings occurred, this stance was no longer tenable. He felt obliged to invite them to hearings at the Sénat after Erwann Binet had already invited them to the Assemblée Nationale out of a stated concern to hear all perspectives, especially as anti-marriage activists were ratcheting up their campaign. Unlike in the United States, however, the presence of religious groups was one-sided. Indeed, in the public hearings, Binet said he was constrained by the centralization of religious hierarchies, an artifact of French secularization policies in which the state, using the Catholic Church as a model, only formally interacts with an official representative of each of five major faiths (Catholicism, Protestantism, Judaism, Islam, and Buddhism) even when those religions are decentralized. These linear and hierarchical interactions meant that clergy and religious community members supporting gay family rights were never invited to give testimony in public hearings but were heard privately by some lawmakers. An example includes David et Jonathan, an ecumenical faith-based activist organization whose founders claim is the oldest LGBTQ organization in France. Even if Binet had wanted to add pro-marriage religious voices to the mix to counter the protests, many of which were organized with support from the Catholic Church, the state's formalized channels of communications with religious groups made that option impossible.

French experts were forced to contend with parliamentary norms and expectations of lawmakers, which shaped how they navigated the hearings and understood their participation in the process. Like their American counterparts, many felt that their presence was requested in response to logics distinct from and sometimes counter to their academic and professional routines. On the one hand, most said it was important to testify when invited to "at least be heard," as Urwicz of the ADFH put it. Hearings were a valuable venue to put their opinions and analyses on the public record. On the other hand, they had the impression that lawmakers were more interested in making a political statement than in using their information to actually modify their legislation in any meaningful way. Experts opposed to same-sex marriage were not under the illusion that their testimony would convince the Socialist majority to drop their bill. They did see themselves as contributing in their own way to a multipronged resistance involving other groups, including social movement organizations. Many of the experts had the impression that legislators held hearings for form in order to claim they had taken all views into account; they were aware of legislators' desires to create an appearance of a legitimate, balanced debate. Indeed, experts' public stances on gay family issues made them part of a political calculus. They were either there to bolster the progressive majority or represent conservative voices so lawmakers could claim the hearings were fair.

Experts called to hearings realized that they were being labeled by most lawmakers as belonging to one or the other side in the debate. Their experiences during the 2012 marriage debates are especially telling. Experts in favor of same-sex marriage and adoption had the accurate impression, which I noted from observing the hearings, that few opposition politicians attended. When they did come, they would come late to the session, leave before it was over, and breaking with parliamentary decorum, interrupt witnesses during their testimony. Several social scientists described feeling unsettled and insulted when Hervé Mariton, a member of one of the opposition parties, loudly exclaimed "Rubbish!" and "Nonsense!" as they described their research on same-sex couples during their allotted speaking time. Conservative lawmakers also rarely asked questions of favorable experts. By essentially boycotting the hearings and attacking experts in favor of the legislation, conservative lawmakers hoped to undermine the legitimacy of the process and discredit expertise they disagreed with.

Experts opposing same-sex marriage felt supported by conservative lawmakers, many of whom they were also meeting in private, but generally ignored by the socialist *rapporteurs*. The hearings gave these experts a formal megaphone to express their perspectives but not an unqualified one. Their participation bolstered the notion that the hearings were fair and balanced, which worked to strengthen the position of the socialist lawmakers they disagreed with who were claiming as much. Some resented lending credibility to the process but evidently decided that access to the hearings was worth the cost. Claire Neirinck, for example, said she was frustrated knowing that she was "serving as a guarantor" by agreeing to testify but did so anyway. Many said they knew the Socialists were determined to pass the bill regardless of what they said or the circumstances, and therefore, in the words of Dekeuwer-Defessez, the lawmakers only "pretended to listen." While progressive lawmakers felt obligated to invite them, conservative experts felt obligated to attend, both sides hoping to get their messages across.

CONCLUSION

Should gay and lesbian couples be allowed to legally marry and raise children? Whose ideas does my audience need to hear to make up their minds about this controversial issue? Whether it be a Parisian newspaper editor deciding whose opinion they want to feature on the editorial page or a team of lawyers at a K Street lobbying firm in Washington, DC, hashing out which authorities to cite in their amicus brief, they all ask themselves these questions. On either side of the Atlantic, they could theoretically interview, cite, or call to testify the same kinds of experts. But, as we have seen, it turns out that French and American audiences, from newspaper readers to judges and lawmakers, are encountering experts with different profiles who talk about gay and lesbian families from sometimes surprising perspectives. While the makeup of French legislative hearings—with its emphasis on ideological balance between experts supporting and opposing gay family rights—might be jarring to an American judge who weighs which side has the best evidence, this chapter has shown that patterns of expertise reflect the choices of gatekeepers working within institutional constraints. Those in charge of organizing expertise have more or less latitude to make their selections and are drawing on a pool of experts that is itself different depending on the context. Moreover, experts themselves, depending on their prestige, public stances, and power, can play an integral role in their own promotion to get a spot at the table.

At the outset, legislators organizing hearings in France and attorneys litigating in bench trials in the United States faced similar tasks. Majority-rules legislative hearings, like those in France, and courtroom trials in the United States gave them the power to control which people and information they wanted decision-making bodies to hear. While in both cases they were looking to transform expertise into political and legal victories, the specific nature of the expert capital they valued was different. In France's closed system, they worried primarily about projecting legitimacy, shielding themselves from criticisms of being closed-minded, and responding to anti-marriage protesters. French lawmakers evaluated the content of expertise and the profile of experts for their suitability according to a political calculus where criteria such as celebrity, representativity, and political connections were priorities. By combining a mixture of different types of expert capital, they aimed to produce an alloy whose combined worth would buttress their own political authority. In U.S. courts, which mattered more than legislatures, lawyers chose expertise for its capacity to support specific legal arguments and withstand the critical scrutiny of judges and opposing litigators. Formal rules defining who qualifies as an expert witness and the adversarial system pushed lawyers to seek researchers whose credibility was grounded in their qualifications and soundness of their research rather than proximity to politicians or journalists.

In addition to academic and professional experts, gay and lesbian people and their children, who know the most about how the law impacts their everyday lives, also told their stories, to varying degrees, in both countries. Moreover, according to some, their voices were especially important for eliciting empathy and making discrimination against their families palpable. But these lay experts also faced institutional and cultural expectations specific to each country. Getting them in front of lawmakers in France was a challenge and could easily have never happened. The *rapporteur* for the marriage hearings was personally determined to break with parliamentary tradition and invite people who "only represent themselves" to make clear that real people's lives were affected by a policy debate that was otherwise abstract. This decision was all the more difficult, and no doubt crucial, given the relative invisibility of gay and lesbian families in French media at the time. In the United States, the open format of the hearings and the almost systematic inclusion of gay family vignettes in journalists' reporting projected their voices across the country. However, in the courts, those plentiful experiences were curated and vetted to fit within judicial rules and support the strategies of the attorneys behind the cases. Only certain gay and lesbian families became litigants who stories would personify the need to rule in favor of all same-sex couples.

Scientific expertise about gay and lesbian families and their children mattered in both countries. However, portrayals of that research reflect how the institutional demands of French legislatures and American courts distort the literature. The science seemed to be saying different things depending to which side of the Atlantic one looked. Because French lawmakers felt obliged or were forced by political circumstances to systematically contrast pro and con views among experts, they created false equivalences, not unlike the bothsidesism in journalism. Their hearings gave the false impression, for example, that researchers and professionals were strongly divided on the outcomes of children raised by same-sex couples. Unlike courts, legislatures have no built-in mechanism to control for the idea of scientific consensus. That logic gave an advantage to anti-same-sex-marriage activists and their allied experts who could make their position seem more mainstream than it actually was.

In contrast, in U.S. courts, the weight of pro-gay-marriage expertise was an asset to litigators defending same-sex marriage, rather than an obstacle that needed to be overcome for the sake of creating balance. They believed they had evidence to convince the judge that the science supported their legal claims, and in fact, anti-same-sex-marriage advocates were at a disadvantage because of that legal framing. Nevertheless, although court logics may appear to value empiricism, they also constrain the nuance, gradation, and subtlety of academic research, pressuring experts to make unequivocal statements. This can, in turn, leave the impression that research is more clear-cut and definitive than it actually is. In this way, courtroom logics also run counter to a feminist approach to empirical research in which the presentation of all data is a collectively agreed upon scientific practice deemed more objective according to a feminist notion of strong objectivity.[59] In addition, American judges, like French lawmakers, generally do not have scientific training even though the institution puts them in the position to act as arbiters of scientific facts. This gives them a significant amount of power to shape public discourse about science, the quality of which can vary widely depending on the judge and their own personal interpretations about what counts as credible research.

Courts and legislatures are not passive venues to which people bring expertise. They also contribute to producing it. Indeed, the same logics that lead lawyers and elected officials to select certain experts over others also drives organizations fighting for and against gay family rights, as well as the experts they collaborate with, to generate knowledge specifically for these legal debates. This chapter has highlighted this feedback relationship between institutional outlets for expertise and knowledge producers, such as academics and professionals, as well as interactions between the political and academic fields. Specifically, in U.S. courts, high-quality, peer-reviewed empirical research has concrete applications for court cases, such as *Hollingsworth* and *DeBoer*, that can dramatically impact the legal landscape. Those researchers capable of producing this kind of scientific expert capital for the policy field may find that their own status in their respective academic fields becomes more elevated.

U.S. advocates and experts on both sides understand that having the research on their side may help them succeed, which also helps stimulate demand for scientific expert capital. Same-sex marriage opponents, for example, deliberately worked to support and encourage academics to publish peer-reviewed material that their experts could present in court. Progressive experts and advocates were pleased by the court's "vindication" of the science, which encouraged them to continue to produce their knowledge. In contrast, in French legislatures, the value of empirical research published in peer-reviewed journals is less relevant, reducing the incentive for its production. Rather, the kind of capital they strive to acquire from experts—notoriety, ideological balance, and capacity to quell critiques—responds to political dynamics. They favor experts who take a clear, strong stance in the media regardless of their empirical grounding or scholarly knowledge of the issues. These nationally differing demands and incentives for knowledge and their effect on expertise also depend on the context in which American and French elite experts work to create their information in the first place. It is to these academic and professional fields—and the ways progressive and conservative knowledge producers negotiate them—that we now turn our attention.

CHAPTER 4

FROM SCRATCH

Experts Work with What They've Got

E xpertise does not create itself. Whether it be historical research about antigay discrimination, studies on children raised by same-sex couples, or legal theories about parenting law, researchers in these academic disciplines had to do the work to produce all the information that ended up cited in legislative reports, amicus briefs, and newspaper articles. But like anything that has to be made, the quality of the materials and the training and working conditions of the creators significantly impact the final product. Not all historians, psychologists, psychoanalysts, legal scholars, economists, sociologists, or any of the other researchers working in fields with relevant information for same-sex marriage debates have enjoyed the same conditions. Examining those circumstances and their impact on the ability of pro- and anti-same-sex marriage experts to do their work is the focus in this chapter.

So far, we have seen how the media, legislatures, and courts have specific demands that shape how American and French experts—as well as the people who use their information, including lawyers, judges, politicians, and activists—deal with expertise in same-sex marriage debates. Differences in the kinds of expert capital that matter in each country are partly the result of divergences in the structure of the expert field and the choices of the people working in their respective national institutions. Focusing again on academics, intellectuals, and professionals, this chapter will argue that those differences are also the result of working conditions for these groups. Specifically, French and U.S. experts who study gay family rights do not have access to the same kinds of resources, recognition, or support in their fields. In the United States, they have a larger, older, and more institutionalized field in academic disciplines and in the professions. In France, the field is smaller, more contested, and lacking in professional and academic recognition. In addition, experts supporting increased legal recognition for same-sex couples and their families now dominate their disciplines in the United States, where conservatives are more marginalized, while in France, they have only recently become more prominent relative to conservatives.

Drawing on interviews and observation, this chapter describes how academic and professional experts work under these nationally divergent conditions. Their experiences can help us better understand why those working on certain issues, such as empirical research on sexual minorities and their families, are more successful in the United States than in France. Knowledge producers, like the elite experts and their social movement allies analyzed in this chapter, are best understood when examined as part of a broader system where their actions and public interventions are constrained and enabled by their circumstances within their specialty areas and the broader context of their countries.[1] Drawing on research about political and academic fields, this chapter places U.S. and French experts within their knowledge production fields, such as disciplines within universities or professions.[2] It pays particular attention to the balance between pro- and anti-same-sex-marriage stances they encounter, as well as their access to resources, including institutionalization of their topics, funding, and the support of professional organizations.

In the United States, which occupies a dominant position in global knowledge production regimes, issues around gender, sexuality, and minority families are more institutionalized within the academy relative to France, where such work remains less common, lacks institutional recognition, and is perceived more negatively.[3] Moreover, because of negative connotations of the United States and discourse about importing "American" ideas into France, people working on such topics in France can face specific challenges if people perceive their work as being brought in from the United States.[4] Experts who have intervened in public debates, most of whom work on these topics within their respective disciplines and professions, confront these contrasting circumstances in each country.

People who produce expertise for policy purposes and who share the same policy stance or ideological outlook form "epistemic communities."[5] And, depending on whether their ideological stance on same-sex marriage is more or less accepted among their peers, they find themselves in a position of collective advantage or disadvantage in their professional and academic fields. Examining these communities in both countries, this chapter analyzes how groups in the ideological minority within their disciplines, such as conservative social scientists in the United States and progressive social scientists in France, navigate marginalization and episodes of exclusion, discrimination, and intimidation because their work challenges local dominant discourse. It also explores how, when some people change their stances and join the epistemic community of their former rivals, as was the case with some French experts formerly opposed to same-sex marriage, it can generate conflict that affects the field more broadly. These configurations impact the capacity of American and French academics to produce expertise.

POWER STRUGGLES IN KNOWLEDGE PRODUCTION FIELDS IN THE 2010s

In the United States and France of the 2010s, when debates over same-sex marriage and parenting were at their apex in both countries, elite experts were working in nationally specific fields where balances of power between gay family rights opponents and supporters differed. While American expert supporters were more dominant relative to opponents within mainstream universities and professional organizations, in France they were more marginalized and had less power in comparison with opponents. These configurations, reflecting the status quo at the time of data collection, are not static; they have changed over time and are likely to evolve as the factors that cause them, which I discuss in the next section, shift.

Relative to France, over the last thirty years in the United States, work on sexual minorities, same-sex couples, and their children has become an established part of academic and professional research agendas. Among the experts I interviewed, this newfound recognition within their disciplines and professions was acquired slowly, starting in the late 1970s, despite intense resistance, including difficulty publishing, securing funding, and getting jobs. For example, William Eskridge, a pioneer of LGBTQ law as a subfield, was denied tenure in the 1980s in part because he was a gay man studying sexual orientation law. Legal professionals faced the same situation. According to Jennifer Pizer of Lambda Legal, in that era, "mainstream law firms would not touch gay rights work." Dealing with discrimination and skepticism was common among experts who had been working on these topics for some time. Gregory Herek's research on the psychology of antigay attitudes was, in his words, "not a very respected area of study" in the early 1980s, a decade after the American Psychiatric Association had removed homosexuality from *The Diagnostic and Statistical Manual of Mental Disorders*.[6] That made it difficult for him to publish in the "big journals" of his field, hindering his career. Overcoming resistance became easier by the 1990s, interviewees said, at least in certain parts of the country, as collective struggles to push academic and professional gatekeepers to accept them started to bear fruit. By then, many were finally receiving funding from major organizations, such as Herek from the National Institute of Mental Health (NIMH), and publishing in some of the most respected peer-reviewed journals in their disciplines.

Recognition of research on gender and sexuality has made it easier for American experts who support LGBTQ rights to do their jobs. By the 2010s, these experts described an academic field where their work is lauded, sometimes funded, and usually supported—or at least not actively thwarted—by most of their colleagues and universities. Such support echoes research suggesting tenure-track faculty in the American academy vote more for Democrats than Republicans and that liberal political stances on women's rights and homosexuality are common, especially among social scientists in non–religiously affiliated institutions.[7] And while it is certainly not true in all law schools, William Eskridge argued at the time of our interview that same-sex marriage had become "embarrassingly . . . accepted" among law professors. Almost all experts supporting gay family rights also said their work was now recognized by their respective professional organizations, such as the American Sociological Association (ASA), the American Psychological Association (APA), the American Psychiatric Association, and the American Bar Association (ABA). Some of these organizations have allowed members to establish working groups devoted to LGBTQ issues for several decades, though sometimes after contentious debates and dissention.

Some pro-marriage experts in the United States have also reached prestigious positions within their universities and organizations. For example, Eskridge is now a professor at Yale, one of the highest ranked law schools in the country. They also pointed to the multiplication of gender studies programs in American universities and faculty members specializing in gender, sexuality, and gay families as proof of their professional mainstreaming. Many have received top prizes in their fields, such as Charlotte Patterson, one of the first psychologists to study same-sex parenting, who was awarded the APA's 2009 Award for Distinguished Contributions to Research in Public Policy. Similarly, Patterson and Gary Gates—a demographer formerly at the Williams Institute, University of

California, Los Angeles's (UCLA) sexual orientation law think tank—have joined committees at the U.S. Census Bureau, one of the most crucial sources of data on the U.S. population. These distinctions reflect the growth of their status in U.S. academic fields over time.

As the topic of gay families has become more respected, interviewees espousing public positions against gay family rights are more marginalized. Their support for "traditional" family views and opposition to the funding, publication, and praise for gay family research have lost a platform for action within mainstream American universities and professional organizations. Indeed, as major professional groups and academic societies take organizational-wide stances in favor of same-sex marriage and parenting, conservatives working in their corresponding disciplines are by definition outside those organizational stances.

Those who agreed to be interviewed said they felt increasing resistance to their work and stances over the last few decades. Academics, such as Brigham Young University law professor Lynn Wardle, and conservative think tank founders, such as activist Maggie Gallagher and former George Mason University professor Jennifer Roback Morse, who all have ties to scientists and lawyers involved in conservative politics, said those sharing their stances were more marginalized in mainstream fields. Some described personally experiencing or hearing about their allies facing challenges from their academic peers over issues including tenure—particularly sociologists Bradford Wilcox and Mark Regnerus, both professors at major public research universities who did ultimately receive tenure—as well as denunciations of their research in specialized journals.

Some said their pro-marriage colleagues refused to collaborate with them on research. Jennifer Roback Morse, for example, who was an assistant professor of economics at Yale and an associate professor at George Mason University before founding a think tank affiliated with the conservative marriage movement, the Ruth Institute, believed most of her colleagues disregarded her scholarship. Before advocating against same-sex marriage, she argued in her work that liberal economic logics, when applied to families, undermine their strength and social benefits.[8] While her work resonated with religious organizations and people outside the academy, she had the impression that economist colleagues ignored it. Similarly, Douglas Allen, an economist at Simon Fraser University, claimed to have contacted sociologists, including Michael Rosenfeld, whose work he and colleagues critiqued, to ask for their data and feedback, "and over all the years *not a single one* has ever replied [his emphasis]."[9] Some pro-marriage researchers share the perception that conservative stances are currently more marginalized. Eskridge, for example, explained that among law scholars he knows, "Almost nobody . . . will sit up and say I think gay people ought to be excluded from marriage. Some might believe it and would vote that way in private, but almost no one will say that in print or publicly." While this may be true among his colleagues at elite institutions, it is unclear that this pro-LGBTQ rights stance is an accurate description of the American legal academic field at large.

Despite their sense of marginalization, U.S. conservatives are far from powerless. On the contrary, they have developed alternative parallel structures to traditional academic institutions and carved out powerful spaces for their ideas within them. Conservative and religiously affiliated groups have their own large and well-funded universities, such as Liberty University in Virginia, Brigham Young University in Utah, and University of Notre Dame in Indiana. These universities have been an institutional home for some of the conservative interviewees and bases for creating expertise to defend antigay political positions. Other anti-marriage experts, such as Robert P. George, a professor at Princeton University, Catholic anti-abortion activist, and behind-the-scenes coordinator of efforts to generate expertise for the cause, have done well for themselves within the academy. In addition, thanks to decades long efforts to reorient the legal profession, and the federal judiciary in particular, they have developed a web of well-funded networks and organizations within mainstream law schools, the Federalist Society being best known among them, to ensure they have legal justifications to back up their antigay stances and a deep roster of lawyers, judges, and law professors to put their plans into action.[10] Moreover, they have also founded American and international professional, advocacy, and funding groups to rival their mainstream counterparts. Examples include the American College of Pediatrics, the International Society of Family Law, and the Witherspoon Institute, where George is a senior fellow. Witherspoon also funded Regnerus's much critiqued study on childhood outcomes that advocates unsuccessfully wielded in U.S. courts to argue against same-sex marriage.[11] These institutions have allowed them to collaborate but do not provide the same professional and scientific recognition as mainstream spaces even as they offer organizational resources.

In France, the balance of power in academic and professional fields between experts supporting and opposing gay family rights was inverted. Although the situation has slowly begun to change since the early 2010s, in general, relative to the United States, experts working on gay families have continued to experience significant professional marginalization. This situation has been especially limiting for those who take public stances in favor of equality for same-sex couples and their children. As recently as the 2000s, sociologists, such as Martine Gross, and anthropologists, including Anne Cadoret, had significant difficulty securing any funding for research on gay families. They described senior colleagues publicly greeting their work on same-sex couples and their children with "violent" hostility. For example, during a seminar at the Collège de France, in the early 2000s, one of Cadoret's colleagues shouted at her to "stop talking" because the colleague "could not stand what [she] was saying" about her research for her book *Des parents comme des autres* [*Parents Like Any Other*], in which she argues that gay and lesbian parents resemble their straight counterparts.[12] She supposed that their aggression toward her stemmed from how her scholarship made the parenting styles and systems of gay families seem "banal."

Only since the 2000s had some researchers who study gay and lesbian families begun to secure permanent positions. Even those who did get hired encountered many barriers along the way. For example, child psychiatrist Stéphane Nadaud (MD in 2000), anthropologist Jérôme Courduriès (PhD in 2008), and sociologist Virginie Descoutures (PhD in 2008) had senior people in their fields, including mentors, explicitly discourage them from working on these topics. One law professor, who began studying surrogacy law after getting a tenured job and who did not want to be named for fear of professional retaliation, said her former dissertation advisor told her she now works on "perverted subjects." When Nadaud—whose supervisor was "a proponent of Anglo-American psychiatric [norms]"—published his 2001 dissertation on the outcomes of children raised by same-sex couples, leaders in his field, such as conservative psychoanalyst Caroline Eliacheff, decried his findings in national newspapers as naïve, unreliable, and partisan.[13]

In terms of prestige, it has been rare for these experts to receive recognition from French institutions. Some notable exceptions began in the wake of the 2013 legalization of same-sex marriage and adoption when President François Hollande awarded the Ordre de Mérite to Gross in 2014 and to gay family lawyer Caroline Mécary in 2013. He gave the Légion d'honneur in 2013 to the sociologist Irène Théry, who, as I analyze in the next section, switched from opposing to supporting gay family rights in the mid-2000s. Nevertheless, these recent accolades notwithstanding, pro-marriage academics have had less peer recognition than their American peers.

Conservative French experts, however, have long held central positions within their fields. In the 2010s, they continued to dominate the most important venues organizing French knowledge production, including top universities, public research institutes, prestigious Parisian hospitals, governmental commissions, and powerful public service advisory boards allocating state funding. Contrary to the American field, this is especially true "among law professors, [where] there are lots of people on the right," Françoise Dekeuwer-Défossez, a family law professor opposed to same-sex marriage, argued. Claire Neirinck is an illustrative example. She had suffered no negative professional consequences because of involvement in antigay family mobilizing. At the time of our interview, she was a distinguished family law professor at the Université de Toulouse, a member of the editorial board of the flagship journal in her specialty, Droit de la Famille, and author of the sections on adoption in the civil law edition of *JurisClasseur*, the reference manual for French legal professionals. Although family law is not a "noble" legal subfield according to the law professors I interviewed—"Women and children basically weren't considered law," Dekeuwer-Défossez said—its direct implications for policy give it place of privilege in political debates. Hughes Fulchiron, professor of law and former president of the Université Jean-Moulin Lyon 3, said that issues in family law "are very bizarre [subjects] at the boundaries of law, morality, and sociology, where one can have a discourse that is more moralistic than legal or a discourse that is more sociological than juridical." Precisely because "it's not only technical [but] . . . also symbolic," family law professors can act as voices of moral opposition to changes they disagree with but do so using the seemingly neutral language of legal theory.

Emphasizing conservative strength in the legal profession, an episode involving an open letter written by 170 jurists to the Sénat in protest against the 2013 marriage bill frequently came up in the interviews.[14] Drafting it required the secretive collaboration of conservatives across generations, ranks, and institutions. Dekeuwer-Défossez described, for example, a group of early career law professors, including Aude Mirkovic, Clotilde de Ponse Brunetti, and Jean-René Binet, who were active in organizing the petition drive and letter writing, which they conducted discreetly through a private electronic network. This discretion was necessary for the sake of some of the people involved, including "several judges, especially those on the Conseil d'État, [who have] a duty of silence that totally forbids them from any form of participation in the public debate," she explained. When the letter was finally published, it sent a signal both to lawmakers and to members of the law profession that conservatives had the upper hand. Because "very well-known law professors at the *grandes universities*" signed the letter, law scholars supporting gay family rights, such as Laurence Brunet, said they felt ostracized. This dominant position has not gone uncriticized. Several progressive French law scholars wrote an online rebuttal to the letter and its arguments.[15] Neirinck and Dekeuwer-Défossez both suggested their junior colleagues behind the letter campaign, whose efforts they supported, may have created professional trouble for themselves in the long term by opposing same-sex marriage, though there is no evidence that those concerns were warranted in the intervening years.

Among French mental health professionals, conservative psychiatrists and psychoanalysts have long spearheaded their professions' resistance to gay family rights.[16] Moreover, French psychologists hold comparatively conservative attitudes toward gay families.[17] They claim their dominance is fading. Christian Flavigny, a psychiatrist at a major Parisian hospital and member of advisory boards on adoption policy, said his peers privately supported his stances but "let him go to the fire" alone to face the media and lawmakers. Deploying a common scapegoat among European conservatives, he claimed that an invasion of "gender theory" was damaging his reputation and that his public opposition to LGBTQ rights no longer resonated as it used to.[18] This intellectual invasion, "which comes from the United States [and] is a way for communitarian American homosexuals to twist a psychological theory to them, [has taken] hold on France." Framing his perceived marginalization this way allows Flavigny to more easily rationalize his stigmatization as the fault of American gay activists. Yet, the decentering of conservatives within psychoanalysis is primarily the result of growing vocal opposition from progressive French psychoanalysts who have undermined their public interventions. One of Flavigny's well-connected conservative colleagues, Pierre-Lévy Soussan, agreed that conservative psychoanalysts are losing legitimacy because of progressive attacks against them. Elisabeth Roudinesco, a famous historian of psychoanalysis popular in the media, has, in her words, made "permanent enemies in the psychoanalytic milieu," because she has denounced experts using psychoanalysis as a form of expertise to argue against gay parenting. Her anti-trans stances, however, have not helped her win allies among more progressive groups.

If the perspective of these anti-marriage experts is accurate, it is possible that conservative dominance in France may be waning and could accelerate as public support for and legal recognition of gay families increases. In addition, contrary to Americans, French conservatives lack powerful alternative knowledge production organizations—at least for now—that they can mobilize as they lose ground to liberals in official state agencies and organizations. Events in the last decade, however, may slow this decline. For example, in 2016, Valérie Pécresse, the president of the Paris region who ran on an anti-gay-family platform—eliminated her region's funding for research on gender and sexuality, which was one of the few French granting sources.[19] Thus, despite recent slippage, French experts opposing gay family rights have continued to wield more power in academic and professional fields than proponents. We now turn our attention to the factors that led to these power distributions.

ACHIEVING FIELD STRENGTH: NATIONAL FACTORS CONSTRAINING AND ENABLING EXPERTS

The relative positions of power in the 2010s of experts who support gay family rights in the United States and those who oppose them in France are the result of nationally specific resources and obstacles they faced in each country. They consist of four interrelated but analytically distinct types: (1) size and centralization of knowledge regimes; (2) disciplinary and university reactions to research on gender and sexuality; (3) social acceptance of gay families; and (4) the degree of division among allied experts. In what follows, I describe how interviewees confronted these factors to arrive at their current circumstances.

Size and Centralization of Knowledge Regimes

The size and centralization of knowledge regimes in the United States and France have both benefitted or hindered different groups of experts. The large, decentralized, and less state-centered American system has advantaged supporters and opponents alike. In a large field with more opportunities than France, American experts supporting gay family rights gained traction in some regions and grew their footholds over time, whereas opponents found homes in alternative organizations or gained support from outside groups to fund their work in mainstream universities. In contrast, in France, the centralized, hierarchical, and largely state-centered system of universities that concentrates power in Paris has limited marriage proponents.[20] Because conservatives continue to occupy high-ranking seats in university policy boards and state-run commissions, almost all of which are in Paris, marriage supporters have had, until recently, fewer opportunities within a smaller academic job market relative to Americans.

Americans on both sides described working in institutions across the country, sometimes when attracted with funding, promotions, or more acceptance. Eskridge, for example, moved to Georgetown University from the University of Virginia, where he found support for his work on LGBTQ law. On the other side, Morse moved from George Mason University to the Hoover Institution, a conservative think tank at Stanford University, before leaving the academy and founding her own conservative advocacy organization. The number and variety of higher education and research institutions give American experts more possibilities than their French counterparts for developing careers and cultivating spaces that fit their political and ideological agendas.

French interviewees have not had such flexibility because universities are less numerous, less independent, and more homogenous. Key steps in academic hiring and promotions, for example, have mostly been nationally centralized. Many progressive interviewees, including law professor Daniel Borrillo and sociologist Eric Fassin, claimed their careers were stifled for decades because well-placed people who opposed gay family rights prevented their promotions. They had few options for overcoming these barriers.

Furthermore, most French non-university knowledge production organizations are linked to the state. Experts opposing gay family rights have held key positions within commissions acting as official governmental advisors, which, in the words of one progressive expert, means that "people who are against a certain social evolution are in strategic positions." For instance, the state nominated Lévy-Soussan to the Agence de la biomédecine [Biomedicine Agency], the state administrative board responsible for regulating assisted reproductive technology (ART). Similarly, Xavier Lacroix, a philosophy professor and theologian, was appointed in 2008 to the Comité consultatif national d'éthique pour les sciences de la vie et de la santé (CCNE) [National Ethics Advisory Committee for Life and Health Sciences], a legally mandated advisory board authoring nonbinding declarations on all bioethics legislation that has opposed ART for lesbians until 2017. Finally, the Union nationale des associations familiales (UNAF) [National Union of Family Associations], a powerful state-mandated family association federation the government is required to consult when drafting policy, overrepresents conservative family groups. It has worked with conservative law professors, such as Claire Neirinck, to draft official stances on gay family rights.[21] Within this system, experts who believe gay and lesbian couples deserve the same rights as straight couples have only begun advancing as conservatives retire or end their terms.

Added to these contrasts, the structure of academic and professional organizations, as well as the capacity and willingness of their leadership to get involved in major social issues, including gay marriage and parenting, are starkly different. In the United States, the size and power of mainstream professional associations, such as the American Medical Association, as well as their conservative rivals give significant mobilizing power to American experts on both sides of the debate, albeit with differing levels of prestige and legitimacy. Their French counterparts, however, not only are much smaller and less professionalized but also have either been unable or disinclined to bring whatever weight they do have to these debates. In that vacuum, conservative experts in France have had the upper hand.

Disciplinary and University Reactions to Research on Gender and Sexuality

Disciplines and universities in each country have historically reacted to gender and sexuality research in ways that have mostly aided American progressives but limited their French colleagues. Mirroring national differences in size and centralization, interviewees experienced the American system as more accommodating to path-breaking research on gay people and their families. Illustrating this, Patterson, one of the first U.S. psychologists to study children raised by same-sex couples, described benefiting from institutional support for her novel work. For example, during a 1989 sabbatical at University of California Berkeley, her peers in the psychology department and the Beatrice Bain Research Group, a feminist studies community, encouraged her to write the first review of the extant literature on childhood outcomes. That paper was eventually published in one of her discipline's flagship journals.[22] Patterson's experience was not uncommon among U.S. interviewees who were the first in their fields to work on these issues. While all said they experienced skepticism, especially in previous decades, they ultimately found support for their unusual work.

Relative to their French peers, this support allowed them to conduct significant empirical research on gay families, creating the "scientific consensus" that children raised by same-sex and different-sex couples fare equally well, which proved central for marriage supporters in trials.[23] Experts who testified before U.S. courts on this consensus, including Gates and Rosenfeld, described how hard-won acceptance of such research in American social sciences multiplied studies with increasingly better data. Both pointed to some open-mindedness from journals, grant providers, review boards, and data collectors. Had U.S. disciplines rejected this research, scholarship on gay families would likely have stagnated, falling short of the perceived critical mass that has buttressed the pro-marriage legal case and given progressive scholars strength in their fields. Indeed, the French case suggests as much.

French experts researching sexual minorities have faced chronic skepticism from their peers and institutions. Each had stories of resistance from colleagues and mentors. Like their American peers, they conducted research on marginal topics but did so in a markedly more hostile environment that remained resistant to their ideas and methodology for longer.[24] Contrary to the United States, French universities did not develop minority studies programs in the wake of post-1960s social movements. Thus, French universities have opened fewer women and gender studies programs, which could have helped experts who support gay family rights. Furthermore, French disciplines have continued to disregard such topics. For example, unlike some U.S. law school curricula, according to Dekeuwer-Défossez, "it's unimaginable in France to open a course on LGBT oriented law." Similarly, decrying the conservativeness of the French academy, renowned anthropologist Maurice Godelier explained that "in the U.S. . . . you have a veritable [literature on] 'gay kinship, lesbian kinship.' " Illustrating this erasure, several cited the omission of gay families from François de Singly's authoritative *Sociologie de la Famille Contemporaine* [*Sociology of the Contemporary Family*] until the third edition, published in 2007, despite his supervision of Virginie Descoutures's dissertation on lesbian mothers and his awareness of gay family organizations.[25]

Refusals to grant academic recognition to sexual minorities in general, and gay families in particular, are consistent with French republican universalism's downplaying of social differences, which also spills over into the way academic gatekeepers conceive of research on topics including race, gender, and sexuality. Some were only able to find positive reinforcement by leaving the country. Daniel Borrillo, for example, a long-time gay rights supporter and law professor, found no support in favor of same-sex marriage from his French jurist colleagues but, as an invited professor at Boston College in 1997, he discovered the "immensity" of favorable U.S. and Canadian legal arguments.

As a result of these circumstances, French scholars have had fewer opportunities and produced less research on gay families than peers in other countries.[26]

French conservative experts have historically benefitted from this environment because academic and professional resistance to gay parenting research aligns with their ideological stances.

Social Acceptance of Gay Families

Social acceptance—or not—of same-sex couples raising children, as measured by their legal recognition, visibility in the media, and representation in organizations, affects the capacity of experts studying them to gain traction in their fields. This factor is most salient in France, where the social, political, and scientific erasure of gay couples and their families has been a lasting feature of the French—but not U.S.—case. Indeed, U.S. experts enjoy both a comparatively more supportive academic environment and work in a country where gay families were legally recognized in some jurisdictions for decades. This made finding and studying them easier than in France. Indeed, academic barriers facing progressive French scholars are made worse by a social climate less sympathetic to gay parenting.

Gay family invisibility in French media and political spheres, noted by other scholars, is both a symptom and cause of the illegitimacy of sexual minorities as research topics.[27] French bans on surrogacy, adoption, and ART for same-sex couples have made it especially difficult for French gays and lesbians to have children in the first place. In addition, as detailed in the introduction to this book, relative to the United States, French public opinion has been historically more negative toward gay parenting. Furthermore, counter to the United States—where, as Gates and Rosenfeld described, scholars have constructed a detailed cartography of gay family demographics with the Census and other national surveys that either indirectly capture or explicitly ask about gay families—French interviewees said national research centers, like the Institut National d'Études Démographiques, have not historically gathered data allowing such measurement. Despite hoping they might eventually do so, some social scientists argued that administrators usually refuse to ask such questions, just as they do with race, because doing so would recognize a minority category and thus violate principles of French universalism. Complicating matters further, the UNAF, which is statutorily required to represent all French family associations, had long systematically refused to admit gay family organizations until the last few years, eliminating their voices from officially sanctioned discourse.[28] In this climate, it has been especially difficult for French researchers to study the experiences of same-sex couples and their children.

Despite the ongoing and historical efforts of France's two gay family organizations—Association des Parents et futurs parents Gays et Lesbiens (APGL) and Association des Familles Homoparentales (ADFH)—to encourage researchers to study their families, most French experts, including those who are gay and lesbian themselves, said gay families have long been socially invisible there relative to countries like the Netherlands, Canada, and the United States.[29] During the late 1990s, it was especially acute. Most interviewees working then, including those who conducted research with the APGL, such as Nadaud and Cadoret, said few people imagined gays and lesbians wanted or already had their own families. Both said gay parenting was "not a visible phenomenon." Gross, also a former president of the APGL, argued that gay parenting was largely underground. This relative erasure seems to have been true even as late as the last few years. For example, in the words of Erwann Binet, the lawmaker responsible for organizing the Assembée Générale's Judiciary Committee hearings in 2012, gay families have been "totally abstract and inexistent in the minds of the French. . . . For them, homosexuals could not have children." This invisibility and the lack of research it exacerbates serve French conservatives. Unlike in the United States, they can more easily minimize the phenomenon of gay families altogether and make claims that are difficult for progressive experts to counter without the data and social support to do so.

Division Among Allied Experts

Finally, the degree of fragmentation among experts on the same ideological side also shapes their position in the field. In the United States, despite some notable discord among more progressive scholars over gay marriage—including debates over radical and queer proposals to undo marriage altogether in favor of a truly emancipatory reimagining of romantic and family formations—the struggle between gay rights supporters and opponents is the more salient division. This progressive-conservative polarization, which is characteristic of the U.S. case and consistent with the national knowledge regimes literature, appears to limit the weakening effects inter-left divisions have on progressive experts' current position in the field.[30] In France, however, long-standing public division among left-leaning experts over gay family rights has made countering conservative dominance more difficult. Contrary to progressives, there are no notable, public divisions among conservative experts over these issues in either country—political tactics or religious stances notwithstanding—other than the degree to which same-sex couples and their family relationship should be recognized, if at all. Fragmentation thus appears to constitute a specific hurdle for pro-marriage experts, especially in France.

Pro-marriage American experts described critique from their peers over concerns that their research might have unintended negative political effects. Their colleagues were anxious that their findings, methodologies, or theoretical orientations could be weaponized by antigay forces. For instance, in the 1980s, psychologist Ilan Meyer encountered pushback in peer reviews and conferences when his research on "minority stress" cast doubt on accepted theory that gay and straight people had the same risk of psychiatric disorders. Some worried that his results, which found higher rates of mental health issues, could hurt gay people's image. But Meyer wondered if "gay people [were] suffering [from] the impact of homophobia" and decided to push ahead with his research to answer that question. He found that experiences of discrimination can have negative psychological consequences on sexual minorities.

Research on relationships and families also faced this kind of skepticism. Anne Peplau, a professor of psychology at UCLA, explained that prior to the 1990s, some psychologists hesitated comparing same-sex and different-sex couples to avoid "imply[ing] heterosexuals were the standard" or that gay couples were somehow deficient. More radical scholars, such as critical theorist Michael Warner and sociologist Judith Stacey, criticized American gay family research for not fully embracing the queer potential of non-heteronormative relationships and parenting.[31] Several interviewees, including Manning, Patterson, and law professor Nan Hunter, personally experienced or witnessed Stacey, who they all knew personally, suggest that most gay family scholarship reinforces heteronormativity by overemphasizing similarities between straight and gay families and their children's outcomes. Patterson, in particular, said Stacey criticized her and her colleagues' work in articles and conferences.

American conservative experts have unsuccessfully tried to exploit these academic divisions in courts. Attempting to cast doubt on the reliability of Patterson and others' research, they frequently cite Stacey in amicus briefs and in expert testimony in federal marriage trials.[32] These strategies, nevertheless, appear to diminish the effects of fragmentation among pro-marriage experts. For example,

Stacey has responded by rejecting conservative manipulation of her work and emphasizing her support for her progressive colleagues. She lays some of this out in a video denouncing antigay distortions of research and in interviews.[33] Furthermore, the way family sociologists reacted to the Regnerus affair—by rallying together through interpersonal networks and the ASA to critique his methods, findings, and conclusions via review boards, journal articles, amicus briefs, and expert testimony—suggests that pro-marriage coalitions can override progressive divisions among academic experts.

The French field, in contrast, is characterized by historic and enduring conflict among experts who would self-identify as politically left leaning. That conflict has been caused, in part, by several famous, high-ranking, and politically connected experts—including anthropologists Françoise Héritier and Maurice Godelier and sociologist Irène Théry—who changed their stances on same-sex marriage in the early 2000s. Before supporting it and arguing for its legalization in the 2010s, they vehemently opposed same-sex marriage and parenting in the press and before lawmakers, denouncing their more progressive peers as radicals. They argued that gender differences were the universal anthropological structure that organized—and should continue to organize—filial relationships.[34] With the exception of David Blankenhorn, an author, activist, and social scientist who explained why he changed his mind in a *New York Times* op-ed, few American academics have publicly shifted from an anti- to pro-same-sex marriage position.[35]

The conflict originated at a time in the 1990s when these scholars, especially Théry, were family policy experts advising, officially and unofficially, the government and the Socialist Party. Sylviane Agacinski, a feminist philosopher and wife of then Socialist Prime Minister Lionel Jospin, who has never stopped fighting against gay families, echoed their views. Théry, though now an outspoken supporter of gay families, opposed the Pacte civil de solidarité (Pacs) and same-sex marriage in the 1990s. "We must continue to refuse homosexual marriage," she explained in an interview to *Le Monde*, "because matrimony is the very institution of sex differences, linking together the couple and *filiation* through the presumption of paternity, which is the heart of marriage."[36] She favored a solution that would preserve reproduction and childrearing for married couples—by her definition heterosexual—and stressed that for the good of the family, people needed to accept the "reality of the finiteness of [homosexual] relationships." She proposed creating domestic partnerships that only same-sex couples would be allowed to enter into—unlike the Pacs, which she also publicly opposed—that would provide some legal recognition, but "not open the right to adoption or assisted reproductive technologies." This conflict between left-leaning French experts erupted at a time when there was a clear demarcation between these key, influential academics, who had relatively conservative stances, and other progressive French academics who supported both the Pacs and full marriage equality.

Many French interviewees discussed the origin of the division and rivalry within the field around the time of the Pacs debates, before Théry and others changed their stances, and when both sides were openly fighting with each other in the press as well as in public and academic conferences.[37] In particular, they described a two-day conference in 1999 on gay couples and parenting, hosted by the APGL, as an especially striking example. At the conference, Théry, Fassin, and Borrillo confronted each other in a debate about whether supposed sex differences between men and women justify prohibiting same-sex couples from joint adoption and full marriage rights or whether principles of equality override such considerations.[38] The debate, which was "explosive" and dramatic according to several interviewees, led Fassin, Borrillo, and their supporters to leave the conference the next day and not publish in the proceedings. They were also simultaneously organizing their own conferences, one in 1998 and another 1999, which involved a critique of the role of experts, including Théry, in the Pacs debates. They also published several academic articles developing these arguments and an edited volume.[39] At the same time, Théry was reiterating her critiques of them, for example, in an interview with the French intellectual journal *Esprit*, and developing her own theorization of experts and their role in politics.[40]

In the intervening decades, experts who had always supported gay family rights—especially those who were politically active, such as Daniel Borrillo, Éric Fassin, and Didier Eribon, a philosopher, sociologist, and memoirist—found their former political and academic rivals now advocating the same positions they had always held themselves. This was also true for advocacy organizations, such as the APGL, Aides, and Homosexualités et Socialisme (HES). During the Pacs debates, these groups had complicated relationships with Théry because of her opposition to marriage and parenting. Yet, once she changed her stance, they found themselves supporting her and relying on her political and academic influence to advance their agendas. As a result of this conflict, left-leaning interviewees who found themselves on one side or the other of this historic division described episodes of career blockages, negative professional side effects, and defamation from their rivals. This clash—regardless of the veracity of each side's claims, which have become legend among French sociologists—limited progressives' capacity to resist conservative dominance in the French academic field. First, in the 1990s, left-leaning anti-gay-marriage experts provided intellectual coverage to conservative arguments. Second, according to every pro-marriage French expert I interviewed, the conflict has left people feeling caught in an ongoing battle requiring one to take sides. This fragmentation continues to complicate work for French experts who favor pro-LGBTQ rights in a small field where research is already underfunded, marginalized, and under attack by conservatives.

CONCLUSION

By testifying for and against gay families in the United States and France, academics and professionals provide expert capital to activists and decision-makers. Yet, as this chapter demonstrates, their capacity to produce, accumulate, and share that capital depends on how they overcome barriers and mobilize resources specific to their respective fields, in this case academic and professional. Just as activists contend with political opportunity structures in the political field to accomplish their goals, elite experts I interviewed produced expertise in contentious fields where competition for resources and recognition is ideologically oriented and conditioned by nationally specific knowledge regimes.[41] Circumstances in the United States and France relative to university and professional organizational structure, social and academic acceptance of gay families, and ideological division have all shaped how experts supporting and opposing gay family rights have fared.

By the 2010s, American pro-marriage experts had leveraged their way into a position of relative strength by pushing their universities and professional organizations to gradually acknowledge their work. They did so in a large field that presented more opportunities for better data collection than their French peers, who found themselves limited by a smaller, more hierarchical field where their institutions have been less receptive to their work, which already suffers from a chronic lack of social acceptance. Pro-marriage experts in both countries also faced fragmentation within their ranks that hindered their work but that proved especially constraining in France. American conservative experts, though facing some pushback from mainstream academics and official organizations, have mobilized networks that are strong in a decentralized American system in order to counter progressive expert capital with varying degrees of success. Conservative French experts are also facing criticism for their views but, because they have historically held top academic and advisory board positions in the top-down French field, especially among legal professionals, they have been able to maintain some dominance.

The current relative positions of experts in their fields, this chapter argues, are the result of historical processes contingent on the nationally specific circumstances described above. Their positions are likely to continue to change. For example, the relative strength of American progressive experts may only be temporary if conservative scholars and their allies successfully attack funding for research on gay families or sexual minorities more generally, as they have done in the past.[42] Recent right-wing attacks on progressive American academics and tepid university administrative responses in defending them could signal a shifting climate.[43] Indeed, in the ten years since I conducted the interviews and in the wake of Donald Trump's first term as president, an increasing number of Republican-dominated states have begun attacks on higher education, with Florida going so far as to push a bill that would close programs in women and gender studies in public universities.[44] This has been accompanied by a hard rightward shift in the federal judiciary, most notably at the Supreme Court, thanks in part to the successful strategies of organizations such as the Federalist Society and the conservative movement more generally.[45] In France, legalization of same-sex marriage and parenting as well as positive shifts in public opinion—polling in 2017 found a majority of French people support gay parenting—may help reduce the invisibility of gay families there.[46] That could lead to more support for gay family research in the long run, especially if conservative experts continue to lose ground on official advisory boards. However, like in the United States, attacks against "wokeism" and "gender ideology" have become common in France since 2015. France, like the United States, has been among the countries in which internationally networked anti-LGBTQ activists have made headway in the last decade as part of a global reactionary trend.[47] Under President Emmanuel Macron's administration, criticisms that the university is a hotbed of "wokeist" ideology imported from the United States do not bode well for a political climate that would support research on gender and sexuality.[48]

Because of their central role in U.S. courts and the French legislature, this chapter has analyzed elite academic and professional experts. Although my fieldwork focused primarily on this group, my interviews and observations with social movement organization leaders as well as evidence from the archives suggest that lay experts, such as religious representatives and ordinary citizens, also face nationally specific circumstances that can empower one side over the other. As chapter 3 mentioned, progressive faith-based communities in France are active but face an uphill battle in a context of centralized confessional organizations for each of the major faiths in which conservative perspectives dominate and where leaders have learned to use secular language to be politically audible, shutting out pro-gay voices. Thanks to more religious diversity and decentralization, progressive American religious groups can effectively organize their testimony despite the overwhelming financial wealth of their conservative adversaries. In both countries, social movement organizations are the key producers of lay expertise, cultivating and curating personal testimony. Since ordinary citizens are mostly excluded from French decision-making institutions, it is more difficult to determine which side has the upper hand. It is clear, however, that public hostility to gay families has made it challenging for French LGBTQ groups to tell the stories of their members. In the United States, getting people's lived experiences on the record is much easier, and the success of both sides to be heard no doubt depends on the relative strength and mobilizing capacity of activist groups. Further research investigating social movements will certainly help us better understand the production of lay expertise.

Evidence from this chapter suggests that the global circulation of expertise and distribution of ideological stances in both countries has encouraged conservative American experts, on the one hand, and progressive French experts, on the other, to seek support for their ideas outside of their home settings. Lynn Wardle, for example, found support for his conservative ideas in the International Society of Family Law (ISFL), where he interacted with his French colleague, Hughes Fulchiron. Similarly, Daniel Borrillo described feeling much more supported by law professors and legal professionals in Canada and the United States, especially in the 1990s and 2000s, where he discovered a body of legal research supporting his pro-gay-marriage stance. However, the extent to which they can use what they learn in those international contexts depends on the policy knowledge outlets in their own countries. It also depends on their ability to access the expert field and the decision-making institutions within it. They may be able to develop direct relationships with decision-makers or with advocacy and professional organizations that mediate that access. It is to these channels between knowledge producers and decision-makers that we now turn our attention.

CHAPTER 5

TIES THAT BIND

How Experts Connect with Lawmakers

I n the late 1980s, after receiving his doctorate in social psychology from the University of California Davis, American psychology professor, Gregory Herek, was publishing pathbreaking studies on the psychology of homophobia and homosexuality. After he was invited to give a presentation about the social psychology of homophobia at an NYU School of Law conference, his research started to get the attention of activist organizations. His talk was published as part of the proceedings in the *New York University Review of Law and Social Change*, a journal founded in the 1960s by a group of radical faculty and students with the goal of producing legal scholarship in support of progressive social causes.[1] Matt Coles, an acquaintance of Herek's, who directed the American Civil Liberties Union's (ACLU) Lesbian and Gay Rights Project, reached out to him. Coles was hoping Herek could provide them with a snapshot of research on the psychology of sexual orientation they could use in upcoming litigation. They thought that if they had scientific research to back up their claims, it could help them win their cases. As Herek reviewed the literature for the ACLU, it became clear that there was a growing demand from gay rights supporters for accessible and scientifically accurate information about gays and lesbians. So, he began working within the American Psychological Association (APA) to pool psychological research findings that the organization could deliver to policymakers and other advocacy groups. That initial research was published in 1991 under the title, "Myths About Sexual Orientation: A Lawyer's Guide to Social Science Research," in the journal *Law & Sexuality: A Review of Lesbian and Gay Legal Issues*, operated by students at the University of Tulane School of Law.[2] The APA project endured and grew, eventually becoming a clearinghouse for expertise that has informed gay rights lawmaking for decades. Thinking back on the active participation of his professional organization in providing information to advance gay rights causes, Herek remarked: "It's amazing how big of a role they've been willing to play."

In contrast, in France, professional organizations have been largely silent on gay family rights issues even in the years immediately before same-sex marriage and adoption were legalized. According to the anthropologist Anne Cadoret, "It's not their habit [or] their way of being. They don't make that commitment." Indeed, most French mental health and social science associations do not get directly involved in the political process unless lawmakers are meddling with the regulations related to their professions. It is almost impossible to find even a cursory public statement—let alone a whole unit devoted to producing expertise for litigation and policymaking—from the learned societies in social and mental health sciences or efforts on their part to summarize the research in their disciplines that might inform debates on gay family rights. Without these organizational support systems, French experts manage their policy interventions in more informal ways. For example, with no scientific organizations or professional groups she could turn to for guidance on how her research could be useful to French lawmakers, Anne Cadoret worked with other social scientists who had direct, personal connections to lawmakers and their staff in order to bring her research to their attention.

These examples illustrate the differing structures of the expert field in each country, where elite experts lend their capital to decision-makers, and the routines both groups have developed within it to get access to one another. The existence or not of third-party organizations is key to how this exchange takes place and the consequences it can have. Whether it be because of the political and legal opportunity structures in each country or the way social movement organizations, professional associations, universities, think tanks, and other bodies have responded to a demand for expertise—or lack thereof—experts on either side of the Atlantic are distributing their knowledge through distinct networks and channels. Building on the previous chapters' analysis of the academic and professional fields where progressive and conservative experts work to create their expertise, this chapter focuses on the paths they take to deliver that information. It also explains how different organizations with invested stakes in supporting or combatting gay rights—or with defending their professional and scientific reputations—produce knowledge with their help in an effort to cultivate expert capital. Understanding these circumstances helps explain why certain kinds of experts and expertise are more or less successful in providing information to decision-makers in each country.

As chapter 3 laid out, interactions between experts and decision-makers can take multiple forms, depending on the institutional context, each with its own power dynamics, rules, norms, and forms of access.[3] One form of power is social capital: who you know—maybe a journalist or parliamentary assistant—and the resources they have, including connections to important people.[4] Getting quoted in a *New York Times* article and obtaining a seat at the hearing table in the Assemblée Nationale are different processes, but both require having the right kind of contacts and a sought-after profile. In the United States, making these connections—as well as managing interactions between experts, decision-makers, and the media more generally—has become an institutionalized and professionalized process with significant involvement of the private and non-profit sectors.[5] This is partly the result of the high barriers to access to courts as well as a need for organizations to handle the sheer number of jurisdictions in the U.S. federal system.

In this context of high demand and a large market for expertise, interest groups that specialize in nurturing experts, such as think tanks, have developed routinized procedures to make these connections. Indeed, with the courts and legislatures on both the state and federal levels, proponents and opponents of same-sex marriage have constantly needed expertise to engage in the debates since at least the 1980s. This situation has lent itself to the development of powerful, well-funded organizations to satisfy the demand for expertise on both sides. Indeed, just as mainstream professional bodies such as the APA have defended LGBTQ causes, major groups working to advance a host of conservative priorities, including preventing legal recognition of gay families, have countered them.[6] These groups have worked as pipelines between knowledge producers and decision-makers, consolidating expertise for public debates along the way.

In contrast, French professional organizations, think tanks, and other groups, except for the Catholic Church, are comparatively small and financially weak. They have not developed the governance structure or organizational capacity to channel knowledge to the same degree as their American counterparts. Moreover, the many state and local-level opportunities for reform, which help sustain demand for knowledge in the United States, are absent in France. French experts and their allies of all ideological stances must therefore navigate through less formal channels, through state-run bodies, or through the media to access lawmakers. Indeed, consistent with my observations of the French expertise field more generally, French experts and policymakers worked in a smaller, more informal field, where personal connections and proximity to lawmakers are the norm. Channels to the expert field are therefore primarily ad hoc and organized around interpersonal networks. As a result, there is less consistency of expertise over time and little systematized accumulation within organizations that can then provide it for future debates.

Relatively unmediated interpersonal interactions and close ties between experts—especially intellectual elites—and politicians have been a historically defining feature of the French case.[7] Indeed, because of its small size and concentration in Paris, the French expert field is at the geographic epicenter of knowledge production, the media, and political decision-making.[8] These personal relationships—some experts attend the same dinner parties as politicians and journalists—are one reason why French lawmakers have asked certain academics and intellectuals for personal advice, as President François Holland did over lunch with a group of academics, or commissioned them to draft official reports on French family law. As this chapter will argue, thanks to these relationships, some experts can become full-fledged political counselors, "prophesying" the social outcomes of potential reforms and playing an outsized role in determining public policy.[9] In short, the fields of academics and politicians in France overlap enough that the debates can easily become personalized: Disagreements involving a few academics or politicians can dominate much of the discussion both in the halls of parliament and in the seminar room. In the United States, the mediating influence of organizations buffers the interactions between decision-makers and experts. The unique opportunities and constraints of these fields determine not only how expert capital is traded but also the forms that it takes and the consequences that exchange has for both parties.

SCIENTIFIC KNOWLEDGE BANKS SUPPORTING AMERICAN GAY FAMILIES

Advocates working in favor of the legal rights of same-sex couples and their children in the United States have needed scientific research to support their work, particularly in courts, going back decades. To meet that need, they created their own organizations, which have become professionalized and institutionalized, as well as worked with already existing academic and professional associations, such as the APA, who have organized and provided knowledge to pro-gay causes.

The significance of the American juridical field and of the involvement of legal organizations in systemizing expertise on behalf of gay rights cannot be overstated. Activists with legal training began laying the groundwork in the post-Stonewall era of the gay rights movement. For example, Nan Hunter, who has since become a professor at the prestigious Georgetown University Law Center, created a feminist law collective with Nancy Polikoff in Washington during the 1970s, focusing on "employment, family law, [and other] issues of gender and sexuality." She then moved on to work for the ACLU and the Lambda Legal Defense Fund, the oldest and largest LGBTQ legal advocacy organization, bringing her organizing experience with her.[10] Terry Stewart, who was the chief deputy city attorney of San Francisco and a celebrated LGBTQ activist that assisted the attorneys in the Hollingsworth trial before her appointment as associate justice to the First Appellate District Court of California in 2014, told me about how some collaborations between scientists and activists started. She explained that Donna Hitchens, who is now a retired San Francisco Superior Court judge, founded the Lesbian Rights Project.

In the late 1970s and early 1980s, the Lesbian Rights Project worked to defend lesbians who sought to maintain custody of their children after their former husbands or other family members contested their parental rights because of their sexual orientation. During that time, Stewart said that Hitchens developed a "Lesbian Mother Custody Manual" because "they couldn't represent everybody in every state that had these issues, but they were trying to be supportive of attorneys who were doing it elsewhere." In addition to legal strategies and advice, the manual also included expertise, such as research on gay and lesbian parenting, that attorneys could use in their cases.

In the years following, many similar organizations have grown and built repositories of knowledge, both legal and scientific, that they could use to push the legal environment in a direction that would be less repressive and more accepting of LGBTQ relationships and families. These efforts became especially urgent in the 1980s and 1990s, as the AIDS crisis decimated the gay community and gay men in particular experienced the violence of a family law system that refused to recognize their relationships, making them vulnerable to the whims of their homophobic landlords, healthcare workers, employers, and the heirs of their deceased partners. LGBTQ legal organizations and advocates, including even some gay Republicans, as well as newly formed collectives fighting against the epidemic, mobilized to try and protect gay families from these assaults.[11]

Since then, these groups, prominent examples of which include Lambda Legal, GLBTQ Legal Advocates and Defenders (GLAD), the Human Rights Campaign, the National Center for Lesbian Rights, the LGBT project at the ACLU, Freedom to Mary, the LGBT Bar Association, the LGBT Judge's Association, and many others, have become so established and professionalized that they are known colloquially as, in the words of Stewart, "Gay inc." Leaders at these organizations, such as Jennifer Pizer at Lambda Legal, consider that developing a repository of expertise is an important part of their success. "Those of us representing same-sex couples and families of LGBT people are benefiting from there being more research and good quality research," Pizer said. Putting together these expertise knowledge banks started out as a practical response to a movement strategy: winning cases with credible expertise that could pass muster in courts and hopefully convince judges to rule in favor of gay and lesbian clients.

In order for this cause lawyering to be most effective, advocates working to advance gay family rights in U.S. courts needed to persuade mainstream legal organizations to join them. They would be especially important as partners in helping to draft briefs and pursue cases. In the 1980s, major law firms would rarely participate, Pizer explained, because "it was just too controversial and dubious." But after this early initial resistance, "there's been such a shift," she said. Looking back, Terry Stewart observed that "the legal community's been really on the forefront in many ways of LGBT equality." She described how when she was a private practice lawyer and president of the San Francisco Bar Association, "we got the bar to adopt the policy advocating for firms to provide domestic partner benefits." Over the decades, as their strategy began to yield major results and the public opinion began to shift in their favor, "the major law firms [have become] insistent on being able to [produce] . . . amicus briefs in the marriage cases," she explained.

Through collaborations between experts and legal advocacy organizations, advocates fighting for same-sex couples have oriented the production of scientific expertise, particularly in the areas of childhood outcomes and the economics of sexuality. Attorneys at these organizations have reached out to scholars for many years to ask them to provide information they could use, assuming that academic information was important for its authoritativeness. For example, the renowned feminist historian and Harvard professor, Nancy Cott, explained how lawyers at GLAD reached out to her in 1999 to give "a history lesson" to the Vermont legislature. The Vermont Supreme Court had ruled that same-sex couples must be provided with legal rights but left it up to the legislature to determine whether to legalize marriage or create some other system. "The lawyers who were working at GLAD thought that history was important," she said. At that point, she was already known as a specialist of the history of marriage in the United States and for having supervised the doctoral dissertation of George Chauncey at Yale, whose groundbreaking scholarship on American gay history would itself make its way into numerous amicus briefs and expert testimony. In another example, psychologist Charlotte Patterson described how Evan Wolfson, founder of Freedom to Marry, contacted her in the early 1990s when he was litigating before the Hawaii Supreme Court to prove that the state had no compelling justification for banning same-sex marriage. They asked her and other academics who had published psychological research on gay couples and families to testify as expert witnesses about childhood outcomes.

As organizations worked in different jurisdictions in the United States, they reached out to each other to learn about which experts their peers had used and what kinds of knowledge they had presented with success. Networks of lawyers were trading war stories and wanted to emulate winning strategies across counties and states. By the time the battle for same-sex marriage was at its apex, these solid collaboration routines were firmly in place and ready for action. For example, Stewart, who successfully litigated for same-sex marriage in California, forcing the state to briefly legalize it in 2008 before it was overturned by Proposition 8, joined the celebrity attorneys, Ted Olson and David Boies, who argued against the proposition in federal court. Part of her responsibility was contacting allied organizations, such as GLAD, Lambda Legal, and the ACLU, to ask them about which experts they had already worked with. "Look, when you go through the process, you look at lots of people, and you try to figure out who's doing the current work, what other testimony have they given," she told me. Finding and vetting the best experts is expensive and time-consuming. When Olson and Boies were putting their case together, they could mobilize decades of collective work by LGBTQ organizations who had identified a reliable group of high-quality experts. These organizations acted like a catalogue from which Stewart could draw to craft her legal argument in tandem with the main team.

Social movement organizations are not the only groups in the United States cultivating same-sex marriage experts. American academic and professional organizations have also been active participants in legal and political debates and used the knowledge of scientists and scholars in their respective domains. What makes their work distinct from social movement organizations is what it says about the role and position of experts within them. These academic and professional organizations are making a case for the policy value of the research of their members. Their interventions in public policy are a form of promotion, showcasing how their disciplines produce science "for the public interest," thereby justifying ongoing support from universities and funders. Their interventions are also a way for experts to use their respective professional organizations to send a message to their peers about what their disciplines should—or should not—be saying about gay family rights. When their organizations do take a stand, it reflects the degree to which organizational leadership is willing to use the name of the discipline to help advance progressive causes.

The most obvious organization is the APA, which has both professional and public credibility. Several lawyers I interviewed explained their long relationship with the APA and how its outreach, policy papers, and briefs have been effective in litigating gay rights because it brings with it the symbolic weight of an entire profession. The organization, which is highly professionalized and includes in-house staff to draft legal briefs that meet the standard of federal courts, has a vibrant and well-instituted unit devoted to sexual minority issues: the Lesbian, Gay, Bisexual, and Transgender Concerns Office. Its associate executive director, Clinton Anderson, described how the APA has worked to issue public position statements and policy resolutions supporting a variety of gay right issues, including same-sex marriage and gay parenting.[12] The organization has also filed briefs on behalf of LGBTQ people, same-sex couples, and sexual minority parents in legal cases throughout the country and going back decades. To create these policy documents, Anderson has worked with some of the most respected psychologists who have had expertise in these areas for decades, including, for example, Anne Peplau, Charlotte Patterson, and Greg Herek.

Though less involved in the debates and less prepared than the APA to draft a high volume of legal briefs, the American Sociological Association (ASA) has also worked to produce and centralize knowledge on gay families in order to make a contribution. As the marriage cases began wending their way through federal court, Sally Hillsman, ASA's executive director from 2002 to 2016, and the Executive Council decided to listen to demands from members within the organization that it take an official stance rejecting sociologist Mark Regnerus's claims, published in *Social Science Research*, that children fare poorly when raised by same-sex couples.[13] Because the study was brandished by conservatives and Regnerus as definitive proof that their crusade to thwart same-sex marriage was justified in the name of sociology, pressure from within the ASA to respond was mounting. This stemmed in part from a campaign Gary Gates, Charlotte Patterson, and other social scientists organized leading *Social Science Research* to investigate the review and editorial process behind the article's publication, including undeclared conflicts of interest.

Agreeing that Regnerus had evidently mischaracterized the sociological research, the ASA provided research funding to Wendy Manning, a professor of sociology at Bowling Green State University (Ohio) specializing in families but who had not taken a public stance on the Regnerus affair—unlike many of her equally qualified colleagues—to fully review the scientific literature. In our interview, Manning described how she conducted the review as she would for any other project and then provided her findings to the ASA, finding no evidence of harm to children and debunking Regnerus's claims. The association then transformed her report into an amicus brief filed in support of same-sex marriage.[14] She and her co-authors—graduate students who received a small stipend from the ASA to help with the review—eventually also published their findings in a peer-reviewed journal.[15]

Advocates and researchers have also founded think tanks, such as the Williams Institute on Sexual Orientation and Gender Identity Law and Public Policy, founded in 2001, whose primary purpose is to fund and produce high-quality empirical research for direct application to the policy sphere. It occupies a unique space in the U.S. expert field because it is housed at a university, UCLA, and is devoted to social science but its members include lawyers and law professors who can apply that information to legal and political transformation. In essence, thanks to generous funding from private donors who support LGBTQ causes, including its founder Charles Williams, this group represents the ultimate formalization and institutionalization of the expertise knowledge bank that developed more organically over the last few decades. Most pro-gay marriage and family researchers working in the United States who I interviewed had either worked with the Williams Institute, been funded to some degree by them, or participated in some way in their scholarly activities.

CONSERVATIVE THINK TANKS AND LOBBYING GROUPS
FIGHT BACK

Opponents to same-sex marriage and parenting in the United States have developed their own set of structures to provide information to lawmakers. They have made good use of the dense and interconnected network of very well-funded conservative and right-wing groups that run the gamut from the relatively small, such as the Ruth Institute, to the large and powerful, such as the Heritage Foundation, that have played an influential role in American politics.[16] Indeed, claiming to be on the margins within their fields and professional organizations that have publicly advocated for same-sex couples and families, including the APA and the ASA, anti-same-sex marriage experts, including some academics at major research universities, have benefited from generous support from conservative organizations and even founded some of their own. Many academic experts I interviewed told me that their peers who have fought against gay family rights are relatively absent from their mainstream professional organizations. I myself have observed, for instance, how Mark Regnerus did not attend the annual meeting or have detectable involvement with the ASA in the years following the publication of his article. Lynn Wardle echoed these feelings of exclusion when he told me that he is the "token conservative" in American law societies and prefers to work in international organizations that appear to defend "traditional families," such as the International Society of Family Law (ISFL), where he has met with French colleagues who share his views. That these anti-marriage academics feel marginalized within their fields does not signify that they lack political power, but it does mean that they have to rely on the resources of their own epistemic communities outside of their mainstream disciplinary organizations to get their expertise into the public eye.

Such experts and their allies within conservative movements have developed a constellation of dozens of organizations and think tanks that have regularly been involved in same-sex marriage debates in the United States and other countries since at least the 1990s. These include the National Organization for Marriage, the Marriage Law Foundation (MLF), the American College of Pediatricians, the Family Research Council, the Federalist Society, the Heritage Foundation, and the American Legislative Council Exchange. Like their progressive counterparts, these conservative organizations have centralized information and facilitate networking between experts and advocates. Wardle described how conservative legal advocacy organizations that he has worked with, such as the Alliance Defending Freedom, propose a counter-model to progressive groups, such as the ACLU, whose operations inspired their own. And, like those groups, they perform litigation and expertise cultivation, including summer legal training via their Blackstone Legal Fellowship program. For example, as William Duncan told me, his organization, the MLF, has worked with lawyers who come to him to learn about which kinds of experts to rely on and what kinds of information they can use in their briefs and trials. Many—but not all—of these organizations are also linked to religiously affiliated universities that also provide alternatives to their public and secular counterparts. Law schools at these universities train future lawyers and judges—Supreme Court Justice Amy Coney Barrett who earned her law degree at the University of Notre Dame, a renowned Catholic institution in Indiana, is a good example—and sponsor their own law review journals in which conservative scholars can publish legal expertise to influence courts.

Other well-established think tanks, such as the Heritage Foundation, help sponsor events through which different conservative experts, who no longer interact with their peers at their respective professional annual conferences, can meet and network. Most of the conservatives I interviewed met one another this way. For example, Douglas Allen, the economist from Simon Fraser University, told me that he met his future co-author Joseph Price, a professor of economics at Brigham Young University, at a Heritage Foundation conference. The Ruth Institute, which has a "circle of experts," helps facilitate similar contacts. One of its experts, Robert P. George, the influential conservative professor of jurisprudence at Princeton University, is the founder of the Witherspoon Institute. This think tank was the major funder for Mark Regnerus's data collection on the New Family Structures Study on which his research was based.

These various forums have become an important component to the conservative cause against same-sex marriage. Maggie Gallagher, an activist who has worked in several of these organizations, described that it is "precisely because of the rarity of intellectual conservatives [in] sociology and a lot of professions" that conservatives need to fund and support the production of expertise to contribute to the political debate. She and her colleagues were missing opportunities to impact the scientific and political process if they did not get involved in producing their own information to compete with that of mainstream professional groups and LGBTQ advocacy organizations. Though relatively small in number, anti-same-sex marriage academic experts have used the power of these organizations to punch above their weight in terms of media exposure, access to lawmakers in hearings, and production of knowledge for amicus briefs. Yet despite the significant financial investment in their work—the Regnerus study being a prominent example—recognition for their publications on same-sex marriage and parenting has been mostly marginal from their peers in the academy and its quality seriously criticized by the courts.

FRENCH EXPERTS SUPPORTING GAY FAMILY RIGHTS: INTERPERSONAL NETWORKS AND PROXIMITY TO LAWMAKERS

From a French perspective, American experts benefit from what looks like industrial-scale systems to get them before decision-makers and disseminate their research. On this side of the Atlantic, access to lawmakers might best be described as "artisanal." French experts in support of marriage and parenting for same-sex couples have not had the same kinds of institutionalized and organized resources at their disposal. Many French professional groups, such as the Association Française de Sociologie [French Sociological Association] and the Société Française de Psychologie [French Psychological Association], are small, have low budgets, lack professional staffs, and have not produced significant contributions of any stance on gay family policy, or public policy at all for that matter. Though French proponents have had the support and backing of some advocacy organizations and think tanks, the influence of such groups remains limited. The budgets of French social movement organizations fighting on behalf of LGBTQ people are no doubt a tiny fraction of their American counterparts. French think tanks, though generally more professionalized than French gay rights groups, are far less numerous and well-funded than in the United States. In the absence of such institutionalized and formalized support systems, progressive French experts' access to the policy sphere has largely depended on media exposure, their individual reputations, and the personal connections and networks they established with each other and with lawmakers. French advocacy organizations also worked through these interpersonal networks via the friendships and connections their members made with scholars or because scholars had founded and worked within them.

France does not have powerful and well-financed LGBTQ organizations that would be capable of mounting large-scale efforts to coordinate expertise in part because debates over gay rights there did not create that need. Indeed, because the judicial branch is a weak avenue of reform for gay family rights issues, unlike in the United States, French activist organizations, like the Inter-LGBT, a federation of social movement groups, do not have the same incentive to reach out to experts for court cases as their American counterparts do. Reflecting on her situation in France, the lawyer Caroline Mécary explained, "The Inter-LGBT has not understood the potential importance or interest of mounting judicial proceedings." Although Mécary was involved with Didier Eribon, Éric Fassin, and other intellectuals, activists, and politicians to set up the Bègles marriage as a test case, as mentioned in chapter 2, the courts invalidated the marriage and deferred to the legislature.[17] This lack of judicial mobilization, which has also affected the French feminist movement, leaves French advocates both without the demand for court-ready scientific expertise and the opportunities to test that knowledge so as to accumulate and perfect it over time.[18]

Despite the relative lack of judicial opportunity for reform, some French gay and lesbian advocacy organizations have played an important role in bridging the gap between academic experts and the public policy sphere. Much like their American counterparts, members created them to mobilize to protect the families of their members. The legal services clinic at the AIDS prevention organization Aides, co-organized by Daniel Borrillo in the 1990s, is a good example. The group used the legal expertise they gained from helping partners of gay AIDS victims deal with their lack of legal protection to then pressure the Socialist Party to recognize gay couples.[19] Indeed, the fallout from the epidemic made stark the unjust reality faced by gay couples in a country that refused to recognize their relationships and was a major catalyst driving efforts to reform family law.[20]

Because of its deliberate and early actions to build an epistemic community for the purposes of generating expertise, the Association des Parents et futurs parents Gay et Lesbiens [The Association of Gay and Lesbian Parents and Future Parents] (APGL) is also an excellent example that is reminiscent of what happened in the early days of similar groups in the United States. The association faced an uphill battle because many of its members were skeptical that raising children in gay relationships or having children as gay couples could ever be a viable option. Martine Gross, who had seen the changing status of gay parenting in France as the former president of the APGL and as a sociologist pioneering

French empirical research on gay families, confirmed that gay parenting was, to a large extent, underground in France in the early 1990s. She suggested that the idea of raising children as a same-sex couple seemed impossible not only legally but also intellectually to her and other lesbians and gay men she knew. Except for her and her partner, "there were very few people who were trying to have children after having already accepted their homosexuality," she explained.

According to Gross, perspectives at the APGL began to slowly change in the mid-1990s when the Hawaii Supreme Court issued its ruling in favor of gay marriage. The court justified its decision citing expertise—including Charlotte Patterson's—confirming the well-being of children raised by same-sex couples. It was eye opening for Gross and other APGL members that the Hawaii court "was for marriage because [same-sex couples] were good parents." Not only did this change their minds about their own families, but it also demonstrated how gay family visibility among researchers could impact gay family rights. At this point, Gross and her colleagues created the neologism "*homoparentalité* [gay parenting]" to describe their experiences and make them legible to the media and academics.[21] The APGL also created a series of initiatives to try and attract scholarly attention based on the assumption that if they could get recognized scientists to start acknowledging and studying gay families, it would give them more legitimacy and political leverage.[22]

In 1997, at a time when not a single academic article had been published in France on same-sex couples raising children, Gross wrote letters to all French research units and scientists she could identify who study family and childrearing—over three hundred—asking them if they would be interested in conducting research on gay families, offering their members as a recruiting base. Yet, despite these efforts, "they weren't interested [because] . . . it's about gays," she said. Gross received two positive responses, one of which was from Anne Cadoret, but, as we have already seen, unlike in the United States, the French academic community was not a conducive environment even for those few scholars willing to carry out novel work. In the 2010s, following in the footsteps of the APGL, the newer gay family rights group, the Association des Familles Homoparentales [Association of Gay Families] (ADFH), commissioned nationally representative surveys from opinion polling companies, including the Institut Français d'Opinion Publique [French Institute of Public Opinion] (IFOP). Their goal has been to use public opinion data to attempt to demonstrate that gay families are not as controversial or divisive as their opponents claim they are.

These French groups are less numerous, smaller, and often newer than their American counterparts. Importantly, most French LGBTQ advocacy organizations are almost entirely volunteer run and lack the professional staff and resources of groups such as Lambda Legal or the Williams Institute. Therefore, relative to their U.S. equivalents, they rarely finance their own research and sparingly engage in other costly and time-consuming tasks, such as organizing conferences, sponsoring consultations, or reaching out to the media. Rather, they have relied on individuals like Gross and Borrillo, who personally bridge the gap between the academic and activist fields because of their posts within the university and involvement in advocacy organizations. These groups also rely on the networks they build with other experts who have direct access to lawmakers.

Many of the experts I interviewed who support gay family rights had informal networks and direct relationships with decision-makers in the Socialist Party and other parties on the left. In a context where advocacy and professional organizations have relatively limited power to harness or channel expertise to get it into the hands of decision-makers, well-connected experts gain access to and influence the debate through direct, personal connections. Some experts, such as the philosophers Élisabeth Badinter and Sylviane Agacinski, whose respective husbands, Robert Badinter and Lionel Jospin, were both major Socialist politicians, had direct relationships via their spouses to decision-makers. Though they were quite well-known in their own right as intellectuals, their personal proximity to elected officials made their access to the debates that much easier. Many other interviewees, including Eric Fassin, described working relationships with lawmakers with varying degrees of success in persuading them to adopt their stances.

For some prominent, famous experts who have been active in the debates over the last few decades, these relationships with decision-makers were not only enduring but also allowed them to act as personal advisors and political sponsors. Maurice Godelier, for example, described his relationship with Christiane Taubira—the minister of justice during the marriage debates—and his role as a "counselor" to the Socialist Party. Other examples include Françoise Héritier and Elisabeth Roudinesco, both of whom described their friendships with senators, ministers, and Socialist Party members, two of whom asked them for their personal support in their bids as presidential candidates. By having their anointment, these politicians seek to benefit from the prestigious reputations of these famous intellectuals whose expert capital they hope they can cash in on to advance their own political careers.

In addition to these behind-the-scenes interactions, in which prominent experts lent their legitimacy and public recognition to politicians, some experts also worked to actively shape Socialist Party stances on policy issues. Irène Théry, in particular, described close working relationships with many Socialist politicians, including successive ministers who have commissioned official expert reports from her, as discussed in chapter 3. These reports, dealing with family rights issues, gave her the opportunity to officially and unilaterally advance her own arguments to French lawmakers. Although she was in conflict with politicians fighting for the Pacte civil de solidarité (Pacs), such as Jean-Pierre Michel, as both she and the party became more progressive over gay rights issues, these relationships strengthened. Indeed, according to her, she was one of two people heard by the Socialist Party in 2006 as it was considering including the legalization of same-sex marriage in its official platform. Reflecting the legal specificities of the French debate and the controversy of gay parenting more generally, she argued that legalizing same-sex marriage would only work if the Civil Code maintained the presumption of paternity for heterosexual married couples—where the husband is automatically the legal father of the children born to his wife—and carved out an exclusion for same-sex couples, who would have to seek a second-parent adoption for the nonbiological parent.[23] Party leaders had "understood her," she said, and moved ahead with their decision to support same-sex marriage with the caveats Théry carved out.

These interpersonal political connections make some experts central nodes in larger networks, shaping the form and meaning of expertise more generally. Indeed, Théry, with the support of government mandates to draft reports as well as her relationships to politicians, had the capacity to produce, organize, channel, and distribute expertise for public policy purposes in her own right. Indeed, she had collaborated with seventeen of the French experts I interviewed and is friends and acquaintances with many others that she feels comfortable working with or that share her specific policy perspectives on gay family rights. Théry drew extensively on this network as she carried out official expertise work for the government. Her dominant position in the French expert field and her high status within French academia have several consequences. First, they give her the unique power to craft a seemingly authoritative picture of expertise for lawmakers, framing who and what they are exposed to by selecting collaborators according to her own criteria and presenting them as the most trustworthy. Second, alternative sources of expertise, whether they be organizations such as the

APGL and Aides or other academics, must therefore compete with her if they happen to disagree with whatever her recommendations may be. Third, lawmakers cannot easily discount her. Politicians, including those on the left who may prefer more expansive or different kinds of gay family rights, must contend with her influence.

These kinds of informal interpersonal networks, which lack the stability, longevity, and institutional memory of the professionalized organizations of the United States, were characteristic of the ways French experts interacted with each other as they worked to bring information to policymakers. They all knew each other and regularly worked together. I saw how the same groups of experts, without much support from organizations, worked within and outside academic spaces to co-publish books and other materials they hoped would influence the political debates. Notable examples include Fassin and Borrillo's edited volume, published during the Pacs debates, and an "analysis document" supporting same-sex marriage published by the École des Hautes Études en Sciences Sociales in the midst of the marriage battle in 2013 by a group of experts working with Théry.[24]

These networks also showed up in other contexts, including the rare French think tanks that took a stance on gay family rights. For example, in the mid-2000s, Terra Nova, a centrist think tank associated with the Socialist Party, established a temporary working group to draft recommendations for updating French family law. Geneviève Delaisi de Parseval, who co-led the group, recruited from within the same pool of experts that have participated with Théry in other settings, including Martine Gross, Serge Hefez, and others. Nevertheless, according to many, these organizations do not have much impact. Absent strong professional organizations receptive of their work, and the relative weakness of think tanks, French progressives' best option is to increase their representation in state advisory commissions, which grant more access to real policymaking influence, where conservatives have dominated until recently. Yet, because appointment to such positions is both political—elected officials are responsible for nominating some members—and collegial, this long-term strategy is contingent, in part, on elections.

The Continued Influence of Conservative French Experts in State Organizations Conservative French experts have been able to access the expert field relatively easily through multiple channels. Although, like their progressive French colleagues, they did not have professionalized advocacy organizations to support them, they could count on groups affiliated with the Catholic Church as well as representation within state or quasi-state agencies and organizations that provided them with resources, contacts, and positions of power. In addition, like American conservatives, they also developed extensive—but usually private—collaborations with protest movements and religious organizations to provide them with expertise they could use to fight against gay family reforms.[25] Finally, much like French progressives, most conservatives knew each other and activated interpersonal networks to collaborate and gain direct access to lawmakers.

There were several examples of conservative academics and professionals within quasi-state organizations that act as official consultive bodies to the government, giving their voices a guaranteed audience. For instance, the government nominated Pierre Lévy-Soussan to the board of the Agence de la biomédecine, the state administrative body responsible for regulating transplants, embryology, human genetics, and procreation. Given the way gay and lesbian parenting—and particularly the question of whether it should be legally possible for a child to have two parents of the same sex—caused such controversy in French same-sex marriage debates, these bioethics councils had a prominent position. Xavier Lacroix, who was a professor of philosophy and moral theology, as well as a longtime adversary of legal recognition for gay families, had an important position in such an organization. In 2008, he was appointed by the administration of conservative French president, Nicolas Sarkozy, to the Comité consultatif national d'éthique pour les sciences de la vie et de la santé (CCNE), a state-mandated advisory board responsible for authoring nonbinding opinions on draft legislation relating to all areas of bioethics. Thanks in part to the influence of such conservative experts, the CCNE consistently advised against allowing lesbian couples—and single women—to benefit from artificial insemination or other medically assisted reproductive treatments. Moreover, as described previously, official family organizations that work with the state, especially the Union Nationale des Associations Familiales (UNAF), have collaborated with conservative law professors, such as Claire Neirinck, to help them draft their public stances on government reforms over same-sex marriage and parenting in which they express reservations.[26]

In addition to their influence within these agencies, several conservative experts also developed connections to social movement organizations, advocacy groups, and churches fighting against same-sex marriage.[27] For example, the Manif Pour Tous [Demo for All], a group created by anti-same-sex marriage activists to fight against the 2012 bill and organize massive protests, invited experts to speak out at their rallies, public debates, conferences, and demonstrations. I observed Neirinck at one such rally in February 2013 in Toulouse, where she was a guest of honor. She described to the audience of mostly wealthy Catholic families that allowing same-sex couples to marry would be dangerous for children. Several interviewees were also involved in helping the Catholic Church prepare its public interventions against the marriage bill, including statements made before lawmakers and the press. Law professor Françoise Dekeuwer-Défossez said that the Bishop's Conference of France invited her and a theologian for private hearings so that they could help them prepare their public arguments. Similarly, Xavier Lacroix, who is affiliated with the Church hierarchy, told me he works regularly with the bishops. In these exchanges of expert capital, conservative experts provide church leaders with secular information that is less likely to be disqualified in a debate structure favoring strict secularism, making them potentially more audible.

Anti-same-sex marriage experts also collaborated with each other in ad hoc interpersonal epistemic communities to share information and resources. A notable example was a small working group that psychiatrists and psychologists Pierre Lévy-Soussan, Christian Flavigny, and their colleague Maurice Berger, created to lend each other moral support—"because we get beat up a lot," Flavigny explained—and give each other ideas about their shared experiences combatting public discourse in favor of gay families. According to Flavigny, they found out about Mark Regnerus's study, which had circulated widely outside the United States thanks to intellectual networks within the Catholic Church and conservative organizations, and discussed it among themselves. They began to refer to Regnerus's research in their interviews with journalists and meetings with lawmakers. That they felt comfortable drawing on an American study in their public interventions even as they denounced so-called "gender theory" suggests that the symbolic value of U.S. intellectual "imports" depends on the degree to which they ideologically oppose them.

Conservative experts described some direct relationships to lawmakers, but unlike their pro-same-sex marriage rivals, none of them said they were close friends with them. This may reflect a reluctance on their part to talk about such relationships with me. Nevertheless, conservative politicians, who were in the minority during the Pacs and marriage debates, called conservative experts to private, party-only hearings, where they asked them for legal and intellectual arguments against the reforms. Moreover, Xavier Lacroix and the philosopher

Thibaud Collin described indirect contact with legislators that none of the progressive experts mentioned. Salvator, a Catholic publishing house, sent free copies of Collin's book, *Les lendemains du mariage gay* [The day after gay marriage], to "many lawmakers," which Collin believes brought his arguments to their attention.[28] Similarly, Lacroix explained that a friend and personal benefactor paid to have his book, *La confusion des genres* [Confusing the genders], sent to every lawmaker in both chambers of parliament. This strategy likely reinforced the notoriety and access both experts had to French lawmakers.[29]

CONCLUSION

Getting expertise into the hands of the people who want it is a complicated business. Experts who think they have information to contribute may have no idea how to bring it to the attention of the elected officials and judges they think need to hear it. Those decision-makers—and their staff who are responsible for much of this invisible, yet crucial, work—might not know who to ask to get the expertise they believe they need. The result is a certain amount of confusion and uncertainty, a gap that has important strategic implications. Indeed, parties who are interested in influencing legal outcomes or bolstering their own credibility—activist organizations, think tanks, and professional organizations, for example—have the opportunity to push their preferred expertise into the hands of decision-makers. If they can boost that information through press releases and get it to the top of the pile of reports aides will have to sift through, these groups may be more likely to reach their goals. The stakes around connecting decision-makers to experts and distributing expertise are therefore high. And, as this chapter has shown, the dynamics around this distribution have played out in distinctly different ways depending on the country, determining which groups of people have the power to shape the role of expertise more broadly in same-sex marriage debates.

Experts on both sides of the issues face nationally specific circumstances that impact how they interact with decision-makers, from differences in scale and longevity of the legal debates, to formal rules of engagement and expectations about how directly they should pursue involvement. What most distinguishes the countries is the degree to which French experts rely on personal connections in a context where most organizations are not set up to facilitate the transaction of expert capital. Some French academics and professionals may sometimes work with activist groups, providing them with information, advice, and prestige, but they generally collaborate with lawmakers directly. The world of French politics is small. So is the French academy, especially at the elite level. The tradition of people moving between the two is old and well documented.[30] Such proximity is evidently at play in this case too. For some well-connected experts, their relationships and long involvement with decision-makers have endured to the point that they themselves come to coordinate the production and distribution of expertise through their ad hoc peer networks, giving them the power to shape the information that gets into the debate and how it is understood.

Because of the limited number of political and legal outlets and opportunities in France for expertise on same-sex marriage, professional, academic, and advocacy organizations have not needed to systematize its production and distribution. Nor have they had the capacity to do so even if they thought it might be useful. In the absence of the incentive structures that buoy and drive American experts and the organizations that rely on them, their French counterparts do not benefit from the kinds of synergies that can result from sustained interaction between these two groups. It is possible that this situation may be specific to gay family debates and an artifact of the historical period I studied. Organizations, such as think tanks, may play a more significant role in the transmission of expertise for political issues where the demand for information is higher and longer lasting, such as climate change or fiscal policy. In addition, the growing deregulation and privatization of the French higher education sector as well as an interest among wealthy individuals to fund efforts to produce expertise that supports their political goals—such as the conservative Catholic billionaire Pierre-Édouard Stérin who has committed 150 million euros to establish a structure that aims to become the French equivalent of the Heritage Foundation—may signify a change in the French knowledge regime where organizations will come to matter more.[31]

Save for a few exceptions, individual academics and professionals in the United States did not describe personal ties with lawmakers. Instead, they usually entered the expert field through the intermediary of professionalized organizations that centralize their knowledge and adapted it for specific political and legal environments. The creation and growth of these relationships have been facilitated by the demand for their information generated by the size of the U.S. legal field and the outlets it creates for their expert capital.[32] These connections have created a "feedback loop" between U.S. policy outlets, organizations, and experts more generally.[33]

Indeed, the process of connecting experts to decision-makers has led to the production of scientific expertise specifically for the purpose of influencing policy debates. In other words, these organizations are not simple distributors, taking information from experts, on the one hand, and directing it toward decision-makers, on the other. Rather, whether unintentionally or not, by establishing a link between these two groups, they open a relationship of influence that flows in both directions. Indeed, these organizations translate political and legal demands into commissions for expertise that they order from independent experts or from those they employ directly. Whether they are fighting for or against same-sex marriage rights, U.S. organizations sustain this feedback loop, crystalizing political debates into organizational routines that shape the production of science over the long term. Wendy Manning's literature review for the ASA, which became a piece of academic scholarship directly triggered by court cases on same-sex marriage, is a good example.[34] The situation of same-sex marriage opponents, no longer able to determine how mainstream professional organizations respond to gay rights, is another. They have used their own think tanks, advocacy groups, and alternative conservative professional organizations to fund and facilitate the research of social scientists, such as Mark Regnerus. Even as the political circumstances change, the relationships created by these processes can endure. In France, without organizations to maintain them, these routines and connections tend to dissipate over time.

In addition to institutionalizing political and legal incentives for expertise, collaboration between organizations and experts serves other important strategic purposes. Organizations provide financial resources, infrastructure, and relationships with lawyers, elected officials and their staff, and journalists and other people who can help advance a political agenda. Because of these resources and their position at the intersection between experts and decision-makers, they can help experts shield themselves from losing credibility or sustaining reputational damage, protecting the value of their expert capital. Rather than directly exposing themselves to politics, organizations allow experts to create a perception of distance between themselves and the political field, acting as a safety buffer that preserves their aura of neutrality. At the same time, the organizations can take a share of this expert capital in the form of perceived scientific credibility and ideological neutrality that working with academic experts provides them.

Indeed, think tanks and social movement organizations that defend specific causes or promote certain positions, such as free-market capitalism or robust welfare programs, may be able to deploy expert capital to temper perceptions of those biases. This kind of ideological laundering could help them better hide the objectives of their donors or clients, allowing them to more easily achieve their political goals in a context where outright ideological stances hurt their chances. How experts maintain their legitimacy and share it with organizations and other groups that want to take advantage of it is the subject of the next chapter.

CHAPTER 6

TO HAVE AND TO HOLD

Expert Capital as a Scarce Resource

Terry Stewart put it to me like this: You want experts "whose credentials are impeccable." The chief deputy city attorney of San Francisco and celebrated LGBTQ activist was faced with a challenge. She was in the process of helping Ted Olson and David Boies put together their witnesses for the *Hollingsworth v. Perry* trial. She knew a lot of people who could fit the bill—economists, historians, sociologists, political scientists, psychologists. The list was long. But the stakes were also incredibly high. The first federal bench trial in which the judge had called for both sides to prove their arguments that same-sex couples should—or should not—be allowed to marry had huge implications. What was said before the court would enter the record, shape the judge's ruling, and ultimately end up before the Supreme Court where conservatives did not yet have a supermajority. Finally winning gay marriage was a real possibility. But losing on a national scale could set the movement back decades. There was no room for error. Only the absolute best experts should be called to testify. But who, exactly, to choose? And based on what criteria? Defining "impeccability" depends not only on the content of what the expert says and how that information answers specific legal questions, as was discussed in Chapter 3, but also on the reputation of experts themselves. In other words, the message cannot easily be separated from the messenger, and people who need experts, like Stewart, must contend with both of them. We turn our attention to that dynamic in this chapter.

Expertise is a currency that lawyers, lawmakers, journalists, and activists want to get ahold of to further their goals. Whether it be to associate scientific authority or the emotional valence of personal experience to their projects, the specific capital of experts can be exploited for many purposes. It can help social movements gain access to elite groups and make people take their claims more seriously. Reporters and editorialists frame their articles with it. Lawyers use it to attempt to convince judges who then use it in turn to justify their legal opinions. Elected officials can use it to guide their decisions—or at least claim that it has—and make their reforms seem necessary and credible. In short, expert capital is versatile and takes many forms.

But it also has limits and constraints. First, not everyone can produce expert capital. Only certain types of people can call themselves or be considered by their audiences as experts. For example, the expert capital of scientists accumulates over time. Their reputations, the quality of their academic publications, or their fame cannot be created overnight. Years, maybe even decades, are necessary to develop these traits. Second, not all forums where people might use expert capital, such as newspaper articles, public hearings, friend of the court briefs, or behind-the-scenes political dealings, value it in the same ways. Scientific rigor, for example, which matters in courts, might not get politicians to show up for hearings the way the fame of a celebrity intellectual would. In sum, what gives expert capital its value, from the kinds of people who produce it to the places where it is spent, is contingent on context.

The same conditions that make expertise valuable also make it vulnerable to attack. Winning the political and legal battle over same-sex marriage and parenting is as much about increasing the value of the expert capital on one's side as it is about diminishing that of one's adversaries. If high-quality empirical research published in peer-reviewed journals is what seems to work to convince a judge in a U.S. court who is relying in good faith on the Federal Rules of Evidence, possessing that expertise is crucial. So is criticizing the scientific accuracy of the opponents' evidence. Similarly, in places where the perception that experts must be neutral and objective for their expertise to be credible, groups will talk about all of the things they assume will undermine experts on the other side: their sexuality, their religious convictions, their involvement in activism, and their public opinions. These kinds of dynamics resemble what sociologist Steven Epstein calls "credibility struggles."[1] They consist in simultaneously protecting the value of one's expert capital while sapping that of opponents. Navigating this fraught terrain guides how experts make decisions about their involvement in these debates. Indeed, as Epstein argues, they are "keenly attuned to the potential disruptions in the social circulation of credibility" and are intent on maintaining their own.[2]

Thinking about credibility struggles within particular decision-making institutions also helps explain the tactics around expertise in same-sex marriage debates more generally. This chapter analyzes the kinds of things that make expert capital valuable and how that can be different depending on the needs and objectives of people using it. It underscores how credibility struggles play out in the United States and France and offers a close look at how accusations of bias create economies of worth that can qualify and disqualify experts for who they are and what they believe.

RENOWN, PRESTIGE, AND ACADEMIC STATUS

Experts with big reputations are among the most sought-after group of people in some contexts, especially France.[3] It just so happens that some of these experts also work in disciplines, such as anthropology and law, that give them some subject area knowledge that relates at least indirectly to gay family rights. Activists and politicians want to associate these kinds of well-known academics and public intellectuals with their projects because they expect that their celebrity and rank within French academic circles will somehow burnish their own reputations and make people take them more seriously. What makes these experts famous in the first place depends on the situation. In France, where elevated institutional status in the academy, attention from television and print journalists, and name recognition by political elites go together and reinforce one another, famed professors play an important role in same-sex marriage debates. In addition to this symbolic appeal, their connections to politicians and the media, which are likely both a cause and effect of their celebrity, make them attractive. Irène Théry, whose authorship of official government reports, close work with the Socialist Party, and professorship at the prestigious École des Hautes Études en Sciences Sociales, France's most elite institution for social science research, is a good example. Importantly, this expertise is not necessarily tied to validation in peer-reviewed journals, which, as we will see below, contrasts with the United States. When I asked Théry what kind of scholarship she does, she told me, "I don't write many articles. . . . I never submit articles to journals because I don't have the time. . . . In fact, I mainly do articles by request or book chapters by request. But mainly, I try to give priority to books." Unlike articles published in academic journals, books can earn their authors more media attention in France. Théry's publication patterns thus make her well suited to the expectations of lawmakers and activists who seek experts with renown.

One example of the attractiveness of expert capital in the form of fame comes from French gay and lesbian family organizations who have sought their public approval or collaboration in order to overcome the stigma of same-sex parenting in France. Alexandre Urwicz of the Association des Familles Homoparentales (ADFH) [Association of Gay Families] explained how he sought to enroll Irène Théry in the late 2000s and early 2010s in the activities of his organization. He was particularly interested in how being a "well-known figure" that places her "among the women recognized by the government" came with potential access to important political figures within the Socialist administration that was in power during the marriage debates, including the prime minister and minister of the family. Urwicz cited her nomination by President François Hollande to the National Order of the Legion of Honour, France's highest civil distinction. Urwicz also courted the public support of specific famous academics as he was working to coordinate an editorial in support of surrogacy—at a moment when that issue had become a wedge to derail the same-sex marriage bill—that he planned to have published in a major newspaper, ideally *Le Monde*.

His strategy had two prongs. On the one hand, he wanted the "endorsement" of the "best specialist in each of the domains" related to surrogacy, including "a philosopher, a sociologist, a judge, a psychoanalyst, and a grass-roots organization." On the other hand, this breadth of experts would be most effective if it consisted of "renowned" experts, whose fame itself he sought out. The list of people he most wanted to have sign on included Maurice Godelier—"who is, after all, a gold medalist of the French National Centre for Scientific Research [CNRS]"—and Élisabeth Badinter, whose reputation as a feminist philosopher and wife of a former beloved minister would send a strong signal. France's other— and first—gay and lesbian parenting organization, the Association des Parents et futurs parents Gays et Lesbiens (APGL), had a similar strategy about a decade and a half before the ADFH when it invited prominent social scientists to study the families of its members. When I asked the anthropologist Anne Cadoret, who was a research scientist with the prestigious CNRS, what she thought the APGL was seeking from her when she agreed to work with them, she said, "I think they were expecting a kind of legitimacy." Asked to define what she meant about those expectations, Cadoret explained, "That researchers work on them, that we talk about them, that we show what they go through. I say my last name and I say my job title. That alone gives them something else." This "something else" is precisely the kind of expert capital that only famous academic experts provide.

In this case, it is distinct from, but also complementary to, the scientific quality of their research.

Several French experts who have worked in support of gay family rights for the last few decades explained that in the early years of the gay family debates in the 1990s, efforts were made to try to convince one of their most famous colleagues to take a public stand: Claude Lévi-Strauss. The story was told to me by at least three interviewees about the efforts of the sociologist Éric Fassin, who also corroborated the account and wrote about it in a collective volume in the years following the Pacte civil de solidarité (Pacs) debates.[4] At the height of those debates, Fassin was coordinating with other academics and gay rights activists to counter expertise from those working to thwart the bill. Some prominent anthropologists and sociologists, including Françoise Héritier and Irène Théry, were arguing that gay and lesbian parenting should not be legalized, although they would both change their stances in the 2000s. Structural anthropology, they said, demonstrated conclusively that different-gender parenting structures were fundamental, universal human rules that civil law must respect. How can someone discredit that kind of argument?

Fassin thought going to the source would be the best option. He wrote a letter to Lévi-Strauss, the world-famous French anthropologist and founder of structural anthropology, who was ninety-one at the time. He had not spoken out during the Pacs debates despite how frequently people were using his theories to justify antigay family stances. Fassin felt Lévi-Strauss would probably agree that "you don't subscribe to this partisan use of anthropology, which seems to me to distort the scientific project presented in your books." In his solicitation letter, Fassin encouraged Lévi-Strauss to say something. "A sentence from you today would count for a lot," he wrote. Authorizing him to make his response public, Lévi-Strauss responded to Fassin's letter, writing "the range of human cultures is so wide, so varied (and so easy to manipulate) that it's easy to find arguments to support any claim." Casting doubt on how his acolytes were using anthropology, he went on to argue that experts should not substitute themselves for the democratic process. He wrote, "societal choices do not belong to the *savant* as such, but—and he himself is one—to the citizen."[5] Though perhaps not as attention-grabbing as a press conference or newspaper editorial, this open letter gave Fassin and his allies the opportunity to attempt to prevent their opponents from claiming Lévi-Strauss's fame and prestige for their own ends.

French organizations working against allowing same-sex couples to marry and raise children also sought out the support of well-known experts. One example is how the Bishop's Conference of France invited a group of scholars to help them elaborate their public responses to the marriage bill, such as judicial hearings and press interviews. Among those people invited, which included a list of lawyers, bioethicists, and psychoanalysts, was law professor Françoise Dekeuwer-Défossez. Her input was not just important because it allowed the bishops to understand the complex legal dimensions of family law, including, as she explained, the concepts of "*filiation*, the presumption of paternity, etc. [which] are far from obvious when you're not a lawyer." Indeed, her involvement was also beneficial for their campaign because the law professor was well-known among high-ranking politicians, having already authored an official report on the state of the family for the Socialist administration in the 1990s and for her nomination by the government to the Haut Conseil de la Famille [High Council of the Family], a quasi-governmental body created after World War II to provide the state with nonbinding opinions on demographic and family policy.[6] Moreover, her secular credentials and specialized legalized knowledge gave the Catholic Church the cover they needed to be audible in a cultural context where overtly religious arguments can be discrediting.

Lawmakers at the Assemblée Nationale and the Sénat were just as interested as other groups in having the same kinds of academic luminaries, and in some cases the same list of people, attend their hearings. Erwann Binet, the *rapporteur* on the marriage bill who organized the hearings for the Judiciary Committee at the Assemblée Nationale, strove to have the best-known anthropologists, sociologists, philosophers, and psychoanalysts speak in favor of the law because opponents of the legislation, including the representatives of the Catholic Church, were claiming the mantle of those disciplines to counter him and pro-marriage advocates. In the words of Anne Cadoret, who was also invited to the hearings, Binet was especially interested in the "*grands noms* [the big names]." Indeed, the list of experts speaking in support of the bill was impressive, with people who were both at the top of French academic hierarchies and also household names among educated French elites. It included Maurice Godelier, Françoise Héritier, Irène Théry, and, as Cadoret described him, "the great media shrink of the day," Serge Héfez. In addition to their specialized knowledge about parenting and relationships, each of these experts contributed the aura of their reputations in support of the legislation.

In the United States, although fame did not seem to matter to people soliciting experts as much as it did to those in France, probably because the phenomenon of celebrity intellectuals is rarer there, institutional prestige and academic accolades did. For Mary Bonauto, the civil rights project director of GLBTQ Legal Advocates and Defenders (GLAD), who helped coordinate amicus briefs on behalf of gay and lesbian litigants in major federal trials on same-sex marriage, having authors from the most prestigious universities and their professional associations was important. I discussed this strategy with the historian Nancy Cott, who has taught at both Harvard and Yale. Cott helped author several amicus briefs and was called as an expert witness to testify in *Perry v. Schwarzenegger*. When Cott was working on a brief for *U.S. v. Windsor* in support of the respondents who were arguing that the Defense of Marriage Act was unconstitutional, Bonauto explained to her that the endorsement of an important organization would be helpful. Cott worked with other historians, including George Chauncey, a pioneer in gay history who also testified as an expert witness, to enroll the American Historical Association for the brief.[7] Chauncey also strove to gain the signatures of the Organization of American Historians and the American Studies Association for another brief for *Hollingsworth v. Perry*.[8] These professional organizations lent their respectable institutional reputations to the historical and legal arguments in the briefs, perhaps making them more credible than they might otherwise have been if only signed in the name of individual historians.

The elite reputations of individual experts in the United States were nevertheless a crucial element that led to decisions about which kinds of expert witnesses to call to the stand in court cases. People with positions at the most well-known academic institutions were of particular interest. Michael Rosenfeld, a sociologist at Stanford University who testified in *Deboer v. Snyder*, described his perception of how prestige played an important role in the strategy of expert testimony. When I asked him how status might have been part of the calculus of the attorneys arguing in favor of same-sex marriage and parenting, he responded:

> I think being a professor at Stanford University was certainly an element
> of status that affected my credibility. . . . Because Stanford is a high-status
> institution . . . I think that there was definitely credibility associated with
> that, and, . . . while the defense had professors from Brigham Young . . .
> and Simon Fraser, . . . which are all good schools, and it's . . . possible to do

world-class research from any of those places, I think it's probably true that there's an advantage to being from, you know, the famous elite institution.

In this reflection on his position, Rosenfeld articulates a clear distinction between scholarship and renown, revealing how the economy of prestige adds to the value of expert capital in the contest between opposing sides.

Terry Stewart described how Olson and Boies used the same logic when considering which economists to have testify on their behalf. She remembered that "David Boies . . . was worried, that while Lee Badgett [an economist at the University of Massachusetts Amherst] was substantively good, that we needed some really high-powered Harvard type to testify who would have, like, you know, the gold standard credentials." Although a Harvard economist was deposed, he ultimately did not testify because the opposing side withdrew its economic experts, making the need for a high-status expert less important. He would have been "the icing on the cake," but Stewart convinced Boies that Badgett's testimony was more germane to the content of the case. This arbitration between substantive knowledge and reputation makes clear that these attorneys understand expertise as multifaceted. Renown, prestige, and status are among its many values. But their worth depends on the circumstances and is often not sufficient. Other kinds of expert capital must come into play.

EMPIRICAL KNOWLEDGE IN THE UNITED STATES

Scientific experts who conduct peer-reviewed research in disciplines related to same-sex marriage and parenting, from economics and psychology to sociology and demography, are uniquely situated to provide a type of expert capital that matters in places where the quality of evidence is judged according to clear norms and written rules. Chapter 3 described how courts in the United States, because of these institutional logics, increase the relevance of such expertise, leading advocates on both sides to invest in acquiring it. At the same time, these pressures and the strategic decisions lawyers make about expertise as well as the way judges read the evidence presented to them can sometimes distort the science by flattening nuance or driving research agendas. Regardless of these side effects, those who produce and wield such expertise understand it as a coveted and limited resource.

"My sense is that social sciences are a really important commodity in our world, particularly in the United States. And the ability to say, hey, you know what? Social scientists agree with me is really, really—it appears to be really, really valuable." In this phrase, William Duncan, a former visiting professor at Brigham Young University and executive director of the Utah-based Marriage Law Foundation, which advocates against same-sex marriage and parenting, articulates a widely shared view. Being in the position to realistically claim that "social scientists agree with me" is a highly sought after resource but one that is difficult to mine.

Scientific experts are an autonomous group whose voices are uniquely effective at giving one's arguments the credibility they need to win a contentious judicial battle. Yet the characteristics that give their expertise its special value also make it especially challenging and complicated to acquire. Because these scientific experts are autonomous—or at least there must be a sincere impression that they are—advocates cannot directly command the production of their expertise. If they do, or if scientific experts are seen as working to reach explicitly political ends, they run the serious risk of tainting their expertise and damaging its value. Because of these constraints, people who work outside of the academy in activist organizations cannot produce expertise of the same value, even when it might use some of the same language and codes common in academic research. Duncan explained how Ryan Anderson, who has a PhD in political philosophy and was a research fellow at the conservative U.S. think tank, the Heritage Foundation, in the late 2010s, could not give his side the value of scientific expertise. Anderson's claims that same-sex marriage should be banned because it harms children could easily be brushed aside. "If Ryan Anderson feels one way, that's kind of Ryan's issue . . . but if a social scientist is saying, 'hey, it's best for children to be in this setting' and other people can point and say, look, I've got empirical research that supports me, that's a whole different thing in our world," Duncan explained. Without empirical social science, the information advocates give to decision-makers, especially in courts, will be disregarded at best or undermine their case at worst.

The reputational purity of scientific expertise, which gives it its value in these policy debates, must respond to the logics of the scientific field, especially the validation of peer review, which advocates cannot control. Furthermore, conducting research takes resources to produce and time for the literature to accumulate enough so that credible conclusions can be drawn about what "scientists say." Those conclusions cannot be dictated from the outset in a good faith scientific process. Terry Stewart made this point clear when she explained that "you can't create something that isn't legitimate. . . . You've got to do peer-reviewed studies that have some legitimacy, and if you do them, it's not going to prove what they want to say."

Academic and leadership staff at the Williams Institute on Sexual Orientation and Gender Identity Law and Public Policy, which is affiliated with the UCLA School of Law, embrace this commitment to empirically rigorous research, convinced of its unique value for policy purposes. That commitment requires transparency and willingness to publish the results of their research, which focuses on a variety of issues related to sexual orientation and gender identity, regardless of where the data lead. That can create tensions with LGBTQ advocacy organizations who rely on their research. Nan Hunter, a pioneering professor of gay rights law who has been involved for decades in these issues, was the legal scholarship director at the Williams Institute. She explained the importance of maintaining scientific autonomy:

> We have to be willing to say the things that our allies don't like if that's what we find. . . . We have to not skew the press release summaries of the work and all the different levels of ways that you're under pressure to highlight the findings that are consistent with the . . . messaging strategy, even if they're not terribly scientifically interesting, and downplay findings that are inconsistent with the messaging strategy, even if they're the most interesting findings in a particular . . . study. Those pressures are just enormous.

Resisting those pressures to color the research is key to protecting their expert capital. Lee Badgett, who in addition to being an economics professor at the University of Massachusetts Amherst is a distinguished scholar at the Williams Institute, emphasized the explicit policy at the Williams Institute to adhere to the standards of science and publish what the data show, even if it does not conform to what some LGBTQ activist groups think is best for their strategies. When Gary Gates, one of the leading researchers of LGBTQ demography in the United States and affiliated with the Williams Institute, published findings showing that the LGBTQ population was lower than earlier estimates, activists were worried that it would damage their message.[9] The reactions, according to Badgett, were sharp:

There are people who would really like us to say something else, and so we say what we say, and then they call us up and they're angry . . . get other people who they think we will listen to call us up, and we say the same thing to everybody. This is what we found. . . . It's not the end of the world if . . . there aren't as many gay people as you think. . . . But this is what we have to do. . . . The best way that we know of to talk about this issue, the data that we have on it.

This commitment to publishing their research regardless of how it could be interpreted acts as a quality guarantee and boosts the credibility of their expertise. Attorneys who need that expertise for their arguments recognize the value of that commitment. Terry Stewart explained what it meant for her: "These are people who have done really careful research. Not all of it always comes out good for us. You know? I don't like all the results. But . . . they take the demographic data, and they crunch it, and then sometimes they've made mistakes and they go back and fix it and even if it works the other way." In fact, some of the Williams Institute scholars find confirmation in the value of their process when their research is mobilized by their opponents. Hunter described how anti-marriage advocates cited some of their studies in their amicus briefs, and for her, "it's like a marker that you've . . . totally, you know, aced it in terms of this because the other side is acknowledging your validity." Because their scholarship is cited by organizations on both sides, it is more difficult to attack as biased—though of course that still happens—and could be more influential in litigation.

The researchers I interviewed were fully aware of these stakes around their research in the courts and its capacity to persuade judges. Gary Gates, who testified in *Deboer v. Snyder*, understood how the logic of the trial created structural advantages for empirical knowledge. He explained his view of the situation, saying, "[In a court, you] are under oath and you are asked questions by the other side . . . and because courts are adjudicating the science, they evaluate the data and can say what is worthwhile or not." To support their argument that the state of Michigan had a constitutionally valid justification for banning marriage and adoption by same-sex couples, opponents had to try to generate scientific expertise, which meant providing publications from respected peer-reviewed journals. The University of Texas sociologist, Mark Regnerus, did precisely that when he published his article in *Social Science Research*.[10] The results of his study, funded by the conservative think tank, the Witherspoon Institute, claimed to show that children raised by same-sex couples lag behind on psychological measures when compared to children raised by a married man and woman who are their bio-logical parents. The study was presumably carried out with the explicit aim of influencing contemporaneous legal and political debates on same-sex parenting. Upon publication, it immediately began appearing in amicus briefs, testimony, editorials, newsletters, and many other formats by antigay organizations in the United States and beyond. As described in previous chapters, members of the sociological community reacted negatively to its promotion as "proof" that same-sex parenting is harmful to children. Through response articles in the journal, open letters, and other public communications, a group of renowned family sociologists and the American Sociological Association criticized the method-ology, the publication process, and the researcher's reputation.[11] In court, the arguments revolved around the sheer volume of studies that ran counter to Reg-nerus's article and its poor scientific quality.

In the end, the Michigan court ruled to repeal the state's ban on marriage and adoption. The judge, Bernard Friedman, insisted in his reasoning that the scien-tific consensus was in favor of advocates of same-sex parenting. He also described the Regnerus study as "junk science," which, according to several expert wit-nesses and lawyers I interviewed, rendered the study and any future testimony by Regnerus essentially unusable because it fully delegitimated its scientific worthi-ness.[12] In an institution where the value of expert capital is translated primarily as empirical rigor, Friedman's assessment bankrupted him. Leslie Cooper, the deputy director of the American Civil Liberties Union (ACLU) LGBT and HIV Project, argued that once a judge's opinion clearly states an expert's claims are unfounded, it can negatively impact their credibility in the courts going forward.

These clear, trenchant positions on research in a major court decision gave comfort to experts supporting the rights of same-sex families. Gary Gates, who exemplifies this perspective, shared his impression of how the trial format ele-vated scientific expertise, exposing the weaknesses of the other side's expertise:

It was a remarkable defense of both how social science thinks about issues, what consensus in social science means. So, consensus doesn't mean . . . every single social scientist. . . . It doesn't mean there aren't . . . occasional contrar-ian viewpoints out there. But it means there's this broad understanding. The opposing side had literally two and half papers. They had the Regnerus paper, they had the Allen paper, and they had that two and a half page commentary to Rosenfeld. And I think [the case] exposed that as well.

The trial made clear that opponents to same-sex marriage had no substantial scientific proof to support their claims—much less a volume of research that could undermine the notion of a scientific consensus—that children raised by same-sex couples fare less well than their peers raised by different-sex couples. Believing that the science vindicated them in a decision-making forum that favors the use of research-based arguments, experts like Gates and the organizations that support them were committed to producing even more research. It also entrenched the idea that supporters of gay family rights should further invest in scientific expertise to discredit the studies mobilized by their opponents.

CREDIBILITY STRUGGLES OVER SCIENTIFIC EXPERTISE IN FRANCE

French lawmakers who organize hearings want the right mix of people who will lend credibility to their process. As chapter 3 explained, they weigh a variety of factors—fame, scientific credentials, political stances—when deciding who to invite and why. Focusing on a particular subset of those experts, social scientists studying same-sex families, gives a picture of how credibility struggles over expert capital can play out in French legislatures, where the institutional logics emphasize political calculations and do not necessarily accord a special status for scientifically credible expertise. Lawmakers primarily sought them out because their research had gotten press attention or they were already famous. Their expert capital, therefore, was a minimum level of name recognition and, in some cases, knowledge validated through peer review. However, many of these experts had already expressed a public stance that was favorable to legalizing same-sex marriage and adoption. This posed a serious problem for the political calculus of the *rapporteurs* organizing hearings. To maintain the idea that the lawmakers were hearing all sides, these social scientists who conduct empirical research on same-sex couples needed to be balanced out with credentialed experts who opposed same-sex family rights. The legitimacy of these opponents, from the perspective of the lawmakers, rested not on the validity of their research, much of which was not empirical or peer reviewed, but on their capacity to play a political part. The value of their expertise came from their opposition to the reform. In this situation, the meaning of scientific expertise was more ambiguous than in the U.S. courts, leaving academic experts, advocates, and lawmakers without bright lines they could use to make decisions about how to produce and accumulate expert capital.

Treating the credibility of experts primarily through a political lens gives the public a distorted representation of the state of the science on the outcomes of children raised by same-sex couples, a question that was at the heart of French—and American—debates over LGBTQ family law. Several cultural and institutional norms that informed the thinking of the *rapporteurs* and the experts themselves created these distortions. These included the dominant language of the international research, English, and the countries of origin of much of the literature, specifically North America, the United Kingdom, and the Netherlands. I asked French social scientists working on same-sex parenting why they thought little empirical research was brought to bear on French legislative debates leading up to the passage of the marriage and adoption bill in 2012. Jérôme Courduriès, an anthropologist working on gay families who was interviewed by the *rapporteuse* Marie Françoise Clergeau for the Committee on Cultural, Family, and Social Affairs, observed that, "in France, few people work on the topic and the Anglo-American studies haven't been translated, for the most part. I have the impression that these studies are not used enough. Someone should write a digest of these studies and make it available to journalists who could then use those arguments." As was discussed in chapter 4, French scholars working on gay and lesbian couples and families have faced significant barriers to carrying out their research, leading to a gap between French scholarship on childhood outcomes compared to that in other contexts.[13] In addition to this gap in output, the language barrier and the lack of journalistic awareness about international research meant that French legislators and the public had an incomplete picture of the field of research on same-sex parenting.

Beyond the problem of translation, however, French family scholars I interviewed pointed out that the British and American origin of many of the studies examining childhood outcomes elicited a particular disdain on the part of some other French researchers and politicians, even among some allies. Sociologist Martine Gross, who has been called to provide testimony to various French institutions in the last two decades, explained: "Everything that comes from the United States faces a kind of anti-Americanism." Similarly, Courduriès explained that some French mental health professionals spread the idea that American-produced research is incompatible in the French context, as if the results of American studies could not be applied in France. He said, "Intellectuals against [the legal recognition of same-sex couples to adopt or access donor insemination] criticize these studies, saying they are biased, too few, and not conducted in France. As if American and French children were so different from each other."

This cultural distrust is compounded by disciplinary differences between France and the United States, which increases resistance to foreign-produced studies. Much of the literature on childhood well-being uses methodologies and theories from developmental psychology, an approach that was still relatively marginal in the psychology departments of French universities. Gross explained, "In France only clinical psychologists and psychoanalysts have legitimacy. Developmental psychology, people in France don't know about it . . . and because they don't know it, they criticize it." The few French researchers who used tools from developmental psychology to study gay and lesbian families, such as Olivier Vecho, who defended his dissertation in psychology in 2005, or Stéphane Nadaud, who defended a psychiatry dissertation in 2000, faced strong critiques because of their methods.

In our interview, Nadaud explained that before beginning his research, he had intended to use psychoanalytic concepts but that the new director of his program—an American who had trained in the United States—required students to use empirical methods. According to Nadaud, the reaction by the majority of the French psychiatry community to his research was negative. Gross explained that the use of questionnaires to query parents about their children's well-being, such as the Child Behavior Checklist, which is common in developmental psychology, is characterized by many French psychoanalysts as suspicious and unreliable, despite "all kinds of validation by the scientific community to eliminate biases." Describing the psychoanalysts that denounced Stephane Nadaud's research, Gross said, "[Critics argue that] gay parents manipulate their children to prove that they are not harmful as parents, to show that their children are fine. . . . It's: either, 'the children are fine' because you are manipulating them, or 'the children are doing poorly,' just like we told you they would." The lack of familiarity with developmental psychology and distrust of "foreign" methodologies gave critics of gay parenting an opportunity to discount research produced abroad as well as the little empirical research that was produced in France. Legislative debates without the structured opportunity for cross-examination leave experts to duel things out on their own in the hearing room and in the media.

The mental health professionals who provided expertise against same-sex parenting insisted on the idea that American research on childhood outcomes is generally incompatible in France. Christian Flavigny, a psychoanalyst and child psychiatrist at the Hôpital de la Pitié-Salpêtrière in Paris and who regularly provides testimony to French lawmakers, explained that American research on gay parenting does not apply to France. He said, "We don't cite [American studies] because we have a way of thinking about these issues that is quite different from the American way. That is to say, we, we have the idea of '*filiation*,' which, I think, does not exist in the United States. The American family functions differently and the society functions differently." To Flavigny, "*filiation*" is the idea that healthy child-parent relationships are strictly defined in two ways. First, a filial tie is one that links a parent to their biological offspring. Second, filiation is necessarily founded on a male-female dyad in which sex difference is absolutely crucial. Thus, true filiation is both heterosexual and based on biological relatedness. This extends to adoption.

According to this logic, heterosexual couples are permitted to adopt because their children can credibly believe that there is a true filial tie between them. In other words, adopted children need to believe that their adoptive parents could have conceived them. Because children with two mothers or two fathers do not have that option, they will suffer serious psychological trauma. For Flavigny and others who share this perspective, family in the United States is somehow defined more by childrearing, rather than the primacy of biological relatedness, or least the appearance of it. From his point of view, studies produced in the United States do not apply in France because the two systems are fundamentally different and thus cannot be used to make decisions for French law. Flavigny was, however, not hostile to all American empirical research, despite the incompatibilities he claimed disqualified their use in France. He told me that the study by Regnerus, unlike other research, "is the first serious study on these questions carried out in the United States." Flavigny, who is not constrained by the U.S. court's disqualification of the Regnerus study, can feel free to cite it as the one exceptional example of American research that he would bring to the hearing table in France. It also just so happens that that study aligns with his ideological positions.

Flavigny's circle of colleagues who also oppose same-sex parenting construct a similar symbolic boundary between foreign research and the French context. Pierre Lévy-Soussan, a psychoanalyst, child psychiatrist specializing in adoption, and professor at the University Paris-Diderot, who is also a frequent expert witness, shared a distrust of American research with Flavigny. He saw the literature as biased and activist. In our interview, he said that the American context, which is characterized by a "real combat" for gay rights, disqualifies research produced there. "The whole history of homosexuality in the United States has meant that there has been a real . . . fight for identity," he said. According to Lévy-Soussan, the mobilization around gay rights in the United States led to the production of activist and biased "social [and] psychological discourse around the homosexual that is extremely identity-based, even for absurd things [such as the right to adoption]." From this perspective, research on gay and lesbian parenting is the result of activist projects coming from the gay movement that therefore have no real scientific basis for informing political debate. Moreover, like Flavigny, Lévy-Soussan argues that American research is unable to deal with the question of *filiation*, which he sees as a uniquely French form of family structure. He explained:

> I've stuffed myself with [those studies] too, because after talking to Martine Gross from the APGL, I said to myself: I'm going to delve into this famous study by Golombok, Tasker et al., telling us that everything's fine, the famous "everything's fine." . . . The question was about *éducation* [childrearing]. Fortunately, sexuality has nothing to do with *éducation*. I can understand why these hyper-activist studies were carried out, and even why they distorted them, etc., because the question asked was a discriminatory one, i.e., because of your homosexuality, you can't take in this child after your divorce. What's that got to do with anything? So, in response to a poorly posed question, they carried out some extremely questionable studies. Then, the problem is that these studies, which were designed to answer a question about childrearing, they used them to make conclusions about *filiation*. But they have nothing to do with *filiation*. For us, a child raised by two women or two men has nothing to do with childrearing. It's very different from a law that says "you have two dads or two moms."

From Lévy-Soussan's point of view, American studies suffer from two major flaws that make them incompatible in France. First, they are primarily the result of activism and politically motivated discourse that makes them particularly biased and unscientific. Second, they only deal with childrearing, rather than the more fundamental question, from his perspective, about the unique legal definition of parenthood, which, he argues, must be based in *filiation*. For Lévy-Soussan, these studies—he was referring in particular to pioneering work by the British psychologists Susan Golombok, Fiona Takser, and their colleagues—may suggest that children can be raised by two people of the same sex, but they cannot inform French legislators about the consequences of legally permitting two men or two women to each be considered the parents of a child.[14] From this perspective, leaving aside the accusations of bias, the empirical quality of such research is irrelevant because it is fundamentally incompatible with French legal conceptions of the family.

As described above, the small quantity of French-produced studies on same-sex parenting and the resistance from experts like Flavigny and Lévy-Soussan have an impact on how French lawmakers draw on scientific expertise when putting together legal reforms addressing gay and lesbian family rights. Erwann Binet, in particular, who organized the Judiciary Committee hearings at the Assemblée Nationale, had very clear ideas about what qualified or disqualified scientific expertise. The empirical rigor of their testimony did not seem to be his first priority. His options, it seemed, were limited. He said, "The problem is that on this question of gay marriage . . . I think that it's a question that must be a little different in the United States because it's an older question for you." From his perspective, the French hearings were constrained by the relative newness of French research on gay parenting. The pool of potential experts who had actually published in peer-reviewed journals was relatively small. And from within this pool, Binet said he was unable to find experts from across the ideological spectrum.

His primary concern was putting together a panel of social scientists and other scholars that would represent opinions both for and against his party's bill. But, just as was the case for attorneys fighting against same-sex marriage in U.S. courts, Binet found that qualified anti-marriage social scientists were hard to come by. Among the experts, he was aware that "a few sociologists and especially child psychiatrists had written a few articles, but very few." Beyond those exceptions, the rest of the experts he considered were not ideal. Despite the quality of their empirical research, their publicly stated opinions made them problematic choices to invite to the hearing. Not unlike French anti-marriage experts themselves, Binet saw French research on gay and lesbian families as biased:

> Initially, when you work on the subject in France, on gay marriage, you're faced with studies, expert reports, people who are activists and who are all in favor of gay marriage. In November [2012], when the text was presented,

all I knew at the time was that 90 percent of people were in favor of the text: jurists, sociologists, psychologists, etc., who had spoken out in favor of the text, who had worked on the subject. In other words, in France, this subject only interested people who were in favor of it. The sociologists had done studies on the subject because they were in favor of gay marriage, because they were perhaps homosexuals themselves, or because they had a favorable a priori view of the issue.

For the *rapporteur*, the overwhelming support for same-sex marriage from the community of scientists who study gay families was a problem.

Faced with the political imperative to create balanced hearings, rather than, say, rally as much high-quality scientific expertise as he could find to support his bill, the specialized knowledge of potential French experts was largely overshadowed by their stances on same-sex marriage and their own sexual orientations. Moreover, Binet appeared to limit his assessment to the French field. He did not take into consideration the overwhelmingly favorable public stances or sexual orientations of researchers outside of France. As a result, he had the view that research produced in other contexts was perhaps less biased than in France. But, given the lack of familiarity with foreign research and the way opponents of these studies delegitimized them as incompatible in France, Binet did not expand the scope of experts called to testify before the committee to those where much of the literature was from, specifically North America, the United Kingdom, the Netherlands, or Scandinavia. This suggests that local expertise, produced in France, was more valuable than that from abroad in a political institution where scientific experts are weighed relative to one another according to a political calculation. To be clear, Binet's sensitivity to the ideologies, sexualities, and political opinions of experts is not unique to France. Indeed, attention to the lives and personal views of experts is a thread that underlines the debates in both countries and something to which we now turn.

TAINTED: NEGOTIATING BIAS AND NEUTRALITY

The credibility struggles around scientific expertise in the United States and France, in which opponents criticize the worthiness of experts fighting against them, is illustrative of a general phenomenon that characterizes the role of experts on both sides of the Atlantic. Attempting to discredit experts because of who they are is a hallmark of same-sex marriage debates—and certainly other contentious political debates as well. It is perhaps one of their most consistent features. On a general level, these credibility struggles follow a simple logic: Experts and their allies on one side argue that the expert capital of their opponents is valueless because the person who produced it has some conflict of interest. Their expertise is tainted or, as sociologist Steven Epstein and historian Michelle Murphy have respectively called it, "impure" or "political."[15]

The causes of this alleged contamination can take many forms. In debates over gay family rights, it usually involves accusations of activism and/or bias because of one's perceived (homo)sexuality, religious convictions, or party affiliations. People engage in these delegitimatizing tactics across contexts and institutional spaces, sometimes tailoring their strategies for the setting or the type of expertise they aim to undermine. When the value of an opponent's expert capital comes from their claiming that the weight of scientific evidence supports their argument, attacking the legitimacy of that evidence by accusing the scientists who produced it of having a personal stake in their research is common.

All of the elite experts I interviewed were keenly aware that everyone's reputations matter. They had spent time thinking about how their choices, opinions, and personal lives, as well as those of their peers, would impact their positions in these debates. Indeed, some were reluctant to let me interview them precisely because they feared that what I would write in this book could be used against them in the future. In contrast, among the few lay experts I interviewed, whose invitation to speak before decision-makers is based on their personal experience, these concerns were less important.

Can scientific experts have strong feelings about the laws they are asked to comment on? If they do, can they express those opinions and take steps to try and bring about their preferred outcomes? In other words, to what degree is being an expert compatible, or not, with activism, or at least the perception of activism? These were the kinds of questions American and French experts were confronted with regularly and to which they often did not have clearcut answers. The French lawmaker, Erwann Binet, was not incorrect in his idea that most academics who study families, childhood well-being, and other questions related to same-sex marriage and parenting care about these issues in some way. In fact, I asked interviewees about whether they thought same-sex couples should be allowed to marry and raise children. All of them had answers to the question one way or another, and few believed that other experts had no opinion either. William Duncan, who has long been involved in promoting "traditional families," provided a typical response when he said, "I think almost everybody involved—and this is one of the slight challenges of the issue—. . . has some degree of interest in the outcome." Yet despite their feelings, most experts were reluctant to consider themselves as activists, despite their direct implication in political action. Instead, they had carefully formulated views about what being an expert entailed and integrated the idea that they needed to maintain some kind of distance from "politics," or least the perception of it.

Accusations of activism can damage the reputations of experts whose value in the debates derives from the perception that they are neutral, independent, and detached from politics. Experts understand the threat these accusations pose. Those who took the stand in U.S. courts were directly exposed to these critiques because attorneys on either side used this tactic explicitly. For example, Nancy Cott, who testified that the legal and cultural meanings of marriage in the United States had changed over time, and which attorneys defending the legalization of same-sex marriage were using to counter the idea that marriage was natural and unchanging, was grilled on her political and personal opinions. "They were, first of all, basically trying to undermine my credibility as a neutral expert. . . . They wanted to paint me as an advocate and try to undermine my historical credibility that way," she remembered. Lynn Wardle, a law professor at Brigham Young University who has long been involved in coordinating movements to thwart gay family rights, explained how academic experts need to be careful about the visibility of the relationships they have with social movement organizations. "Activist work, it's about the alliances and the people that are surrounding and promoting and putting you forward, and sometimes that brings a lot of negative baggage that impacts the credibility of your academic work," he said.

And indeed, involvement in actively organizing political campaigns can plainly disqualify an expert. Jennifer Roback Morse, a formerly tenured economics professor and founder of the conservative religious think tank, the Ruth Institute, explained the vetting process she underwent as a potential expert witness testifying against same-sex marriage in *Perry v. Schwarzenneger*: "The lawyers decided that because I had been a Prop 8 campaign spokesman that I was tainted and that the other side would make so much hay about that that I would be completely discredited and would fall apart on the stand." For some, the activist label is so potentially toxic that they asked to speak off the record when we got to this portion of the interview. One U.S. social scientist working at a major university who had been involved as an expert for decades explained that they did not want to be identified on this point. Years of attempts to discredit their expertise mobilized to support LGBTQ rights taught them to be cautious:

> I was being labeled an activist and . . . I don't consider myself an activist because I think an activist's first priority is to the cause and everything else is, you know, secondary to that and for me the primary value is what we can do and what can we say based on empirical data and as a it turns out usually what we can say based on empirical data . . . it's actually quite consistent with what the activists would like, not completely in all cases but . . . it tends to refute all of these sole stereotypes. So . . . I like to think of myself as a scientist. I certainly . . . have been involved in advocacy efforts in that I have . . . testified . . . on a particular side in legal cases or before congress or . . . other sorts of settings. The distinction I would make between what I do and what an activist does is that really that thing about needing . . . to be true to the data at least as well as I understand it.

This expert's commitment to their understanding of themselves as a scientist who follows the data was echoed by many others. These interviewees drew clear lines between their activities and those of activists, which they described as leading political campaigns and engaging in movement organizing.

They saw their work as distinct and, sometimes, complementary. Lee Badgett, for example, argued that "it is possible to be an activist and to be a very good academic, but it just so happens in my case that I'm much more of an academic than I am an activist." Characterizing their work as fundamentally distinct from activism helped them justify their unique—and precarious—position in a contentious political setting. From the perspective of Terry Stewart, maintaining these boundaries was key to the success of the experts who testified on behalf of same-sex marriage:

> You know, what the other side was going to try to do—and this is what I would've done if I were in their shoes—is you try to show that they're biased . . . and that their research has been skewed by their bias, and that they haven't looked at the other side of the issue. They weren't very effective in doing that because our experts were both well-prepared for it and because,

frankly, I think they're all more committed to science than they are to an
outcome, even though they care about the outcome.

Any evidence that an expert was under the influence of unscientific forces or
had a stronger commitment to the political goal than to faithfully communi-
cating the scientific research—albeit through the unequivocal language of the
courts—was exploited as a potential weakness. Experts whose self-understanding
and public behavior were as removed from activism as possible were more likely
to survive accusations of contamination.

Indeed, independence from outside influence was often a key component to
many experts' self-conceptions. They upheld a separateness from political action
from which they could strategically engage with the political field without getting
so involved that it would undermine their credibility. French respondents who
made these distinctions used a particular rhetoric, rejecting the label "*militant*
[activist]" but sometimes calling themselves "*engagé* [committed]," an adjective
that signified a desire to impact the political process within the confines of their
roles as academics or intellectuals, similar to the way some U.S. respondents were
willing to call themselves advocates but not activists.

Many also made clear that to maintain their independence, they avoided all
formal affiliations with *associations* [activist organizations]. The philosopher Élisabeth Badinter's perspective was common. When I asked if she had ever supported organizations defending gay family rights, she answered, "No, and I'll tell
you what, I think it was more politically astute. Precisely so that I don't seem
to be the voice of an association, but to express my opinion, well that gave me
more independence, so I could be heard better." For their voices to be taken
seriously, these experts made clear that they were not speaking on behalf of an
interested group. In French legislatures, where the fame of experts is especially
important, Badinter aimed to speak "for herself," emphasizing her persona. This
personalization makes sense in a context where renowned experts are mobilized
for who they are. In addition, the power of reputation may be enough for certain
especially well-known French experts to protect against accusations of political
contamination because of their personal relationships with politicians and political parties.

Experts intervening in U.S. courts, where scientific evidence is valuable, also
insisted on their distance from politics. But unlike famous French intellectuals, such as Badinter, these experts fashioned themselves as spokespeople of the

research and not necessarily as speaking for themselves. Michael Rosenfeld, the social demographer at Stanford, for example, spoke about how his autonomy made his testimony audible to the court: "I mean, my work was just, you know, paid for out of my own time. I didn't have any—I wasn't answering to anybody, I felt like that also made me an especially strong potential advocate for social science." In both countries, such elite experts were invested in portraying themselves as uncorrupted from the influence—financial, political, or otherwise—of groups outside their peer community.

STRAIGHTS SAY IT BEST: HOMOSEXUAL DISQUALIFICATION

Among the kinds of accusations of conflict of interest that could constitute a particular liability for experts in these debates is their real or supposed homosexuality. According to this logic, because of their presumed "personal attachment" to the legal question, they cannot provide credible expertise to decision-makers. This attack, generally leveled by activists or experts fighting against same-sex marriage, explicitly posits that all information, whether validated by peer review or not, is inherently untrustworthy because gay, lesbian, or bisexual experts have a vested interest in the outcomes of their research. They are, in short, fabricating dubious science in order to help a cause they stand to benefit from. Moreover, even as they claim that same-sex marriage risks destroying the traditional family, these groups do not argue that straight experts are also personally impacted by the reform, despite the fact that their own arguments imply as much. To be clear, allegations of disqualification because of intimate connection to the issues—because of an expert's race, class, gender, or ethnicity, for example—are common in many credibility struggles across a range of contentious political issues. But accusations of bias because of presumed homosexuality—there is no evidence that accusations of presumed heterosexuality were leveled in these debates—are especially important here. They both highlight and reinforce the structural dimensions of heterosexism upon which regimes of expert capital are structured in same-sex marriage debates.

Many of the academic experts in the United States and France who study questions related to same-sex marriage and parenting debates, such as psychologists researching childhood outcomes, sociologists mapping the patterns of same-sex partnerships, or historians analyzing the history of anti-LGBTQ discrimination, did indeed embark on their careers for personal reasons. They wanted to contribute to the scientific and intellectual understanding of people in their communities, often in a context where such research was largely disregarded at first, as discussed in chapter 4. The risk that decision-makers and opponents, and sometimes even their colleagues, might look at their expertise as less valuable was always a possibility.

The stigma surrounding research on these topics also leads people to assume that anyone who studies same-sex couples and their children must be directly concerned by the question. The historian Nancy Cott and the sociologists Michael Rosenfeld and Virginie Descoutures—as well as several other experts who asked not to be explicitly identified on this particular issue—all said that people had assumed that they were not straight because of their research. However, unlike their gay, lesbian, and bisexual peers, they could choose to invoke their heterosexuality to shield themselves from the disqualification that comes with homosexuality. Indeed, the French lawyer, and lesbian, Caroline Mécary, summed this idea up when referring to one of the experts called to provide testimony before lawmakers on queer parenting: "[They're] lucky, because [they] can say: 'I'm heterosexual.' I don't say that because I've never hidden my life. But we don't refer to the sexuality of heterosexuals who intervene in the field of heterosexuality." Although clearly unequal and discriminatory, this double standard creates a unique opportunity for heterosexual experts in these competitions.

Taking advantage of the fortified legitimacy of straight experts to defend the cause of gay families is one of the paradoxes that emerges from these credibility struggles. Indeed, the strategy is actively supported, albeit not uncritically, by the very people who aim to advance the rights of same-sex couples and their children. Because they understand that heterosexuality itself is a form of expert capital for elite experts, they realize it should be deployed tactically. In the United States, LGBTQ activists and their allies, especially those working in advocacy lawyering, learned through decades of experience that the sexualities of their experts would always be on the table. Gregory Herek, a pioneering professor of psychology who studied public attitudes about homosexuality and also a gay man, told me stories about how he was regularly questioned in pretrial depositions about his private life:

> It was Lambda Legal suing the county and this [attorney from the district attorney's office] was doing a deposition and he did in fact ask me if I was gay. . . . It's out there publicly so you know I said yes and he asked if I was

in a domestic partnership and that also was public record and I said yes. . . . He asked me something to the respect of, well do you have a stake in this case? You know, would you benefit from a particular ruling and I just pointed out to him that one of his main arguments was . . . that essentially gay people would not benefit from . . . being married. There was nothing special about it and but you know so I guess you know based on your argument, no. I wouldn't . . . be affected by this.

Herek's story, drawn from a long history of providing testimony, illustrates how anti-marriage advocates systematically exploit the homosexuality of potential expert witnesses. Although in this example Herek deflected the attack on his legitimacy by using his opponent's logic against him, if groups defending gay family rights can avoid these questions altogether, they will consider it.

Discussions about the risks of homosexuality were common. Don Haider-Markel, a political scientist who has conducted extensive research on gay and lesbian elected officials and the political power of the LGBTQ movement, recalled conversations he was involved in when he was under consideration to be an expert witness for *Perry v. Schwarzenegger*. Haider-Markel, who is straight but criticizes how opponents weaponize the homosexuality of researchers, talked with his colleague who was ultimately selected by the attorneys to testify. That expert is gay. "I understood he was more concerned about, you know, whether his legitimacy would be called into question as an expert witness," Haider-Markel explained. Although it did not prevent that expert from taking the stand, concerns about his sexuality as a potential liability were never off the table. Sometimes these concerns are tacit. The historian Nancy Cott explained how she and Michael Grossberg, an historian at Indiana University, were solicited to contribute an amicus brief. "Both Michael and I are not gay, and while that was never asked, I think it probably helped in saying, you know, these are historians who for historians' reasons are, you know, writing these things on the history of marriage," she recalled. These experts understand that heterosexual privilege makes the credibility of their voices less open to attack. When I asked Cott how LGBTQ advocates might think about the fact that she is not lesbian, she replied, "I would guess that they see it as an advantage because I'd be less likely to be seen as . . . self-interested." Indeed, when Cott and other straight witnesses took the stand, whether or not it was explicitly mentioned, their sexualities could not be used to derail their testimony.

Experiences with constant accusations that their expertise is biased and understanding the disadvantages of homosexuality caused some gay or lesbian experts to push advocates to find an equally qualified straight expert who could replace them. One of them, who asked not to be named for their own protection, recounted how they were thrilled to be asked to take the stand in one of the major U.S. federal trials but had no illusions that it would be a bad idea. They explained the story: "They called me and asked me, will I testify? And I said, yeah, sure, I would, but I thought they should ask [another expert] first because he's a straight guy, and he's a wonderful witness, and he is a very smart guy . . . and he has wonderful credentials, and, you know, he'll do a better job. I said, I mean, we want to win. . . . I don't need to be famous. I just want to win."

When I asked the interviewee why they felt the witness they recommended would be specifically better than them on the stand, they said, "He can't be impugned. He's validly heterosexual." Despite their impressive publication record in peer-reviewed journals and many professional accolades, this social scientist's commitment to seeing same-sex marriage legalized led them to recuse themselves from the process. They were convinced that even if they could have provided the expertise the team was looking for in terms of scientific content, it was not worth taking the risk that the value of their expert capital might be tainted in the eyes of the judge. In the end, they provided extensive consulting to those involved, including to the professor who would ultimately take the stand, convinced that his straight voice would resonate with more authority.

DON'T TAKE IT ON FAITH: RELIGIOUS DISQUALIFICATION

Just as the romantic and family lives of gay and lesbian scientific experts were a potential liability for them when they testified on behalf of same-sex marriage supporters, the real or assumed religious convictions of experts were an issue for those on the other side. People had questions about whether their faith and involvement in religious organizations made their testimony partial and thus unusable. For same-sex marriage advocates working on U.S. trials, by showing that a person's views were grounded in religious beliefs condemning homosexuality rather than in good-quality empirical research, they could potentially damage their testimony as an expert witness.

For example, Leslie Cooper of the ACLU, who assisted in the *DeBoer v. Snyder* trial, discussed how in previous trials in other states, the attorneys she worked with used this tactic on George Rekers. Rekers, a Baptist minister, psychologist, and former professor of neuropsychiatry and behavioral science at the University of South Carolina School of Medicine, had long-outspoken views against same-sex couples and same-sex couples raising children in particular. In a case over adoption in Arkansas where Rekers had been called as an expert witness to testify on the supposed dangers of gay parenting for children's well-being, the team involving the ACLU was able to demonstrate that his testimony was unreliable. "It wasn't just that he held a religious belief," she explained. "He had written a number of things that showed that his religious views and his scientific views were all one and the same and intertwined. . . . That was helpful in demonstrating to the court that here's someone who's testifying not based on what the science shows, but based on something else unscientific and that's relevant for . . . evaluating the credibility."

Rekers had a long history of involvement with antigay Christian organizations, such as Focus on the Family, and a record of public statements condemning homosexuality for religious reasons. In addition, his peer-reviewed research did not address issues related to gay parenting. Because of their efforts to disqualify him, judges in several trials, first in Arkansas and then in Florida, wrote opinions in which they explicitly discredited Rekers because of this bias. To Leslie Cooper's mind, this demonstrated that "you just can't find somebody credible to support an unsupportable position." After those scathing opinions, "we haven't heard from him again," she added. While effective in cultural and institutional contexts where evidence of religious bias matters, these tactics may not necessarily work in other settings.

Whether effective of not, academic experts with conservative Christian beliefs decried what they saw as a form of discrimination, saying that they felt their religious views should not be used to undermine their authority. It was something most of them said they had confronted or thought about. In our discussion of his participation as an expert witness, I asked Douglas Allen, an economist at Simon Fraser University, about why his testimony was being attacked and whether his being Christian had something to do with it. He replied:

> Oh, no question. It's just . . . like how people say, oh, you're funded by some right-wing group, therefore, your evidence is useless. Oh, you're a Christian. You must've made up the numbers, and, therefore, it's dismissed. And people explicitly said this in their emails that, you know, how could we ever trust a

> Christian on this topic. I mean, the same thing applies to . . . how could you trust somebody who was a supporter of same-sex marriage on empirical work done, right? . . . There's a larger social question, but I think, you know, a lot of people believe there's no such thing as truth. And so, it's just you're just judging by one advocate versus another. And so, once you recognize somebody as an advocate and an enemy, well, then you just don't trust them. And so that question just pointed out to people he's an advocate. He's an enemy. Can't trust a thing he says. . . . End of story.

Allen, like many other academic experts on both sides of the debate, has a strong sense of his own identity as a scientist with a commitment to following the data. Unlike the majority of his peers in the social sciences who study same-sex couples and their children, he believes that scholarship supports his view that children should be raised by married heterosexual couples, ideally their biological parents. And like many of his peers who are gay and lesbian, his view was perceived as having been informed by his intimate convictions and personal life, in this case, his faith. But in a setting where his academic credentials and research are the source of his credibility, his personal life can undermine his status as an expert, reducing him to the role of an "advocate" who can no longer provide expert capital to enlighten the public about "the truth."

Xavier Lacroix, who was a professor of philosophy and moral theology at the Catholic University of Lyon, also expressed frustration about threats to his expert capital because of his religious ties. He was irritated with the way same-sex marriage experts and advocates never failed to mention his Catholic faith and his job as a theologian. He recalled, in particular, his many public interactions with Daniel Borrillo, a professor of law, lawyer, and former law policy advocate at the HIV prevention organization Aides. Lacroix said:

> Borrillo always starts the same way. I know in advance how he's going to start: "Monsieur Lacroix is a theologian. Monsieur Lacroix is a Christian. Monsieur Lacroix is even a canonist, he once told me. So, he's a Christian. He's a believer. It's his right. It's his strictest right. We're in a Republic. The Republic respects all beliefs, etc., but he shouldn't impose his personal options on everyone." So, we're locked into denominational categories, as if we were only defending what our faith tells us. But we are defending what we believe to be the common good of all.

Lacroix resented that experts defending same-sex marriage, such as Daniel Bor-rillo, should consistently center his religious beliefs and affiliation with the Catholic Church. Although there were no formal mechanisms to disqualify him because of this—and in fact Lacroix had an official position in a state advisory body precisely in order to be the representative of a Catholic perspective on bioethics—he knew that if his expertise seemed religiously tinged, it could face more skepticism from the secular French public. He wanted to ensure that his faith would not hamper his power to influence the public debate. Lacroix's resentment over his being constantly reminded about his religious views illustrates how the lives and convictions of experts become potential weaknesses that either side can exploit to damage one another. Because the authority of scientific experts is predicated on the collective belief that what they say is unbiased and neutral—even when almost everyone involved acknowledges that such a thing is an illusion—these delegitimating strategies will likely continue.

CONCLUSION

An impeccable expert is one who can provide information that withstands repeated attacks from adversaries. It requires walking a fine line, intervening in public controversies on behalf of others without getting damaged in the process. Experts serve a political purpose—persuading an audience, demonstrating seriousness, backing up a policy goal—but cannot be "political." What they provide, expert capital, is both precious but also difficult to handle.

Avoiding accusations of political contamination—what Michelle Murphy calls "the politics of politics"—is indispensable.[16] Indeed, because much of scientific experts' worth comes from the perception that they are different and autonomous from precisely the groups that seek their knowledge, interacting with them is potentially dangerous for both parties. Experts could lose their credibility if they seem tainted by the political process, and people who use experts must not be seen to be manipulating them; otherwise, it defeats the purpose of calling on experts in the first place.[17] Indeed, expert capital is strongest when it is perceived as providing authority without taking sides. This is especially true of scientific expertise. Decision-makers can try to use it to pass their stances off as simple, unbiased truths. Or, as David Swartz argues, they seek to create a legitimation for their goals, "where the vested interests of some authority are misperceived as being disinterested."[18] For political actors to be able to benefit from this effect, the experts they rely on cannot be seen to be too involved. As research on vaccine hesitancy has shown, if they seem untrustworthy because of a perceived conflict of interest, experts can lose their ability to serve as a justification for public policies.[19]

Sometimes organizations, such as professional groups or think tanks that are transparent about their activities, can act as a buffer, reducing the risks for interacting with policymakers, as we saw in the previous chapter. Speaking collectively or via these larger entities, experts are less exposed to individual disqualification. Commitment to publishing research regardless of findings, including and perhaps even especially when it goes against the goals of their social movement allies, is another way for organizations, such as the Williams Institute, to maintain a credible distance from politics. Its success in maintaining a reputation of reliable and transparent scholarship may also account for its attractiveness among academic experts whose own reputations are protected when they collaborate with it.

This chapter has examined how the complexities of this mining process, in which experts share their expertise in political and legal institutions, expose everyone involved to the dynamics of credibility struggles. People who rely on expert capital, whether it be politicians crafting a hearing on a bill or lawyers selecting witnesses to take the stand, want experts who will contribute their value in the most effective ways possible. But it is not just a matter of extracting expertise from them. Experts are inseparable from the special kind of currency that decision-makers, activists, journalists, and other groups want from them. Who they are and what they say must be taken together. French activists and lawmakers often want famous French intellectuals whose celebrity will make observers take them more seriously. Sometimes peer-reviewed research will matter, but only if it is produced in France and if the stances of the experts who conducted it match with other competing political objectives. U.S. attorneys putting together trials search for scientists whose empirical research will stand up to judicial scrutiny. The research, however, cannot speak for itself. They feel they have a better chance when it is presented by a straight tenured professor from Stanford or Harvard.

In this light, we see that both the qualification and disqualification of experts are multifaceted. For example, professional and academic experts whose worth comes from the quality of their scientific research are likely to face accusations that their expertise is tainted by bias. The stories of credibility discussed in this chapter thus confirm what feminist and antiracist scholarship has already shown: Expert worth is determined by systems of domination that posit the inherent value of white heterosexual cisgender men. They are most likely to be given the benefit of the doubt that their expertise is neutral and pure. Most—but not all—of the experts I interviewed were white. Race may have been a component of the credibility struggles that went into the processes behind their selection, though that was not mentioned explicitly. This fact may also be a reflection of the hierarchies of elite knowledge production more generally that marginalize people of color in the United States and France, making their voices less often heard by decision-makers.

Thinking simultaneously about the things that qualify and disqualify an expert, as this chapter has done, is a useful way for understanding the value of expert capital in a particular institutional and cultural setting. Its specific qualities, such as fame, prestige, or empirical rigor, each has its own constraints. None of these things is produced in the same way, and each has its own vulnerabilities. Analyzing these phenomena gives us insight into the interaction between politics and expertise more broadly. Because the value of their legitimacy depends on the places where it is heard, people who want to mobilize experts—whether it be activists trying to advocate their cause, lawyers defending a constitutional argument in court, or lawmakers putting together a hearing—have limited options. For example, scientific expertise cannot be created quickly and takes time to change, especially if the notion of scientific "consensus" becomes central to the debate. While these challenges do not stop some groups from trying—as Tom Waidzunas has shown for "ex-gay" research or Naomi Oreskes and Erik Conway have shown for tabacco and fossil fuel industries—producing scientific expertise is a long-term strategy that requires time and money.[20]

Once it is mobilized for legal purposes, different kinds of expert capital become vulnerable. Indeed, because institutional logics give judges the opportunity to determine what counts as good expertise, they have the power to permanently destroy or enhance its worth, along with the reputations of the specific experts who produce it. A judge's determination can create a feedback effect on the scientific field. On the other hand, experts whose power derives from their renown have their own advantages and disadvantages. If activists or lawmakers want to benefit from the expert capital of a famous intellectual, they convince that person to lend them their voice. Achieving their support looks very different than investing in scientific research published in peer-reviewed journals whose results may not end up supporting political goals. But rallying famous intellectuals to one's cause is also a fraught endeavor. There is no clear roadmap to convince them to lend their aura to support a political stance, and once they speak on a party's behalf, their future behavior, for better or worse, could lead to unwanted publicity. To make sure it is worth the risk and effort, people who use experts must therefore think very carefully before deciding whom to call.

This chapter has focused on elite experts, most of whom are social scientists and mental health professionals, given their outsized role in U.S. courts and French legislatures on gay family debates. Lay experts no doubt face credibility struggles around the value of their expert capital as well. Future research could explore these dynamics more specifically. In particular, whereas things like irreproachable credentials or celebrity status may matter for academics, the reasons why decision-makers seek lay experts make the sources of their expert capital different. For example, unlike scientific experts, ordinary citizens are valued precisely because of their personal connection to the issue. They are not meant to not be neutral. Among other things, their power comes from their capacity to make the legal stakes legible on an emotional level to their audiences in policy institutions that are set up to hear them.

In addition to the kinds of things they say, such as wrenching stories about, say, how their lives were upended by the death of a partner that the law prevented them from marrying, who they are is also important. For example, if authenticity is a key component of being seen as trustworthy, lay experts must also deal with the "politics of politics." The value of their expert capital can be tainted if people think it is polluted by political manipulation. Their reputations as "real" ordinary people may be subject to damage if their adversaries accuse them of being politically motivated, insincere, and fabricating their stories to fit a predetermined narrative. Criticisms of "astroturfing" are a good example of this kind of delegitimization strategy.[21] At the same time, much like academic experts who had to learn to use the right kind of language in the courtroom, lay experts who develop the skills necessary to tell their stories effectively, perhaps with the coaching of an activist group or others who have been through the process, are more effective. The trick is in learning those techniques without it costing them their credibility.

Just as the pressures to preserve the value of one's expert capital according to the demands of the expert field can create feedback loops between the academic and political fields and produce distortions in representations of information, the same is true for lay experts. Organizations involved in curating and cultivating lay experts select and determine who the "best" kind of person is to represent personal testimony. The messenger needs to be the perfect, respectable, and relatable example. This can lead to biased depictions about who, exactly, ordinary gay families are. And, if research on this question is any indication, respectability politics lead to the overrepresentation of white middle-class gays and lesbians and their families.[22] This leads to the erasure of racialized gay families, making it possible for anti-same-sex marriage activists to claim that same-sex marriage is a "white" issue. Indeed, perhaps in order to counter this specific line of attack, attorneys put author and activist for Asian American civil rights, Helen Zia, on the stand as an expert witness in the *Perry* trial. Thinking about these dynamics through the prism of expert capital helps us better understand the specific national and institutional conditions that give weight to certain voices, attaching specific values to them and shaping the strategic choices of the people who covet it.

CONCLUSION

Authoritative Knowledge, Authorizing Families

EXPERTS IN THE AGE OF ILLIBERAL DEMOCRACIES

The politics of knowledge production are essential for understanding our current political situation and the role of experts within it. One of the features of the mid-twenty-first century is the rise of illiberal democracies across the globe, from Hungary and Poland to Brazil and the United States. This process is also sometimes called de-democratization. Scholars have shown an important feature that seems common among these regimes: establishing control of knowledge production in universities and organizations autonomous from their political authority in order to thwart critique and impose their own ideological agendas.[1] Their goal is to "influence public history," and they do so by defending or even banning programs they deem threatening, often targeting especially the social sciences and gender studies programs in particular, as well as reducing state funding for research on unworthy topics, increasing resources to researchers who are faithful to the regime, and founding parallel institutions that are beholden to them.[2] Through these mechanisms, these illiberal states suppress critical academic voices and ensure that their own version of the truth prevails in public discourse.

In this light, it is clear that experts of all stripes play an important role in the future of democracy across the globe. On the one hand, many academic experts are targets of oppression by these authoritarian projects. Scholars studying topics related to contentious political issues, including poverty, race, gender, sexuality, and climate change, are seeing their capacity to produce expertise drastically reduced. In the United States, elimination of tenure, bans on teaching critical race theory, and the shuttering of gender studies programs are just some examples. In France, while the situation seems less dire for now, conservative politicians and their allies have decried the invasion of so-called "woke" ideologies from the United States that they claim are taking over the French academy.[3] On the other hand, experts who produce information that supports authoritarian projects or who follow along with restrictions on academic freedom see their status maintained or even elevated. This book has shown how academic expertise can help advance gay rights causes in policy forums where that information matters, such as courts. As illiberal regimes gain more power, they crack down on such research, working to ensure that academic autonomy is undermined and that knowledge production explicitly serves their political aims.

The rollback of rights for sexual minorities and women is a central component of this illiberal turn. Things have shifted rapidly since I began work on this book in 2012. When I started research, it seemed that people who supported expanding the rights of women and LGBTQ people had gained enough power to maintain momentum on both sides of the Atlantic. Afterall, thanks to the hard work of activists, politicians, lawyers, judges, and many other people, both the United States and France had gone from condemning homosexuality to legalizing same-sex marriage in a matter of decades. This vision, however, did not account for the long-term strategies of those opposed to sexual democracy. Their efforts have started to come to fruition since at least the election of Donald Trump in the United States, and it is possible that rights gained for gay families described in this book will not last.

Since 2020, the Supreme Court is dominated by a conservative supermajority rendering decisions that have rolled back constitutional protections to abortion—*Dobbs v. Jackson Women's Health Organization* (2022)—and enlarged the scope of religious liberty and free speech to allow groups to discriminate against same-sex couples—*303 Creative LLC v. Elenis* (2023), *Masterpiece Cakeshop v. Colorado Civil Rights Commission* (2018), and *Fulton v. City of Philadelphia* (2021). These decisions—along with state politicians banning transgender healthcare and forbidding any teaching or discussion of gender identity and sexuality in schools—threaten the lives of women and LGBTQ people. Advocates fighting on behalf of these people have their work cut out for them. Not only are they facing an increasingly hostile political and legal climate, but they may also have trouble securing the expertise they need. Their adversaries will do what they can to make sure that knowledge production is oriented toward their own goals and will, wherever possible, change the terms of the debate so that the experts they do have can make their arguments effective.

Questions about who has access to authoritative sources of information and how political actors can marshal them to reach their political goals—for better or worse—are not new. As this book as shown, when it comes to gay family rights in the United States and France, journalists, lawmakers, judges, lawyers, activists, and other groups have grappled with getting their hands on the kinds of expertise they wanted. From at least the 1990s to the legalization of same-sex marriage in both countries in the mid-2010s, they have been figuring out the types of expertise that matters and determining who is best suited to give it to them. For some, that painstaking work paid off. But it also triggered some unintended consequences.

WHAT HAPPENS WHEN DECISION-MAKERS USE EXPERTS?

The *rapporteur* for the Judiciary Committee of the Assemblée Nationale had spent many months in 2012 and 2013 carefully crafting a long series of hearings. While leaders of the anti-same-sex marriage organizations spent their time giving interviews to journalists and leading massive marches all over France, Erwann Binet was thinking about their arguments and responding to the political pressure he was under to get the marriage and adoption bill through parliament. He invited experts from both sides, anticipating that the tension in the streets and the angry calls from the opposition parties might abate if he could demonstrate that all ideological views had a seat at the hearing table. The calculations were complex. He wanted people who had media reputations but also scientific legitimacy. At the same time, the social scientists who had studied gay families were either lesbian or gay themselves or had already supported the legalization of same-sex marriage and adoption. Those situations made their expertise less credible, in his view. In the end, he rendered a report consisting of two tomes and almost fifteen hundred pages. In it, he described the work of the Committee and why, according to the experts, the Socialist Party's bill was justified. Binet was proud of this incredible effort: "I'd like to share with you my thoughts on the wide-ranging hearings we've been conducting over the past seven weeks, which will conclude on Thursday. They have enabled us to gather an exhaustive range of opinions, expertise and experience: in almost fifty hours, we have met over 120 people. Since the bill calls on everyone to take a stand, we felt it necessary to make all the elements of our reflection accessible to the French people: we did this by opening these hearings to the press."[4] These hearings were widely disseminated in the media. Evening news shows and radio broadcasts played particularly interesting clips, interspersing them with interviews of pro- and anti-same-sex marriage activists and protestors.

Whether they wanted to or not, the experts were lending the credibility of their voices to a multilayered political strategy of which they were only one part. Thanks to media amplification, their involvement influenced how gay families were framed, bringing discussions of the Oedipus complex and "universal anthropological rules" directly into people's living rooms. This involvement did not come without a cost. Some academic experts saw the trajectories of their careers change, for better or worse, because of the attention the hearings brought them. The field of scientific knowledge production itself was transformed by the process as researchers from different disciplines took divergent stances, some mobilizing their celebrity and their personal connections to lawmakers. Some experts rejoiced as they and the people they study finally saw French law extend the rights and responsibilities of marriage and adoption to gay and lesbian couples. Others, of course, were bitterly disappointed and would continue to battle against what they saw as an attack on anthropological truth.

A continent away, the stakes were just as high. Gay and lesbian couples in the United States had been embroiled in battles for decades to have their intimate and family relationships afforded the same state-certified recognition as those of their straight peers. By 2014, after much strategizing, several viable legal challenges had made their way into federal courts. Despite the risks involved, attorneys defending same-sex couples gambled that they could win in the Supreme Court, guaranteeing equal access to marriage across the states. The suit against the state of Michigan, *DeBoer v. Snyder*, was one of the cases that would ultimately prove them right when it was consolidated into *Obergefell v. Hodges*.

Before it reached the nine justices in Washington, DC, the case was before judge Bernard Friedman, a Ronald Reagan nominee, in the District Court for the Eastern District of Michigan. He presided over a trial in which attorneys faced off over the constitutionality of Michigan's laws that both limited second-parent adoption to married couples and prevented same-sex couples from marrying. One side argued that the state's restrictions were a violation of the constitutional rights of April DeBoer and Jayne Rowse, a lesbian couple who could not legally marry and were thus prevented from adopting one another's children. The other side claimed that the Michigan laws were justified. The goal was not to discriminate against gays and lesbians but to ensure that children would be raised in optimal conditions, they said.

Once their legal claims were staked out, attorneys had to convince judge Friedman that their positions were based on verifiable facts and not unfounded opinions. In addition to the reams of amicus briefs and reports that flooded the court from the outside, the lawyers on both sides put the best expert witnesses they could find on the stand. In the end, the judge ruled in favor of the plaintiffs, represented by a team of lawyers that included the American Civil Liberties Union and the Gay and Lesbian Advocates and Defenders. His reasoning was based on "the evidence presented at the trial, including the testimony of various expert witnesses, the exhibits, and stipulations."[5] In his opinion, he wrote: "Throughout the trial, the state defendants asserted that Michigan has a legitimate interest in proceeding with caution before altering the traditional definition of marriage. The state defendants' experts all concluded that it is too soon to understand the societal impact of allowing same-sex couples to marry because further study is required. This 'wait-and-see' justification is not persuasive." In his position as an arbiter of the expertise, Judge Friedman reserved particular critique for the anti-same-sex marriage side, dismissing their arguments as unsupported by fact and inadequate justifications for treating gay families differently.

The trial was not only a win for advocates of gay family rights. It also demonstrated that scientific expertise, accumulated over time and supported by disciplines and organizations, could make a difference. But this direct encounter between the scientific and the juridical fields, like the many that took place before it, created an incentive structure to produce expertise on either side that could not leave the scientists indifferent to the impact their research would have. It also led to a series of complicated questions about whether science should indeed be the main way in which gay family rights are justified and whether the personal lives of experts might disqualify them to take the stand.

As these examples illustrate, experts are an integral part of political and legal debates on both sides of the Atlantic. Whether it is journalists calling on them to provide a quote, lawmakers and lawyers inviting them to give testimony, or activists networking with them, experts are a sought-after group of people. Because we perceive them as having the unique ability to make a claim appear authoritative or justified, what they say matters. Whether intentional or not, experts shape the debates they participate in. Not only can what they say impact legal outcomes, but they also contribute to how we understand the meaning of a given social problem. And, at the same time, their participation influences them and their fields. The efforts that go into bringing expertise to the people who want it can have long-lasting effects. These can be as big as organizations creating routines to keep the flow of expertise coming or as small as a scientific expert talking about her experience about being a witness at a trial with her a colleague who then decides not to publish some research for fear of how it might be interpreted.

Focusing on debates over same-sex marriage and parenting in the United States and France, this book has looked at the role of experts and expertise from several angles. The overarching question has been to explain the following puzzle: Despite dealing with the same legal questions, the media and decision-makers in these countries appear to be drawing on different types of experts who use specific kinds of expertise. In explaining why we observe, for example, more economists and ordinary citizens in the United States and more philosophers and psychoanalysts in France, this book has brought to light other important issues.

First, it has shown that the special value of experts—conceptualized as expert capital—is contextually specific. Rather than simply reflect their social class on the one hand or an inherent value of their knowledge on the other, their value depends on interactions conditioned by institutions and culture. Second, relying on experts, especially those who draw their legitimacy from their status as scientists, is a risky business. It can be expensive to fund research for policy purposes, and the payoff, in terms of legal outcomes, is not guaranteed. But, more importantly, foregrounding scientific expertise can transform questions about human rights into technical questions about "what the science says." Lay experts talking about their personal lives can help counter this by incarnating the otherwise abstract terms of the debate, but only in decision-making institutions that give them the space to be heard. Third, by analyzing the conditions under which experts produce, protect, and share their expert capital, this book provides observation that can be useful for understanding other contentious policy debates. The remainder of the conclusion discusses each of these contributions in turn.

YOU SAY EXPERTS, I SAY *LES EXPERTS*— LET'S CALL THE WHOLE THING OFF

After comparing newspaper coverage, legal and political archives, and interviews and observations in both countries, the answer to the underlying question of this book is clear: In debates over gay family rights, U.S. and French media and decision-makers use experts in ways that follow distinct national patterns. Although there is overlap in the kinds of experts and expertise in the debates—activists and legal professionals are common kinds of experts in both countries, for example—there are many ways in which they diverge.

People reading articles published in *The New York Times* and *Le Monde* between 1990 and 2013 will have encountered markedly different stories about the intimate and family lives of gay and lesbian people as well as the political battles for their recognition. In U.S. coverage, ordinary citizens providing information about their lived experiences are the most commonly cited group of people. French reporting, on the other hand, prioritizes elite experts, such as professors and mental health professionals, who talk about them from an analytical distance. While of course there is diversity and variation in these expertise patterns—which chapter 1 describes—on the broadest level, U.S. framing treats gay families as fact, whereas French framing treats them as theory. As chapter 2 detailed, these specificities are mirrored, to different degrees, in political and legal institutions in both countries. Both U.S. courts and legislatures draw on the testimony of ordinary citizens either as litigants in specific cases or through testimony in hearings. U.S. courts also scaffold that testimony with precise information from elite experts who bring empirical evidence tailored to specific legal questions. French political institutional debates, which are dominated by the legislature, rely on similar kinds of experts as the French media: elite professionals, intellectuals, and academics who often discuss the issues in the abstract.

What explains these patterns? This book argues that they are the result of how experts and decision-makers navigate (1) the institutional logics of legislatures and courts; (2) the fields where knowledge producers work; and (3) the channels between knowledge producers and decision-makers. Each of these three components is configured in nationally specific ways that constrain and enable the presence of certain kinds of experts and expertise. In addition to these proximate circumstances, expertise in these debates is also contingent on broader legal structures, such as federalism in the United States and centralization in France, as well as on policy differences, such as those on adoption and medically assisted reproduction, that shape the availability, usability, legitimacy, and demand for specific kinds of information.

The abundance of favorable empirical research on same-sex couples and their children in the United States relative to France is a good example. This disparity is not only the result of the marginalization of such research in the French academy and weaker relationships between academics and social movement organizations that could have encouraged it but also the result of the legal structural conditions that allowed American scholars to study these nontraditional families in the first place. Specifically, federalism in the United States and free market approaches to artificial insemination have meant that gay families have actually existed, and publicly, for at least a decade and a half earlier than in France and have therefore been available for research purposes. Moreover, the plethora of court cases across the range of jurisdictions in the United States has fueled a demand for that information, sustaining it over time and encouraging professional and advocacy organizations to institutionalize it.

Abstract psychoanalytic information has long been an integral part of French public debates in the twentieth century.[6] Such information, especially that provided by experts opposed to same-sex marriage and parenting, continues to be important in French decision-making institutions partly because of the historic invisibility of same-sex couples—itself a result of conservative French family law—that prevented French researchers from analyzing them. Elite conservative experts could thus more easily discuss same-sex couples and their children without confronting information that could prove them wrong, whether for fellow academics or from gay and lesbian families themselves. Legislators invited these opponents to hearings in part because of their reputations in the media, which made them known figures. Lawmakers felt they would face critique and attack on their legitimacy if they did not invite them. Furthermore, the legislative arena, unlike courts, provided no systemic way for other experts to effectively counter and debunk same-sex marriage opponents' abstract psychoanalytic claims.

The presence of such expertise in France is also related to conditions of scientific knowledge production. French scholars who might have provided more empirical research found themselves marginalized in the academy, without resources or the support of professional organizations. They faced resistance from official French family organizations. French legal circumstances—particularly the absence of many jurisdictions to pursue reforms—did not create a high demand for their information, which could have sustained more knowledge production, as it did in the United States. Finally, unlike in the United States, several high-status anthropologists and sociologists were originally opposed to same-sex parenting, and although they eventually lent their legitimacy to both research on the topic and the political advancement of gay family rights, their initial stances contributed to the systemic delegitimization of such topics.

We can also explain the presence or absence of other kinds of expertise, such as economics, personal experience, and religion, by examining how experts and decision-makers navigate the institutional and cultural circumstances outlined above. As we saw in chapters 1 and 2, economic expertise is present in the U.S. media, courts, and legislatures but almost entirely absent in France. This discrepancy is consistent with other analyses finding that market-based justifications are more common in the United States relative to France and constitute a common cultural repertoire in that country.[7] In the case of gay family rights debates, this kind of expertise also matters because marriage has more direct economic consequences through its corollary effects, such as companies whose benefits plans cover the healthcare costs for the spouses of their employees. Furthermore, interstate competition and legal experimentation in the United States created the conditions of a natural experiment on a national level, allowing economists, activists, and think tanks to study the financial effects of same-sex partnership rights within the country's borders. Because the research finds that same-sex marriage has positive economic benefits for states, pro-gay advocacy organizations have created relationships with academic economists and members of the business community to channel that information to legislators, who may be persuaded by economic arguments.[8] Moreover, in courts, when opponents argue that same-sex marriage hurts states, proponents can bring economic evidence to prove them wrong.

In France, in the absence of interstate economic competition and with direct individual access to public healthcare and other social services regardless of marital status, French economists have not found a reason to generate much information relevant for same-sex marriage debates. Unlike in the United States, French business organizations and companies operate in a country with uniform marriage policies and therefore have little perceivable economic arguments to make about same-sex marriage and parenting. French LGBTQ advocacy organizations have not created alliances with members of the business community in part because, unlike in the United States, they do not have a shared economic interest in the legalization of same-sex partnership rights. Even if French economic expertise were hypothetically available, given how market justifications have not been part of French cultural frameworks more broadly, it is possible that the lawmakers in charge of hearings might not have invited any economists to provide it anyway.[9]

The disparate presence of lay experts, such as citizens talking about the effects of gay marriage laws on their lives, reveals how common cultural modes of communication are shared (or not) across institutions in the United States and France. This book has shown how personal experience is shared by a variety of actors—from politicians to academics and ordinary citizens—across institutional contexts in the United States. Different institutional logics appear to operate in different ways to make this possible. In the media, U.S. journalists personalize their coverage by systematically reaching out to people for vignettes. In state legislatures where providing testimony is open to the public, ordinary citizens can share their stories in an effort to persuade lawmakers. In courts, personal experience enters the record through the lives of the litigants and opinion witnesses who provide some of the facts for judges to consider. Social movement organizations on both sides have been instrumental in working with individuals in specific cases but also in packaging their stories and bringing them to decision-makers more broadly. This kind of expertise also fits into broader U.S. cultural narratives and common law traditions that emphasize the personal and the particular relative to France.[10]

As we saw in the first two chapters, personal experience is not a shared form of expertise in French debates. Testimony from ordinary citizens, especially queer people and their families, was marginal in French media reporting and in legislatures until more recently. This is partly due to the way neither media nor lawmakers have systematically reached out to invite them to share their stories. One of the reasons they have not done so is because French law—by formally barring same-sex couples from joint adoption, second-parent adoption, and reproductive technologies—made them invisible. They existed on the margins of the law, facing significant stigma. They have had few effective channels to reach the political field except through family organizations like the Association des Parents et futurs parents Gays et Lesbiens (APGL) and Association des Familles Homoparentales (ADFH), which are relatively new and small compared to their U.S. equivalents. On top of all these barriers, French legislators face entrenched political routines that put them in stark contrast with their American peers. Even when they believe that hearing the lived experiences of ordinary citizens is important, as Erwann Binet did, they face serious critique from their peers who explain that the role of law is to deal with the common good and the universal, not the particular or specific. Because French legislators have the power to determine who has access to hearings, they have prioritized witnesses who speak about the law from a distance, such as academic and professional experts, rather than lay witnesses.

The analysis of the media and decision-making institutions shows that religious representatives are present in both the United States and France but that they draw on different kinds of information when speaking out. In the United States, they frequently draw on religious knowledge, such as information about scriptures and appeals to God, to defend and condemn gay family rights in the media and legislatures. Neither of these forums delegitimizes that kind of expertise. They also provide information through amicus briefs to courts, which advocacy organizations on both sides encourage because they believe it helps project popular support for their side to the judges. These findings are consistent with other work on the historic and contemporary value of religion as a legitimate form of public knowledge in U.S. politics across many policy issues.[11]

In France, religious representatives write op-ed pieces in the press and journalists interview them. Surprisingly, despite French rhetoric around *laïcité*, French lawmakers also invite them to legislative hearings either because they feel they have to or because they believe it will defuse conservative opposition. Unlike their American peers, however, when clergy make public statements, they draw less often on religious knowledge and rely instead on secular information, such as psychoanalysis, anthropology, and law. In other words, they rely on the most widely diffused kinds of expertise in French debates, joining the common discourse. This tactic, which other scholars have also observed, helps cover the stigma of their religious affiliations, which might otherwise be disqualifying.[12] In addition, religious organizations with official representation to the French government, such as the Catholic Church and the Israelite Central Consistory of France, have coordinated with secular conservative experts, as described in the book, who provide them with information for their hearings. This strategy resembles the way U.S. anti-same-sex marriage activists sought out allies in the social sciences to produce peer-reviewed information for courts. In both instances, they were motivated to find experts whose expert capital best corresponded to the cultural and institutional expectations of the decision-makers they were trying to convince.

SCIENTIFIC EXPERTS, DEMOCRACY, AND RADICAL CRITIQUE

In addition to cataloging and explaining differences in expertise across national contexts, this book has shown how political debates and expertise inform one another. That interrelationship is knotty and consequential. Experts can help journalists, activists, lawyers, judges, and lawmakers accomplish their goals. But their involvement is not a simple matter of answering a phone call, speaking at a hearing, or taking the stand and then walking away. When experts get involved in the political process, they bring not only their personal reputations with them but also the reputations of their respective communities, whatever they may be. Among the different kinds of experts this book has described, scientists warrant some specific attention here. Whether they be sociologists, demographers, developmental psychologists, psychoanalysts, historians, or economists, their implication in the debate has a feedback effect on their disciplines. It also has an effect on how we think about the appropriate place of scientific expertise in democracies more generally.

In so doing, this book includes a warning about the potential risks involved in relying on and lauding science as the answer to political questions. By providing their expertise to decision-makers, researchers heighten the stakes around their work and—intentionally or not—increase the circulation of influence between science and politics. They also participate in the enmeshing of the empirical—what research says about a phenomenon—and the normative—what political decisions ought to be made, if any, to respond to a social problem. This is not to say that science could or should strive to isolate itself from politics. Indeed, following in the footsteps of feminist and social constructionist conceptions, this book has demonstrated that scientific knowledge production is inherently political, contingent on material, cultural, and institutional conditions that vary across time and place. However, if science is to be a distinct way of knowing, attention to its political dimensions is salutary. This requires that we be lucid about what happens when political authorities and the people hoping to persuade them enroll science to solve contentious social issues with ethical implications.[13]

The specific issue of whether or not same-sex couples should have the same parenting rights as different-sex couples to have children, adopt, or otherwise raise them is a good example. This question could be answered in terms of equality and nondiscrimination. And in part, it was. Yet supporters of gay family rights also invested heavily in the scientific research, materially and symbolically. Their adversaries did the same. As the book explains, as it turns out, evidence from social science about children raised by same-sex couples was an asset to gay rights groups because it unambiguously supported their cause. This was especially useful in U.S. courts, as the sociologist, Michael Rosenfeld, described in a book about his experience as an expert witness that he published ten years after I interviewed him for this book.[14]

Yet, if the research consensus were to demonstrate that children suffer psychologically or socially because of gay parenting, what would that mean? Although this is not at all what the data show, this counterfactual argument warrants our attention. If we let the scientific question prevail over the political one, the answer seems clear. Many of the scientific experts I interviewed who had testified in favor of same-sex marriage were aware of these implications. When I put forward the hypothesis of this fictitious scientific consensus to them, the responses varied. Some experts supporting gay families ultimately argued that the political question should not be subordinated to the scientific one. They said that their position would not change along with what the research showed. Instead, other principles, such as equality and justice, were all that they needed to make up their minds. That the scientific consensus supported same-sex marriage was a good thing but not a requirement. Other experts asserted, however, that if the results showed that gay parenting was somehow harmful to children, they would be more circumspect about supporting same-sex marriage. In a context where gay rights advocates use scientific expertise as a key justification for their stance, the counterfactual scenario shows how slippery this strategy can be. It seems that advocates would either have to admit defeat, following the science to its logical conclusion that children should not be raised by same-sex couples, or claim that scientific expertise is irrelevant, flawed, or incomplete. This quandary puts into focus the problematic role science can play in human rights debates more broadly even when social movement organizations are the ones mobilizing that expertise in the first place.

Another dimension of this issue is the way the scientific argument, and the research that supported it, took for granted the standardness of heterosexual families. In the predominant framework, if same-sex couples wanted to have the same rights to raise children as their straight peers, they would need to demonstrate they are just as capable and that their children fare just as well. And indeed, much of the scholarship uses heterosexual married couples, ideally with biological ties to their children, as the standard to which queer family structures are compared. Among the wealth of expertise presented to the media and decision-makers, one might have expected to hear critical positions coming from academics sensitive to this heterosexist position—one that centralizes straight families as the norm—especially in the United States, where social science research on gay families is older and more abundant than in France. The critical perspective that asks why gay families are required to justify their ability to raise children has indeed been present for decades on both sides of the Atlantic. Since the early 2000s, there have been voices in the scientific literature arguing that the comparison with heterosexual families does not necessarily make scientific sense and represents a theoretical error.[15] However, it seems that these perspectives were deliberately downplayed by the majority of lawyers and experts testifying on behalf of same-sex families.

Some researchers, notably Judith Stacey, a sociologist at New York University, have observed that even if sociologists continue to make this comparison between different and same-sex couples, the results of these studies are more nuanced than they sometimes appear. They show some interesting differences between children raised in these two types of families. For example, some studies have shown that children raised by same-sex couples are more open to the idea that they themselves could one day be in a relationship with a person of the same sex.[16] They also tend, on average, to have less stereotypical ideas about gender. As early as 2001, Stacey and others claimed that the public debate had created a kind of distortion in the scientific literature, encouraging researchers to relegate to the background results that showed these differences between the two groups.[17]

However, more than a decade later when the federal marriage trials were at their peak, this critical perspective was mainly mobilized by conservative lawyers and experts to delegitimize pro-same-sex marriage expertise. As a result, Stacey and other researchers decided to declare publicly that their criticisms of the scientific literature could in no way justify a refusal to legally recognize same-sex families. The weaponization of scientific doubt or nuance has been important in other debates at the intersection of science and politics. Research on climate change and its countervailing forces of climate denial or climate confusion are good examples. Scientific disagreements, which are a crucial part of the scientific process, are either mobilized to delegitimate the authority of scientific expertise in general or created artificially to give the impression that scientists have no consensus about the causes and responses to climate change. All of this is made possible by the comingling of empirical and normative questions that underline contentious political issues.

The scientization of human rights debates, such as same-sex marriage, may also limit radical critique. Despite their differences, what the U.S. and French debates have in common is the reification of the heterosexual family and a symbolic reinforcement of the institution of marriage. The involvement of scientific expertise in these debates has not led to a questioning of the heterosexual, married family as the measuring stick. On the contrary, whether before parliamentarians or judges, supporters and opponents have clashed on similar terms: the capacity of gay families to live up to a supposedly "natural" model. Indeed, these debates were never an opportunity to sincerely raise the question of the potentially harmful effects of the heterosexual family on children. Nor was there any question of trying to see if gay, lesbian, bisexual, or trans people could show a better way forward with more egalitarian and supportive family models that other families could emulate. No doubt for strategic reasons, particularly on the part of certain mainstream advocates of same-sex couples, a radical critique of the merits of marriage and parenting was off the table.

This book shows what can happen to the texture of democratic debate when an issue of fundamental rights slips into a technical framework that gives place of prominence to scientific expertise. U.S. courts are particularly problematic in this respect. The formal rules of expertise can minimize democratic debate in favor of an apparently apolitical technical logic. This situation has at least two significant effects. First, it introduces considerable incentive into the scientific field to produce court-worthy expertise. That alone is cause for concern because it puts researchers in a position to influence the legal process whether they realize it or not. Second, it places judges in the position of arbiters of scientific truth in the context of their courtrooms, giving them a fundamental power to guide scientific knowledge production even as they determine legal outcomes. Even for those who think that judges ought to have that authority over science, there is no requirement that they undergo certified training that would allow them to engage in arcane scientific debates that surpass the capacities of nonspecialists.

Debates in French parliaments also mobilize expertise in utilitarian ways. But the logics underlying them, as this book has shown, respond to immediate political dynamics, including political and social power. Their goal is not to make some kind of definitive decision about the state of the scientific literature. This situation leaves more room than the U.S. judicial system for a diversity of voices across a range of normative positions. It also makes it easier to talk about and respond to the political context. This is not to say, of course, that U.S. courts are apolitical. Ample research has argued that decisions of the U.S. Supreme Court are as much about partisan calculations as they are about legal principle or a judge's detached reading of the evidence presented. Nevertheless, the explicit institutional logic of the courts—as long as judges decide to continue to respect it—puts scientific expertise in a unique position that can give advocates on one side or the other the upper hand if they are willing to run the risk that this strategy implies.

EXPERTISE: A COMMODITY UNLIKE ANY OTHER

Expert capital, the concept developed in this book, allows us to conceptualize the nexus where experts and politics meet at the point of political decision-making. This work is inspired by Ferree and colleagues' idea of discursive "forums" and builds on Bourdieu's idea of scientific fields and juridical fields.[18] But it is also distinct in that it foregrounds the place where multiple fields overlap and expert capital is transferred (or not) between them. Defining experts inductively—by looking at who provides testimony in courts, legislatures, and the media—has allowed me to track them back to the scientific, religious, professional, and other fields from which they hail and then unpack the choices they made within their circumstances as they transformed their knowledge and positions into the specific power journalists and decision-makers sought them out for: expert capital. Conceptualizing expertise in this way gives insights that may also be helpful for analyzing other issues that involve moral and technical dimensions, including, for example, antivaccine organizing, climate change denial, or antiabortion activism.

One insight is the understanding that expertise is interactional. Expert capital, the worth that only experts can provide in a given setting, is not inherently valuable per se. Rather, people working within institutions, such as journalists in the press, lawyers and judges in courts, and politicians in political bodies, all contribute to recognizing certain people as uniquely situated to produce the information they believe will be credible. Moreover, the value of expert capital is shaped by the cultural repertoires and institutional logics in which it is deployed as well as by the circumstances in which experts produce it. Interactions between experts and those who seek their capital work within these structural conditions. This approach makes clear that some kinds of expertise, from personal experience to peer-reviewed research, are more useful than others in a given setting. For example, scientific credibility, including credentials, publication record, or prestige, will only add value to one's expert capital in contexts where those characteristics matter for accomplishing strategic aims. These variations are also important to analyze in light of the fact that the appropriate kind of expertise is not always available when and where people need it.

In addition to its not having an inherent worth outside of the interactions that create it, the value of expert capital depends on interactions between groups as they collectively struggle to determine what criteria should be used to draw the boundaries around what "counts" as expertise in the first place and the inevitable fights that spring up to contest them. Those battles impact the experts themselves as they face efforts to undermine and delegitimize them. The valences of other kinds of capital that go into these contests can be both empowering and hazardous. For example, economic capital gives scientific experts the means to conduct research or lay experts to produce, curate, and bring their personal experience to the field. At the same time, money can pose a problem if it is seen as coming from a source—perhaps a rich donor or an industry group—that is seen to bias scientific information or makes lay expertise appear bought and inauthentic.

This interactional approach can be helpful for scholars who are interested in contentious political debates by encouraging them to look at how different interest groups compete to make their own claims appear credible and legitimate. One of the ways they do this is by mobilizing expert capital, which, when conceived as the result of social interactions rather than intrinsically valuable, allows us to focus on how experts play an important role in political processes without making a priori judgements about their profiles and backgrounds. In other words, stripped of the idea that experts are a fixed category of people whose information always matters, we are better able to look at the work that goes into making and unmaking their worth across time and space.

This perspective can be useful, for example, in the current context of a "crisis of expertise," characterized by mistrust in science, especially among certain political and social groups.[19] Despite their apparent hostility to expertise, it is not the case that such groups reject the idea of authoritative information altogether. Instead, they work to create alliances with people who can produce the expert capital that they believe helps them reach their goals. Within the examples of activists who oppose mandatory vaccines and climate change denialists, classifying these groups as simply groups of people who reject expert authority fundamentally misunderstands the story.

These groups seem to understand that in order to be taken seriously and gain credibility in public discourse, they need to use the language and codes of expertise. For these reasons, they work to get access to expert capital they can deploy in these settings, cultivating relationships with the kinds of people who can produce it. For instance, anti-climate-change activists worked to find people with academic credentials in fields germane to environmental issues and used the backing of industry organizations and wealthy donors to generate the idea of doubt about human impacts on the climate. Similarly, parents opposed to childhood vaccines have built relationships with allied doctors and researchers to effectively buttress their claims. Moreover, they also organize to share lay expertise, providing lawmakers with stories about how vaccines hurt their children. In both of these examples, their determinations about what kind of voices they would need to get the respect they sought led these groups to anticipate the sorts of expert capital that would serve their purposes in their given contexts. At the same time, they had to find experts willing to put their own reputations on the line and, when necessary, compensate for the potential damage that their involvement might incur.

Some might say my argument that the value of expert capital is determined by its context—the conditions of its production and exchange—is all just relativism. Such critics would probably be especially troubled by the inductive approach that treats any kind of person heard by a decision-making institution as an "expert," arguing that this makes it impossible to distinguish between truth claims and the qualifications of the people who make them. To be clear, I do not argue that truth does not exist, that there is no inherent worth to science, or that we cannot or should not rank the trustworthiness and value of information in the public sphere. Understanding expertise as a socially constructed commodity contingent on context does not mean that we can no longer tell the difference between fact and fiction or that types and sources of information are equally valuable. On the contrary, an interactive and inductive theorization of expertise is meant to make us better able to unpack the power structures that lead people to attribute worth to some types of expertise over others and better understand how and why, say, misinformation gets into the hands of decision-makers.

We cannot take for granted that the kind of information we believe is the most valid will be seen as such by the people we are hoping to convince. Expertise is not science. That is a key lesson of this book. Science can be inherently valuable. So can personal experience. But whether those kinds of information become "expertise" is another matter, and it behooves us to understand how and why that happens. In fact, in certain circumstances, expert capital can be composed of claims that look like science but are either questionable or even fully fabricated, or what some call pseudoscience or junk science. Even if that information is rejected by the scientific community, such information can become expertise, giving power to those who use it, if the intended audience is willing and able to treat it as such. A good example includes the circulation of several studies, since retracted, purporting to find serious side effects of the medication mifepristone that U.S federal judge Matthew Kacsmaryk used to justify his ruling against the Food and Drug Administration (FDA) in a case that is part of an effort to ban medication abortion.[20] Expertise, therefore, does not speak for itself. Regardless of which kinds of information we think should be given consideration—scientific research, ethical arguments grounded in religious texts, or stories about the impacts of the law on a person's life—we will all benefit from a critical understanding of expertise. Being attentive to these questions means that those who observe and participate in public debates can better perceive the mechanisms that shape the value of expert capital and the people who produce and deliver it. This book has revealed those dynamics for same-sex marriage debates in the United States and France. Scholars, including those who are skeptical of relativism, can use these insights to investigate the production and deployment of expertise for other questions and in other periods and locations.

METHODOLOGICAL APPENDIX

This book was based on the analysis of a variety of data collected from multiple sources in France and the United States, which were only briefly described in the introduction and substantive chapters. These data include (1) content analysis of 2,335 articles covering gay partnership and parenting reforms published in *The New York Times* and *Le Monde*; (2) content analysis of legislative and judicial archives of proceedings, debates, hearings, briefs, and reports of major bills and cases in California and Texas, on the U.S. federal level, on the French national level, and European cases affecting France; (3) interviews with seventy-two people involved in the debates, including experts who provided oral or written testimony to courts and legislatures, lawyers who coordinated experts and expertise in court cases, and legislators who set up hearings; and (4) participant observation of experts at public events sponsored by think tanks, professional organizations, and advocacy groups, as well as at research meetings and seminars. In this appendix, I describe in greater detail how I gathered and analyzed these data and conclude with a discussion of my standpoint doing cross-national comparative research.

MEDIA ANALYSIS (CHAPTER 1)

I used the Lexis-Nexis electronic archives to search *The New York Times* and *Le Monde*, both newspapers of record in the United States and France, respectively, for all articles that discuss same-sex couples and their families in relation to laws and legal reform. Conducting media analysis of gay parenting rights requires search terms that can capture a complex and fluctuating social and linguistic object. Journalists, editorialists, and letter writers describe sexual minorities and their rights using several words, such as homosexual, gay, lesbian, or queer. Moreover, their usage has changed over time. For example, *The New York Times* gradually shifted from using homosexual to gay or lesbian around the turn of the twenty-first century. Also, although it was common to talk about "domestic partnerships" and "civil unions" in the 1990s and early 2000s, "gay marriage," "same-sex marriage," and "same-sex unions" became more politically and journalistically popular in the last ten years. Because of individual habits, there can be systematic differences in word preference between journalists. Similarly, barriers to legal recognition of gay parenting cover the many ways in which same-sex couples gain access to parenthood, from custody battles with former different-sex spouses to surrogacy contracts, adoption, and artificial insemination. No single term sufficiently captures all of these modes of access. I thus designed my search query to deal with these linguistic and historical complexities.

I queried the database for articles whose full text contains co-occurrences of words in English, and their French equivalents, for sexual minorities—such as gay, lesbian, homosexual, and same-sex—for gay family issues—such as partnership, marriage, civil union, spouse, couple, adoption, assisted reproduction, surrogacy, and parenting—and for legal reforms—such as right, proposal, law, bill, committee, hearing, court, senate, and house of representatives. I expected this search to generate a list of all articles covering legal issues germane to my research question.

Consistent with the historical scope of the broader project, I limited my search to articles published between January 1, 1990, and July 31, 2013. This covers the period of legal debates, ending two months after the French legislature passed a law allowing marriage and adoption for same-sex couples and one month after U.S. Supreme Court decisions invalidated certain provisions of the Defense of Marriage Act (DOMA), allowing federal recognition to same-sex couples legally married in their home states. I also limited my search to newspaper articles, excluding blogs hosted on the newspapers' websites. This search yielded a total of 1,166 articles in *Le Monde* and 3,534 articles in *The New York Times*.

I used two criteria to filter out articles from this initial list that were unrelated to my research question. First, I eliminated articles that do not actually discuss gay family rights. These newspapers cover an especially broad variety and number of legal and political questions that fall under the umbrella of "gay rights." Workplace discrimination, hate crimes, military service, youth and sex education, sexual minorities in the media, the lives of public figures, and the ordination of gay and lesbian clergy are some examples. Because of the overlap between gay rights issues and the way journalists treat the question as a coherent field, many articles that do not center on gay family rights still mention them in passing. In addition, articles describing parliamentary strategies, lobbying, fundraising, and political campaigning in electoral and legislative seasons also often mention gay family rights issues, but in a cursory manor. I also eliminated all articles that do not cover national or local gay partnership and/or parenting rights, per se, but only mention them as part of a story on another topic. An example of such an article describes a legislative session in detail but only makes mention of a same-sex marriage bill under consideration.

I eliminated other articles using criteria specifically adapted to my analytical framework. Unlike frame analysis, which considers all articles as having a frame, "expertise" analysis, which I developed for this project, must identify whether or not an article does, in fact, contain "expert" knowledge. I therefore removed all articles describing gay family rights but that did not cite or include any form of expertise. Consistent with my theoretical approach, I broadly define "expertise" as any statements that include justifications on a stance or information that clarifies a point of view. Therefore, articles only containing quotes or phrases simply asserting stances, such as, "I am against gay marriage," were excluded. Those that included quotes or ideas with justifications, such as, "I am against gay marriage because homosexuality is a sin," were retained.

This filtration yielded a total of 652 articles in *Le Monde* and 1,683 in *The New York Times*, representing 55 percent and 47.6 percent, respectively, of the initial search results, a rate not uncommon in news media analysis of gay marriage.[1] To develop my analytical framework of expertise, I read a sample of two hundred articles from both newspapers, examining the factual information and quotes, inductively coding for the content of expertise and the types of people quoted. After identifying and labeling all of the information observed, I developed a list of nineteen types of "expertise" appearing across the newspapers. Some types are rooted in scientific or academic disciplines, such as "anthropology," "economics," "sociology," and "psychology." Other kinds, like "personal experience," are forms of lay expertise, in which speakers draw on their lives to justify their stances. Some arguments, which I label "religion," draw on scriptural and moral justifications. Some people justify their stances with knowledge too broad or arguments too unspecific—such as politicians who say they support gay marriage because it is "the right thing to do"—to belong to a category. I call these sorts of arguments "general" expertise. When they do so, I use the same label journalists, op-ed writers, or the people they quote use to qualify their statements. For example, when a journalist writes that "psychological studies show that children of same-sex couples fare as well as their peers," I label that occurrence of expertise as "psychology." For each type of expertise, I also observed whether it takes a neutral, affirmative, or negative stance on gay parenting rights. Table A.1 provides the complete list of types of "expertise."

To distinguish between types of knowledge and the people who provide it, I developed a list of eighteen types of "experts" that journalists quote or who write letters and op-ed pieces. This list encompasses people from the professions—such as professors, doctors, and lawyers—from the political sphere—such as judges, politicians, and activists—and from civil society—such as religious representatives and members of the public. It also includes labels for when people speak in the name of organizations or think tanks. Experts can belong to multiple categories. For instance, I would include someone such as Mary Bonauto, the director of the Civil Rights Project for the Gay and Lesbian Advocates and Defenders, in three categories: "activist," "lawyer," and "organization." Table A.2 provides the complete list of types of expertise and categories of experts. I analyzed experts' stances for or against gay family rights, but save for several exceptions, those patterns reflect their overall proportions and are therefore not represented in the chapter. In other words, if a category of expert is more often cited in one newspaper, that category is higher in arguments both for and against gay family rights. Where pertinent, exceptions are described in the text.

Using these lists, I created a spreadsheet database by recording every occurrence of expertise for each article. Take for example an article about a U.S. civil union debate describing a lawyer affiliated with a liberal activist organization who argues that civil unions are inadequate because they are not recognized by other states. I would code that occurrence as "legal expertise 'for' " and note the speaker's expert category as "lawyer, activist, organization." The same article quotes a Catholic bishop and member of the Conference of Bishops stating that civil unions are unacceptable because homosexuality is a sin; I would code that as "religious expertise 'against' " and the speaker as a "religious representative, organization."

With information on the content of expertise by category and expert for each article and newspaper, I used the database to quantify and compare trends in time, stance, category of expertise, and type of expert, as well as compare across newspapers. When conducting direct comparisons, I performed chi-square tests of each

Type of expertise	Description	Example
Activism	Discusses activist organization practices; knowledge activists have gathered about the issues	"Ending DOMA will not end the legal and personal issues gays and lesbians face."
Anthropology	Cites an anthropologist or uses the word anthropology	"Marriage is a universal anthropological truth."
Demography	Demographic information	"In 2008 about 116,000 same-sex couples across the country were raising a total of about 250,000 [children]."
Economy	Public and private finances; businesses and the private sector	"Legalizing same-sex ceremonies in the state would result in about $63.8 million in government tax and fee revenue over three years."
Ethics	Specifically labels ethics or bioethics	"The Catholic Church does not emphasize ethics, nor beliefs."
General	Provides justification for stance but in general/ unspecific terms	"We should pass gay marriage because it is fair and the right thing."
History	Appeals to history or past events or cites historian	"For thousands of years marriage has been between a man and woman."
Law	Legal code; the status of a legal issue; juridical arguments	"Proposition 8 essentially nullifies the equal protection guarantee."
Medicine/biology	Medical and biological research	"Soon it will be possible for same-sex couples to reproduce using their own genes."
Other	Does not fit into another category but too few articles to justify new category	"Same-sex couples require new linguistic categories."
Personal	Person's experience; descriptions of same-sex couples' lives	"This is about the possibility that half of the state of Oregon thinks that I don't deserve to be treated equally as the majority."
Philosophy	Specifically sites philosophical principles or concepts; cites philosophy	"There is no philosophical obstacle to gay parenting in terms of the rights of children."
Politics	Cites political science; uses political institutional arguments	"It should be clear that these religious institutions have the right to refuse to marry anyone within their own religious houses."
Psychiatry	Discusses mental and emotional well-being, specifically mentioning psychiatry	"The psychiatric literature shows no harm to children of same-sex couples."

(continued)

Type of expertise	Description	Example
Psychoanalysis	Citing psychoanalysts or psychoanalytic ideas	"Gays that want to have children suffer from a pathological narcissist fantasy of self-reproduction."
Psychology	Discusses mental and emotional well-being	"Studies show children need a mother and father to develop properly."
Public opinion	Polling	"Recent polls show that the electorate is now evenly split."
Religion	Scripture, moral concepts, appeals to deities	"Same-sex marriage is against the word of God."
Sociology	Discusses norms, and social structures; cites sociology	"Regnerus finds that children do best with intact families."

TABLE A.2 Complete List of Categories of Experts

Type of expert	Description
Activist	Belonging to an activist organization or doing activist work, such as phone banking
Artist	Member of a creative field, such as actor, visual artist, performer, etc.
Author	Having published but not a professor or academic within an institution
Average person	Members of the public
Government agency	Organization affiliated with the state, such as the Census Bureau
Industry	Business owners, investors, a private sector worker
Intellectual	Unaffiliated academic
Journalist	Author of the article or other journalists cited
Judge	Judges of any type
Lawyer	A person practicing law
Medical/mental health professional	Doctors, psychiatrists, psychologists, psychoanalysts
Organization	Associations and groups of any kind, including professional organizations
Philosopher	A person specifically labeled philosopher, particularly in the French case
Politician	Any elected official
Professor	Affiliated academic in any field
Public figure	Person with notoriety but not belonging to another category, such as the child of a politician, like Chelsea Clinton
Religious representative	Member of the clergy or religious organization
Think tank	Organization specifically calling itself a think tank

table using Stata in order to verify the statistical significance of the differences between coverage. Some of the tables were used to elaborate figures that represent the patterns graphically. My analysis examined each kind of expertise independently, but to ease understanding, in the data presentation, I grouped together similarly themed types into clusters. "Social sciences" includes anthropology, economy, politics, and sociology. "Mental health" combines psychiatry, psychology, and psychoanalysis. Some types of expertise, such as "medicine and biology," had limited occurrences of expertise in either newspaper. These were grouped together as "all other." Statistical tests were done both for the independent types of expertise and for these aggregate clusters. When pertinent, I discuss differences within the clusters. Full results of the statistical tests are available on request.

LEGISLATIVE AND JUDICIAL ARCHIVAL ANALYSIS (CHAPTER 2)

I analyzed the role of experts and expertise in the content of proceedings in courts and legislatures in the United States and France. Because of the jurisdictional structures on the issues of same-sex couples' partnership and parenting rights, I included several analytical levels to these national cases. As explained in the introduction, in the United States, individual states have primary jurisdiction over these issues. It was therefore necessary to examine legal reforms on the state level. Rather than analyze all fifty states in detail, to make this study feasible, I selected two comparable states: California and Texas. They are the first and second most populous states, with active think tanks, strong local and national gay and antigay social movement organizations, and significant media presence on the national stage. They differ, however, in their political alignments—California has traditionally been more Democratic and Texas more Republican—as well as on their laws on gay families. Before 2015, whereas both states had constitutional amendment referenda banning same-sex marriage, California briefly recognized such unions and had a domestic partnership law offering almost all of the same rights, while Texas did not. Because of the role of U.S. federal courts in constitutional law, as well as the role of Congress in passing DOMA, I also examined the U.S. federal level.

In France, I focused on the national level because only the national Parliament, with the approval of the Conseil Constitutionnel, has the power to create or modify laws relative to marriage and parenting. Furthermore, although lower-level courts can sometimes vary in their judgments on issues, such as adoption and custody cases, they do not build case law. Because French citizens can appeal rulings in France's highest courts—the Conseil Constitionnel, the Conseil d'État, and the Cour de Cassation—to the European Court of Human Rights, I also analyzed those decisions that had an impact—or not—on French law.

To identify the major legislation and court cases on the relevant issues, I surveyed the secondary scholarly literature on gay family rights in the United States and France, concentrating especially on surveys detailing legal reforms.[2] I also consulted the extensive online legal analysis of U.S. and international LGBTQ rights organizations, which provide maps and detailed up-to-date descriptions of constantly evolving legislation and jurisprudence.[3] Finally, I searched the databases of the relevant legal institutions for bills and cases with pertinent keywords in both languages, such as adoption, marriage, and partnership.

Because of the high number of cases and bills and the amount of data they implied, I narrowed my analytical focus to those that had significant implications for the rights of same-sex couples and their families. In California legislation, I focused on AB 1982 (1995), which attempted to prevent the recognition of out-of-state same-sex marriages and eventually inspired Proposition 22, which banned same-sex marriage in statutory law; AB 205 (2003), the California Domestic Partner Rights and Responsibilities Act, which established civil unions for same-sex couples; AB 43 (2006), which would have legalized same-sex marriage; and hearings held before the passage of Proposition 8 (2008). In Texas, which had fewer bills overall, I focused on SB 7 (2003), which banned same-sex marriage and civil unions in law, and HJR 6 (2005), which created a referendum that inscribed that ban into the state's constitution. On the U.S. federal level, I examined DOMA (1996) and later attempts to create a federal anti-gay-marriage amendment in 2004 and repeal DOMA in 2011. In courts, I focused on the case *In Re Marriage Cases* (2008), which legalized same-sex marriage before Proposition 8, *United States v. Windsor* (2013), *Hollingsworth v. Perry* (2013), and *DeBoer v. Snyder* (2014).[4] In the French case, I focused on the Pacte civil de solidarité (Pacs) of 1999, which authorized civil unions, and the 2013 bill authorizing same-sex marriage and adoption.[5] At the European Court of Human Rights (ECtHR), I studied the cases originating in France: *Fretté v. France* (2002), *E.B. v. France* (2008), and *Gas and Dubois v. France* (2012).[6] Table A.3 summarizes these laws and court cases.

After identifying the cases and legislation, I used the online archives of the relevant institutions to access the records of proceedings, debates, hearings, reports,

TABLE A.3 Laws and Legal Cases Most Frequently Discussed in the Book

Legal institution	Date	Title	Description
United States			
U.S. Congress	1996	The Defense of Marriage Act (DOMA)	This bill (passed) banned federal recognition of same-sex marriage and allowed states to refuse to recognize those granted under the laws of other states.
U.S. Congress	2004	The Federal Marriage Amendment	This bill (not passed) proposed an amendment to the U.S. Constitution that would define marriage as between one man and one woman.
U.S. Congress	2011	The Respect for Marriage Act	This bill (not passed) would have repealed DOMA and required the federal government and states to recognize same-sex marriage.
U.S. Judiciary	2013	*United States v. Windsor*	The U.S. Supreme Court invalidated DOMA.
U.S. Judiciary	2013	*Hollingsworth v. Perry* (*Perry v. Schwarzenegger*)	The U.S. Supreme Court invalidated California's Proposition 8, legalizing same-sex marriage in that state. This case was originally titled *Perry v. Schwarzenegger* before appeal.
U.S. Judiciary	2014	*DeBoer v. Snyder*	The U.S. District Court (Michigan) struck down Michigan's constitutional amendment prohibiting same-sex marriage. It was consolidated with other cases on appeal to be heard as *Obergefell v. Hodges* in the U.S. Supreme Court.
U.S. Judiciary	2015	*Obergefell v. Hodges*	The U.S. Supreme Court found that state laws and constitutional amendments prohibiting same-sex marriage violate the Constitution of the United States.
California			
California legislature	1995	AB 1982: An act to amend Section 300 of the Family Code, relating to family law	Sparked by the Hawaii Supreme Court's then pending decision in *Baehr v. Miike* (1996) that California lawmakers feared would legalize same-sex marriage, they proposed a bill (not passed) that would have defined marriage as heterosexual and banned the recognition of out-of-state same-sex marriages.

(continued)

Legal institution	Date	Title	Description
California legislature	2003	AB 205: The California Domestic Partner Rights and Responsibilities Act of 2003	This bill (passed) granted most of the rights and responsibilities of marriage to registered domestic partners (same-sex couples or heterosexual couples where one member is at least sixty-two).
California legislature	2006	AB 43: Religious Freedom and Civil Marriage Protection Act	This bill (not passed) would have legalized same-sex marriage in California, overturning Proposition 22 (2000), which defined marriage as heterosexual in the California Family Code.
California judiciary	2008	*In Re Marriage Cases*	The Supreme Court of the State of California ruled that state law defining marriage as heterosexual (Proposition 22) violated the state's constitution.
California referendum	2008	Proposition 8: Amending the Constitution to Eliminate the Right of Same-Sex Couples to Marry	This referendum (passed) modified California's constitution to define marriage as heterosexual, overturning the California Supreme Court's decision in the *In Re Marriage Cases* (2008).
Texas			
Texas legislature	2003	SB 7: The Defense of Marriage Act	This bill (passed) modified Texas law to explicitly prohibit any legal recognition of same-sex partnerships and also defined marriage as a heterosexual union.
Texas legislature	2005	HJR 6: Proposing a constitutional amendment providing that marriage in this state consists only of the union of one man and one woman	This bill (passed) proposed an amendment to Texas's constitution (passed) defining marriage as heterosexual and prohibiting the passage of any legal relationship statuses similar or identical to marriage (i.e., civil unions).
Europe			
European Court of Human Rights (ECtHR)	2002	*Fretté v. France*	The ECtHR determined that France could use a potential adoptive father's homosexuality as a reason to deny his application to adopt.
European Court of Human Rights	2008	*E.B. v. France*	The ECtHR determined that France could not use a potential adoptive mother's homosexuality as a reason to deny her application to adopt, reversing the justification behind their previous decision.

European Court of Human Rights	2012	*Gas and Dubois v. France*	The ECtHR determined that France had infringed on the rights of a lesbian couple who were in a civil partnership by refusing to allow the non-birth mother to adopt the child of her partner.
France			
French legislature	1999	Pacte civil de solidarité (Pacs) [Civil Solidarity Pact]	This bill (passed) allowed different-sex and same-sex couples to enter into civil unions granting many of the same rights as marriage, excluding those related to parenting and immigration.
French legislature	2013	Loi ouvrant le mariage aux couples de personnes de même sexe [Law opening marriage to same-sex couples]	This ball (passed) modified the Civil Code to allow marriage, and by extension adoption, to be available to both same-sex and different-sex couples.

briefs, and other materials on file. These records represented more than fourteen thousand cumulative pages of judicial and legislative work around these reforms. Some legislative hearings were only available in video format. These included those for California and Texas and the hearings during the marriage debates in France. I downloaded those from Texas and France and traveled to the State Archives in California to access the physical copies, which could only be consulted in person before being prepared for duplication. These video records totaled more than one hundred hours of testimony.

In analyzing these records, I concentrated particularly on the parts of the process involving experts, such as briefs and full trials in courts and oral and written testimony during hearings in legislatures. I studied the number of people who provided this information and categorized them according to the same typology I use in the media analysis. This allowed me to identify the categories of experts, such as professors, mental health professionals, religious representatives, or ordinary people, that provided information most often to decision-makers. I also examined the kinds of information these people shared in their testimony. I traced whether there were differences in the categories of experts and kinds of knowledge they used across courts and legislatures as well as across national cases and jurisdictions.

INTERVIEWS AND OBSERVATION (CHAPTERS 3, 4, 5, AND 6)

I directly solicited interviews from experts who had participated in either French or American debates. I used the media, legislative, and judicial data to identify them. I prioritized people who had spoken in front of legal institutions, such as courts or legislatures, as well as people who have organized or brought expertise to legal institutions, such as lawyers and lawmakers. I aimed to speak to experts who had testified either in favor of or against gay family reforms. To have a variety of perspectives, I also sought to speak with people from multiple academic disciplines and who had been involved in the debates for different lengths of time. I hoped to speak to scholars and professionals who had been involved in the debates for the entire twenty-five-year historical period as well as those who were involved more recently.

I contacted interviewees by email. In France, I contacted several experts via handwritten letters after French researchers told me this would be more effective. My interview request stated the objective of my research, my institutional affiliations, and my motivation for contacting them specifically. During the course of the interview, I asked respondents if they had personal or professional connections with other experts I hoped to interview. If they did, I asked if they could either put me in touch with those people or if I could use their name to request an interview on their behalf. I suspected this approach would be helpful in opening doors. It proved especially necessary for gaining access to conservative experts. It was also essential for gaining access to famous respondents whose email addresses and telephone numbers are private and who receive constant solicitation. I also knew that I was more likely to get a positive response, or at least an acknowledgement of my request and a denial, if another well-known expert or trusted friend of theirs could vouch for me. In one case that I am aware of, unbeknownst to me, the potential interviewee contacted one of my faculty mentors to ask whether I was trustworthy.

I interviewed seventy-two experts, thirty-seven who participated in French debates and thirty-five who participated in American debates. Fifty-seven interviewees (twenty-eight in France and twenty-nine in the United States) were supportive of allowing same-sex couples to marry at the time of the interview. Of these, eight (seven in France and one in the United States) were formerly opposed but later changed their minds. Though also generally supportive of their access to adoption, assisted reproductive techniques, and surrogacy, several interviewees in support of same-sex marriage expressed some reservations about one or more of these questions. Fifteen interviewees (nine French and six American) did not support either relationship or parenting rights for same-sex couples. Tables A.4 and A.5 list the interviewees, their professions, their affiliations, and their stance at the time of the interview.

Although there is a preponderance of supporters among the pool of experts heard in courts and legislators, I strove to interview as many opponents as possible. Despite considerable effort, their limited representation in my sample likely reflects a distrust to speak to a sociologists who has published on sexual minorities and gay parenting. They likely assumed that my political stance reflects that of most sociologists who appear to dominate the American field today and that I would portray them unfavorably. Moreover, some have had their scholarly reputations and personal reputations publicly questioned, which probably makes them leery of interviews.

Many interview solicitations to them went unacknowledged and unanswered. I attempted to contact them through multiple avenues. For example, I had three interviewees contact researchers at the Heritage Foundation who were among their personal contacts but never got a response. Similarly, I contacted David Blankenhorn on behalf of several interviewees and over the course of several months, but my requests went unacknowledged. Three people, Bradford Wilcox, professor of sociology at the University of Virginia, Monseigneur André Vingt-Trois, a French cardinal, and Tony Anatrella, a Parisian priest, author, and psychoanalyst, all wrote back but declined to be interviewed. They said they were unavailable or did not see a reason why I should interview them. A senior researcher at the Family Research Council, whom I met at one of their public conferences, agreed to be interviewed pending permission from his organization's public relations department. They denied my request.

Two conservative experts, Mark Regnerus, professor of sociology at the University of Texas at Austin, and Robert P. George, professor of jurisprudence at Princeton and founder of several advocacy organizations, initially agreed to interviews but then, after repeated communication to set up a time, stopped responding. One conservative respondent, who asked not to be identified, agreed to an interview and we spoke for several hours. They called back several days later and asked to be retracted from the study. They cited

TABLE A.4 Interviewees in U.S. Debates (n = 35)

Name	Profession/activity	Organization/affiliation
Opponents		
Allen, Douglas	Professor economy	Simon Fraser University
Duncan, William	Activist organization researcher	Marriage Law Foundation
Gallagher, Maggie	Activist organization founder/scholar	Institute for Marriage and Public Policy
Lund, Nelson	Professor law	George Mason University
Morse, Jennifer Roback	Activist organization founder/scholar	The Ruth Institute
Wardle, Lynn	Professor law	Brigham Young University
Supporters		
Anderson, Clinton	Professional organization staff	American Psychological Association
Avery, Shannon	Judge	State of Maryland
Badgett, Lee	Professor economy/think tank researcher	UMass Amherst/Williams Institute
Boaz, David	Think tank executive vice president	The Cato Institute
Bonauto, Mary	Activist lawyer	Gay and Lesbian Alliance and Defenders
Carpenter, Dale	Professor law	University of Minnesota
Cherlin, Andrew	Professor sociology	Johns Hopkins University
Cooper, Leslie	Activist lawyer	American Civil Liberties Union
Cott, Nancy	Professor history	Harvard University
Egan, Edmund	Economist/professor economy	City of San Francisco
Eskridge, William	Professor law	Yale University
Galatzer-Levy, Robert	Professor psychology/psychoanalyst	University of Chicago
Gates, Gary	Think tank researcher	The Williams Institute
Haider-Markel, Donald P.	Professor political science	University of Kansas
Herek, Gregory	Professor psychology	University of California Davis
Hillsman, Sally	Professional organization executive	American Sociological Association
Hunter, Nan	Professor law	Georgetown University
Lamb, Michael	Professor psychology	Cambridge University
Manning, Wendy	Professor sociology	Bowling Green State University
Meyer, Ilan	Professor psychology	The Williams Institute
Patterson, Charlotte	Professor psychology	University of Virginia
Peplau, Letitia Anne	Professor psychology	University of California Los Angeles
Pizer, Jennifer	Activist lawyer	Lambda Legal
Rosenfeld, Michael	Professor psychology	Stanford University
Shapiro, Ilya	Think tank researcher	The Cato Institute
Stein, Edward	Professor law	Cardozo School of Law
Stern, Marc D.	Activist lawyer	American Jewish Committee
Stewart, Therese	City government lawyer	City of San Francisco
Zia, Helen	Author/activist/average person	None

Name	Profession/activity	Organization/affiliation
Opponents		
Collin, Thibaud	Professor philosophy	Collège Stanislas
Dekeuwer-Defossez, Françoise	Professor law	Université Catholique de Lille
Flavigny, Christian	Psychoanalyst/psychiatrist	Hôpital de la Pitié-Salpétrière
Fulchiron, Hugues	Professor law	Université de Lyon III
Lacroix, Xavier	Professor philosophy/theology	Université Catholique de Lyon
Levy-Soussan, Pierre	Psychoanalyst/psychiatrist	Psychology practice / Université Paris-Diderot
Neirinck, Claire	Professor law	Université de Toulouse I
Ménard, Claire	Agency staff	Union National des Associations Familiales
Vallat, Jean-Philipe	Agency under director	Union National des Associations Familiales
Supporters		
Badinter, Elisabeth	Professor philosophy	École Polytechnique
Binet, Erwann	Legislator	Assemblée Nationale
Bloche, Patrick	Legislator	Assemblée Nationale
Borrillo, Daniel	Professor law	Université Paris Ouest Nanterre
Brunet, Laurence	Scholar law/bioethics	Université de Paris / Hôpital Cochin
Cadoret, Anne	Professor anthropology	Centre National de le Recherche Scientifique
Courduriès, Jérôme	Professor anthropology	Université de Toulouse II
Delaisi de Parseval, Geneviève	Psychoanalyst/professor	Multiple
Descoutures, Virginie	Researcher sociology	Institut National d'Études Démographiques
Fassin, Eric	Professor sociology	Université Paris 8
Godelier, Maurice	Professor anthropology	École des Hautes Études en Sciences Sociales
Gross, Martine	Researcher sociology	Centre National de le Recherche Scientifique
Hefez, Serge	Psychoanalyst/psychiatrist	Hôpital de la Pitié-Salpétrière
Héritier, Françoise	Professor anthropology	Collège de France
Jouannet, Pierre	Doctor/professor	Université Paris Descartes, Multiple
Le Déroff, Joël	Activist organization staff	ILGA—Europe
Mécary, Caroline	Lawyer	None
Michel, Jean-Pierre	Legislator	Sénat
Nadaud, Stéphane	Psychoanalyst/psychiatrist	Hôpital de Ville-Évrard
Neiertz, Nicolas	Activist organization president	Association David et Jonathan
Quinqueton, Denis	Activist organization president	Association Homosexualités et Socialismes
Roudinesco, Élisabeth	Professor of history	École Normale Supérieure, Multiple
Sanguinetti, Patrick	Activist organization president	Association David et Jonathan
Schulz, Marianne	Ministry staff member	Ministère des solidarités
Seban, Pablo	Average person/activist	Indépendent
Théry, Irène	Professor sociology	École des Hautes Études en Sciences Sociales
Urwicz, Alexandre	Activist organization	Association des Familles Homoparentales
Wintemute, Robert	Professor law/lawyer	King's College, London

fears of retribution and potential harm to their ability to engage in future policy debates. I offered to let them read and correct any quotes of theirs I would include in the write up as well as exclude any information they felt uncomfortable seeing published, but they refused. Some American experts supporting gay family rights, such as Jonathan Rauch and Andrew Sullivan, both conservative gay intellectuals, declined to be interviewed or did not respond to requests. Similarly, in France, Nicolas Gougain, the spokesperson of the Inter-LGBT, a French advocacy organization, and François de Singly, a sociologist, declined or did not acknowledge my interview request, despite repeated solicitation.

Several respondents, both supporters and opponents, asked to see my complete interview guide before agreeing to speak with me. One submitted his responses in writing but then agreed to a follow-up interview. One respondent asked to read and edit the transcript of our interview. Two respondents also declined to allow me to quote them verbatim, and two others asked to read any work before publication to ensure that I was not misquoting them. Finally, most respondents, at least once during the interview, asked to speak off the record. All of these requests suggest their desire to control their public image and manage their reputations. These requests make sense in light of the elevated political stakes of gay family rights and the pressure they exert on experts; anything and everything they say is scrutinized and could be used to undermine their credibility in their professions and before lawmakers and judges.

I conducted interviews in person, over the telephone, and via videoconferencing technology. Interviews ranged from one to four hours. Interviews were shortest with professionals who bill by the hour. I had the interviews fully transcribed and used HyperResearch to code and analyze them.

I supplemented these interviews with ethnographic fieldwork in both countries. Between 2008 and 2015, I attended workshops, public debates, academic seminars, professional conferences, academic meetings, and other events featuring knowledge producers I identified through my media and institutional analysis. Table A.6 includes the complete list of events I attended in person but does not list the webinars and online conferences I also watched. Throughout this ethnographic fieldwork, I had hundreds of informal conversations with experts—some of whom I was able to later formally interview—and observed their interactions with one another.

TABLE A.6 Conferences, Seminars, and Events Attended in Person

Type	Organization/event	Title	Date	Location
United States				
Think tank conference	The Williams Institute	14th Annual Update: Marriage and Beyond	4/17/15	Los Angeles
Public conference	KPCC Radio	Forcing the Spring: Inside the Fight for Marriage Equality. Featuring Terry Stewart, Torie Osborne, and Jo Becker	4/28/14	Los Angeles
Think tank conference	The Williams Institute	More Progress, More Stagnation, More Setbacks: A Global Picture of Legal Recognition of Same-Sex Orientation	4/13/14	Los Angeles
University seminar	UCLA School of Law	Comparative Sexual Orientation Law Featuring Robert Wintemute	4/8/14	Los Angeles
Think tank conference	The Family Research Council	Pro-life Con	1/22/14	Washington
Professional conference	American Sociological Association	When the Professional Becomes Political: Responding to the New Family Structures Survey	8/19/13	New York
Professional conference	Eastern Sociological Association	Infertility and Assisted Reproductive Technologies	2/21/13	Boston
Think tank conference	The Williams Institute	11th Annual Update: Fair Play? LGBT People, Civic Participation, and Political Process	4/13/12	Los Angeles
Academic conference	The Williams Institute UCLA Department of History	Why History Matters. Same-Sex Marriage: Past, Present, and Future	2/24/11	Los Angeles
Academic conference	UCLA School of Law	The Aftermath of Prop 8: Is Gay Really the New Black?	11/13/08	Los Angeles
France				
Professional conference	Association Française de Sociologie	Vers une dénaturalisation du genre, de la sexualité et de la famille?	7/2/15	Saint Quentin en Yvelines
University seminar	EHESS "Genre, Personne, Interlocution," directed by Irène Théry	"Etat civil des enfants nés de GPA: quand la politique interfère dans l'application du droit positif" Featuring Caroline Mécary	5/26/15	Paris
University conference	Centre de recherche Droit, sciences et techniques at Univ. Paris I and Centre d'études et de recherches en sciences administratives et politiques at Univ. Paris II	Don, contre-don et rémunération des gamètes dans l'assistance médicale à la procréation: Perspectives de droit comparé	12/10/14	Paris

(continued)

TABLE A.6 (*continued*)

Type	Organization/event	Title	Date	Location
Professional hearing	Académie Nationale de Médicine	Audition sur l'accès aux PMA et la GPA aux couples homosexuels	11/16/13	Paris
University conference	EHESS	History Politics and the Supreme Court in the U.S. Debate Over Same-Sex Marriage	10/25/13	Paris
University seminar	Université de Toulouse, Master Anthropologie	Procéation et parentalité	10/9/13	Toulouse
Professional conference	Association Française de Sociologie	La science au service de la religion	9/4/13	Nantes
University conference	EHESS	Contre la tyrannie du genre	6/5/13	Paris
University conference	Université de Toulouse	Les familles homoparentales aujourd'hui: les enjeux	4/18/13	Toulouse
University conference	Association Master 2 Droit Privé at Droit Privé Général de l'Université Panthéon-Assas, Paris II	L'ouverture du mariage aux personnes de même sexe	4/15/13	Paris
Activist conference	Manif Pour Tous	Grand Meeting Régional La Manif Pour Tous	3/12/13	Toulouse
Think tank conference	Terra Nova	"Poings de vue," PMA–GPA: un débat en gestation?	3/6/13	Paris

Some of these events I attended were part of my standard academic activities as a sociologist. For example, I attended the meetings of the American Sociological Association and the French Sociological Association, at which experts held panels and gave papers. I also audited seminars and classes run by experts, such as Irène Théry and Martine Gross. I was also formally heard by the French Académie Nationale de Médecine about the state of the U.S. empirical research on the outcomes of children raised by same-sex couples because of a review article I co-authored with one of my graduate school mentors, Mignon Moore.[7] Working on that article provided me with an insider's view into the way American family sociologists collaborate and work together. Beginning in 2014, toward the very end of the field work, I participated as a volunteer researcher with France's first large-scale interdisciplinary cohort study of children raised by same-sex couples, DEVHOM, and ultimately co-authored several articles based on this work.[8] This opportunity gave me an ethnographic perspective of the opportunities and challenges facing French researchers who are working in a changing field.

STANDPOINT IN COMPARATIVE RESEARCH

In conducting this comparative cultural sociological research, I brought my perspective as a person raised in the United States but who had lived and worked in France regularly for a decade at the time of the fieldwork to study people working in both countries. I attempted to remain conscious of my position as a relative insider in the United States and outsider in France in order to remain sensitive to the ways I might be relying on my own cultural assumptions as I interpreted how American and French experts and policymakers worked. Cultural sociologists and anthropologists describe how working in a cultural context that is new and unfamiliar can help bring to light people's taken-for-granted assumptions and worldviews in ways that might be difficult for locals to perceive. At the same time, researchers run the risk of imposing their own culturally informed frameworks on the people they are studying. And, if they conduct comparative work, they may reify their own cultures as normal relative to the other contexts they study. I strived to be aware of these issues as I lived and carried out fieldwork in both countries.

Gaining a more than superficial understanding of the cultural contexts that shape how people think and work requires living and immersing oneself in those countries. I was raised in the United States and learned French in high school—which I now speak fluently—before pursuing a bachelor's degree in French studies. After college and spending a "year abroad" in France, I moved there to work and study for four years. I earned a master's degree in American studies from the University of Toulouse, which gave me a French academic perspective of the United States, and taught post-secondary and high school English and U.S. government courses. I began my PhD training at the University of California, Los Angeles in the United States and ultimately defended my dissertation in 2015 in a dual diploma with the École des hautes études en sciences sociales (EHESS). During graduate school, I spent my time living between both countries. These experiences have not only helped me to gain a deeper understanding of French culture but have also helped me to see American cultural norms in ways that would not be possible if I had not lived abroad for so long. I now have family, friends, and colleagues in both places. My discussions with them as I gathered and analyzed my data helped make me sensitive to the perspectives and assumptions I brought to my work.

My status as an American in France provided some unique advantages in conducting interviews with and observing French academics, professionals, activists, and policymakers. First, I believe that they may have been more willing to meet and speak with me because they perceived me as an outsider who did not have political stakes in the conflicts and struggles between and among French experts and political actors. As described in chapter 4, the French knowledge production field is small and conflictual. Therefore, my interviewees might have perceived a French sociologists as a potential threat or expected him to represent a particular intellectual or political "camp." I was likely exempted from some of those issues. Second, because French respondents assumed I was not especially familiar with their context, they were probably willing to answer questions and be more explicit about their processes, challenges, and issues in ways they might not have been with a French native. In the United States, although I was not perceived as a cultural outsider, I emphasized that I was conducting comparative work and the fact I had received a grant from the French government, which may have encouraged interviewees to respond to my request for interviews.

I also tried to be attentive to my connection to the issues I was analyzing and the impact that could have on my reactions to ideas, stances, and power dynamics I encountered in the field. One connection is related to my scholarship and position within sociology. By the time I began data collection for this book, I had already published or was in the process of publishing work related to gay and lesbian people and their families in the United States and France. Thus, as it concerns the role of sociologists in these debates, my position as a junior member of this academic community may have given me easier access to some internal discussions but also potentially exposed me to issues of status hierarchies and critical distance. I attempted to navigate as best I could the fractures among sociologists on both sides of the Atlantic—but especially in France—that their involvement in gay family debates created.

My other connection to these issues is personal. This book has shown that people will attempt to disqualify those who are involved as experts or decision-makers in gay family rights debates—sometimes successfully—because of their religious beliefs, ideological stances, or romantic and family lives. Whether or not these tactics are fair, such credibility struggles are characteristic of the legal and political debates I analyze. And, perhaps ironically, I am not immune from the very dynamics I bring to light in this book. For this reason, I am aware that discussing this dimension of my life may lead some to disqualify my analyses as biased. Nevertheless, I am committed to a feminist epistemological stance that rigorous empirical scholarship benefits from acknowledging that all researchers are socially situated and none are neutral. Thanks to my position, I have a unique vantage on these questions that has made my research stronger. Not only do I study gay family rights because it is an issue I care very much about as a citizen and a social scientist, but as a married gay man—whose relationship was made legally recognizable thanks to the French parliament—and as a child of lesbian mothers who raised me and my sister in Baltimore during a time when lesbian parenting was only beginning to become more common, I feel compelled to understand how experts and decision-makers dissect families like my own. When it felt appropriate or when I was asked, I disclosed this fact to interviewees. And even when I did not, some may have made assumptions about my life based on my research interests anyway. I am confident that the quality of my data and the transparency about my methodological choices in analyzing them give readers the tools to come to their own conclusions about my findings.

NOTES

INTRODUCTION: ON WHAT GROUNDS? HOW SAME-SEX MARRIAGE EXPERTS ESTABLISH POWER IN THEIR COUNTRIES

1. *Perry v. Schwarzenneger*, 685 F. Supp. 4 (U.S. D.C. N. CA. 2010).

2. Jean-Pierre Michel, "Rapport (437 Tome II) fait au nom de la commission des lois constitutionnelles, sur le projet de loi, adopté par l'assemblée nationale, ouvrant le mariage aux couples de personnes de même sexe" (Sénat: Commission des Lois, March 20, 2013), 94. Unless otherwise stated, all quotations in French have been translated into English by the author.

3. Some notes on terminology. Legal and political struggles dealing with the intimate and familial lives of gay, lesbian, bisexual, and transgender people are complex and multifaceted. The language to describe them is as well. This book focuses on debates over partnership rights—whether the state should give any recognition to the romantic relationships between two men or two women—and on parenting rights—whether the state should allow gay and lesbian people to have access to parenthood, via adoption or medically assisted reproductive techniques, and recognize that children can legally have two mothers or two fathers. In this book, except where precision is necessary, the term "gay family debates" or "gay family rights" refers to all of these legal questions. In addition, this book uses the terminology "same-sex" rather than "same-gender" marriage. This decision is twofold. On the one hand, perhaps out of habit, much extant literature uses the term "same-sex" when referring to relationships among men or among women, on the (sometimes unquestioned) assumption that these people are cisgender. There is, however, a growing body of work on the romantic and familial relationships of trans people. On the other hand, many of the legal debates center specifically on whether people with the same legal "sex" can indeed marry one another and adopt children. That is, the gender identity of the person may not be what matters for legal purposes as much as the "sex" on their official state documentation. Inasmuch as two people have different "sexes," they may be able to marry regardless of their gender identities even in jurisdictions that prohibit same-sex marriage. For these reasons, despite its imperfections, this book uses the terminology of "same-sex" rather than "same-gender" when talking about gay family rights. For research on families in which one or more of the parents is transgender, the

following sources are a good place to start: Timothy J. Biblarz and Evren Savci, "Lesbian, Gay, Bisexual, and Transgender Families," *Journal of Marriage and Family* 72, no. 3 (June 2010): 480–97, https://doi.org/10.1111/j.1741-3737.2010.00714.x; Mignon R. Moore and Michael Stambolis-Ruhstorfer, "LGBT Sexuality and Families at the Start of the Twenty-First Century," *Annual Review of Sociology* 39, no. 1 (2013): 491–507, https://doi .org/10.1146/annurev-soc-071312-145643; Olivia Fiorilli, "Reproductive Injustice and the Politics of Trans Future in France," *TSQ: Transgender Studies Quarterly* 6, no. 4 (November 1, 2019): 579–92, https://doi.org/10.1215/23289252-7771737; Trish Hafford-Letchfield et al., "What Do We Know about Transgender Parenting?: Findings from a Systematic Review," *Health and Social Care in the Community* 27, no. 5 (2019): 1111–25, https://doi.org/10.1111 /hsc.12759.

4. Scott Barclay, "In Search of Judicial Activism in the Same-Sex Marriage Cases: Sorting the Evidence from Courts, Legislatures, Initiatives and Amendments," *Perspectives on Politics* 8, no. 01 (March 2010): 111–26, https://doi.org/10.1017/S1537592709992696; Miriam Smith, *Political Institutions and Lesbian and Gay Rights in the United States and Canada* (Taylor & Francis, 2008).

5. Timothy P. Carney, "Opinion: Biden Says He's Pro-Science. Why Is His Schools Plan Based on Fear?," *New York Times*, February 19, 2021, sec. Opinion, https://www.nytimes .com/2021/02/19/opinion/coronavirus-schools-biden.html.

6. Maya J. Goldenberg, *Vaccine Hesitancy: Public Trust, Expertise, and the War on Science* (University of Pittsburgh Press, 2021); Aaron M. McCright and Riley E. Dunlap, "Defeating Kyoto: The Conservative Movement's Impact on U.S. Climate Change Policy," *Social Problems* 50, no. 3 (August 1, 2003): 348–73, https://doi.org/10.1525/sp.2003.50.3.348; Dorothy McBride Stetson, *Abortion Politics, Women's Movements, and the Democratic State: A Comparative Study of State Feminism* (Oxford University Press, 2001).

7. Patrick J. Egan and Megan Mullin, "Climate Change: US Public Opinion," *Annual Review of Political Science* 20, no. 1 (2017): 209–27, https://doi.org/10.1146/annurev-polisci -051215-022857; Ruth Hubbard, *The Politics of Women's Biology* (Rutgers University Press, 1990); Ted G. Jelen and Clyde Wilcox, "Causes and Consequences of Public Attitudes Toward Abortion: A Review and Research Agenda," *Political Research Quarterly* 56, no. 4 (December 1, 2003): 489–500, https://doi.org/10.1177/106591290305600410; Rachael Shwom et al., "Understanding U.S. Public Support for Domestic Climate Change Policies," *Global Environmental Change*, Governance, Complexity and Resilience, 20, no. 3 (August 1, 2010): 472–82, https://doi.org/10.1016/j.gloenvcha.2010.02.003; Jeremy K. Ward and Patrick Peretti-Watel, "Understanding Vaccine Mistrust: From Perception Bias to Controversies," *Revue francaise de sociologie* 61, no. 2 (October 6, 2020): 243–73.

8. Daniel Hirschman, "Rediscovering the 1 Percent: Knowledge Infrastructures and the Stylized Facts of Inequality," *American Journal of Sociology* 127, no. 3 (November 1, 2021): 739–86, https://doi.org/10.1086/718451.

9. Sheila Jasanoff, *Designs on Nature: Science and Democracy in Europe and the United States* (Princeton University Press, 2005); Harry Collins and Robert Evans, *Rethinking Expertise* (University of Chicago Press, 2008); Naomi Oreskes and Erik M. Conway, *Merchants of Doubt: How a Handful of Scientists Obscured the Truth on Issues from Tobacco Smoke to Global Warming* (Bloomsbury, 2010).

10. Aaron M. McCright and Riley E. Dunlap, "The Politicization of Climate Change and Polarization in the American Public's Views of Global Warming, 2001–2010," *Sociological Quarterly* 52, no. 2 (March 1, 2011): 155–94, https://doi.org/10.1111/j.1533-8525.2011.01198.x; Melissa Lane, "Political Theory on Climate Change," *Annual Review of Political Science* 19, no. 1 (2016): 107–23, https://doi.org/10.1146/annurev-polisci-042114-015427; Doug McAdam, "Social Movement Theory and the Prospects for Climate Change Activism in the United States," *Annual Review of Political Science* 20, no. 1 (2017): 189–208, https://doi.org/10.1146/annurev-polisci-052615-025801.

11. Anna Grzymala-Busse, "Why Comparative Politics Should Take Religion (More) Seriously," *Annual Review of Political Science* 15, no. 1 (2012): 421–42, https://doi.org/10.1146/annurev-polisci-033110-130442.

12. Isabelle Engeli et al., eds., *Morality Politics in Western Europe* (Palgrave Macmillan, 2012); Mildred A. Schwartz and Raymond Tatalovich, *The Rise and Fall of Moral Conflicts in the United States and Canada* (University of Toronto Press, 2018).

13. Tom Waidzunas, *The Straight Line: How the Fringe Science of Ex-Gay Therapy Reoriented Sexuality* (University of Minnesota Press, 2015); Guillaume Marche, "Flawed Science: mobilisations conservatrices, sexualité et discours scientifique," *Revue française d'études américaines* 133, no. 3 (2012): 67–81, https://doi.org/10.3917/rfea.133.0067; Joanna Wuest, *Born This Way: Science, Citizenship, and Inequality in the American LGBTQ+ Movement* (University of Chicago Press, 2023).

14. Jimi Adams and Ryan Light, "Scientific Consensus, the Law, and Same Sex Parenting Outcomes," *Social Science Research* 53 (September 2015): 300–310, https://doi.org/10.1016/j.ssresearch.2015.06.008; M. V. Lee Badgett, *When Gay People Get Married: What Happens When Societies Legalize Same-Sex Marriage* (NYU Press, 2009); Daniel Borrillo and Éric Fassin, eds., *Au delà du Pacs: l'expertise familiale à l'épreuve de l'homosexualité* (Presses Universitaires de France, 2001); Bette L. Bottoms, Margaret Bull Kovera, and Bradley D. McAuliff, *Children, Social Science, and the Law* (Cambridge University Press, 2002); Susan Gluck Mezey, *Gay Families and the Courts: The Quest for Equal Rights* (Rowman & Littlefield, 2009); Kathleen E. Hull, "The Role of Social Science Expertise in Same-Sex Marriage Litigation," *Annual Review of Law and Social Science* 13, no. 1 (2017): 471–91, https://doi.org/10.1146/annurev-lawsocsci-110615-084729; Michael J. Rosenfeld, *The Rainbow After the Storm: Marriage Equality and Social Change in the U.S.* (Oxford University Press, 2021).

15. Tina Fetner, *How the Religious Right Shaped Lesbian and Gay Activism* (University of Minnesota Press, 2008); Roman Kuhar, "Playing with Science: Sexual Citizenship and the Roman Catholic Church Counter-Narratives in Slovenia and Croatia," *Women's Studies International Forum* 49 (March 2015): 84–92, https://doi.org/10.1016/j.wsif.2014.07.005.

16. Lisa Dilling and Maria Carmen Lemos, "Creating Usable Science: Opportunities and Constraints for Climate Knowledge Use and Their Implications for Science Policy," *Global Environmental Change*, Special Issue on The Politics and Policy of Carbon Capture and Storage, 21, no. 2 (May 2011): 680–89, https://doi.org/10.1016/j.gloenvcha.2010.11.006; R. E. Dunlap and P. J. Jacques, "Climate Change Denial Books and Conservative Think Tanks: Exploring the Connection," *American Behavioral Scientist* 57, no. 6 (June 1, 2013): 699–731, https://doi.org/10.1177/0002764213477096.

17. Elizabeth A. Armstrong and Mary Bernstein, "Culture, Power, and Institutions: A Multi-Institutional Politics Approach to Social Movements," *Sociological Theory* 26, no. 1 (2008): 74–99, https://doi.org/10.1111/j.1467-9558.2008.00319.x; Francesca Polletta and Beth Gharrity Gardner, "Culture and Movements," in *Emerging Trends in the Social and Behavioral Sciences*, ed. Robert Scott and Stephen Kosslyn (Wiley & Sons, 2015), 1–13, https://doi.org/10.1002/9781118900772.etrds0108.

18. Engeli et al., *Morality Politics in Western Europe.*

19. Ellen Ann Andersen, *Out of the Closets and Into the Courts: Legal Opportunity Structure and Gay Rights Litigation* (University of Michigan Press, 2005); David Paternotte, *Revendiquer le "mariage gay": Belgique, France, Espagne* (Editions de l'Université de Bruxelles, 2011); Smith, *Political Institutions and Lesbian and Gay Rights in the United States and Canada*; Charles Tilly and Sidney G. Tarrow, *Contentious Politics* (Paradigm Publishers, 2007); Manon Tremblay et al., eds., *The Lesbian and Gay Movement and the State: Comparative Insights Into a Transformative Relationship* (Ashgate, 2011); Engeli et al., *Morality Politics in Western Europe*; Christopher Z. Mooney, ed., *The Public Clash of Private Values: The Politics of Morality Policy* (Chatham House Publishers, 2001); Donald P. Haider-Markel, "Morality in Congress? Legislative Voting on Gay Issues," in *The Public Clash of Private Values: The Politics of Morality Policy*, ed. Christopher Z. Mooney (Chatham House Publishers, 2001), 115–29; Smith, *Political Institutions and Lesbian and Gay Rights in the United States and Canada.*

20. Rodney Benson and Abigail Cope Saguy, "Constructing Social Problems in an Age of Globalization: A French-American Comparison," *American Sociological Review* 70, no. 2 (April 2005): 233–59; Joel Best, *Social Problems* (Norton, 2012); Tilly and Tarrow, *Contentious Politics*; Sara L. Wiest et al., "Framing, Partisan Predispositions, and Public Opinion on Climate Change," *Global Environmental Change* 31 (March 1, 2015): 187–98, https://doi.org/10.1016/j.gloenvcha.2014.12.006.

21. Kathrin S. Zippel, *The Politics of Sexual Harassment: A Comparative Study of the United States, The European Union, and Germany* (Cambridge University Press, 2006); Gil Eyal, "For a Sociology of Expertise: The Social Origins of the Autism Epidemic," *American Journal of Sociology* 118, no. 4 (January 1, 2013): 863–907, https://doi.org/10.1086/668448.

22. Deborah Stone, *Policy Paradox: The Art of Political Decision Making*, 3rd ed. (Norton, 2011).

23. Dilling and Lemos, "Creating Usable Science"; Sheila Jasanoff, *Science at the Bar: Law, Science, and Technology in America* (Harvard University Press, 2009); Timothy L. O'Brien, "Scientific Authority in Policy Contexts: Public Attitudes About Environmental Scientists, Medical Researchers, and Economists," *Public Understanding of Science (Bristol, England)* 22, no. 7 (October 2013): 799–816, https://doi.org/10.1177/0963662511435054; Timothy L. O'Brien et al., "Scientific Disciplines and the Admissibility of Expert Evidence in Courts," *Socius* 8 (January 1, 2022): 23780231221108044, https://doi.org/10.1177/23780231221108044; Hull, "The Role of Social Science Expertise in Same-Sex Marriage Litigation."

24. Armstrong and Bernstein, "Culture, Power, and Institutions."

25. Edwin Amenta and Francesca Polletta, "The Cultural Impacts of Social Movements," *Annual Review of Sociology* 45, no. 1 (2019): 279–99, https://doi.org/10.1146/annurev-soc-073018-022342; Dilling and Lemos, "Creating Usable Science."

26. Carole E. Joffe et al., "Uneasy Allies: Pro-Choice Physicians, Feminist Health Activists and the Struggle for Abortion Rights," *Sociology of Health and Illness* 26, no. 6 (2004): 775–96, https://doi.org/10.1111/j.0141-9889.2004.00418.x; Oscar Javier Maldonado, "The Decriminalisation of Abortion in Colombia as Cautionary Tale: Social Movements, Numbers and Socio-Technical Struggles in the Promotion of Health as a Right," *Global Public Health* 14, no. 6–7 (July 3, 2019): 1031–43, https://doi.org/10.1080/17441692.2018.1504101.

27. Marianna Y. Smirnova and Sergey Y. Yachin, "Epistemic Communities and Epistemic Operating Mode," *International Journal of Social Science and Humanity* 5, no. 7 (2015): 646–50.

28. Oreskes and Conway, *Merchants of Doubt*.

29. Elizabeth Chiarello, "Where Movements Matter: Examining Unintended Consequences of the Pain Management Movement in Medical, Criminal Justice, and Public Health Fields," *Law and Policy* 40, no. 1 (2018): 79–109, https://doi.org/10.1111/lapo.12098; Nancy Felipe Russo and Jean E. Denious, "Controlling Birth: Science, Politics, and Public Policy," *Journal of Social Issues* 61, no. 1 (2005): 181–91, https://doi.org/10.1111/j.0022-4537.2005.00400.x.

30. Neil Fligstein and Doug McAdam, *A Theory of Fields* (Oxford University Press, 2012).

31. Sheila Jasanoff, ed., *States of Knowledge: The Co-Production of Science and the Social Order* (Routledge, 2004); Dilling and Lemos, "Creating Usable Science."

32. Daniel Béland and Robert Henry Cox, eds., *Ideas and Politics in Social Science Research* (Oxford University Press, 2010).

33. Dunlap and Jacques, "Climate Change Denial Books and Conservative Think Tanks."

34. Mieke Verloo, "Gender Knowledge, and Opposition to the Feminist Project: Extreme-Right Populist Parties in the Netherlands," *Politics and Governance* 6, no. 3 (September 14, 2018): 20–30, https://doi.org/10.17645/pag.v6i3.1456.

35. Karin Knorr-Cetina, *Epistemic Cultures: How the Sciences Make Knowledge* (Harvard University Press, 1999).

36. Sally Jones et al., " 'We Were Fighting for Our Place': Resisting Gender Knowledge Regimes Through Feminist Knowledge Network Formation," *Gender, Work and Organization* 26, no. 6 (2019): 789–804, https://doi.org/10.1111/gwao.12288.

37. Pauline Cullen et al., "Introduction to Special Issue: Gender, Knowledge Production and Knowledge Work," *Gender, Work and Organization* 26, no. 6 (2019): 765–71, https://doi.org/10.1111/gwao.12329.

38. Kristin Luker, *Abortion and the Politics of Motherhood* (University of California Press, 1984).

39. Sandra G. Harding and Merrill B. Hintikka, eds., *Discovering Reality: Feminist Perspectives on Epistemology, Metaphysics, Methodology, and Philosophy of Science*, Synthese Library, vol. 161 (D. Reidel, 1983); Patricia Hill Collins, *Black Feminist Thought: Knowledge, Consciousness, and the Politics of Empowerment*, Perspectives on Gender, vol. 2 (Routledge, 1991).

40. Patrick Murphy, a professor at the University of Alabama at Birmingham's Bill L. Harbert Institute of Innovation and Entrepreneurship, and his colleagues appear to have been the first to coin the term "expert capital" in a 2007 article, but they have not developed it conceptually since then and it seems not to have diffused within or beyond

business studies. Patrick J. Murphy et al., "Expert Capital and Perceived Legitimacy," *International Journal of Entrepreneurship and Innovation* 8, no. 2 (May 1, 2007): 127–38, https://doi.org/10.5367/000000007780808002.

41. Pierre Bourdieu, "The Specificity of the Scientific Field and the Social Conditions of the Progress of Reason," *Social Science Information* 14, no. 6 (December 1, 1975): 19–47, https://doi.org/10.1177/053901847501400602; Pierre Bourdieu, *La distinction: critique sociale du jugement* (Minuit, 1979); Pierre Bourdieu, "The Forms of Capital," in *Handbook of Theory and Research for the Sociology of Education*, ed. John Richardson (Greenwood Press, 1986), 46–58.

42. The sociologist David Swartz also describes experts as possessing cultural capital—without going into further detail—in the political field, contrasting it with the "social/organizational" capital of political operatives who draw their power from "popular support and/or bureaucratic inertia." David L. Swartz, *Symbolic Power, Politics, and Intellectuals: The Political Sociology of Pierre Bourdieu* (University of Chicago Press, 2013), 63.

43. Bourdieu, "The Forms of Capital."

44. Swartz, *Symbolic Power, Politics, and Intellectuals*, 103.

45. In her analysis of feminist self-help movements in 1970s California, the technoscience studies scholar and historian, Michelle Murphy, calls the process by which something is understood as political or not as the "politics of 'politics.' " Michelle Murphy, *Seizing the Means of Reproduction: Entanglements of Feminism, Health, and Technoscience* (Duke University Press, 2012).

46. Swartz explains that "symbolic capital points to a type of legitimation where the vested interests of some authority are misperceived as being disinterested." Swartz, *Symbolic Power, Politics, and Intellectuals*, 103.

47. Bourdieu, "The Forms of Capital," 18.

48. Steven Brint, *In an Age of Experts* (Princeton University Press, 1996); Irène Théry, "Expertises de service, de consensus, d'engagement: essai de typologie de la mission d'expertise en sciences sociales," *Droit et société* 60, no. 2 (June 1, 2005): 311–27.

49. Abigail C. Saguy, *What's Wrong with Fat?* (Oxford University Press, 2013); Frank Fischer, *Citizens, Experts, and the Environment: The Politics of Local Knowledge* (Duke University Press, 2000); Sarah Franklin, "Science as Culture, Cultures of Science," *Annual Review of Anthropology* 24, no. 1 (1995): 163–84, https://doi.org/10.1146/annurev.an.24.100195.001115.

50. Steven Epstein, *Impure Science: AIDS, Activism, and the Politics of Knowledge* (University of California Press, 1996).

51. Gil Eyal and Larissa Buchholz, "From the Sociology of Intellectuals to the Sociology of Interventions," *Annual Review of Sociology* 36, no. 1 (2010): 117–37, https://doi.org/10.1146/annurev.soc.012809.102625; Francis Chateauraynaud, *Argumenter dans un champ de forces: Essai de balistique sociologique* (Editions Pétra, 2011).

52. Bourdieu, "The Specificity of the Scientific Field and the Social Conditions of the Progress of Reason"; Pierre Bourdieu, "Le champ scientifique," *Actes de la Recherche en Sciences Sociales* 2, no. 2 (1976): 88–104, https://doi.org/10.3406/arss.1976.3454; Pierre Bourdieu, *Les usages sociaux de la science: Pour une sociologie clinique du champ scientifique* (Editions Quae, 2019).

53. Monica Di Gregorio, "Gaining Access to the State: Political Opportunities and Agency in Forest Activism in Indonesia," *Social Movement Studies* 13, no. 3 (July 3, 2014): 381–98,

https://doi.org/10.1080/14742837.2013.856297; David S. Meyer, "Protest and Political Opportunities," *Annual Review of Sociology* 30 (2004): 125–45; Thomas Medvetz, *Think Tanks in America* (University of Chicago Press, 2012).

54. Dilling and Lemos, "Creating Usable Science."

55. Eyal and Buchholz, "From the Sociology of Intellectuals to the Sociology of Interventions."

56. Andrew Abbott, *The System of Professions: An Essay on the Division of Expert Labor* (University of Chicago Press, 1988); Marion Fourcade, *Economists and Societies: Discipline and Profession in the United States, Britain, and France, 1890s to 1990s* (Princeton University Press, 2009); Jasanoff, *Designs on Nature*.

57. Bourdieu, "Le champ scientifique"; Andrew M. McKinnon et al., "Bourdieu, Capital, and Conflict in a Religious Field: The Case of the 'Homosexuality' Conflict in the Anglican Communion," *Journal of Contemporary Religion* 26, no. 3 (October 2011): 355–70, https://doi.org/10.1080/13537903.2011.616033; Pierre Bourdieu, "The Force of Law: Toward a Sociology of the Juridical Field," *Hastings Law Journal* 38 (1987): 805–53; Swartz, *Symbolic Power, Politics, and Intellectuals*.

58. Thomas F. Gieryn, *Cultural Boundaries of Science: Credibility on the Line* (University of Chicago Press, 1999).

59. O'Brien et al., "Scientific Disciplines and the Admissibility of Expert Evidence in Courts."

60. Henri Bergeron, "The Soft Power of the European Centre for Drugs and Drug Addiction," in *European Drug Policies: The Ways of Reform*, ed. Henri Bergeron (Routledge, 2017), 40–56.

61. Luc Boltanski and Laurent Thévenot, *De la justification: les économies de la grandeur*, Essais (Gallimard, 1991).

62. Myra Marx Ferree, "Resonance and Radicalism: Feminist Framing in the Abortion Debates of the United States and Germany," *American Journal of Sociology* 109, no. 2 (2003): 304–44; Myra Marx Ferree et al., *Shaping Abortion Discourse: Democracy and the Public Sphere in Germany and the United States* (Cambridge University Press, 2002).

63. Michèle Lamont and Laurent Thévenot, eds., *Rethinking Comparative Cultural Sociology: Repertoires of Evaluation in France and the United States* (Cambridge University Press, 2000); Erik Bleich, *Race Politics in Britain and France: Ideas and Policymaking Since the 1960s* (Cambridge University Press, 2003); Hank Johnston and John A. Noakes, *Frames of Protest: Social Movements and the Framing Perspective*, ed. Hank Johnston and John A. Noakes (Rowman & Littlefield, 2005); Abigail C. Saguy, *What Is Sexual Harassment?: From Capitol Hill to the Sorbonne* (University of California Press, 2003); Saguy, *What's Wrong with Fat?*

64. Jasanoff, *Designs on Nature*. In this work, Jasanoff is particularly interested in scientific knowledge, arguing that the influence of science on policy varies significantly from one country to another because of factors including, for example, how governments support and guide the scientific process. While I am also interested in science, I expand my analysis to other kinds of knowledge.

65. Sheila Jasanoff, "Cosmopolitan Knowledge: Climate Science and Global Civic Epistemology," in *The Oxford Handbook of Climate Change and Society*, ed. John S. Dryzek et al. (Oxford University Press, 2011), 129–43, https://doi.org/10.1093/oxfordhb/9780199566600.003.0009.

66. Roger Friedland and Robert Alford, "Bringing Society Back In: Symbols, Practices and Institutional Contradictions," in *The New Institutionalism in Organizational Analysis*, ed. Walter Powell and Paul Dimaggio (University of Chicago Press, 1991), 232–63; Patricia H. Thornton et al., *The Institutional Logics Perspective: A New Approach to Culture, Structure, and Process* (Oxford University Press, 2012).

67. Stefan Vogler, *Sorting Sexualities: Expertise and the Politics of Legal Classification* (University of Chicago Press, 2021).

68. Jan Beyers and Caelesta Braun, "Ties That Count: Explaining Interest Group Access to Policymakers," *Journal of Public Policy* 34, no. 1 (2014): 93–121; Cornelia Woll, "Lobbying in the European Union: From Sui Generis to a Comparative Perspective," *Journal of European Public Policy* 13, no. 3 (April 1, 2006): 456–69, https://doi.org/10.1080/13501760600560623.

69. Jasanoff, *States of Knowledge*.

70. Abbott, *The System of Professions*.

71. Paul Starr, *The Social Transformation of American Medicine: The Rise of a Sovereign Profession and the Making of a Vast Industry* (Basic Books, 1982).

72. Steven Epstein and Stefan Timmermans, "From Medicine to Health: The Proliferation and Diversification of Cultural Authority," *Journal of Health and Social Behavior* 62, no. 3 (September 2021): 240–54, https://doi.org/10.1177/00221465211010468.

73. These concepts are most useful for understanding how groups of professionals work to define, establish, control, and expand their "jurisdiction" and "authority" over certain areas of social life, such as doctors over health. They also see them as competing with other professionals, sometimes using the state as a means to solidify their positions. Jurisdiction and authority could be useful tools for explaining why, for example, psychoanalysts, relative to other types of mental health professionals, have held sway over family policy in France—as Camille Robcis has shown—and why their authority may be waning. Expert capital could then be used to help unpack how professionals struggle with one another to exert their expertise or claim authority. Indeed, one could argue that one of the ways professionals maintain jurisdiction is by augmenting the value and desirability of their expert capital relative to that of other groups. In this way, expert capital is different from jurisdiction and authority because it asks us to think about the specific social value (rhetorical, reputational, etc.) professionals—as well as other groups—provide to decision-makers within particular national settings as well as the risks and advantages that come along with sharing it. Camille Robcis, *The Law of Kinship: Anthropology, Psychoanalysis, and the Family in France* (Cornell University Press, 2013).

74. Steven Shapin, *A Social History of Truth: Civility and Science in Seventeenth-Century England*, Science and Its Conceptual Foundations Series (University of Chicago Press, 1995); Steven Shapin, "Cordelia's Love: Credibility and the Social Studies of Science," *Perspectives on Science* 3, no. 3 (1995): 255–75.

75. Epstein, *Impure Science*.

76. Epstein, *Impure Science*, 3.

77. Phillip M. Ayoub, *When States Come Out: Europe's Sexual Minorities and the Politics of Visibility* (Cambridge University Press, 2016); Haider-Markel, "Morality in Congress? Legislative Voting on Gay Issues"; H. N. Hirsch, ed., *The Future of Gay Rights in America* (Routledge, 2005); Kathleen E. Hull, *Same-Sex Marriage: The Cultural Politics of Love and*

Law (Cambridge University Press, 2006); Leigh Moscowitz, *The Battle Over Marriage: Gay Rights Activism Through the Media* (University of Illinois Press, 2013); Gary Mucciaroni, *Same Sex, Different Politics: Success and Failure in the Struggles Over Gay Rights* (University of Chicago Press, 2008); Gary Mucciaroni, "Are Debates About 'Morality Policy' Really About Morality? Framing Opposition to Gay and Lesbian Rights," *Policy Studies Journal* 39, no. 2 (May 1, 2011): 187–216, https://doi.org/10.1111/j.1541-0072.2011.00404.x; Jason Pierceson et al., *Same-Sex Marriage in the Americas: Policy Innovation for Same-Sex Relationships* (Lexington Books, 2010); Smith, *Political Institutions and Lesbian and Gay Rights in the United States and Canada.*

78. Borrillo and Fassin, *Au delà du Pacs*; Éric Fassin, "Le savant, l'expert et le politique: la famille des sociologues," *Genèses* 32, no. 1 (1998): 156–69, https://doi.org/10.3406/genes .1998.1533; Éric Fassin, "Usages de la science et science des usages," *L'Homme. Revue française d'anthropologie* 154–55 (January 1, 2000): 391–408, https://doi.org/10.4000/lhomme .39; Martine Gross, "Quand et comment l'homoparentalité est-elle devenue un objet « légitime » de recherche en sciences humaines et sociales?," *Socio-logos* 2 (October 16, 2007), http://socio-logos.revues.org/803; Ashveen Peerbaye, "L'invention de l'homoparentalité: acteurs, arènes et rhétoriques autour de la question de la filiation homosexuelle" (master's thesis [DEA], Cachan, France, ENS, 2000); Anne Verjus and Marine Boisson, "Quand connaître, c'est reconnaître? Le rôle de l'expertise familiale dans la production d'un sens commun du parent (homosexuel)," *Droit et société* 60, no. 2 (June 1, 2005): 449–67; Emmanuelle Yvert, "Des mobilisations victorieuses sans mouvement social. La construction de la cause de l'homoparentalité et sa traduction législative en France (1986–2013)" (PhD dissertation, Université Paris-Saclay, 2021), https://theses.fr /2021UPASU006.

79. Hull, "The Role of Social Science Expertise in Same-Sex Marriage Litigation"; Rosenfeld, *The Rainbow After the Storm.*

80. Brian Doherty and Graeme Hayes, "Having Your Day in Court: Judicial Opportunity and Tactical Choice in Anti-GMO Campaigns in France and the United Kingdom," *Comparative Political Studies* 47, no. 1 (2014): 3–29; Sidney Tarrow, "The Strategy of Paired Comparison: Toward a Theory of Practice," *Comparative Political Studies* 43, no. 2 (2010): 230–59.

81. Lamont and Thévenot, *Rethinking Comparative Cultural Sociology.*

82. Scholarship by Anne Stoler and Vrushali Patil is helpful for thinking through the way imperialism and colonialism develop legal regimes that define sexuality and gender through processes of racialization. I would like to thank the third anonymous reviewer of this manuscript for their helpful wording here, which I have borrowed. Ann Laura Stoler, *Race and the Education of Desire: Foucault's History of Sexuality and the Colonial Order of Things* (Duke University Press, 1995); Vrushali Patil, *Webbed Connectivities: The Imperial Sociology of Sex, Gender, and Sexuality* (University of Minnesota Press, 2022).

83. Michèle Lamont, *The Dignity of Working Men: Morality and the Boundaries of Race, Class, and Immigration* (Harvard University Press, 2002).

84. Rogers Brubaker, *Citizenship and Nationhood in France and Germany* (Harvard University Press, 1992); T. Jeremy Gunn, "Religious Freedom and Laicite: A Comparison of the United States and France," *Brigham Young University Law Review* 2004 (2004): 419–506;

Enda McCaffrey, *The Gay Republic: Sexuality, Citizenship and Subversion in France* (Ashgate, 2005).

85. Eléonore Lépinard, *L'égalité Introuvable: La parité, les feministes, et la République* (Presses de Sciences Po, 2007); Saguy, *What Is Sexual Harassment?*; Michael Stambolis-Ruhstorfer, "Labels of Love: How Migrants Negotiate (or Not) the Culture of Sexual Identity," *American Journal of Cultural Sociology* 1, no. 3 (October 2013): 321–45, https://doi.org/10.1057/ajcs.2013.11; Pauline Delage, *Violences conjugales: Du combat féministe à la cause publique* (Presses de Sciences Po, 2017); Christophe Broqua and Olivier Fillieule, "The Making of State Homosexuality: How AIDS Funding Shaped Same-Sex Politics in France," *American Behavioral Scientist* 61, no. 13 (November 1, 2017): 1623–39, https://doi.org/10.1177/0002764217744136; Omar Slaouti and Olivier Le Cour Grandmaison, eds., *Racismes de France* (La Découverte, 2020).

86. Patrick Simon, "The Choice of Ignorance the Debate on Ethnic and Racial Statistics in France," *French Politics, Culture and Society* 26, no. 1 (April 30, 2008): 7–31, https://doi.org/10.3167/fpcs.2008.260102.

87. Lamont and Thévenot, *Rethinking Comparative Cultural Sociology*.

88. Mezey, *Gay Families and the Courts*.

89. Andersen, *Out of the Closets and Into the Courts*; Patricia Cain, *Rainbow Rights: The Role of Lawyers and Courts in the Lesbian and Gay Civil Rights Movement* (Westview Press, 2000).

90. John L. Campbell and Ove K. Pedersen, *The National Origins of Policy Ideas: Knowledge Regimes in the United States, France, Germany, and Denmark* (Princeton University Press, 2014); Fourcade, *Economists and Societies*.

91. Brint, *In an Age of Experts*, 134.

92. Brint, *In an Age of Experts*; Eyal and Buchholz, "From the Sociology of Intellectuals to the Sociology of Interventions"; Fischer, *Citizens, Experts, and the Environment*; Frank Fischer, *Democracy and Expertise* (Oxford University Press, 2009); Andrew Rich, "Ideas, Expertise, and Think Tanks," in *Ideas and Politics in Social Science Research*, ed. Daniel Béland and Robert Henry Cox (Oxford University Press, 2010), 191–207; Gil Eyal, *The Crisis of Expertise* (Polity, 2019).

93. Charles E. Lindblom, *Usable Knowledge: Social Science and Social Problem Solving* (Yale University Press, 1979); Medvetz, *Think Tanks in America*; Rich, "Ideas, Expertise, and Think Tanks."

94. Scott L. Cimmings and Douglas NeJaime, "Lawyering for Marriage Equality," *UCLA Law Review* 57 (2010 2009): 1235–331.

95. Andrea Louise Campbell, "Policy Makes Mass Politics," *Annual Review of Political Science* 15, no. 1 (2012): 333–51, https://doi.org/10.1146/annurev-polisci-012610-135202; Elisabeth S. Clemens and James M. Cook, "Politics and Institutionalism: Explaining Durability and Change," *Annual Review of Sociology* 25, no. 1 (1999): 441–66, https://doi.org/10.1146/annurev.soc.25.1.441.

96. Brint, *In an Age of Experts*, 192–93.

97. Jacques Commaille, "La famille, l'état, le politique: une nouvelle économie des valeurs," *Informations sociales* 136, no. 8 (December 1, 2006): 100–111.

98. Yann Bérard and Renaud Crespin, eds., *Aux frontières de l'expertise: dialogues entre savoirs et pouvoirs* (Presses Universitaires de Rennes, 2010).

99.   Pierre Bourdieu, *Homo academicus* (Minuit, 1984); Christophe Charle, *Naissance des "intellectuels": 1880–1900* (Minuit, 1990); Charles Kurzman and Lynn Owens, "The Sociology of Intellectuals," *Annual Review of Sociology* 28 (January 1, 2002): 63–90; Gisèle Sapiro, "Modèles d'intervention politique des intellectuels," *Actes de la recherche en sciences sociales* 176–77, no. 1 (March 6, 2009): 8–31; Swartz, *Symbolic Power, Politics, and Intellectuals.*

100.   Lamont and Thévenot, *Rethinking Comparative Cultural Sociology.*

101.   Elizabeth Popp Berman, *Thinking Like an Economist: How Efficiency Replaced Equality in U.S. Public Policy* (Princeton University Press, 2022).

102.   Marion Fourcade et al., "The Superiority of Economists," *Journal of Economic Perspectives* 29, no. 1 (2015): 89–114.

103.   David C. Barker et al., "Intellectualism, Anti-Intellectualism, and Epistemic Hubris in Red and Blue America," *American Political Science Review* 116, no. 1 (February 2022): 38–53, https://doi.org/10.1017/S0003055421000988; Eric Merkley, "Anti-Intellectualism, Populism, and Motivated Resistance to Expert Consensus," *Public Opinion Quarterly* 84, no. 1 (March 1, 2020): 24–48, https://doi.org/10.1093/poq/nfz053.

104.   Jeremy Ahearne, "Public Intellectuals and Cultural Policy in France," *International Journal of Cultural Policy* 12, no. 3 (November 1, 2006): 323–39, https://doi.org/10.1080/10286630601020603; Pierre Bourdieu, *La noblesse d'état: grandes écoles et esprit de corps* (Minuit, 1989); Charle, *Naissance des "intellectuels."*

105.   *Obergefell v. Hodges*, 135 S. Ct. 1039 (2015); Loi n° 2013–404 du 17 mai 2013, J.O. n° 0114 du 18 mai 2013, p. 8253.

106.   Relative to more precursor countries, such as Spain and Belgium, who legalized same-sex marriage in 2005 and 2003, respectively, the United States and France joined a larger list of countries who legalized same-sex marriage when it had already begun to be more common in Western Europe and North America. Work in political science and political sociology provides explanations for these differences in when and under what circumstances countries legalize same-sex marriage. Ayoub, *When States Come Out*; Mary Bernstein and Nancy A. Naples, "Altared States: Legal Structuring and Relationship Recognition in the U.S., Canada, and Australia," *American Sociological Review* 80, no. 6 (2015): 1226–49; Paternotte, *Revendiquer le "mariage gay."*

107.   Table A.3 in the methodological appendix provides a summary of the laws and court cases most frequently discussed in the book.

108.   Stéphanie Hennette-Vauchez, *Le droit de la bioéthique* (Editions La Découverte, 2009); Caroline Mécary, *L'amour et la loi* (Alma Editeur, 2012); Irène Théry and Anne-Marie Leroyer, *Filiation origines parentalité: Le Droit face aux nouvelles valeurs de responsabilité générationnelle* (Odile Jacob, 2014).

109.   Mary Bernstein and Verta Taylor, eds., *The Marrying Kind? Debating Same-Sex Marriage Within the Lesbian and Gay Movement* (University of Minnesota Press, 2013).

110.   *Baehr v. Miike*, 910 P. 2d 112, 80 Haw. 341—Hawaii: Supreme Court, 1996.

111.   Pub.L. 104–199, 110 Stat. 2419, enacted September 21, 1996, 1 U.S.C. § 7 and 28 U.S.C. § 1738C.

112.   Andersen, *Out of the Closets and Into the Courts.*

113.   *Hollingsworth v. Perry*, 133 S. Ct. 2652 (2013); *United States v. Windsor*, 133 S. Ct. 2675, 2694 (2013).

114. In 2022, Congress passed and then president Joseph Biden signed into law the Respect for Marriage Act (RFMA; H.R. 8404) officially repealing the Defense of Marriage Act (DOMA). It required the U.S. federal government and all U.S. states to recognize same-sex and interracial civil marriages contracted in states and abroad.

115. Mezey, *Gay Families and the Courts*; Kimberly D. Richman, *Courting Change: Queer Parents, Judges, and the Transformation of American Family Law* (New York University Press, 2009).

116. Rene Almeling, *Sex Cells: The Medical Market for Eggs and Sperm* (University of California Press, 2011).

117. Andersen, *Out of the Closets and Into the Courts*; Bernstein and Naples, "Altared States"; Mary Bernstein, "United States: Multi-Institutional Politics, Social Movements, and the State," in *The Lesbian and Gay Movement and the State: Comparative Insights Into a Transformative Relationship*, ed. Manon Tremblay et al. (Ashgate, 2011), 197–212; Cain, *Rainbow Rights*; Jason Pierceson, *Courts Liberalism and Rights: Gay Law and Politics in the United States and Canada* (Temple University Press, 2005).

118. Council of Europe, European Convention for the Protection of Human Rights and Fundamental Freedoms, 4 November 1950, ETS 5, available at http://www.unhcr.org/refworld/docid/3ae6b3b04.html (accessed May 2, 2012). See, in particular, Protocol 12, Art. 1 § 1, General Prohibition of Discrimination. Mécary, *L'Amour et la Loi*; Paternotte, *Revendiquer le "mariage gay."*

119. *Fretté v. France* (Application no. 36515/97, March 26, 2002); *E.B. v. France* (Application no. 43546/02, January 22, 2008). Éric Garnier, *L'homoparentalité en France: La bataille des nouvelles familles* (Thierry Marchaisse Editions, 2012); Mécary, *L'amour et la loi.*

120. *Gas and Dubois v. France* (no. 25951/07, March 15, 2012).

121. Loi n° 99-944 du 15 novembre 1999, J.O. n° 265 du 16 novembre 1999, p. 16959.

122. Massimo Prearo, *Le moment politique de l'homosexualité: mouvements, identités, et communautés en France* (Presses Universitaires de Lyon, 2014); Christophe Broqua and David M. Halperin, *Action = Vie: A History of AIDS Activism and Gay Politics in France* (Temple University Press, 2020); David Caron, *AIDS in French Culture: Social Ills, Literary Cures* (University of Wisconsin Press, 2001); McCaffrey, *The Gay Republic.*

123. Yvert, "Des mobilisations victorieuses sans mouvement social."

124. Hennette-Vauchez, *Le droit de la bioéthique*; Sylvie Mennesson and Dominique Mennesson, *La gestation pour autrui: l'improbable débat* (Editions Michalon, 2010).

125. Virginie Descoutures, *Les mères lesbiennes* (PUF, 2010); Martine Gross et al., "Le recours à l'AMP dans les familles homoparentales: état des lieux. Résultats d'une enquête menée en 2012," *Socio-logos. Revue de l'association française de sociologie*, no. 9 (February 24, 2014), http://socio-logos.revues.org/2870.

126. Andersen, *Out of the Closets and Into the Courts.*

127. These divergent approaches to family in the United States and France also have roots in their respective colonial and imperial histories. Although different in their details, in both cases, marginalized groups were framed as having inferior or even deviant types of families. Policies were put into place to control them. The families of dominant groups were largely understood as normal and benefited from social and political support. While not central to the argument of this book, it is important to mention here that political debates around whether or not to normalize queer families are mixed together

with these historical and ongoing racial and class politics of defining the "right kind" of family. Mignon R. Moore, *Invisible Families: Gay Identities, Relationships, and Motherhood Among Black Women* (University of California Press, 2011); Bruno Perreau, *The Politics of Adoption. Gender and the Making of French Citizenship* (MIT Press, 2014); Robcis, *The Law of Kinship*; Camille Robcis, "Liberté, Égalité, Hétérosexualité: Race and Reproduction in the French Gay Marriage Debates," *Constellations* 22, no. 3 (September 1, 2015): 447–61, https://doi.org/10.1111/1467-8675.12168; Dorothy E. Roberts, *Killing the Black Body: Race, Reproduction, and the Meaning of Liberty* (Pantheon Books, 1997); Sébastien Roux, *Sang d'encre: enquête sur la fin de l'adoption internationale* (Vendémiaire, 2022); Amy C. Steinbugler, *Beyond Loving: Intimate Racework in Lesbian, Gay, and Straight Interracial Relationships* (Oxford University Press, 2012).

128. Robert Neelly Bellah et al., *Habits of the Heart: Individualism and Commitment in American Life* (University of California Press, 1985); Andrew J. Cherlin, *The Marriage-Go-Round: The State of Marriage and the Family in America Today* (Knopf Doubleday, 2010); Neil Gross, "The Detraditionalization of Intimacy Reconsidered*," *Sociological Theory* 23, no. 3 (2005): 286–311, https://doi.org/10.1111/j.0735-2751.2005.00255.x.

129. Andrew J. Cherlin, "American Marriage in the Early Twenty-First Century," *Future of Children* 15, no. 2 (2005): 33–55; Andrew J. Cherlin, "Demographic Trends in the United States: A Review of Research in the 2000s," *Journal of Marriage and Family* 72, no. 3 (June 1, 2010): 403–19.

130. Kelly Musick and Katherine Michelmore, "Cross-National Comparisons of Union Stability in Cohabiting and Married Families with Children," *Demography* 55, no. 4 (June 7, 2018): 1389–421, https://doi.org/10.1007/s13524-018-0683-6.

131. Melanie Heath, *One Marriage Under God: The Campaign to Promote Marriage in America* (NYU Press, 2012); Jennifer Randles, *Proposing Prosperity?: Marriage Education Policy and Inequality in America* (Columbia University Press, 2016).

132. Ange-Marie Hancock, "Contemporary Welfare Reform and the Public Identity of the 'Welfare Queen,'" *Race, Gender and Class* 10, no. 1 (2003): 31–59; Bart Landry, *Black Working Wives: Pioneers of the American Family Revolution* (University of California Press, 2002); Moore, *Invisible Families*.

133. Anna Marie Smith, *Welfare Reform and Sexual Regulation* (Cambridge University Press, 2007).

134. François De Singly, *Sociologie de la famille contemporaine*, 6th ed. (Armand Colin, 2017); Robcis, *The Law of Kinship*; Théry and Leroyer, *Filiation origines parentalité*.

135. Éric Fassin, "Same Sex, Different Politics: 'Gay Marriage' Debates in France and the United States," *Public Culture* 13 (2001): 215–32; Abigail Ocobock, "Leveraging Legitimacy: Institutional Work and Change in the Case of Same-Sex Marriage," *American Journal of Sociology* 126, no. 3 (November 2020): 513–44, https://doi.org/10.1086/712501; Brian Powell et al., *Counted Out: Same-Sex Relations and Americans' Definitions of Family* (Russel Sage Foundation, 2010); Gianfranco Rebuccini, "Du 'mariage pour tous' à la 'famille pour tout le monde?' Pour une politique queer populaire des parentés dépareillées," *Eigensinn* 1, no. 1 (2022): 111–31; Rosenfeld, *The Rainbow After the Storm*.

136. ADFH and IFOP, "La Position Des Français Sur La PMA et La GPA," Association des Familles Homoparentales (ADFH), May 29, 2019, https://adfh.net/wp-content

/uploads/2019/06/115524_Rapport_Ifop_ADFH_2019-3.pdf; Gayle Kaufman and D'Lane Compton, "Attitudes Toward LGBT Marriage and Legal Protections Post-Obergefell," *Sexuality Research and Social Policy* 18, no. 2 (June 1, 2021): 321–30, https://doi.org/10.1007/s13178-020-00460-y.

137. Research used in this book was funded in part by grants from the National Science Foundation (Doctoral Dissertation Research Improvement Grant, Law and Social Sciences Division, Grant No. SES 1226663); the Chateaubriand Fellowship program organized by the French Ministry of Foreign Affairs and the Fulbright Foundation; the UCLA Center for European and Eurasian Studies; and the UCLA Graduate Division.

138. It is important to mention that much of the time-consuming labor that goes into making exchanges between experts and decision-makers happen is carried out by people I did not interview: paralegals, secretaries, law clerks, parliamentary assistants, and other staff members. In the future, research could look at their contribution to decisions around expertise.

1. ACCORDING TO AUTHORITIES: EXPERTISE IN THE MEDIA

1. Jean-Pierre Winter, *Homoparenté* (Albin Michel, 2010).
2. Jean-Pierre Winter, "Ne Jouons Pas Aux Apprentis Sorciers !," *Le Monde*, October 23, 2010.
3. Maggie Astor, "Illinois Clergy Members Support Same-Sex Marriage in Letter Signed by 260," *New York Times*, December 24, 2012.
4. Erik Bleich, *Race Politics in Britain and France: Ideas and Policymaking Since the 1960s* (Cambridge University Press, 2003); Dominique Brossard et al., "Are Issue-Cycles Culturally Constructed? A Comparison of French and American Coverage of Global Climate Change," *Mass Communication and Society* 7, no. 3 (July 1, 2004): 359–77, https://doi.org/10.1207/s15327825mcs0703_6; Abigail C. Saguy, *What Is Sexual Harassment?: From Capitol Hill to the Sorbonne* (University of California Press, 2003); Abigail C. Saguy, *What's Wrong with Fat?* (Oxford University Press, 2013).
5. Michèle Lamont and Laurent Thévenot, eds., *Rethinking Comparative Cultural Sociology: Repertoires of Evaluation in France and the United States* (Cambridge University Press, 2000).
6. Rodney Benson and Abigail Cope Saguy, "Constructing Social Problems in an Age of Globalization: A French-American Comparison," *American Sociological Review* 70, no. 2 (April 2005): 233–59.
7. Éric Fassin, *Le sexe politique : Genre et sexualité au miroir transatlantique*, Cas de figure (Éditions de l'EHESS, 2009); Saguy, *What Is Sexual Harassment?*; Joan Wallach Scott, *Parité!: Sexual Equality and the Crisis of French Universalism* (The University of Chicago Press, 2005).
8. Judith Ezekiel, "Le Women's Lib: Made in France," *European Journal of Women's Studies* 9 (2002): 345–61; Fassin, *Le sexe politique*; Juliet A. Williams and Paul Apostolidis, "Introduction: Sex Scandals and Discourses of Power," in *Public Affairs: Politics in the Age of Sex Scandals*, ed. Juliet A. Williams and Paul Apostolidis (Duke University Press, 2004), 1–38.
9. Lamont and Thévenot, *Rethinking Comparative Cultural Sociology*.

10. Abigail Cope Saguy, "Puritanism and Promiscuity? Sexual Attitude in France and the United States," *Comparative Social Research* 18 (1999): 227–47; Alexis de Tocqueville, *De la démocratie en Amérique*, ed. Eduardo Nolla, Revised (Vrin, 1990).

11. Kevin M. Carragee and Wim Roefs, "The Neglect of Power in Recent Framing Research," *Journal of Communication* 54, no. 2 (June 1, 2004): 214–33, https://doi.org/10.1111/j.1460-2466 .2004.tb02625.x.

12. Rodney Benson and Daniel C. Hallin, "How States, Markets and Globalization Shape the News: The French and US National Press, 1965–97," *European Journal of Communication* 22, no. 1 (March 1, 2007): 27–48, https://doi.org/10.1177/0267323107073746; Benson and Saguy, "Constructing Social Problems in an Age of Globalization"; Brossard et al., "Are Issue-Cycles Culturally Constructed?"

13. Guy Golan, "Inter-Media Agenda Setting and Global News Coverage," *Journalism Studies* 7, no. 2 (April 1, 2006): 323–33, https://doi.org/10.1080/14616700500533643; Jean-Sébastien Rioux and Douglas A. Van Belle, "The Influence of *Le Monde* Coverage on French Foreign Aid Allocations," *International Studies Quarterly* 49, no. 3 (September 1, 2005): 481–502, https://doi.org/10.1111/j.1468-2478.2005.00374.x.

14. David E. Campbell and J. Quin Monson, "The Religion Card: Gay Marriage and the 2004 Presidential Election," *Public Opinion Quarterly* 72, no. 3 (January 1, 2008): 399–419, https:// doi.org/10.1093/poq/nfn032; Jeremiah J. Garretson, "Changing with the Times: The Spillover Effects of Same-Sex Marriage Ballot Measures on Presidential Elections," *Political Research Quarterly* 67, no. 2 (June 1, 2014): 280–92, https://doi.org/10.1177/1065912914521897.

15. Daniel Garcia, *La folle histoire du mariage gay* (Flammarion, 2004).

16. Adam Liptak, "Justices Say Time May Be Wrong for Ruling on Gay Marriage," *New York Times*, March 27, 2013, Late Edition, sec. A.

17. Maurice Berger, "L'homoparentalité est-elle porteuse d'un risque affectif?," *Le Monde*, February 8, 2013.

18. Abby Goodnough, "A Push Is on for Same-Sex Marriage Rights Across New England," *New York Times*, April 5, 2009, sec. A.

19. Pascale Kremer, "Sociologues, psychiatres et psychanalystes sont divisés," *Le Monde*, March 15, 1999.

20. Daniel Borrillo and Éric Fassin, eds., *Au delà du Pacs : l'expertise familiale à l'épreuve de l'homosexualité* (Presses Universitaires de France, 2001); Éric Fassin, "Same Sex, Different Politics: 'Gay Marriage' Debates in France and the United States," *Public Culture* 13 (2001): 215–32; Camille Robcis, *The Law of Kinship: Anthropology, Psychoanalysis, and the Family in France* (Cornell University Press, 2013).

21. Samuel G. Freedman, "Focus on the Family Works to Invite Discussion and Transform Message," *New York Times*, March 9, 2013, sec. A.

22. Tara Siegel Bernard and Ron Lieber, "The Costs of Being a Gay Couple Run Higher," *New York Times*, October 3, 2009, sec. A.

23. Marion Fourcade, *Economists and Societies: Discipline and Profession in the United States, Britain, and France, 1890s to 1990s* (Princeton University Press, 2009); Lamont and Thévenot, *Rethinking Comparative Cultural Sociology*; Michelle Marzullo, "Through a Glass, Darkly: U.S. Marriage Discourse and Neoliberalism," *Journal of Homosexuality* 58, no. 6–7 (2011): 758–74, https://doi.org/10.1080/00918369.2011.581919.

24. Michael Stambolis-Ruhstorfer and Josselin Tricou, "Resisting 'Gender Theory' in France: A Fulcrum for Religious Action in a Secular Society," in *Anti-Gender Campaigns in Europe*, ed. Roman Kuhar and David Paternotte (Rowman & Littlefield, 2017), 79–98.

25. Tony Anatrella, "Une précipitation anxieuse," *Le Monde*, October 10, 1998, sec. Divers.

26. Patrick Healy, "Hopefuls Differ as They Reject Gay Marriage," *New York Times*, November 1, 2008, sec. A.

27. Jackie Calmes and Peter Baker, "Obama Endorses Same-Sex Marriage, Taking Stand on Charged Social Issue," *New York Times*, May 10, 2012, sec. A.

28. Sheryl Gay Stolberg, "Hillary Clinton Backs Same-Sex Marriage," *New York Times*, March 19, 2013, sec. A.

29. Pascale Kremer, "Jean-Luc Romero, élu RPR, présente son compagnon à la télévision," *Le Monde*, September 20, 2001; Hugo Bouvard, *Gays et lesbiennes en politique: représenter les minorités sexuelles en France et Aux États-Unis* (Presses Universitaires du Septentrion, 2024).

30. Anne Chemin, "Une homosexuelle se voit refuser une adoption pour la deuxième fois," *Le Monde*, February 2009.

31. Hélène Bekmezian and Gaëlle Dupont, "Mariage gay: la droite veut s'opposer sans déraper," *Le Monde*, October 23, 2012.

2. THE FLOOR IS YOURS: EXPERTISE IN COURTS AND LEGISLATURES

1. The methodological appendix details my sampling and analytic techniques. Table A.3 in that section provides a summary of the laws and court cases I focus on in most depth.

2. Note that there is no official neutral stance because those providing testimony to Texas legislative committees register as either in favor or opposition to the bill under consideration.

3. Francesca Polletta, "Storytelling in Social Movements," in *Culture, Social Movements, and Protest*, ed. Hank Johnston (Ashgate, 2009), 33–53.

4. Carlos A. Ball, *The Right to Be Parents: LGBT Families and the Transformation of Parenthood* (NYU Press, 2012).

5. Access to parenting through adoption and other means has varied widely on the state level, as described in the introduction. Moreover, preventing same-sex couples from adopting was a goal in some jurisdictions, and as 2021 Supreme Court Case *Fulton v. City of Philadelphia* has demonstrated, hostility toward same-sex parenting, especially on the part of conservative religious organizations, such the Catholic Social Services, has continued in the wake of *Obergefell v. Hodges*.

6. Elizabeth Popp Berman, *Thinking Like an Economist: How Efficiency Replaced Equality in U.S. Public Policy* (Princeton University Press, 2022).

7. M. V. Lee Badgett and Brad Sears, "The Bottom Line on Family Equality: The Impact of AB 205 on California's Businesses," The Williams Institute, August 1, 2003, https://escholarship.org/uc/item/9s3603j4; M. V. Lee Badgett and Brad Sears, "The Impact on California's Budget of Allowing Same-Sex Couples to Marry," Institute for Gay and Lesbian Strategic Studies, May 1, 2004, https://policycommons.net/artifacts/1171661/the-impact-on-californias-budget-of-allowing-same-sex-couples-to-marry/1724790/.

8. Anthony Castet, "Guerres culturelles, idéologies et égalité des droits aux Etats-Unis : Le cas du mariage homosexuel," These de doctorat, Tours, 2016, https://www.theses .fr/2016TOUR2014; Melinda D. Kane and Thomas Alan Elliott, "Turning to the Courts: A Quantitative Analysis of the Gay and Lesbian Movement's Use of Legal Mobilization," *Sociological Focus* 47, no. 4 (October 2, 2014): 219–37, https://doi.org/10.1080/00380237.2014.939901.

9. Susan Gluck Mezey, *Gay Families and the Courts: The Quest for Equal Rights* (Rowman & Littlefield, 2009).

10. Allison Orr Larsen, "The Trouble with Amicus Facts," *Virginia Law Review* 100, no. 8 (2014): 1757–818; Allison Orr Larsen and Neal Devins, "The Amicus Machine," *Virginia Law Review* 102, no. 8 (December 2016): 1901–68.

11. Paul M. Collins Jr., "Friends of the Court: Examining the Influence of Amicus Curiae Participation in U.S. Supreme Court Litigation," *Law and Society Review* 38, no. 4 (2004): 807–32, https://doi.org/10.1111/j.0023-9216.2004.00067.x; Paul M. Collins Jr. et al., "The Influence of Amicus Curiae Briefs on U.S. Supreme Court Opinion Content," *Law and Society Review* 49, no. 4 (2015): 917–44, https://doi.org/10.1111/lasr.12166; Richard L. Pacelle Jr. et al., "Assessing the Influence of Amicus Curiae Briefs on the Roberts Court*," *Social Science Quarterly* 99, no. 4 (2018): 1253–66, https://doi.org/10.1111/ssqu.12480.

12. Larsen and Devins, "The Amicus Machine."

13. Brief of American Companies as *Amici Curiae* in Support of Respondents, *Hollingsworth v. Perry*, 570 U.S. 12–144 (2013).

14. Brief of the States of Indiana, Virginia, Alabama, Alaska, Arizona, Colorado, Georgia, Idaho, Kansas, Montana, Nebraska, North Dakota, Oklahoma, South Carolina, South Dakota, Texas, Utah, West Virginia, and Wisconsin as *Amici Curiae* in Support of Petitioners, *Hollingsworth v. Perry*, 570 U.S. 12–144 (2013).

15. "How Different Are the Adult Children of Parents Who Have Same-Sex Relationships? Findings from the New Family Structures Study," *Social Science Research* 41, no. 4 (2012): 752–70, https://doi.org/10.1016/j.ssresearch.2012.03.009.

16. Jo Becker, *Forcing the Spring: Inside the Fight for Marriage Equality* (Penguin Books, 2015).

17. Didier Eribon, *Sur cet instant fragile: carnets, janvier-août 2004* (Fayard, 2004).

18. ECHR, *Fretté* v. France no. 36515/97 (26 Feb. 2002); EHCR *E.B.* v. France no. 43546/02 (22 Jan. 2008).

19. "Usages de la science et science des usages," *L'Homme. Revue française d'anthropologie*, no. 154–155 (January 1, 2000): 391–408, https://doi.org/10.4000/lhomme.39; "Same Sex, Different Politics: 'Gay Marriage' Debates in France and the United States," *Public Culture* 13 (2001): 215–32.

20. Christèle Fraïssé, ed., *L'homophobie: Et les expressions de l'ordre hétérosexiste* (Presses universitaires de Rennes, 2011).

21. Françoise Dekeuwer-Défossez, "Rénover Le Droit de La Famille: Propositions Pour Un Droit Adapté Aux Réalités et Aux Aspirations de Notre Temps," Rapport au Garde des Sceaux (Ministère de la Justice, September 1999); Irène Théry, *Couple, filiation et parenté aujourd'hui: le droit face aux mutations de la famille et de la vie privée : Rapport à la Ministre de l'emploi et de la solidarité et au Garde des Sceaux, Ministre de la justice* (Odile Jacob, 1998).

22. Michèle Lamont and Laurent Thévenot, eds., *Rethinking Comparative Cultural Sociology: Repertoires of Evaluation in France and the United States* (Cambridge University Press, 2000).

23. Éric Fassin, "Same Sex, Different Politics: 'Gay Marriage' Debates in France and the United States," *Public Culture* 13 (2001): 215–32; Éric Fassin, "Same-Sex Marriage, Nation, and Race: French Political Logics and Rhetorics," *Contemporary French Civilization* 39, no. 3 (January 1, 2014): 281–301, https://doi.org/10.3828/cfc.2014.17; Camille Robcis, *The Law of Kinship: Anthropology, Psychoanalysis, and the Family in France* (Cornell University Press, 2013); Elisabeth Roudinesco, *La Bataille de Cent Ans: Histoire de la psychanalyse en France, 2* (Seuil, 1986).

24. Daniel Borrillo and Éric Fassin, eds., *Au delà du Pacs: L'expertise familiale à l'épreuve de l'homosexualité* (Presses universitaires de France, 2001).

25. Patrice Gélard, "Rapport (258): Fait au nom de la commission des lois constitutionnelles, sur la proposition de loi, adopté par l'assemblée nationale, relative au pacte civil de solidarité," Sénat, Commission de Lois, January 27, 1999, http://www.senat.fr/rap/l98-258/l98-258.html.

26. Éric Garnier, *L'homoparentalité en France: La bataille des nouvelles familles* (Thierry Marchaisse Éditions, 2012); Martine Gross, "Quand et comment l'homoparentalité est-elle devenue un objet « légitime » de recherche en sciences humaines et sociales ?," *Socio-logos*, no. 2 (October 16, 2007), http://socio-logos.revues.org/803; Ashveen Peerbaye, "L'invention de l'homoparentalité: acteurs, arènes et rhétoriques autour de la question de la filiation homosexuelle" (master's thesis [DEA], Cachan, France, ENS, 2000).

27. Borrillo and Fassin, *Au delà du Pacs*; Robcis, *The Law of Kinship*.

28. Gélard, "Rapport (258)."

29. Fassin, "Same Sex, Different Politics."

30. Erwann Binet, "Rapport (568 Tome I) fait au nom de la commission des lois constitutionnelles, de la légalisation et de l'administration générale de la république sur le projet de loi (n°344), ouvrant le mariage aux couples de personnes de même sexe," Assemblée Nationale, January 17, 2013.

31. Binet, "Rapport (568 Tome I)," 217.

32. David Brodzinsky and Adam Pertman, eds., *Adoption by Lesbians and Gay Men: A New Dimension in Family Diversity* (Oxford University Press, 2012); Gary J. Gates et al., "Adoption and Foster Care by Gay and Lesbian Parents in the United States," The Williams Institute, 2007, http://williamsinstitute.law.ucla.edu/research/parenting/adoption-and-foster-care-by-gay-and-lesbian-parents-in-the-united-states/.

33. Juliette Halifax and Catherine Villeneuve-Gokalp, "L'adoption en France: Qui sont les adoptés, qui sont les adoptants?," *Population et Sociétés* 417 (2005): 1–4.

34. Jean-Pierre Michel, "Rapport (437 Tome II) fait au nom de la commission des lois constitutionnelles, sur le projet de loi, adopté par l'assemblée nationale, ouvrant le mariage aux couples de personnes de même sexe," Sénat, Commission des Lois, March 20, 2013, 64.

35. Michel, "Rapport (437 Tome II)," 70.

36. Binet, "Rapport (568 Tome I)," 171.

3. FOR THE RECORD: BECOMING AND CREATING EXPERTS

1. The list of interviewees and the list of events I attended to conduct observations are available in the methodological appendix.

2. Based on my inductive approach, I chose to focus on the experts that were both easier to identify in the archival material and who constituted the core group of experts across

institutions and the two national cases. Indeed, it is often impossible to find contact information for many of the ordinary citizens who provide testimony in legislatures. Furthermore, unless they are members of activist organizations, their involvement in legal and political debates is often sporadic and isolated. Unlike academics and professionals, ordinary citizens do not constitute a group of experts with a relatively consistent set of norms that I could analyze. Nevertheless, by virtue of giving information to decision-makers, it is possible to think about the nature of their expert capital and its place in decision-making institutions. Despite not interviewing them, I do explain how they found themselves in a position to provide testimony—or not—and the impact their presence had on the overall landscape of expertise in these debates.

3. Gil Eyal and Larissa Buchholz, "From the Sociology of Intellectuals to the Sociology of Interventions," *Annual Review of Sociology* 36, no. 1 (2010): 117–37, https://doi.org/10.1146/annurev.soc.012809.102625.

4. Lisa Dilling and Maria Carmen Lemos, "Creating Usable Science: Opportunities and Constraints for Climate Knowledge Use and Their Implications for Science Policy," *Global Environmental Change, Special Issue on the Politics and Policy of Carbon Capture and Storage*, 21, no. 2 (May 2011): 680–89, https://doi.org/10.1016/j.gloenvcha.2010.11.006; Robin Stryker et al., "Employment Discrimination Law and Industrial Psychology: Social Science as Social Authority and the Co-Production of Law and Science," *Law and Social Inquiry* 37, no. 4 (2012): 777–814, http://dx.doi.org/10.1111/j.1747-4469.2011.01277.x; Peter Wagner et al., eds., *Social Sciences and Modern States: National Experiences and Theoretical Crossroads* (Cambridge University Press, 1991); Roger Friedland and Robert Alford, "Bringing Society Back In: Symbols, Practices and Institutional Contradictions," in *The New Institutionalism in Organizational Analysis*, ed. Walter Powell and Paul Dimaggio (University of Chicago Press, 1991), 232–63.

5. Eyal and Buchholz, "From the Sociology of Intellectuals to the Sociology of Interventions"; Michel Foucault, "Truth and Power," in *Essential Works of Michel Foucault (Power)*, ed. James Faubion, vol. 3 (New Press, 2000), 111–33; Scott Frickel and Kelly Moore, *The New Political Sociology of Science: Institutions, Networks, and Power* (University of Wisconsin Press, 2006).

6. Andrea Louise Campbell, "Policy Makes Mass Politics," *Annual Review of Political Science* 15, no. 1 (2012): 333–51, https://doi.org/10.1146/annurev-polisci-012610-135202; Elisabeth S. Clemens and James M. Cook, "Politics and Institutionalism: Explaining Durability and Change," *Annual Review of Sociology* 25, no. 1 (1999): 441–66, https://doi.org/10.1146/annurev.soc.25.1.441.

7. Frank R. Baumgartner et al., "The Evolution of Legislative Jurisdictions," *Journal of Politics* 62, no. 2 (May 1, 2000): 321–49, https://doi.org/10.1111/0022-3816.00015; Frank R. Baumgartner and Bryan D. Jones, "Agenda Dynamics and Policy Subsystems," *Journal of Politics* 53, no. 4 (November 1991): 1044–74, https://doi.org/10.2307/2131866; Walter J. Jatkowski, "Subsystem Contexts and Policy Information: Conditional Effects on Information in Congressional Hearings," University of Oklahoma, 2013, https://shareok.org/handle/11244/319339.

8. Francesca Polletta, *It Was Like a Fever: Storytelling in Protest and Politics* (University of Chicago Press, 2006).

9. Pierre Bourdieu, "The Force of Law: Toward a Sociology of the Juridical Field," *The Hastings Law Journal* 38 (1987): 834.

10. Ellen Ann Andersen, *Out of the Closets and into the Courts: Legal Opportunity Structure and Gay Rights Litigation* (University of Michigan Press, 2005); Byron Sheldrick, "Law, Representation, and Political Activism: Community-Based Practice and the Mobilization of Legal Resources," *Canadian Journal of Law and Society/Revue Canadienne Droit et Societe* 10, no. 2 (1995): 155–84.

11. Banks Miller and Brett Curry, "Expertise, Experience, and Ideology on Specialized Courts: The Case of the Court of Appeals for the Federal Circuit," *Law and Society Review* 43, no. 4 (2009): 839–64, https://doi.org/10.1111/j.1540-5893.2009.00390.x; Joseph Sanders, "Expert Witness Ethics," *Fordham Law Review* 76 (2007): 1539.

12. Brief of the Cato Institute and Constitutional Accountability Center as *Amicus Curiae* in Support of Respondents, *United States v. Windsor*, 570 U.S. 12–307 (2013).

13. Polletta, *It Was Like a Fever*; Deborah Stone, *Policy Paradox: The Art of Political Decision Making*, 3rd ed. (Norton, 2011).

14. Natasha Vargas-Cooper, "Raw Drama of Case Against Proposition 8 Given a Slice of Hollywood A-List Ham," *The Guardian*, March 4, 2012, sec. World News, https://www.theguardian.com/world/2012/mar/04/proposition-8-hollywood-stars-staged-reading.

15. *Perry v. Schwarzenegger*, 704 F. Supp. 2d 921 (N.D. Cal. 2010), No. C 09–2292 VRW, p. 11.

16. Robert F. Kelly and Sarah H. Ramsey, "Standards for Social Science Amicus Briefs in Family and Child Law Cases," *Journal of Gender, Race and Justice* 13 (2010): 81.

17. Brief of 278 Employers and Organizations Representing Employers as *Amicus Curiae* in Support of Respondent, *United States v. Windsor*, 570 U.S. 12–307 (2013).

18. Brief of the Cato Institute and Constitutional Accountability Center as *Amicus Curiae* in Support of Respondent, *United States v. Windsor*, 570 U.S. 12–307 (2013).

19. Brief of the American Psychological Association, the American Medical Association, the American Academy of Pediatrics, the California Medical Association, the American Psychiatric Association, the American Psychoanalytic Association, the American Association for Marriage and Family Therapy, the National Association of Social Workers and Its California Chapter, and the California Psychological Association as *Amicus Curiae* in Support of Respondents, *Hollingsworth v. Perry*, 570 U.S. 12–144 (2013).

20. Brief of the Ethics and Religious Liberty Commission of the Southern Baptist Convention as *Amicus Curiae* in Support of Defendants-Intervenors, *Perry v. Schwarzenegger*, 570 U.S. 12–144 (2010).

21. *Baehr v. Miike*, 910 P. 2d 112, 80 Haw. 341-Haw: Supreme Court (1996); *Perry v. Schwarzenegger*, 704 F. Supp. 2d 921 (N.D. Cal. 2010); *DeBoer v. Snyder*, 973 F. Supp. 2d 757, 775 (E.D. Mich. 2014). Jo Becker, *Forcing the Spring: Inside the Fight for Marriage Equality* (Penguin Books, 2015); William N. Eskridge and Nan D. Hunter, *Sexuality, Gender and the Law*, 3rd ed. (Foundation Press, 2011); Melinda D. Kane and Thomas Alan Elliott, "Turning to the Courts: A Quantitative Analysis of the Gay and Lesbian Movement's Use of Legal Mobilization," *Sociological Focus* 47, no. 4 (October 2, 2014): 219–37, https://doi.org/10.1080/00380237.2014.939901; Lee Walzer, *Gay Rights on Trial: A Reference Handbook*, ABC-CLIO's on Trial Series (ABC-CLIO, 2002).

22. *Obergefell v. Hodges*, 135 S. Ct. 1039 (2015)

23. Fed. R. Evid. 701–706. David S. Caudill and Lewis H. LaRue, "Why Judges Applying the Daubert Trilogy Need to Know About the Social, Institutional, and Rhetorical—and

Not Just the Methodological—Aspects of Science," *Boston College Law Review* 45 (2003): 1; Sarah H. Ramsey and Robert F. Kelly, "Social Science Knowledge in Family Law Cases: Judicial Gate-Keeping in the Daubert Era," *University of Miami Law Review* 59 (2004): 1.

24. Fed. R. Evid. 702.

25. Michael A. Helfand, "Usual Suspect Classifications: Criminals, Aliens and the Future of Same-Sex Marriage," *University of Pennsylvania Journal of Constitutional Law* 12 (2009): 1–56.

26. *Perry v. Schwarzenegger*, 1207 F. Supp. 5 (U.S. D.C. N. CA. 2010).

27. Becker, *Forcing the Spring*; Walzer, *Gay Rights on Trial*; Kenji Yoshino, *Speak Now: Marriage Equality on Trial* (Broadway Books, 2015).

28. *Perry v. Schwarzenegger*, opinion 11 (U.S. D.C. N. CA. 2010).

29. *Perry v. Schwarzenegger*, opinion 49 (U.S. D.C. N. CA. 2010).

30. "How Different Are the Adult Children of Parents Who Have Same-Sex Relationships? Findings from the New Family Structures Study," *Social Science Research* 41, no. 4 (2012): 752–70, https://doi.org/10.1016/j.ssresearch.2012.03.009.

31. *DeBoer, et al. v. Snyder, et al.*, 12–10285, 13 (E.D. Mich., March 21, 2014).

32. Wendy D. Manning et al., "Child Well-Being in Same-Sex Parent Families: Review of Research Prepared for American Sociological Association Amicus Brief," *Population Research and Policy Review* 33, no. 4 (August 1, 2014): 485–502, https://doi.org/10.1007/s11113-014-9329-6; Mignon R. Moore and Michael Stambolis-Ruhstorfer, "LGBT Sexuality and Families at the Start of the Twenty-First Century," *Annual Review of Sociology* 39, no. 1 (2013): 491–507, https://doi.org/10.1146/annurev-soc-071312-145643.

33. Timothy J. Biblarz and Judith Stacey, "Ideal Families and Social Science Ideals," *Journal of Marriage and Family* 72, no. 1 (February 1, 2010): 41–44, https://doi.org/10.1111/j.1741-3737.2009.00682.x; Judith Stacey and Timothy J. Biblarz, "(How) Does the Sexual Orientation of Parents Matter?," *American Sociological Review* 66, no. 2 (April 2001): 159–83.

34. Arnaud Lerch, Judith Stacey, and Arnaud Lerch, " 'Au nom de la famille.' Entretien avec Judith Stacey," *Actes de la recherche en sciences sociales* 214, no. 4 (August 9, 2016): 94–103.

35. Judith Stacey, "Cruising to Familyland: Gay Hypergamy and Rainbow Kinship," *Current Sociology* 52, no. 2 (March 1, 2004): 181–97, https://doi.org/10.1177/0011392104041807; Judith Stacey, *Unhitched: Love, Marriage, and Family Values from West Hollywood to Western China* (NYU Press, 2011).

36. Décision no. 2010–92 QPC du 28 janvier 2010.

37. Paul Johnson, *Homosexuality and the European Court of Human Rights* (Routledge, 2013).

38. Jeremy Ahearne, "Public Intellectuals and Cultural Policy in France," *International Journal of Cultural Policy* 12, no. 3 (November 1, 2006): 323–39, https://doi.org/10.1080/10286630601020603.

39. Michele Lamont, "How to Become a Dominant French Philosopher: The Case of Jacques Derrida," *American Journal of Sociology* 93, no. 3 (November 1, 1987): 584–622; Gisèle Sapiro, "Modèles d'intervention politique des intellectuels," *Actes de la recherche en sciences sociales* 176–77, no. 1 (March 6, 2009): 8–31; David L. Swartz, *Symbolic Power, Politics, and Intellectuals: The Political Sociology of Pierre Bourdieu* (University of Chicago Press, 2013).

40. AFP, "Mariage pour tous : 170 juristes contre le 'marché des enfants,' " *Le Monde.fr*, March 15, 2013, http://www.lemonde.fr/societe/article/2013/03/15/mariage-pour-tous-170-juristes-contre-le-marche-des-enfants_1849346_3224.html.

41. Marie-Joëlle Gros and Catherine Mallaval, "Et toujours cette norme du papa, maman et moi . . .," *Libération*, October 10, 2012, http://www.liberation.fr/societe/2012/10/10/et-toujours-cette-norme-du-papa-maman-et-moi_852366.

42. Françoise Héritier, *Masculin/féminin: La pensée de la différence* (Editions Odile Jacob, 1995); Françoise Héritier, *Masculin/féminin II: Dissoudre la hiérarchie* (Odile Jacob, 2012).

43. Elisabeth Badinter et al., "Mariage pour tous: La gestation pour autrui ne doit pas être le bouc émissaire," *Le Monde.Fr*, December 19, 2012, http://www.lemonde.fr/idees/article/2012/12/19/mariage-pour-tous-la-gestation-pour-autrui-ne-doit-pas-etre-le-bouc-emissaire_1808271_3232.html.

44. Ingrid Seyman, "Homoparentalité: Dessine-moi tes mamans!," *MarieClaire.Fr*, September 3, 2013, http://www.marieclaire.fr/,homoparentalite-dessine-moi-tes-mamans,697050.asp#?slide=7.

45. Christian Flavigny, "L'enfant bientôt privé de 'père et mère'?," *Le Monde*, November 9, 2012, sec. Débats; Chantal Delsol et al., "Touche pas à 'père-et-mère,'" *Le Monde.Fr*, November 11, 2012, http://www.lemonde.fr/idees/article/2012/11/08/touche-pas-a-pere-et-mere_1788107_3232.html.

46. Stéphane Nadaud, *Homoparentalité: une nouvelle chance pour la famille?* (Fayard, 2002).

47. Denis Quinqueton, "L'éthique de notre engagement," *Le Monde.Fr*, February 14, 2013, http://www.lemonde.fr/idees/article/2013/02/14/l-ethique-de-notre-engagement_1832580_3232.html.

48. Sylviane Agacinski, "Deux mères = un père ?," *Le Monde*, February 2, 2013, sec. Débats.

49. Irène Théry, "La filiation doit évoluer," *Le Monde*, February 10, 2013, sec. Débats.

50. Irène Théry, *Couple, filiation et parenté aujourd'hui: le droit face aux mutations de la famille et de la vie privée: rapport à la Ministre de l'emploi et de la solidarité et au Garde dess Sceaux, Ministre de la justice* (Odile Jacob, 1998); Françoise Dekeuwer-Défossez, "Rénover le droit de la famille: Propositions pour un droit adapté aux réalités et aux aspirations de notre temps," Rapport au Garde des Sceaux, Ministère de la Justice, September 1999.

51. Irène Théry and Anne-Marie Leroyer, *Filiation origines parentalité: Le Droit face aux nouvelles valeurs de responsabilité générationnelle* (Odile Jacob, 2014).

52. Théry, *Couple, filiation et parenté aujourd'hui*, 6–7.

53. *Concubinage*—sometimes called common-law marriage in parts of the United States—is a legal category for a situation in which two people live together in a "marriage-like" relationship that the state can recognize and can sometimes afford certain limited rights. At the time of the PACS debates, only heterosexual couples could benefit from this recognition.

54. Dekeuwer-Défossez, "Rénover Le Droit de La Famille."

55. Théry and Leroyer, *Filiation origines parentalité*.

56. French lawmakers would not legalize medically assisted procreation for lesbian couples and single women until 2021.

57. Hearings for the Pacs in 1998 were organized by MPs Jean-Pierre Michel for the *Assemblée Nationale*'s Judiciary Committee and Patrick Bloche for the Cultural, Family, and Social Affairs Committee. Hearings in 2012 and 2013 for the marriage bill were organized by the MPs Erwann Binet for the *Assemblée Nationale*'s Judiciary Committee and Marie Françoise Clergeau for the Cultural, Family, and Social Affairs Committee. Michel, who

was a senator by then, organized the senatorial marriage hearings. In addition, in 2006, Bloche also organized hearings for a special "fact-finding missing on family and the rights of children" commissioned by the president of the Assemblée Nationale. I interviewed Binet, Bloche, and Michel.

58. Gaëlle Dupont, "Entretien: 'L'humanité n'a cessé d'inventer de nouvelles formes de mariage,'" *Le Monde*, November 18, 2012, sec. Société.

59. I would like to thank reviewer 3 for helping me see this point and for providing the language I use here to make it. For more on feminist approaches to science and technology studies, readers can begin with the following sources: Sandra G. Harding and Merrill B. Hintikka, eds., *Discovering Reality: Feminist Perspectives on Epistemology, Metaphysics, Methodology, and Philosophy of Science*, Synthese Library, vol. 161 (D. Reidel, 1983); Sandra Harding, "After Absolute Neutrality: Expanding 'Science,'" in *Feminist Science Studies* (Routledge, 2001); Paige L. Sweet, "Who Knows? Reflexivity in Feminist Standpoint Theory and Bourdieu," *Gender and Society* 34, no. 6 (December 1, 2020): 922–50, https://doi.org/10.1177/0891243220966600; and Patricia Hill Collins, *Black Feminist Thought: Knowledge, Consciousness, and the Politics of Empowerment*, Perspectives on Gender, vol. 2 (Routledge, 1991).

4. FROM SCRATCH: EXPERTS WORK WITH WHAT THEY'VE GOT

1. Pierre Bourdieu, "Les conditions sociales de la circulation internationale des idées," *Actes de la recherche en sciences sociales* 145, no. 5 (December 1, 2002): 3–8.

2. Pierre Bourdieu and Loïc Wacquant, *An Invitation to Reflexive Sociology* (University of Chicago Press, 1992); Pierre Bourdieu, *Sociology in Question* (Sage, 1993); David L. Swartz, *Symbolic Power, Politics, and Intellectuals: The Political Sociology of Pierre Bourdieu* (University of Chicago Press, 2013).

3. Leandro Rodriguez Medina, *Centers and Peripheries in Knowledge Production* (Routledge, 2013); Joan Wallach Scott, ed., *Women's Studies on the Edge* (Duke University Press, 2008); Martine Gross, "Quand et comment l'homoparentalité est-elle devenue un objet « légitime » de recherche en sciences humaines et sociales?," *Socio-logos*, no. 2 (October 16, 2007), http://socio-logos.revues.org/803; Olivier Vecho and Benoît Schneider, "Homoparentalité et développement de l'enfant: bilan de trente ans de publications," *La psychiatrie de l'enfant* 48, no. 1 (March 1, 2005): 271–328, https://doi.org/10.3917/psye.481.0271; Olivier Vecho and Benoît Schneider, "Attitudes Toward Gay and Lesbian Parents: A Comparison Among French and Quebec Psychologists," *Canadian Journal of Behavioural Science* 47, no. 1 (2015): 102–12, https://doi.org/10.1037/a0037607; Bruno Perreau, ed., *Le choix de l'homosexualité: Recherches inédites sur la question gay et lesbienne* (EPEL, 2007).

4. Judith Ezekiel, "Le Women's Lib: Made in France," *European Journal of Women's Studies* 9 (2002): 345–61; Abigail C. Saguy, *What Is Sexual Harassment?: From Capitol Hill to the Sorbonne* (University of California Press, 2003).

5. Peter M. Haas, "Introduction: Epistemic Communities and International Policy Coordination," *Knowledge, Power, and International Policy Coordination* 43, no. 3 (1992): 1–35; Karin Knorr-Cetina, *Epistemic Cultures: How the Sciences Make Knowledge* (Harvard University Press, 1999); Marianna Y. Smirnova and Sergey Y. Yachin, "Epistemic Communities and

Epistemic Operating Mode," *International Journal of Social Science and Humanity* 5, no. 7 (2015): 646–50.

6. Michael J. Maher et al., "Hirschfeld to Hooker to Herek to High Schools: A Study of the History and Development of GLBT Empirical Research, Institutional Policies, and the Relationship Between the Two," *Journal of Homosexuality* 56, no. 7 (2009): 921–58, https://doi.org/10.1080/00918360903187861.

7. Christopher F. Cardiff and Daniel B. Klein, "Faculty Partisan Affiliations in All Disciplines: A Voter-Registration Study," *Critical Review* 17, no. 3–4 (June 1, 2005): 237–55, https://doi.org/10.1080/08913810508443639; Daniel B. Klein and Charlotta Stern, "Professors and Their Politics: The Policy Views of Social Scientists," *Critical Review* 17, no. 3–4 (June 1, 2005): 257–303, https://doi.org/10.1080/08913810508443640; Deborah A. Prentice, "Liberal Norms and Their Discontents," *Perspectives on Psychological Science* 7, no. 5 (September 1, 2012): 516–18, https://doi.org/10.1177/1745691612454142; Matthew Woessner and April Kelly-Woessner, "Reflections on Academic Liberalism and Conservative Criticism," *Society* 52, no. 1 (February 1, 2015): 35–41, https://doi.org/10.1007/s12115-014-9864-0.

8. Jennifer Roback Morse, *Love and Economics: Why the Laissez-Faire Family Doesn't Work* (Spence Publishing Company, 2001).

9. Michael J. Rosenfeld, "Nontraditional Families and Childhood Progress Through School," *Demography* 47, no. 3 (2010): 755–75, https://doi.org/10.1353/dem.0.0112; Michael J. Rosenfeld, "Reply to Allen et al," *Demography* 50, no. 3 (June 2013): 963–69, https://doi.org/10.1007/s13524-012-0170-4; Douglas W. Allen, Catherine Pakaluk, and Joseph Price, "Nontraditional Families and Childhood Progress Through School: A Comment on Rosenfeld," *Demography* 50, no. 30 (2013): 955–61, https://doi.org/10.1007/s13524-012-0169-x.

10. Amanda Hollis-Brusky, *Ideas with Consequences: The Federalist Society and the Conservative Counterrevolution* (Oxford University Press, 2019); Steven M. Teles, *The Rise of the Conservative Legal Movement: The Battle for Control of the Law* (Princeton University Press, 2008).

11. Mark Regnerus, "How Different Are the Adult Children of Parents Who Have Same-Sex Relationships? Findings from the New Family Structures Study," *Social Science Research* 41, no. 4 (2012): 752–70, https://doi.org/10.1016/j.ssresearch.2012.03.009.

12. Anne Cadoret, *Des parents comme les autres* (Odile Jacob, 2002).

13. Caroline Eliacheff, "Malaise dans la psychanalyse," *Esprit* 273 (2001): 62–77; Éric Garnier, *L'homoparentalité en France: La bataille des nouvelles familles* (Thierry Marchaisse Editions, 2012).

14. AFP, "Mariage pour tous: 170 juristes contre le 'marché des enfants,' " *Le Monde.fr*, March 15, 2013, http://www.lemonde.fr/societe/article/2013/03/15/mariage-pour-tous-170-juristes-contre-le-marche-des-enfants_1849346_3224.html.

15. Eric Millard et al., "Mariage pour tous: Juristes, taisons-nous!," *Raison-Publique.Fr* (blog), March 20, 2013, http://www.raison-publique.fr/article601.html.

16. Daniel Borrillo and Éric Fassin, eds., *Au delà du Pacs: L'expertise familiale à l'épreuve de l'homosexualité* (Presses Universitaires de France, 2001); Camille Robcis, *The Law of Kinship: Anthropology, Psychoanalysis, and the Family in France* (Cornell University Press, 2013).

17. Vecho and Schneider, "Attitudes Toward Gay and Lesbian Parents."

18. Roman Kuhar and David Paternotte, eds., *Anti-Gender Campaigns in Europe: Mobilizing Against Equality* (Rowman & Littlefield, 2017).

19. Cécile Daumas, "Valérie Pécresse coupe les bourses au genre," *Libération.Fr*, December 14, 2016, http://www.liberation.fr/debats/2016/12/14/valerie-pecresse-coupe-les-bourses-au-genre_1535283.

20. Pierre Bourdieu, *Homo academicus* (Minuit, 1984); Marion Fourcade, *Economists and Societies: Discipline and Profession in the United States, Britain, and France, 1890s to 1990s* (Princeton University Press, 2009); Christine Musselin, *The Long March of French Universities* (Routledge, 2013); Gisèle Sapiro, "Modèles d'intervention politique des intellectuels," *Actes de la recherche en sciences sociales* 176–77, no. 1 (March 6, 2009): 8–31.

21. UNAF, "Les questions du mariage, de la filiation et de l'autorité parentale pour les couples de même sexe," Union Nationale des Associations Familiales, October 29, 2012, http://www.unaf.fr/IMG/pdf/dossier_d_analyse___mariage_et_filiation_v_finale.pdf.

22. Charlotte J. Patterson, "Children of Lesbian and Gay Parents," *Child Development* 63, no. 5 (October 1, 1992): 1025–42, https://doi.org/10.1111/j.1467-8624.1992.tb01679.x.

23. Jimi Adams and Ryan Light, "Scientific Consensus, the Law, and Same Sex Parenting Outcomes," *Social Science Research* 53 (September 2015): 300–310, https://doi.org/10.1016/j.ssresearch.2015.06.008.

24. Bruno Perreau, *Queer Theory: The French Response* (Stanford University Press, 2016).

25. François de Singly, *Sociologie de la famille contemporaine*, 3rd ed. (Armand Colin, 2007).

26. Vecho and Schneider, "Homoparentalité et développement de l'enfant."

27. Garnier, *L'homoparentalité en France*; Vecho and Schneider, "Homoparentalité et développement de l'enfant"; Emmanuelle Yvert, "Des mobilisations victorieuses sans mouvement social. La construction de la cause de l'homoparentalité et sa traduction législative en france (1986–2013)" (PhD diss., Université Paris-Saclay, 2021), https://theses.fr/2021UPASU006.

28. Garnier, *L'homoparentalité en France*; Robcis, *The Law of Kinship*.

29. Gross, "Quand et comment l'homoparentalité est-elle devenue un objet « légitime » de recherche en sciences humaines et sociales?"; Ashveen Peerbaye, "L'invention de l'homoparentalité: Acteurs, arènes et rhétoriques autour de la question de la filiation homosexuelle" (master's thesis [DEA], Cachan, France, ENS, 2000).

30. John L. Campbell and Ove K. Pedersen, *The National Origins of Policy Ideas: Knowledge Regimes in the United States, France, Germany, and Denmark* (Princeton University Press, 2014).

31. Michael Warner, "Normal and Normaller: Beyond Gay Marriage," *GLQ: A Journal of Lesbian and Gay Studies* 5, no. 2 (1999): 119–71; Timothy J. Biblarz and Judith Stacey, "Ideal Families and Social Science Ideals," *Journal of Marriage and Family* 72, no. 1 (February 1, 2010): 41–44, https://doi.org/10.1111/j.1741-3737.2009.00682.x; Judith Stacey, *Unhitched: Love, Marriage, and Family Values from West Hollywood to Western China* (NYU Press, 2011).

32. See, for example, Brief of Robert P. George, Sherif Girgis, and Ryan T. Anderson as *Amici Curiae* in Support of Hollingsworth and Bipartisan Legal Advisory Board, *Hollingsworth v. Perry* and *Windsor v. Bipartisan Legal Advisory Board*, 570 U.S. 12–144 (2013). *Perry v. Schwarzenneger* 274 F. Supp. 4 (U.S. D.C. N. CA. 2010).

33. http://respectmyresearch.org/scientists/dr-judith-stacey/. Accessed 10/18/2015. See also http://www.prweb.com/releases/2006/07/prweb412920.htm. Accessed 06/25/2017. Paige Schilt, "Sociologist Judith Stacey: Get Rid of Marital Privilege," The Bilerico Project,

March 25, 2017, http://www.bilerico.com/2014/03/unhitching_the_movement_from_marital
_privilege.php.

34. Borrillo and Fassin, *Au delà du Pacs*; Robcis, *The Law of Kinship*.

35. David Blankenhorn, "How My View on Gay Marriage Changed," *New York Times*, June 22, 2012, http://www.nytimes.com/2012/06/23/opinion/how-my-view-on-gay-marriage-changed.html.

36. Michelle Aulagnon, "La fausse bonne idée du contrat d'union sociale, c'est de tout mélanger," *Le Monde*, November 25, 1997, sec. Sports, http://www.lemonde.fr/archives/article/1997/11/25/la-fausse-bonne-idee-du-contrat-d-union-sociale-c-est-de-tout-melanger_3806704_1819218.html?xtmc=la_fausse_bonne_idee_du_contrat_d_union_sociale&xtcr=11.

37. Borrillo and Fassin, *Au delà du Pacs*; Daniel Borrillo and Pierre Lascoumes, *Amours Égales? Le Pacs, les homosexuels et la Gauche* (La Découverte, 2002); Gross, "Quand et comment l'homoparentalité est-elle devenue un objet « légitime » de recherche en sciences humaines et sociales?"; Massimo Prearo, *Le moment politique de l'homosexualité: mouvements, identités, et communautés en France* (Presses Universitaires de Lyon, 2014); Robcis, *The Law of Kinship*.

38. Peerbaye, "L'Invention de l'homoparentalité."

39. Éric Fassin, "L'intellectuel spécifique et le Pacs: Politiques des savoirs," *Mouvements*, no. 7 (January 2000): 68–76; Éric Fassin, "Le Savant, l'expert et Le Politique: La Famille des Sociologues," *Genèses* 32, no. 1 (1998): 156–69, https://doi.org/10.3406/genes.1998.1533; Éric Fassin, "Usages de la science et science des usages," *L'Homme. Revue française d'anthropologie*, no. 154–55 (January 1, 2000): 391–408, https://doi.org/10.4000/lhomme.39; Borrillo and Fassin, *Au delà du Pacs*.

40. Olivier Abel et al., "Les occasions manquées du Pacs (entretien)," *Esprit*, November 1998, 201–14; Irène Théry, "Expertises de service, de consensus, d'engagement: essai de typologie de la mission d'expertise en sciences sociales," *Droit et société* 60, no. 2 (June 1, 2005): 311–27.

41. David S. Meyer, "Protest and Political Opportunities," *Annual Review of Sociology* 30 (2004): 125–45; Swartz, *Symbolic Power, Politics, and Intellectuals*.

42. Steven Epstein, "The New Attack on Sexuality Research: Morality and the Politics of Knowledge Production," *Sexuality Research and Social Policy* 3, no. 1 (2006): 1–12.

43. Peter Schmidt, "Professors' Growing Risk: Harassment for Things They Never Really Said," *The Chronicle of Higher Education*, June 22, 2017, http://www.chronicle.com/article/Professors-Growing-Risk-/240424/.

44. Sharon Bernstein, "Florida Bill Would Ban Gender Studies Majors, Diversity Programs at Universities," *Reuters*, February 25, 2023, sec. United States, https://www.reuters.com/world/us/florida-bill-would-ban-gender-studies-majors-diversity-programs-universities-2023-02-25/.

45. Hollis-Brusky, *Ideas with Consequences*; Teles, *The Rise of the Conservative Legal Movement*.

46. Ifop, http://www.ifop.com/media/poll/3798-1-study_file.pdf; Copyright © 2017 Ifop, Inc. All rights reserved.

47. Phillip M. Ayoub and Kristina Stoeckl, *The Global Fight Against LGBTI Rights: How Transnational Conservative Networks Target Sexual and Gender Minorities* (NYU Press, 2024).

48. Mattea Battaglia, Violaine Morin, and Sylvie Lecherbonnier, "Jean-Michel Blanquer: « La France et sa jeunesse doivent échapper à l'idéologie woke »," *Le Monde.fr*, October 13, 2021, https://www.lemonde.fr/societe/article/2021/10/13/jean-michel-blanquer-la-france-et -sa-jeunesse-doivent-echapper-a-l-ideologie-woke_6098250_3224.html.

5. TIES THAT BIND: HOW EXPERTS CONNECT WITH LAWMAKERS

1. Gregory M. Herek, "The Social Psychology of Homophobia: Toward a Practical Theory," *New York University Review of Law and Social Change* 14 (1986): 923.

2. Gregory M. Herek, "Myths About Sexual Orientation: A Lawyer's Guide to Social Science Research," *Law and Sexuality: A Review of Lesbian and Gay Legal Issues* 1 (1991): 133–72.

3. Mayer N. Zald and Michael Lounsbury, "The Wizards of Oz: Towards an Institutional Approach to Elites, Expertise and Command Posts," *Organization Studies* 31, no. 7 (July 1, 2010): 963–96, https://doi.org/10.1177/0170840610373201.

4. Pierre Bourdieu, "The Forms of Capital," in *Handbook of Theory and Research for the Sociology of Education*, ed. John Richardson (Greenwood Press, 1986), 46–58.

5. Thomas Medvetz, *Think Tanks in America* (University of Chicago Press, 2012).

6. Kim Phillips-fein, *Invisible Hands: The Making of the Conservative Movement from the New Deal to Reagan* (Norton, 2009); Amanda Hollis-Brusky, *Ideas with Consequences: The Federalist Society and the Conservative Counterrevolution* (Oxford University Press, 2019).

7. Pierre Bourdieu, *Homo academicus* (Minuit, 1984); Christophe Charle, *Naissance des "intellectuels": 1880–1900* (Minuit, 1990); Charles Kurzman and Lynn Owens, "The Sociology of Intellectuals," *Annual Review of Sociology* 28 (January 1, 2002): 63–90.

8. Éric Fassin, "Le savant, l'expert et le politique: La famille des sociologues," *Genèses* 32, no. 1 (1998): 156–69, https://doi.org/10.3406/genes.1998.1533; Gisèle Sapiro, "Modèles d'intervention politique des intellectuels," *Actes de la recherche en sciences sociales* 176–177, no. 1 (March 6, 2009): 8–31.

9. Sapiro, "Modèles d'intervention politique des intellectuels."

10. Ellen Ann Andersen, *Out of the Closets and Into the Courts: Legal Opportunity Structure and Gay Rights Litigation* (University of Michigan Press, 2005); Patricia Cain, *Rainbow Rights: The Role of Lawyers and Courts in the Lesbian and Gay Civil Rights Movement* (Westview Press, 2000); Susan Gluck Mezey, *Queers in Court: Gay Rights Law and Public Policy* (Rowman & Littlefield Publishers, 2007).

11. Barbara A. Misztal and David Moss, eds., *Action on AIDS: National Policies in Comparative Perspective*, Contributions in Medical Studies, No. 28 (Greenwood Press, 1990); Mary Bernstein and Verta Taylor, eds., *The Marrying Kind? Debating Same-Sex Marriage Within the Lesbian and Gay Movement* (University of Minnesota Press, 2013); Neil J. Young, *Coming Out Republican: A History of the Gay Right* (University of Chicago Press, 2024).

12. American Psychological Association, "Lesbian and Gay Parenting," American Psychological Association, 2005, http://www.apa.org/pi/lgbt/resources/parenting-full.pdf.

13. Mark Regnerus, "How Different Are the Adult Children of Parents Who Have Same-Sex Relationships? Findings from the New Family Structures Study," *Social Science Research* 41, no. 4 (2012): 752–70, https://doi.org/10.1016/j.ssresearch.2012.03.009.

14. Brief of the American Sociological Association as *Amicus Curiae* in Support of Perry and Windsor, *Hollingsworth v. Perry* and *Windsor v. Bipartisan Legal Advisory Board*, 570 U.S. 12–144 (2013).

15. Wendy D. Manning et al., "Child Well-Being in Same-Sex Parent Families: Review of Research Prepared for American Sociological Association Amicus Brief," *Population Research and Policy Review* 33, no. 4 (August 1, 2014): 485–502, https://doi.org/10.1007/s11113-014-9329-6.

16. Steven M. Teles, *The Rise of the Conservative Legal Movement: The Battle for Control of the Law* (Princeton University Press, 2008); Hollis-Brusky, *Ideas with Consequences*; Phillips-fein, *Invisible Hands*.

17. Didier Eribon, *Sur cet instant fragile: carnets, janvier-août 2004* (Fayard, 2004).

18. Abigail C. Saguy, *What Is Sexual Harassment?: From Capitol Hill to the Sorbonne* (University of California Press, 2003).

19. Daniel Borrillo and Pierre Lascoumes, *Amours égales ? Le Pacs, les homosexuels et la Gauche* (La Découverte, 2002).

20. Christophe Broqua and David M. Halperin, *Action = Vie: A History of AIDS Activism and Gay Politics in France* (Temple University Press, 2020); Julian Jackson, *Living in Arcadia Homosexuality, Politics, and Morality in France from the Liberation to AIDS* (University of Chicago Press, 2009).

21. Martine Gross, "Quand et comment l'homoparentalité est-elle devenue un objet « légitime » de recherche en sciences humaines et sociales?," *Socio-logos*, no. 2 (October 16, 2007), http://socio-logos.revues.org/803.

22. Gross, "Quand et comment l'homoparentalité est-elle devenue un objet « légitime » de recherche en sciences humaines et sociales?"; Ashveen Peerbaye, "L'invention de l'homoparentalité: Acteurs, arènes et rhétoriques autour de la question de la filiation homosexuelle" (master's thesis [DEA], Cachan, France, ENS, 2000).

23. The requirement that same-sex couples go through a second-parent adoption procedure, which requires that the couple first get married, would not be dropped until 2021.

24. Daniel Borrillo and Éric Fassin, eds., *Au delà Du Pacs: L'expertise familiale à l'épreuve de l'homosexualité* (Presses Universitaires de France, 2001); Irène Théry et al., "Mariage des personnes de même sexe et filiation: Le projet de loi au prisme des sciences sociales," École des Hautes Études en Sciences Sociales-Cerles de Formation, December 16, 2012, www.ehess.fr/mariage.

25. Céline Béraud and Philippe Portier, *Métamorphoses catholiques: Acteurs, enjeux et mobilisations depuis le mariage pour tous* (Maison des Sciences de l'Homme, 2015).

26. UNAF, "Les questions du mariage, de la filiation et de l'autorité parentale pour les couples de même sexe," Union Nationale des Associations Familiales, October 29, 2012, http://www.unaf.fr/IMG/pdf/dossier_d_analyse__mariage_et_filiation_v_finale.pdf.

27. Michael Stambolis-Ruhstorfer and Josselin Tricou, "Resisting 'Gender Theory' in France: A Fulcrum for Religious Action in a Secular Society," in *Anti-Gender Campaigns in Europe*, ed. Roman Kuhar and David Paternotte (Rowman & Littlefield, 2017), 79–98.

28. Thibaud Collin, *Les lendemains du mariage gay: Vers la fin du mariage? Quelle place pour les enfants?* (Salvator, 2012).

29. Xavier Lacroix, *La confusion des genres: Réponses à certaines demandes homosexuelles sur le mariage et l'adoption* (Bayard Jeunesse, 2005).

30. Pierre Bourdieu, *La noblesse d'état: Grandes écoles et esprit de corps* (Minuit, 1989); Gérard Noiriel, *Dire la vérité au pouvoir: Les intellectuels en question* (Agone, 2010).

31. Thomas Lemahieu, "Projet Périclès: le document qui dit tout du plan de Pierre-Édouard Stérin pour installer le RN au pouvoir," https://www.humanite.fr, July 19, 2024, sec. Politique, https://www.humanite.fr/politique/bien-commun/projet-pericles-le-document-qui -dit-tout-du-plan-de-pierre-edouard-sterin-pour-installer-le-rn-au-pouvoir.

32. Daniel Sarewitz and Roger A. Pielke Jr., "The Neglected Heart of Science Policy: Reconciling Supply of and Demand for Science," *Environmental Science and Policy*, Reconciling the Supply of and Demand for Science, with a Focus on Carbon Cycle Research, 10, no. 1 (February 2007): 5–16, https://doi.org/10.1016/j.envsci.2006.10.001; Robin Stryker et al., "Employment Discrimination Law and Industrial Psychology: Social Science as Social Authority and the Co-Production of Law and Science," *Law and Social Inquiry* 37, no. 4 (2012): 777–814, http://dx.doi.org/10.1111/j.1747-4469.2011.01277.x.

33. Andrea Louise Campbell, "Policy Makes Mass Politics," *Annual Review of Political Science* 15, no. 1 (2012): 333–51, https://doi.org/10.1146/annurev-polisci-012610-135202; Elisabeth S. Clemens and James M. Cook, "Politics and Institutionalism: Explaining Durability and Change," *Annual Review of Sociology* 25, no. 1 (1999): 441–66, https://doi.org/10.1146 /annurev.soc.25.1.441; Sheila Jasanoff, ed., *States of Knowledge: The Co-Production of Science and the Social Order* (Routledge, 2004).

34. Research in the United States on the science of the causes of homosexuality, in particular efforts to uncover its genetic origins, is another example of the way policy contexts can lead social movement organizations to create a demand for the production of scientific expertise. Joanna Wuest, *Born This Way: Science, Citizenship, and Inequality in the American LGBTQ+ Movement* (University of Chicago Press, 2023).

6. TO HAVE AND TO HOLD: EXPERT CAPITAL AS A SCARCE RESOURCE

1. Steven Epstein, *Impure Science: AIDS, Activism, and the Politics of Knowledge* (University of California Press, 1996).

2. Epstein, *Impure Science*, 16.

3. Drawing on Bourdieu, David Swartz describes this power as also important for political capital, the kind that politicians need to win elections. He says that "political capital refers to a 'particular kind of symbolic capital,' a 'reputational capital linked to notoriety' that is 'linked to the manner of being perceived.'" David L. Swartz, *Symbolic Power, Politics, and Intellectuals: The Political Sociology of Pierre Bourdieu* (University of Chicago Press, 2013), 65.

4. Daniel Borrillo and Éric Fassin, eds., *Au delà du Pacs: L'expertise familiale à l'épreuve de l'homosexualité* (Presses Universitaires de France, 2001).

5. Borrillo and Fassin, *Au delà du Pacs*, 109–10.

6. Françoise Dekeuwer-Défossez, "Rénover le droit de la famille: Propositions pour un droit adapté aux réalités et aux aspirations de notre temps," Rapport au Garde des Sceaux (Ministère de la Justice, September 1999).

7. Brief of Historians, American Historical Association, Peter W. Bardaglio, Norma Basch, George Chauncey, Stephanie Coontz, Nancy F. Cot, et al. as *Amicus Curiae* in Support of Respondents, *United States v. Windsor*, 570 U.S. 12–307 (2013).

8. Brief of the Organization of American Historians and the American Studies Association as *Amici Curiae* in Support of Respondents, *Hollingsworth v. Perry*, 570 U.S. 12–144 (2013).

9. Gary J. Gates, "How Many People Are Lesbian, Gay, Bisexual and Transgender?" (Williams Institute, April 1, 2011), http://escholarship.org/uc/item/09h684x2.

10. Mark Regnerus, "How Different Are the Adult Children of Parents Who Have Same-Sex Relationships? Findings from the New Family Structures Study," *Social Science Research* 41, no. 4 (2012): 752–70, https://doi.org/10.1016/j.ssresearch.2012.03.009.

11. Wendy D. Manning et al., "Child Well-Being in Same-Sex Parent Families: Review of Research Prepared for American Sociological Association Amicus Brief," *Population Research and Policy Review* 33, no. 4 (August 1, 2014): 485–502, https://doi.org/10.1007/s11113-014-9329-6; Paul R. Amato, "The Well-Being of Children with Gay and Lesbian Parents," *Social Science Research* 41, no. 4 (2012): 771–74, https://doi.org/10.1016/j.ssresearch.2012.04.007.

12. *DeBoer, et al. v. Snyder, et al.*, 12–10285, 13 (E.D. Mich. March 21, 2014).

13. Olivier Vecho and Benoît Schneider, "Homoparentalité et développement de l'enfant: Bilan de trente ans de publications," *La psychiatrie de l'enfant* 48, no. 1 (March 1, 2005): 271–328, https://doi.org/10.3917/psye.481.0271.

14. Susan Golombok et al., "Children with Lesbian Parents: A Community Study," *Developmental Psychology* 39, no. 1 (2003): 20–33, https://doi.org/10.1037/0012-1649.39.1.20; Susan Golombok and Fiona Tasker, "Gay Fathers," in *Role of the Father in Child Development*, ed. Michael E. Lamb (Wiley, 2010), 319–40.

15. Epstein, *Impure Science*; Michelle Murphy, *Seizing the Means of Reproduction: Entanglements of Feminism, Health, and Technoscience* (Duke University Press, 2012).

16. Murphy, *Seizing the Means of Reproduction*.

17. Maya J. Goldenberg, *Vaccine Hesitancy: Public Trust, Expertise, and the War on Science* (University of Pittsburgh Press, 2021); Jeremy K. Ward and Patrick Peretti-Watel, "Understanding Vaccine Mistrust: From Perception Bias to Controversies," *Revue francaise de sociologie* 61, no. 2 (October 6, 2020): 243–73.

18. Swartz, *Symbolic Power, Politics, and Intellectuals*, 103.

19. Goldenberg, *Vaccine Hesitancy*.

20. Tom Waidzunas, *The Straight Line: How the Fringe Science of Ex-Gay Therapy Reoriented Sexuality* (University of Minnesota Press, 2015); Naomi Oreskes and Erik M. Conway, *Merchants of Doubt: How a Handful of Scientists Obscured the Truth on Issues from Tobacco Smoke to Global Warming* (Bloomsbury, 2010).

21. Edward T. Walker and Andrew N. Le, "Poisoning the Well: How Astroturfing Harms Trust in Advocacy Organizations," *Social Currents* 10, no. 2 (April 1, 2023): 184–202, https://doi.org/10.1177/23294965221123808.

22. Mignon R. Moore, *Invisible Families: Gay Identities, Relationships, and Motherhood Among Black Women* (University of California Press, 2011); Mignon R. Moore and Michael Stambolis-Ruhstorfer, "LGBT Sexuality and Families at the Start of the Twenty-First Century," *Annual Review of Sociology* 39, no. 1 (2013): 491–507, https://doi.org/10.1146/annurev-soc-071312-145643; Suzanne Lenon, "White as Milk: Proposition 8 and the Cultural Politics of Gay Rights," *Atlantis: Critical Studies in Gender, Culture and Social Justice* 36, no. 1 (April 1, 2013): 44–54; Amy L. Stone and Jane Ward, "From 'Black People Are

Not a Homosexual Act' to 'Gay Is the New Black': Mapping White Uses of Blackness in Modern Gay Rights Campaigns in the United States," *Social Identities* 17, no. 5 (September 1, 2011): 605–24, https://doi.org/10.1080/13504630.2011.595204.

CONCLUSION: AUTHORITATIVE KNOWLEDGE, AUTHORIZING FAMILIES

1. Weronika Grzebalska and Andrea Pető, "The Gendered Modus Operandi of the Illiberal Transformation in Hungary and Poland," *Women's Studies International Forum* 68 (May 1, 2018): 164–72, https://doi.org/10.1016/j.wsif.2017.12.001; David Paternotte and Mieke Verloo, "De-Democratization and the Politics of Knowledge: Unpacking the Cultural Marxism Narrative," *Social Politics: International Studies in Gender, State and Society* 28, no. 3 (September 1, 2021): 556–78, https://doi.org/10.1093/sp/jxab025; Andrea Pető, "Current Comment: The Illiberal Academic Authority. An Oxymoron?," *Berichte Zur Wissenschaftsgeschichte* 44, no. 4 (2021): 461–69, https://doi.org/10.1002/bewi.202100013.
2. Pető, "Current Comment," 465.
3. Margot Mahoudeau, *La panique woke* (TEXTUEL, 2022).
4. Erwann Binet, "Rapport (568 Tome I) fait au nom de la commission des lois constitutionnelles, de la légalisation et de l'administration générale de la république sur le projet de loi (n°344), ouvrant le mariage aux couples de personnes de même sexe" (Assemblée Nationale, January 17, 2013), 116.
5. *DeBoer, et al. v. Snyder, et al.*, 12–10285, 24 (E.D. Mich. March 21, 2014).
6. John Blevins, "Broadening the Family of God: Debating Same-Sex Marriage and Queer Families in America," *Theology and Sexuality: The Journal of the Institute for the Study of Christianity and Sexuality* 12, no. 1 (September 2005): 63–80, https://doi.org/10.1177/1355835805057787; Daniel Borrillo and Éric Fassin, eds., *Au delà du Pacs: L'expertise familiale à l'épreuve de l'homosexualité* (Presses Universitaires de France, 2001); Éric Fassin, "Usages de la science et science des usages," *L'Homme. Revue française d'anthropologie*, no. 154–55 (January 1, 2000): 391–408, https://doi.org/10.4000/lhomme.39; Éric Fassin, "Same Sex, Different Politics: 'Gay Marriage' Debates in France and the United States," *Public Culture* 13 (2001): 215–32; Douglas Kirsner, "Psychoanalysis and Its Discontents," *Psychoanalytic Psychology* 21, no. 3 (2004): 339–52, https://doi.org/10.1037/0736-9735.21.3.339; Camille Robcis, *The Law of Kinship: Anthropology, Psychoanalysis, and the Family in France* (Cornell University Press, 2013); Elisabeth Roudinesco, *La Bataille de Cent Ans: Histoire de La Psychanalyse En France*, vol. 2 (Seuil, 1986).
7. Elizabeth Popp Berman, *Thinking Like an Economist: How Efficiency Replaced Equality in U.S. Public Policy* (Princeton University Press, 2022); Marion Fourcade, *Economists and Societies: Discipline and Profession in the United States, Britain, and France, 1890s to 1990s* (Princeton University Press, 2009); Marion Fourcade et al., "The Superiority of Economists," *Journal of Economic Perspectives* 29, no. 1 (2015): 89–114; Michèle Lamont and Laurent Thévenot, eds., *Rethinking Comparative Cultural Sociology: Repertoires of Evaluation in France and the United States* (Cambridge University Press, 2000).
8. M. V. Lee Badgett, *When Gay People Get Married: What Happens when Societies Legalize Same-Sex Marriage* (NYU Press, 2009).

9.   Lamont and Thévenot, *Rethinking Comparative Cultural Sociology*.

10.   Lamont and Thévenot, *Rethinking Comparative Cultural Sociology*; Enda McCaffrey, *The Gay Republic: Sexuality, Citizenship and Subversion in France* (Ashgate, 2005); Abigail C. Saguy, *What Is Sexual Harassment?: From Capitol Hill to the Sorbonne* (University of California Press, 2003).

11.   Larry Cata Backer, "Religion as the Language of Discourse of Same Sex Marriage," *Capital University Law Review* 30 (2002): 222–78; Robert Neelly Bellah et al., *Habits of the Heart: Individualism and Commitment in American Life* (University of California Press, 1985); Blevins, "Broadening the Family of God"; Ahmet T. Kuru, *Secularism and State Policies Toward Religion: The United States, France, and Turkey* (Cambridge University Press, 2009); Alexis de Tocqueville, *De La Démocratie En Amérique*, ed. Eduardo Nolla, Revised (Vrin, 1990).

12.   Fassin, "Same Sex, Different Politics"; Éric Fassin, "Same-Sex Marriage, Nation, and Race: French Political Logics and Rhetorics," *Contemporary French Civilization* 39, no. 3 (January 1, 2014): 281–301, https://doi.org/10.3828/cfc.2014.17; Robcis, *The Law of Kinship*.

13.   Joanna Wuest, for example, describes how in the United States, LGBTQ activism and bioessentialist research on sexual orientation grew in tandem, shaping one another. Joanna Wuest, *Born This Way: Science, Citizenship, and Inequality in the American LGBTQ+ Movement* (University of Chicago Press, 2023).

14.   Michael J. Rosenfeld, *The Rainbow After the Storm: Marriage Equality and Social Change in the U.S.* (Oxford University Press, 2021).

15.   Timothy J. Biblarz and Judith Stacey, "Ideal Families and Social Science Ideals," *Journal of Marriage and Family* 72, no. 1 (February 1, 2010): 41–44, https://doi.org/10.1111/j.1741-3737.2009.00682.x.

16.   Mignon R. Moore and Michael Stambolis-Ruhstorfer, "LGBT Sexuality and Families at the Start of the Twenty-First Century," *Annual Review of Sociology* 39, no. 1 (2013): 491–507, https://doi.org/10.1146/annurev-soc-071312-145643.

17.   Judith Stacey and Timothy J. Biblarz, "(How) Does the Sexual Orientation of Parents Matter?," *American Sociological Review* 66, no. 2 (April 2001): 159–83.

18.   Myra Marx Ferree et al., *Shaping Abortion Discourse: Democracy and the Public Sphere in Germany and the United States* (Cambridge University Press, 2002); Pierre Bourdieu, "The Force of Law: Toward a Sociology of the Juridical Field," *The Hastings Law Journal* 38 (1987): 805–53; Pierre Bourdieu, "The Specificity of the Scientific Field and the Social Conditions of the Progress of Reason," *Social Science Information* 14, no. 6 (December 1, 1975): 19–47, https://doi.org/10.1177/053901847501400602.

19.   Gil Eyal, *The Crisis of Expertise* (Polity, 2019).

20.   Lauren Weber et al., "Unpacking the Flawed Science Cited in the Texas Abortion Pill Ruling," *Washington Post*, April 13, 2023, https://www.washingtonpost.com/health/2023/04/13/abortion-pill-safety/.

METHODOLOGICAL APPENDIX

1.   Nathian Shae Rodriguez and Lindsey Blumell, "What a Year! The Framing of Marriage Equality Through Media's Selected Sources in 2013," *Journal of Communication Inquiry* 38, no. 4 (October 1, 2014): 341–59, https://doi.org/10.1177/0196859914551767.

2. See, for example, William N. Eskridge and Nan D. Hunter, *Sexuality, Gender and the Law*, 3rd ed. (Foundation Press, 2011); Clarisse Fabre and Éric Fassin, *Liberté, Egalité, Sexualités* (Belfond, 2003); Caroline Mécary, "Homosexualité, mariage et filiation: où en sommes-nous?," *Informations sociales* 149, no. 5 (October 27, 2008): 136–49; Susan Gluck Mezey, *Gay Families and the Courts: The Quest for Equal Rights* (Rowman & Littlefield Publishers, 2009).

3. The Human Rights Campaign, "Human Rights Campaign State Maps," http://www .selectsurrogate.com/surrogacy-laws-by-state.html; Gay and Lesbian Advocates and Defenders, "GLAD Know Your Rights Information by State," http://www.glad.org /rights/states, consulted January 21, 2015; European Region of the International Lesbian, Gay, Bisexual, Trans, and Intersex Association, "Rainbow Europe," http://www.ilga-europe .org/rainboweurope, consulted August 3, 2015.

4. *In re Marriage Cases*, 43 Cal. 4th 757 (2008); *United States v. Windsor*, 133 S. Ct. 2675, 2694 (2013); *Hollingsworth v. Perry*, 133 S. Ct. 2652 (2013); *DeBoer v. Snyder*, 973 F. Supp. 2d 757, 775 (E.D. Mich. 2014).

5. Loi n° 99–944 du 15 novembre 1999, J.O. n° 265 du 16 novembre 1999, p. 16959; Loi n° 2013–404 du 17 mai 2013, J.O. n° 0114 du 18 mai 2013, p. 8253.

6. *Fretté v. France* (Application no. 36515/97, March 26, 2002); *E.B. v. France* (Application no. 43546/02, January 22, 2008); *Gas and Dubois v. France* (Application no. 25951/07, March 15, 2012).

7. Mignon R. Moore and Michael Stambolis-Ruhstorfer, "LGBT Sexuality and Families at the Start of the Twenty-First Century," *Annual Review of Sociology* 39, no. 1 (2013): 491–507, https://doi.org/10.1146/annurev-soc-071312-145643.

8. Michael Stambolis-Ruhstorfer and Virginie Descoutures, "Licence Required: French Lesbian Parents Confront the Obligation to Marry in Order to Establish Kinship," *International Social Science Journal* 70, no. 235–36 (2020): 79–97, https://doi.org/10.1111/issj.12241; Michael Stambolis-Ruhstorfer and Martine Gross, "Qui lave le linge sale de la famille?," *Travail, genre et societes* 46, no. 2 (November 10, 2021): 75–95; Michael Stambolis-Ruhstorfer, "Lesbian and Gay Families in France: Results from the DEVHOM Study," *International Social Science Journal* 70, no. 235–36 (2020): 7–11, https://doi.org/10.1111/issj.12248.

BIBLIOGRAPHY

Abbott, Andrew. *The System of Professions: An Essay on the Division of Expert Labor*. University of Chicago Press, 1988.

Abel, Olivier, Guy Coq, Antoine Garapon, and Irène Théry. "Les Occassions Manquées Du PACS (Entretien)." *Esprit*, November 1998, 201–14.

Adams, Jimi, and Ryan Light. "Scientific Consensus, the Law, and Same Sex Parenting Outcomes." *Social Science Research* 53 (September 2015): 300–310. https://doi.org/10.1016/j.ssresearch.2015.06.008.

ADFH and IFOP. "La Position Des Français Sur La PMA et La GPA." Association des Familles Homoparentales (ADFH), May 29, 2019. https://adfh.net/wp-content/uploads/2019/06/115524_Rapport_Ifop_ADFH_2019-3.pdf.

AFP. "Mariage pour tous: 170 juristes contre le 'marché des enfants.' " *Le Monde.fr*, March 15, 2013. http://www.lemonde.fr/societe/article/2013/03/15/mariage-pour-tous-170-juristes-contre-le-marche-des-enfants_1849346_3224.html.

Agacinski, Sylviane. "Deux mères = un père ?" *Le Monde*, February 2, 2013, sec. Débats.

Ahearne, Jeremy. "Public Intellectuals and Cultural Policy in France." *International Journal of Cultural Policy* 12, no. 3 (November 1, 2006): 323–39. https://doi.org/10.1080/10286630601020603.

Allen, Douglas W., Catherine Pakaluk, and Joseph Price. "Nontraditional Families and Childhood Progress Through School: A Comment on Rosenfeld." *Demography* 50, no. 30 (2013): 955–61. https://doi.org/10.1007/s13524-012-0169-x.

Almeling, Rene. *Sex Cells: The Medical Market for Eggs and Sperm*. University of California Press, 2011.

Amato, Paul R. "The Well-Being of Children with Gay and Lesbian Parents." *Social Science Research* 41, no. 4 (2012): 771–74. https://doi.org/10.1016/j.ssresearch.2012.04.007.

Amenta, Edwin, and Francesca Polletta. "The Cultural Impacts of Social Movements." *Annual Review of Sociology* 45, no. 1 (2019): 279–99. https://doi.org/10.1146/annurev-soc-073018-022342.

American Psychological Association. "Lesbian and Gay Parenting." American Psychological Association, 2005. http://www.apa.org/pi/lgbt/resources/parenting-full.pdf.

Anatrella, Tony. "Une précipitation anxieuse." *Le Monde*, October 10, 1998, sec. Divers.

Andersen, Ellen Ann. *Out of the Closets and Into the Courts: Legal Opportunity Structure and Gay Rights Litigation*. University of Michigan Press, 2005.

Armstrong, Elizabeth A., and Mary Bernstein. "Culture, Power, and Institutions: A Multi-Institutional Politics Approach to Social Movements." *Sociological Theory* 26, no. 1 (2008): 74–99. https://doi.org/10.1111/j.1467-9558.2008.00319.x.

Astor, Maggie. "Illinois Clergy Members Support Same-Sex Marriage in Letter Signed by 260." *New York Times*, December 24, 2012.

Aulagnon, Michelle. "La fausse bonne idée du contrat d'union sociale, c'est de tout mélanger." *Le Monde*, November 25, 1997, sec. Sports. http://www.lemonde.fr/archives/article/1997/11/25/la-fausse-bonne-idee-du-contrat-d-union-sociale-c-est-de-tout-melanger_3806704_1819218.html?xtmc=la_fausse_bonne_idee_du_contrat_d_union_sociale&xtcr=11.

Ayoub, Phillip M. *When States Come Out: Europe's Sexual Minorities and the Politics of Visibility.* Cambridge University Press, 2016.

Ayoub, Phillip M., and Kristina Stoeckl. *The Global Fight Against LGBTI Rights: How Transnational Conservative Networks Target Sexual and Gender Minorities.* NYU Press, 2024.

Backer, Larry Cata. "Religion as the Language of Discourse of Same Sex Marriage." *Capital University Law Review* 30 (2002): 222–78.

Badgett, M. V. Lee. *When Gay People Get Married: What Happens When Societies Legalize Same-Sex Marriage.* NYU Press, 2009.

Badgett, M. V. Lee, and Brad Sears. "The Bottom Line on Family Equality: The Impact of AB 205 on California's Businesses." The Williams Institute, August 1, 2003. https://escholarship.org/uc/item/9s3603j4.

——. "The Impact on California's Budget of Allowing Same-Sex Couples to Marry." Institute for Gay and Lesbian Strategic Studies, May 1, 2004. https://policycommons.net/artifacts/1171661/the-impact-on-californias-budget-of-allowing-same-sex-couples-to-marry/1724790/.

Badinter, Elisabeth, Irène Théry, Geneviève Delaisi de Parseval, et al. "Mariage pour tous: La gestation pour autrui ne doit pas être le bouc émissaire." *Le Monde.Fr*, December 19, 2012. http://www.lemonde.fr/idees/article/2012/12/19/mariage-pour-tous-la-gestation-pour-autrui-ne-doit-pas-etre-le-bouc-emissaire_1808271_3232.html.

Ball, Carlos A. *The Right to Be Parents: LGBT Families and the Transformation of Parenthood.* NYU Press, 2012.

Barclay, Scott. "In Search of Judicial Activism in the Same-Sex Marriage Cases: Sorting the Evidence from Courts, Legislatures, Initiatives and Amendments." *Perspectives on Politics* 8, no. 1 (March 2010): 111–26. https://doi.org/10.1017/S1537592709992696.

Barker, David C., Ryan Detamble, and Morgan Marietta. "Intellectualism, Anti-Intellectualism, and Epistemic Hubris in Red and Blue America." *American Political Science Review* 116, no. 1 (February 2022): 38–53. https://doi.org/10.1017/S0003055421000988.

Battaglia, Mattea, Violaine Morin, and Sylvie Lecherbonnier. "Jean-Michel Blanquer : « La France et sa jeunesse doivent échapper à l'idéologie woke »." *Le Monde.fr*, October 13, 2021. https://www.lemonde.fr/societe/article/2021/10/13/jean-michel-blanquer-la-france-et-sa-jeunesse-doivent-echapper-a-l-ideologie-woke_6098250_3224.html.

Baumgartner, Frank R., and Bryan D. Jones. "Agenda Dynamics and Policy Subsystems." *The Journal of Politics* 53, no. 04 (November 1991): 1044–74. https://doi.org/10.2307/2131866.

Baumgartner, Frank R., Bryan D. Jones, and Michael C. Macleod. "The Evolution of Legislative Jurisdictions." *Journal of Politics* 62, no. 2 (May 1, 2000): 321–49. https://doi.org/10.1111/0022-3816.00015.

Becker, Jo. *Forcing the Spring: Inside the Fight for Marriage Equality*. Penguin Books, 2015.

Bekmezian, Hélène, and Gaëlle Dupont. "Mariage gay: La droite veut s'opposer sans déraper." *Le Monde*, October 23, 2012.

Béland, Daniel, and Robert Henry Cox, eds. *Ideas and Politics in Social Science Research*. Oxford University Press, 2010.

Bellah, Robert Neelly, Richard Madsen, William M. Sullivan, Ann Swidler, and Steven Tipton. *Habits of the Heart: Individualism and Commitment in American Life*. University of California Press, 1985.

Benson, Rodney, and Daniel C. Hallin. "How States, Markets and Globalization Shape the News: The French and US National Press, 1965–97." *European Journal of Communication* 22, no. 1 (March 1, 2007): 27–48. https://doi.org/10.1177/0267323107073746.

Benson, Rodney, and Abigail Cope Saguy. "Constructing Social Problems in an Age of Globalization: A French-American Comparison." *American Sociological Review* 70, no. 2 (April 2005): 233–59.

Bérard, Yann, and Renaud Crespin, eds. *Aux frontières de l'expertise: dialogues entre savoirs et pouvoirs*. Presses Universitaires de Rennes, 2010.

Béraud, Céline, and Philippe Portier. *Métamorphoses catholiques: Acteurs, enjeux et mobilisations depuis le mariage pour tous*. Maison des Sciences de l'Homme, 2015.

Berger, Maurice. "L'homoparentalité est-elle porteuse d'un risque affectif?" *Le Monde*, February 8, 2013.

Bergeron, Henri. "The Soft Power of the European Centre for Drugs and Drug Addiction." In *European Drug Policies: The Ways of Reform*, edited by Henri Bergeron, 40–56. Routledge, 2017.

Berman, Elizabeth Popp. *Thinking Like an Economist: How Efficiency Replaced Equality in U.S. Public Policy*. Princeton University Press, 2022.

Bernard, Tara Siegel, and Ron Lieber. "The Costs of Being a Gay Couple Run Higher." *New York Times*, October 3, 2009, sec. A.

Bernstein, Mary. "United States: Multi-Institutional Politics, Social Movements, and the State." In *The Lesbian and Gay Movement and the State: Comparative Insights into a Transformative Relationship*, edited by Manon Tremblay, David Paternotte, and Carol Johnson, 197–212. Ashgate, 2011.

Bernstein, Mary, and Nancy A. Naples. "Altered States: Legal Structuring and Relationship Recognition in the U.S., Canada, and Australia." *American Sociological Review* 80, no. 6 (2015): 1226–49.

Bernstein, Mary, and Verta Taylor, eds. *The Marrying Kind? Debating Same-Sex Marriage Within the Lesbian and Gay Movement*. University of Minnesota Press, 2013.

Bernstein, Sharon. "Florida Bill Would Ban Gender Studies Majors, Diversity Programs at Universities." *Reuters*, February 25, 2023, sec. United States. https://www.reuters.com/world/us/florida-bill-would-ban-gender-studies-majors-diversity-programs-universities-2023-02-25/.

Best, Joel. *Social Problems*. Norton, 2012.

Beyers, Jan, and Caelesta Braun. "Ties That Count: Explaining Interest Group Access to Policymakers." *Journal of Public Policy* 34, no. 1 (2014): 93–121.

Biblarz, Timothy J., and Evren Savci. "Lesbian, Gay, Bisexual, and Transgender Families." *Journal of Marriage and Family* 72, no. 3 (June 2010): 480–97. https://doi.org/10.1111/j.1741-3737.2010.00714.x.

Biblarz, Timothy J., and Judith Stacey. "Ideal Families and Social Science Ideals." *Journal of Marriage and Family* 72, no. 1 (February 1, 2010): 41–44. https://doi.org/10.1111/j.1741-3737.2009.00682.x.

Binet, Erwann. "Rapport (568 Tome I) fait au nom de la commission des lois constituionnelles, de la légalisation et de l'administration générale de la république sur le projet de loi (n°344), ouvrant le mariage aux couples de personnes de même sexe." Assemblée Nationale, January 17, 2013.

Blankenhorn, David. "How My View on Gay Marriage Changed." *New York Times*, June 22, 2012. http://www.nytimes.com/2012/06/23/opinion/how-my-view-on-gay-marriage-changed .html.

Bleich, Erik. *Race Politics in Britain and France: Ideas and Policymaking Since the 1960s*. Cambridge University Press, 2003.

Blevins, John. "Broadening the Family of God: Debating Same-Sex Marriage and Queer Families in America." *Theology and Sexuality: The Journal of the Institute for the Study of Christianity and Sexuality* 12, no. 1 (September 2005): 63–80. https://doi.org/10.1177/1355835805057787.

Boltanski, Luc, and Laurent Thévenot. *De la justification: Les économies de la grandeur*. Essais. Gallimard, 1991.

Borrillo, Daniel, and Éric Fassin, eds. *Au delà du Pacs: L'expertise familiale à l'épreuve de l'homosexualité*. Presses Universitaires de France, 2001.

Borrillo, Daniel, and Pierre Lascoumes. *Amours égales? Le Pacs, les homosexuels et la Gauche*. La Découverte, 2002.

Bottoms, Bette L., Margaret Bull Kovera, and Bradley D. McAuliff. *Children, Social Science, and the Law*. Cambridge University Press, 2002.

Bourdieu, Pierre. "Le champ scientifique." *Actes de la Recherche en Sciences Sociales* 2, no. 2 (1976): 88–104. https://doi.org/10.3406/arss.1976.3454.

——. "Les conditions sociales de la circulation internationale des idées." *Actes de la recherche en sciences sociales* 145, no. 5 (December 1, 2002): 3–8.

——. *La distinction: Critique sociale du jugement*. Minuit, 1979.

——. "The Forms of Capital." In *Handbook of Theory and Research for the Sociology of Education*, edited by J. Richardson, 46–58. Greenwood Press, 1986.

——. "The Force of Law: Toward a Sociology of the Juridical Field." *The Hastings Law Journal* 38 (1987): 805–53.

——. *Homo academicus*. Minuit, 1984.

——. *La noblesse d'état: Grandes écoles et esprit de corps*. Minuit, 1989.

——. *Sociology in Question*. Sage, 1993.

——. "The Specificity of the Scientific Field and the Social Conditions of the Progress of Reason." *Social Science Information* 14, no. 6 (December 1, 1975): 19–47. https://doi.org/10.1177 /053901847501400602.

——. *Les usages sociaux de la science: Pour une sociologie clinique du champ scientifique*. Editions Quae, 2019.

Bourdieu, Pierre, and Loïc Wacquant. *An Invitation to Reflexive Sociology*. University of Chicago Press, 1992.

Bouvard, Hugo. *Gays et lesbiennes en politique: Représenter les minorités sexuelles en France et aux États-Unis*. Presses universitaires du Septentrion, 2024.

Brint, Steven. *In an Age of Experts*. Princeton University Press, 1996.

Brodzinsky, David, and Adam Pertman, eds. *Adoption by Lesbians and Gay Men: A New Dimension in Family Diversity*. Oxford University Press, 2012.

Broqua, Christophe, and Olivier Fillieule. "The Making of State Homosexuality: How AIDS Funding Shaped Same-Sex Politics in France." *American Behavioral Scientist* 61, no. 13 (November 1, 2017): 1623–39. https://doi.org/10.1177/0002764217744136.

Broqua, Christophe, and David M. Halperin. *Action = Vie: A History of AIDS Activism and Gay Politics in France.* Temple University Press, 2020.

Brossard, Dominique, James Shanahan, and Katherine McComas. "Are Issue-Cycles Culturally Constructed? A Comparison of French and American Coverage of Global Climate Change." *Mass Communication and Society* 7, no. 3 (July 1, 2004): 359–77. https://doi.org/10.1207/s15327825mcs0703_6.

Brubaker, Rogers. *Citizenship and Nationhood in France and Germany.* Harvard University Press, 1992.

Cadoret, Anne. *Des parents comme les autres.* Odile Jacob, 2002.

Cain, Patricia. *Rainbow Rights: The Role of Lawyers and Courts in the Lesbian and Gay Civil Rights Movement.* Westview Press, 2000.

Calmes, Jackie, and Peter Baker. "Obama Endorses Same-Sex Marriage, Taking Stand on Charged Social Issue." *New York Times*, May 10, 2012, sec. A.

Campbell, Andrea Louise. "Policy Makes Mass Politics." *Annual Review of Political Science* 15, no. 1 (2012): 333–51. https://doi.org/10.1146/annurev-polisci-012610-135202.

Campbell, David E., and J. Quin Monson. "The Religion Card: Gay Marriage and the 2004 Presidential Election." *Public Opinion Quarterly* 72, no. 3 (January 1, 2008): 399–419. https://doi.org/10.1093/poq/nfn032.

Campbell, John L., and Ove K. Pedersen. *The National Origins of Policy Ideas: Knowledge Regimes in the United States, France, Germany, and Denmark.* Princeton University Press, 2014.

Cardiff, Christopher F., and Daniel B. Klein. "Faculty Partisan Affiliations in All Disciplines: A Voter-registration Study." *Critical Review* 17, no. 3–4 (June 1, 2005): 237–55. https://doi.org/10.1080/08913810508443639.

Carney, Timothy P. "Opinion: Biden Says He's Pro-Science. Why Is His Schools Plan Based on Fear?" *New York Times*, February 19, 2021, sec. Opinion. https://www.nytimes.com/2021/02/19/opinion/coronavirus-schools-biden.html.

Caron, David. *AIDS in French Culture: Social Ills, Literary Cures.* University of Wisconsin Press, 2001.

Carragee, Kevin M., and Wim Roefs. "The Neglect of Power in Recent Framing Research." *Journal of Communication* 54, no. 2 (June 1, 2004): 214–33. https://doi.org/10.1111/j.1460-2466.2004.tb02625.x.

Castet, Anthony. "Guerres culturelles, idéologies et égalité des droits aux Etats-Unis: Le cas du mariage homosexuel." Thèse de doctorat, Tours, 2016. https://www.theses.fr/2016TOUR2014.

Caudill, David S., and Lewis H. LaRue. "Why Judges Applying the Daubert Trilogy Need to Know about the Social, Institutional, and Rhetorical—and Not Just the Methodological—Aspects of Science." *Boston College Law Review* 45 (2004): 1.

Charle, Christophe. *Naissance des "intellectuels": 1880–1900.* Minuit, 1990.

Chateauraynaud, Francis. *Argumenter dans un champ de forces: Essai de balistique sociologique.* Editions Pétra, 2011.

Chemin, Anne. "Une homosexuelle se voit refuser une adoption pour la deuxième fois." *Le Monde*, février 2009.

Cherlin, Andrew J. "American Marriage in the Early Twenty-First Century." *The Future of Children* 15, no. 2 (2005): 33–55.

——. "Demographic Trends in the United States: A Review of Research in the 2000s." *Journal of Marriage and Family* 72, no. 3 (June 1, 2010): 403–19.

——. *The Marriage-Go-Round: The State of Marriage and the Family in America Today.* Knopf Doubleday, 2010.

Chiarello, Elizabeth. "Where Movements Matter: Examining Unintended Consequences of the Pain Management Movement in Medical, Criminal Justice, and Public Health Fields." *Law and Policy* 40, no. 1 (2018): 79–109. https://doi.org/10.1111/lapo.12098.

Cimmings, Scott L., and Douglas NeJaime. "Lawyering for Marriage Equality." *UCLA Law Review* 57 (2010 2009): 1235–1331.

Clemens, Elisabeth S., and James M. Cook. "Politics and Institutionalism: Explaining Durability and Change." *Annual Review of Sociology* 25, no. 1 (1999): 441–66. https://doi.org/10.1146/annurev.soc.25.1.441.

Collin, Thibaud. *Les lendemains du mariage gay: Vers la fin du mariage? Quelle place pour les enfants?* Salvator, 2012.

Collins, Harry, and Robert Evans. *Rethinking Expertise.* University of Chicago Press, 2008.

Collins Jr., Paul M. "Friends of the Court: Examining the Influence of Amicus Curiae Participation in U.S. Supreme Court Litigation." *Law and Society Review* 38, no. 4 (2004): 807–32. https://doi.org/10.1111/j.0023-9216.2004.00067.x.

Collins Jr., Paul M., Pamela C. Corley, and Jesse Hamner. "The Influence of Amicus Curiae Briefs on U.S. Supreme Court Opinion Content." *Law and Society Review* 49, no. 4 (2015): 917–44. https://doi.org/10.1111/lasr.12166.

Collins, Patricia Hill. *Black Feminist Thought: Knowledge, Consciousness, and the Politics of Empowerment.* Perspectives on Gender, vol. 2. Routledge, 1991.

Commaille, Jacques. "La famille, l'état, le politique: une nouvelle économie des valeurs." *Informations sociales* 136, no. 8 (December 1, 2006): 100–111.

Cullen, Pauline, Myra Marx Ferree, and Mieke Verloo. "Introduction to Special Issue: Gender, Knowledge Production and Knowledge Work." *Gender, Work and Organization* 26, no. 6 (2019): 765–71. https://doi.org/10.1111/gwao.12329.

Daumas, Cécile. "Valérie Pécresse coupe les bourses au genre." *Libération.Fr,* December 14, 2016. http://www.liberation.fr/debats/2016/12/14/valerie-pecresse-coupe-les-bourses-au-genre_1535283.

De Singly, François. *Sociologie de La Famille Contemporaine.* 6th ed. Armand Colin, 2017.

Dekeuwer-Défossez, Françoise. "Rénover le droit de la famille: Propositions pour un droit adapté aux réalités et aux aspirations de notre temps." Rapport au Garde des Sceaux. Ministère de la Justice, September 1999.

Delage, Pauline. *Violences conjugales: Du combat féministe à la cause publique.* Presses de Sciences Po, 2017.

Delsol, Chantal, Pierre Lévy-Soussan, Sophie Marinopoulos, et al. "Touche pas à 'père-et-mère.'" *Le Monde.Fr,* November 11, 2012. http://www.lemonde.fr/idees/article/2012/11/08/touche-pas-a-pere-et-mere_1788107_3232.html.

Descoutures, Virginie. *Les mères lesbiennes.* PUF, 2010.

Dilling, Lisa, and Maria Carmen Lemos. "Creating Usable Science: Opportunities and Constraints for Climate Knowledge Use and Their Implications for Science Policy." *Global*

Environmental Change, Special Issue on The Politics and Policy of Carbon Capture and Storage, 21, no. 2 (May 2011): 680–89. https://doi.org/10.1016/j.gloenvcha.2010.11.006.

Doherty, Brian, and Graeme Hayes. "Having Your Day in Court: Judicial Opportunity and Tactical Choice in Anti-GMO Campaigns in France and the United Kingdom." *Comparative Political Studies* 47, no. 1 (2014): 3–29.

Dunlap, Riley E., and Peter J. Jacques. "Climate Change Denial Books and Conservative Think Tanks: Exploring the Connection." *American Behavioral Scientist* 57, no. 6 (June 1, 2013): 699–731. https://doi.org/10.1177/0002764213477096.

Dupont, Gaëlle. "Entretien: 'L'humanité n'a cessé d'inventer de nouvelles formes de mariage.'" *Le Monde*, November 18, 2012, sec. Société.

Egan, Patrick J., and Megan Mullin. "Climate Change: US Public Opinion." *Annual Review of Political Science* 20, no. 1 (2017): 209–27. https://doi.org/10.1146/annurev-polisci-051215-022857.

Eliacheff, Caroline. "Malaise dans la psychanalyse." *Esprit* 273 (2001): 62–77.

Engeli, Isabelle, Christoffer Green-Pedersen, and Lars Thorup Larsen, eds. *Morality Politics in Western Europe*. Palgrave Macmillan, 2012.

Epstein, Steven. *Impure Science: AIDS, Activism, and the Politics of Knowledge*. University of California Press, 1996.

——. "The New Attack on Sexuality Research: Morality and the Politics of Knowledge Production." *Sexuality Research and Social Policy* 3, no. 1 (2006): 1–12.

Epstein, Steven, and Stefan Timmermans. "From Medicine to Health: The Proliferation and Diversification of Cultural Authority." *Journal of Health and Social Behavior* 62, no. 3 (September 2021): 240–54. https://doi.org/10.1177/00221465211010468.

Eribon, Didier. *Sur cet instant fragile: carnets, janvier-août 2004*. Fayard, 2004.

Eskridge, William N., and Nan D. Hunter. *Sexuality, Gender and the Law*. 3rd ed. Foundation Press, 2011.

Eyal, Gil. "For a Sociology of Expertise: The Social Origins of the Autism Epidemic." *American Journal of Sociology* 118, no. 4 (January 1, 2013): 863–907. https://doi.org/10.1086/668448.

——. *The Crisis of Expertise*. Polity, 2019.

Eyal, Gil, and Larissa Buchholz. "From the Sociology of Intellectuals to the Sociology of Interventions." *Annual Review of Sociology* 36, no. 1 (2010): 117–37. https://doi.org/10.1146/annurev.soc.012809.102625.

Ezekiel, Judith. "Le Women's Lib: Made in France." *European Journal of Women's Studies* 9 (2002): 345–61.

Fabre, Clarisse, and Éric Fassin. *Liberté, egalité, sexualités*. Belfond, 2003.

Fassin, Éric. "Le Savant, l'expert et Le Politique: La Famille Des Sociologues." *Genèses* 32, no. 1 (1998): 156–69. https://doi.org/10.3406/genes.1998.1533.

——. *Le sexe politique: Genre et sexualité au miroir transatlantique*. Cas de figure. Éditions de l'EHESS, 2009.

——. "L'intellectuel Spécifique et Le PaCS: Politiques Des Savoirs." *Mouvements*, no. 7 (January 2000): 68–76.

——. "Same Sex, Different Politics: 'Gay Marriage' Debates in France and the United States." *Public Culture* 13 (2001): 215–32.

——. "Same-Sex Marriage, Nation, and Race: French Political Logics and Rhetorics." *Contemporary French Civilization* 39, no. 3 (January 1, 2014): 281–301. https://doi.org/10.3828/cfc.2014.17.

——. "Usages de la science et science des usages." *L'Homme. Revue française d'anthropologie*, no. 154–155 (January 1, 2000): 391–408. https://doi.org/10.4000/lhomme.39.

Ferree, Myra Marx. "Resonance and Radicalism: Feminist Framing in the Abortion Debates of the United States and Germany." *The American Journal of Sociology* 109, no. 2 (2003): 304–44.

Ferree, Myra Marx, William Anthony Gamson, Dieter Rucht, and Jürgen Gerhards. *Shaping Abortion Discourse: Democracy and the Public Sphere in Germany and the United States*. Cambridge University Press, 2002.

Fetner, Tina. *How the Religious Right Shaped Lesbian and Gay Activism*. University of Minnesota Press, 2008.

Fiorilli, Olivia. "Reproductive Injustice and the Politics of Trans Future in France." *TSQ: Transgender Studies Quarterly* 6, no. 4 (November 1, 2019): 579–92. https://doi.org/10.1215/23289252 -7771737.

Fischer, Frank. *Citizens, Experts, and the Environment: The Politics of Local Knowledge*. Duke University Press, 2000.

——. *Democracy and Expertise*. Oxford University Press, 2009.

Flavigny, Christian. "L'enfant bientôt privé de 'père et mère'?" *Le Monde*, November 9, 2012, sec. Débats.

Fligstein, Neil, and Doug McAdam. *A Theory of Fields*. Oxford University Press, 2012.

Foucault, Michel. "Truth and Power." In *Essential Works of Michel Foucault (Power)*, edited by James Faubion, 3:111–33. New Press, 2000.

Fourcade, Marion. *Economists and Societies: Discipline and Profession in the United States, Britain, and France, 1890s to 1990s*. Princeton University Press, 2009.

Fourcade, Marion, Etienne Ollion, and Yann Algan. "The Superiority of Economists." *Journal of Economic Perspectives* 29, no. 1 (2015): 89–114.

Fraïssé, Christèle, ed. *L'homophobie: Et les expressions de l'ordre hétérosexiste*. Presses universitaires de Rennes, 2011.

Franklin, Sarah. "Science as Culture, Cultures of Science." *Annual Review of Anthropology* 24, no. 1 (1995): 163–84. https://doi.org/10.1146/annurev.an.24.100195.001115.

Freedman, Samuel G. "Focus on the Family Works to Invite Discussion and Transform Message." *New York Times*, March 9, 2013, sec. A.

Frickel, Scott, and Kelly Moore. *The New Political Sociology of Science: Institutions, Networks, and Power*. University of Wisconsin Press, 2006.

Friedland, Roger, and Robert Alford. "Bringing Society Back in: Symbols, Practices and Institutional Contradictions." In *The New Institutionalism in Organizational Analysis*, edited by Walter Powell and Paul Dimaggio, 232–63. University of Chicago Press, 1991.

Garcia, Daniel. *La folle histoire du mariage gay*. Flammarion, 2004.

Garnier, Éric. *L'homoparentalité en France: La bataille des nouvelles familles*. Thierry Marchaisse Editions, 2012.

Garretson, Jeremiah J. "Changing with the Times: The Spillover Effects of Same-Sex Marriage Ballot Measures on Presidential Elections." *Political Research Quarterly* 67, no. 2 (June 1, 2014): 280–92. https://doi.org/10.1177/1065912914521897.

Gates, Gary J. "How Many People Are Lesbian, Gay, Bisexual and Transgender?" The William's Institute, April 1, 2011. http://escholarship.org/uc/item/09h684x2.

Gates, Gary J., Lee M. V. Badgett, Macomber E. Jennifer, and Kate Chambers. "Adoption and Foster Care by Gay and Lesbian Parents in the United States." The Williams Institute, 2007. http://williamsinstitute.law.ucla.edu/research/parenting/adoption-and-foster-care-by-gay-and-lesbian-parents-in-the-united-states/.

Gélard, Patrice. "Rapport (258): fait au nom de la commission des lois constitutionnelles, sur la proposition de loi, adopté par l'assemblée nationale, relative au pacte civil de solidarité." Sénat: Commission de Lois, January 27, 1999. http://www.senat.fr/rap/l98-258/l98-258.html.

Gieryn, Thomas F. Cultural Boundaries of Science: Credibility on the Line. University of Chicago Press, 1999.

Golan, Guy. "Inter-Media Agenda Setting and Global News Coverage." Journalism Studies 7, no. 2 (April 1, 2006): 323–33. https://doi.org/10.1080/14616700500533643.

Goldenberg, Maya J. Vaccine Hesitancy: Public Trust, Expertise, and the War on Science. University of Pittsburgh Press, 2021.

Golombok, Susan, Beth Perry, Amanda Burston, et al. "Children with Lesbian Parents: A Community Study." Developmental Psychology 39, no. 1 (2003): 20–33. https://doi.org/10.1037/0012-1649.39.1.20.

Golombok, Susan, and Fiona Tasker. "Gay Fathers." In Role of the Father in Child Development, edited by Michael E. Lamb, 319–40. Wiley, 2010.

Goodnough, Abby. "A Push Is on for Same-Sex Marriage Rights Across New England." New York Times, April 5, 2009, sec. A.

Gregorio, Monica Di. "Gaining Access to the State: Political Opportunities and Agency in Forest Activism in Indonesia." Social Movement Studies 13, no. 3 (July 3, 2014): 381–98. https://doi.org/10.1080/14742837.2013.856297.

Gros, Marie-Joëlle, and Catherine Mallaval. "Et toujours cette norme du papa, maman et moi. . . ." Liberation, October 10, 2012. http://www.liberation.fr/societe/2012/10/10/et-toujours-cette-norme-du-papa-maman-et-moi_852366.

Gross, Martine. "Quand et comment l'homoparentalité est-elle devenue un objet « légitime » de recherche en sciences humaines et sociales?" Socio-logos, no. 2 (October 16, 2007). http://socio-logos.revues.org/803.

Gross, Martine, Jérôme Courduriès, and Ainhoa de Federico. "Le recours à l'AMP dans les familles homoparentales: état des lieux. Résultats d'une enquête menée en 2012." Socio-logos. Revue de l'association française de sociologie, no. 9 (February 24, 2014). http://socio-logos.revues.org/2870.

Gross, Neil. "The Detraditionalization of Intimacy Reconsidered*." Sociological Theory 23, no. 3 (2005): 286–311. https://doi.org/10.1111/j.0735-2751.2005.00255.x.

Grzebalska, Weronika, and Andrea Pető. "The Gendered Modus Operandi of the Illiberal Transformation in Hungary and Poland." Women's Studies International Forum 68 (May 1, 2018): 164–72. https://doi.org/10.1016/j.wsif.2017.12.001.

Grzymala-Busse, Anna. "Why Comparative Politics Should Take Religion (More) Seriously." Annual Review of Political Science 15, no. 1 (2012): 421–42. https://doi.org/10.1146/annurev-polisci-033110-130442.

Gunn, T. Jeremy. "Religious Freedom and Laicite: A Comparison of the United States and France." Brigham Young University Law Review 2004 (2004): 419–506.

Haas, Peter M. "Introduction: Epistemic Communities and International Policy Coordination." Knowledge, Power, and International Policy Coordination 43, no. 3 (1992): 1–35.

Hafford-Letchfield, Trish, Christine Cocker, Deborah Rutter, Moreblessing Tinarwo, Keira McCormack, and Rebecca Manning. "What Do We Know About Transgender Parenting? Findings from a Systematic Review." *Health and Social Care in the Community* 27, no. 5 (2019): 1111–25. https://doi.org/10.1111/hsc.12759.

Haider-Markel, Donald P. "Morality in Congress? Legislative Voting on Gay Issues." In *The Public Clash of Private Values: The Politics of Morality Policy*, edited by Christopher Z. Mooney, 115–29. Chatham House Publishers, 2001.

Halifax, Juliette, and Catherine Villeneuve-Gokalp. "L'adoption En France: Qui sont les adoptés, qui sont les adoptants?" *Population et Sociétés* 417 (2005): 1–4.

Hancock, Ange-Marie. "Contemporary Welfare Reform and the Public Identity of the 'Welfare Queen.'" *Race, Gender and Class* 10, no. 1 (2003): 31–59.

Harding, Sandra. "After Absolute Neutrality: Expanding 'Science.'" In *Feminist Science Studies*. Routledge, 2001.

Harding, Sandra G., and Merrill B. Hintikka, eds. *Discovering Reality: Feminist Perspectives on Epistemology, Metaphysics, Methodology, and Philosophy of Science*. Synthese Library, vol. 161. D. Reidel, 1983.

Healy, Patrick. "Hopefuls Differ as They Reject Gay Marriage." *New York Times*, November 1, 2008, sec. A.

Heath, Melanie. *One Marriage Under God: The Campaign to Promote Marriage in America*. NYU Press, 2012.

Helfand, Michael A. "The Usual Suspect Classifications: Criminals, Aliens and the Future of Same-Sex Marriage." *University of Pennsylvania Journal of Constitutional Law* 12 (2009): 1–56.

Hennette-Vauchez, Stéphanie. *Le droit de la bioéthique*. Editions La Découverte, 2009.

Herek, Gregory M. "Myths about Sexual Orientation: A Lawyer's Guide to Social Science Research." *Law and Sexuality: A Review of Lesbian and Gay Legal Issues* 1 (1991): 133–72.

——. "The Social Psychology of Homophobia: Toward a Practical Theory." *New York University Review of Law and Social Change* 14 (1986): 923.

Héritier, Françoise. *Masculin/féminin: La pensée de la différence*. Odile Jacob, 1995.

——. *Masculin/féminin II: Dissoudre la hiérarchie*. Odile Jacob, 2012.

Hirsch, H. N., ed. *The Future of Gay Rights in America*. Routledge, 2005.

Hirschman, Daniel. "Rediscovering the 1 Percent: Knowledge Infrastructures and the Stylized Facts of Inequality." *American Journal of Sociology* 127, no. 3 (November 1, 2021): 739–86. https://doi.org/10.1086/718451.

Hollis-Brusky, Amanda. *Ideas with Consequences: The Federalist Society and the Conservative Counterrevolution*. Oxford University Press, 2019.

Hubbard, Ruth. *The Politics of Women's Biology*. Rutgers University Press, 1990.

Hull, Kathleen E. "The Role of Social Science Expertise in Same-Sex Marriage Litigation." *Annual Review of Law and Social Science* 13, no. 1 (2017): 471–91. https://doi.org/10.1146/annurev-lawsocsci-110615-084729.

——. *Same-Sex Marriage: The Cultural Politics of Love and Law*. Cambridge University Press, 2006.

Jackson, Julian. *Living in Arcadia Homosexuality, Politics, and Morality in France from the Liberation to AIDS*. University of Chicago Press, 2009.

Jasanoff, Sheila. "Cosmopolitan Knowledge: Climate Science and Global Civic Epistemology." In *The Oxford Handbook of Climate Change and Society*, edited by John S. Dryzek,

Richard B. Norgaard, and David Schlosberg, 129–43. Oxford University Press, 2011. https://doi
.org/10.1093/oxfordhb/9780199566600.003.0009.

——. *Designs on Nature: Science and Democracy in Europe and the United States.* Princeton University
Press, 2005.

——. *Science at the Bar: Law, Science, and Technology in America.* Harvard University Press, 2009.

——, ed. *States of Knowledge: The Co-Production of Science and the Social Order.* Routledge, 2004.

Jatkowski, Walter J. "Subsystem Contexts and Policy Information: Conditional Effects on
Information in Congressional Hearings." University of Oklahoma, 2013.

Jelen, Ted G., and Clyde Wilcox. "Causes and Consequences of Public Attitudes Toward Abortion: A Review and Research Agenda." *Political Research Quarterly* 56, no. 4 (December 1,
2003): 489–500. https://doi.org/10.1177/106591290305600410.

Joffe, Carole E., T. A. Weitz, and C. L. Stacey. "Uneasy Allies: Pro-Choice Physicians, Feminist
Health Activists and the Struggle for Abortion Rights." *Sociology of Health and Illness* 26, no.
6 (2004): 775–96. https://doi.org/10.1111/j.0141-9889.2004.00418.x.

Johnson, Paul. *Homosexuality and the European Court of Human Rights.* Routledge, 2013.

Johnston, Hank, and John A. Noakes. *Frames of Protest: Social Movements and the Framing Perspective.* Edited by Hank Johnston and John A. Noakes. Rowman & Littlefield, 2005.

Jones, Sally, Angela Martinez Dy, and Natalia Vershinina. " 'We Were Fighting for Our Place':
Resisting Gender Knowledge Regimes Through Feminist Knowledge Network Formation." *Gender, Work and Organization* 26, no. 6 (2019): 789–804. https://doi.org/10.1111/gwao
.12288.

Kane, Melinda D., and Thomas Alan Elliott. "Turning to the Courts: A Quantitative Analysis
of the Gay and Lesbian Movement's Use of Legal Mobilization." *Sociological Focus* 47, no. 4
(October 2, 2014): 219–37. https://doi.org/10.1080/00380237.2014.939901.

Kaufman, Gayle, and D'Lane Compton. "Attitudes Toward LGBT Marriage and Legal Protections Post-Obergefell." *Sexuality Research and Social Policy* 18, no. 2 (June 1, 2021): 321–30.
https://doi.org/10.1007/s13178-020-00460-y.

Kelly, Robert F., and Sarah H. Ramsey. "Standards for Social Science Amicus Briefs in Family
and Child Law Cases." *Journal of Gender, Race and Justice* 13 (2009): 81.

Kirsner, Douglas. "Psychoanalysis and Its Discontents." *Psychoanalytic Psychology* 21, no. 3 (2004):
339–52. https://doi.org/10.1037/0736-9735.21.3.339.

Klein, Daniel B., and Charlotta Stern. "Professors and Their Politics: The Policy Views of
Social Scientists." *Critical Review* 17, no. 3–4 (June 1, 2005): 257–303. https://doi.org/10.1080
/08913810508443640.

Knorr-Cetina, Karin. *Epistemic Cultures: How the Sciences Make Knowledge.* Harvard University Press,
1999.

Kremer, Pascale. "Jean-Luc Romero, élu RPR, présente son compagnon à la télévision." *Le
Monde*, September 20, 2001.

——. "Sociologues, psychiatres et psychanalystes sont divisés." *Le Monde*, March 15, 1999.

Kuhar, Roman. "Playing with Science: Sexual Citizenship and the Roman Catholic Church
Counter-Narratives in Slovenia and Croatia." *Women's Studies International Forum* 49 (March
2015): 84–92. https://doi.org/10.1016/j.wsif.2014.07.005.

Kuhar, Roman, and David Paternotte, eds. *Anti-Gender Campaigns in Europe: Mobilizing Against
Equality.* Rowman & Littlefield, 2017.

Kuru, Ahmet T. *Secularism and State Policies Toward Religion: The United States, France, and Turkey.* Cambridge University Press, 2009.

Kurzman, Charles, and Lynn Owens. "The Sociology of Intellectuals." *Annual Review of Sociology* 28 (January 1, 2002): 63–90.

Lacroix, Xavier. *La confusion des genres: Réponses à certaines demandes homosexuelles sur le mariage et l'adoption.* Bayard Jeunesse, 2005.

Lamont, Michèle. *The Dignity of Working Men: Morality and the Boundaries of Race, Class, and Immigration.* Harvard University Press, 2002.

——. "How to Become a Dominant French Philosopher: The Case of Jacques Derrida." *American Journal of Sociology* 93, no. 3 (November 1, 1987): 584–622.

Lamont, Michèle, and Laurent Thévenot, eds. *Rethinking Comparative Cultural Sociology: Repertoires of Evaluation in France and the United States.* Cambridge University Press, 2000.

Landry, Bart. *Black Working Wives: Pioneers of the American Family Revolution.* University of California Press, 2002.

Lane, Melissa. "Political Theory on Climate Change." *Annual Review of Political Science* 19, no. 1 (2016): 107–23. https://doi.org/10.1146/annurev-polisci-042114-015427.

Larsen, Allison Orr. "The Trouble with Amicus Facts." *Virginia Law Review* 100, no. 8 (2014): 1757–818.

Larsen, Allison Orr, and Neal Devins. "The Amicus Machine." *Virginia Law Review* 102, no. 8 (December 2016): 1901–68.

Lemahieu, Thomas. "Projet Périclès: le document qui dit tout du plan de Pierre-Édouard Stérin pour installer le RN au pouvoir." L'Humanité, July 19, 2024, sec. Politique. https://www.humanite.fr/politique/bien-commun/projet-pericles-le-document-qui-dit-tout-du-plan-de-pierre-edouard-sterin-pour-installer-le-rn-au-pouvoir.

Lenon, Suzanne. "White as Milk: Proposition 8 and the Cultural Politics of Gay Rights." *Atlantis: Critical Studies in Gender, Culture and Social Justice* 36, no. 1 (April 1, 2013): 44–54.

Lépinard, Eléonore. *L'égalité introuvable: La parité, les feministes, et la république.* Presses de Sciences Po, 2007.

Lerch, Arnaud, Judith Stacey, and Arnaud Lerch. " 'Au nom de la famille.' Entretien avec Judith Stacey." *Actes de la recherche en sciences sociales* 214, no. 4 (August 9, 2016): 94–103.

Lindblom, Charles E. *Usable Knowledge: Social Science and Social Problem Solving.* Yale University Press, 1979.

Liptak, Adam. "Justices Say Time May Be Wrong for Ruling on Gay Marriage." *New York Times*, March 27, 2013, Late Edition, sec. A.

Luker, Kristin. *Abortion and the Politics of Motherhood.* University of California Press, 1984.

Maher, Michael J., Kimberly Landini, Dennis M. Emano, et al. "Hirschfeld to Hooker to Herek to High Schools: A Study of the History and Development of GLBT Empirical Research, Institutional Policies, and the Relationship Between the Two." *Journal of Homosexuality* 56, no. 7 (2009): 921–58. https://doi.org/10.1080/00918360903187861.

Mahoudeau, Margot. *La panique woke.* TEXTUEL, 2022.

Maldonado, Oscar Javier. "The Decriminalisation of Abortion in Colombia as Cautionary Tale. Social Movements, Numbers and Socio-Technical Struggles in the Promotion of Health as a Right." *Global Public Health* 14, no. 6–7 (July 3, 2019): 1031–43. https://doi.org/10.1080/17441692.2018.1504101.

Manning, Wendy D., Marshal Neal Fettro, and Esther Lamidi. "Child Well-Being in Same-Sex Parent Families: Review of Research Prepared for American Sociological Association Amicus Brief." *Population Research and Policy Review* 33, no. 4 (August 1, 2014): 485–502. https://doi.org/10.1007/s11113-014-9329-6.

Marche, Guillaume. "Flawed Science: Mobilisations conservatrices, sexualité et discours scientifique." *Revue française d'études américaines* 133, no. 3 (2012): 67–81. https://doi.org/10.3917/rfea.133.0067.

Marzullo, Michelle. "Through a Glass, Darkly: U.S. Marriage Discourse and Neoliberalism." *Journal of Homosexuality* 58, no. 6–7 (2011): 758–74. https://doi.org/10.1080/00918369.2011.581919.

McAdam, Doug. "Social Movement Theory and the Prospects for Climate Change Activism in the United States." *Annual Review of Political Science* 20, no. 1 (2017): 189–208. https://doi.org/10.1146/annurev-polisci-052615-025801.

McCaffrey, Enda. *The Gay Republic: Sexuality, Citizenship and Subversion in France*. Ashgate, 2005.

McCright, Aaron M., and Riley E. Dunlap. "Defeating Kyoto: The Conservative Movement's Impact on U.S. Climate Change Policy." *Social Problems* 50, no. 3 (August 1, 2003): 348–73. https://doi.org/10.1525/sp.2003.50.3.348.

——. "The Politicization of Climate Change and Polarization in the American Public's Views of Global Warming, 2001–2010." *Sociological Quarterly* 52, no. 2 (March 1, 2011): 155–94. https://doi.org/10.1111/j.1533-8525.2011.01198.x.

McKinnon, Andrew M., Marta Trzebiatowska, and Christopher Craig Brittain. "Bourdieu, Capital, and Conflict in a Religious Field: The Case of the 'Homosexuality' Conflict in the Anglican Communion." *Journal of Contemporary Religion* 26, no. 3 (October 2011): 355–70. https://doi.org/10.1080/13537903.2011.616033.

Mécary, Caroline. "Homosexualité, mariage et filiation: Où en sommes-nous?" *Informations sociales* 149, no. 5 (October 27, 2008): 136–49.

——. *L'amour et la loi*. Alma Editeur, 2012.

Medina, Leandro Rodriguez. *Centers and Peripheries in Knowledge Production*. Routledge, 2013.

Medvetz, Thomas. *Think Tanks in America*. University Of Chicago Press, 2012.

Mennesson, Sylvie, and Dominique Mennesson. *La gestation pour autrui: L'improbable débat*. Editions Michalon, 2010.

Merkley, Eric. "Anti-Intellectualism, Populism, and Motivated Resistance to Expert Consensus." *Public Opinion Quarterly* 84, no. 1 (March 1, 2020): 24–48. https://doi.org/10.1093/poq/nfz053.

Meyer, David S. "Protest and Political Opportunities." *Annual Review of Sociology* 30 (2004): 125–45.

Mezey, Susan Gluck. *Gay Families and the Courts: The Quest for Equal Rights*. Rowman & Littlefield, 2009.

——. *Queers in Court: Gay Rights Law and Public Policy*. Rowman & Littlefield Publishers, 2007.

Michel, Jean-Pierre. "Rapport (437 Tome II) fait au nom de la commission des lois constitutionnelles, sur le projet de loi, adopté par l'assemblée nationale, ouvrant le mariage aux couples de personnes de même sexe." Sénat, Commission des Lois, March 20, 2013.

Millard, Eric, Pierre Brunet, Stéphanie Hennette-Vauchez, and Véronique Champeil-Desplats. "Mariage pour tous: Juristes, taisons-nous!" *Raison-Publique.Fr* (blog), March 20, 2013. http://www.raison-publique.fr/article601.html.

Miller, Banks, and Brett Curry. "Expertise, Experience, and Ideology on Specialized Courts: The Case of the Court of Appeals for the Federal Circuit." *Law and Society Review* 43, no. 4 (2009): 839–64. https://doi.org/10.1111/j.1540-5893.2009.00390.x.

Misztal, Barbara A., and David Moss, eds. *Action on AIDS: National Policies in Comparative Perspective.* Contributions in Medical Studies, No. 28. Greenwood Press, 1990.

Mooney, Christopher Z., ed. *The Public Clash of Private Values: The Politics of Morality Policy.* Chatham House Publishers, 2001.

Moore, Mignon R. *Invisible Families: Gay Identities, Relationships, and Motherhood Among Black Women.* University of California Press, 2011.

Moore, Mignon R., and Michael Stambolis-Ruhstorfer. "LGBT Sexuality and Families at the Start of the Twenty-First Century." *Annual Review of Sociology* 39, no. 1 (2013): 491–507. https://doi.org/10.1146/annurev-soc-071312-145643.

Morse, Jennifer Roback. *Love and Economics: Why the Laissez-Faire Family Doesn't Work.* Spence Publishing Company, 2001.

Moscowitz, Leigh. *The Battle Over Marriage: Gay Rights Activism Through the Media.* University of Illinois Press, 2013.

Mucciaroni, Gary. "Are Debates About 'Morality Policy' Really About Morality? Framing Opposition to Gay and Lesbian Rights." *Policy Studies Journal* 39, no. 2 (May 1, 2011): 187–216. https://doi.org/10.1111/j.1541-0072.2011.00404.x.

——. *Same Sex, Different Politics: Success and Failure in the Struggles Over Gay Rights.* University of Chicago Press, 2008.

Murphy, Michelle. *Seizing the Means of Reproduction: Entanglements of Feminism, Health, and Technoscience.* Duke University Press, 2012.

Murphy, Patrick J., Jill Kickul, Saulo D. Barbosa, and Lindsay Titus. "Expert Capital and Perceived Legitimacy." *The International Journal of Entrepreneurship and Innovation* 8, no. 2 (May 1, 2007): 127–38. https://doi.org/10.5367/000000007780808002.

Musick, Kelly, and Katherine Michelmore. "Cross-National Comparisons of Union Stability in Cohabiting and Married Families with Children." *Demography* 55, no. 4 (June 7, 2018): 1389–421. https://doi.org/10.1007/s13524-018-0683-6.

Musselin, Christine. *The Long March of French Universities.* Routledge, 2013.

Nadaud, Stéphane. *Homoparentalité: Une nouvelle chance pour la famille?* Fayard, 2002.

Noiriel, Gérard. *Dire la vérité au pouvoir: Les intellectuels en question.* Agone, 2010.

O'Brien, Timothy L. "Scientific Authority in Policy Contexts: Public Attitudes about Environmental Scientists, Medical Researchers, and Economists." *Public Understanding of Science (Bristol, England)* 22, no. 7 (October 2013): 799–816. https://doi.org/10.1177/0963662511435054.

O'Brien, Timothy L., Stephen L. Hawkins, and Adam Loesch. "Scientific Disciplines and the Admissibility of Expert Evidence in Courts." *Socius* 8 (January 1, 2022): 23780231221108044. https://doi.org/10.1177/23780231221108044.

Ocobock, Abigail. "Leveraging Legitimacy: Institutional Work and Change in the Case of Same-Sex Marriage." *American Journal of Sociology* 126, no. 3 (November 2020): 513–44. https://doi.org/10.1086/712501.

Oreskes, Naomi, and Erik M. Conway. *Merchants of Doubt: How a Handful of Scientists Obscured the Truth on Issues from Tobacco Smoke to Global Warming.* Bloomsbury, 2010.

Pacelle Jr., Richard L., John M. Scheb II, Hemant K. Sharma, and David H. Scott. "Assessing the Influence of Amicus Curiae Briefs on the Roberts Court*." *Social Science Quarterly* 99, no. 4 (2018): 1253–66. https://doi.org/10.1111/ssqu.12480.

Paternotte, David. *Revendiquer le "mariage gay": Belgique, France, Espagne*. Editions de l'Université de Bruxelles, 2011.

Paternotte, David, and Mieke Verloo. "De-Democratization and the Politics of Knowledge: Unpacking the Cultural Marxism Narrative." *Social Politics: International Studies in Gender, State and Society* 28, no. 3 (September 1, 2021): 556–78. https://doi.org/10.1093/sp/jxab025.

Patil, Vrushali. *Webbed Connectivities: The Imperial Sociology of Sex, Gender, and Sexuality*. University of Minnesota Press, 2022.

Patterson, Charlotte J. "Children of Lesbian and Gay Parents." *Child Development* 63, no. 5 (October 1, 1992): 1025–42. https://doi.org/10.1111/j.1467-8624.1992.tb01679.x.

Peerbaye, Ashveen. "L'invention de l'homoparentalité: Acteurs, arènes et rhétoriques autour de la question de la filiation homosexuelle." Master's Thesis (DEA), ENS, 2000.

Perreau, Bruno, ed. *Le choix de l'homosexualité: Recherches inédites sur la question gay et lesbienne*. EPEL, 2007.

——. *The Politics of Adoption. Gender and the Making of French Citizenship*. MIT Press, 2014.

——. *Queer Theory: The French Response*. Stanford University Press, 2016.

Pető, Andrea. "Current Comment: The Illiberal Academic Authority. An Oxymoron?" *Berichte Zur Wissenschaftsgeschichte* 44, no. 4 (2021): 461–69. https://doi.org/10.1002/bewi.202100013.

Phillips-fein, Kim. *Invisible Hands: The Making of the Conservative Movement from the New Deal to Reagan*. Norton, 2009.

Pierceson, Jason. *Courts Liberalism and Rights: Gay Law and Politics in the United States and Canada*. Temple University Press, 2005.

Pierceson, Jason, Adriana Piatti-Crocker, and Shawn Schulenberg. *Same-Sex Marriage in the Americas: Policy Innovation for Same-Sex Relationships*. Lexington Books, 2010.

Polletta, Francesca. *It Was Like a Fever: Storytelling in Protest and Politics*. University of Chicago Press, 2006.

——. "Storytelling in Social Movements." In *Culture, Social Movements, and Protest*, edited by Hank Johnston, 33–53. Ashgate, 2009.

Polletta, Francesca, and Beth Gharrity Gardner. "Culture and Movements." In *Emerging Trends in the Social and Behavioral Sciences*, edited by Robert Scott and Stephen Kosslyn, 1–13. John Wiley & Sons, 2015. https://doi.org/10.1002/9781118900772.etrds0108.

Powell, Brian, Catherine Bolzendahl, Claudia Geist, and Lala Carr Steelman. *Counted Out: Same-Sex Relations and Americans' Definitions of Family*. Russel Sage Foundation, 2010.

Prearo, Massimo. *Le moment politique de l'homosexualité: Mouvements, identités, et communautés en France*. Presses Universitaires de Lyon, 2014.

Prentice, Deborah A. "Liberal Norms and Their Discontents." *Perspectives on Psychological Science* 7, no. 5 (September 1, 2012): 516–18. https://doi.org/10.1177/1745691612454142.

Quinqueton, Denis. "L'éthique de notre engagement." *Le Monde.Fr*, February 14, 2013. http://www.lemonde.fr/idees/article/2013/02/14/l-ethique-de-notre-engagement_1832580_3232.html.

Ramsey, Sarah H., and Robert F. Kelly. "Social Science Knowledge in Family Law Cases: Judicial Gate-Keeping in the Daubert Era." *University of Miami Law Review* 59 (2005 2004): 1.

Randles, Jennifer. *Proposing Prosperity?: Marriage Education Policy and Inequality in America.* Columbia University Press, 2016.

Rebuccini, Gianfranco. "Du 'mariage pour tous' à la 'famille pour tout le monde?' Pour une politique queer populaire des parentés dépareillées." *Eigensinn* 1, no. 1 (2022): 111–31.

Regnerus, Mark. "How Different Are the Adult Children of Parents Who Have Same-Sex Relationships? Findings from the New Family Structures Study." *Social Science Research* 41, no. 4 (2012): 752–70. https://doi.org/10.1016/j.ssresearch.2012.03.009.

Rich, Andrew. "Ideas, Expertise, and Think Tanks." In *Ideas and Politics in Social Science Research*, edited by Daniel Béland and Robert Henry Cox, 191–207. Oxford University Press, 2010.

Richman, Kimberly D. *Courting Change: Queer Parents, Judges, and the Transformation of American Family Law.* New York University Press, 2009.

Rioux, Jean-Sébastien, and Douglas A. Van Belle. "The Influence of Le Monde Coverage on French Foreign Aid Allocations." *International Studies Quarterly* 49, no. 3 (September 1, 2005): 481–502. https://doi.org/10.1111/j.1468-2478.2005.00374.x.

Robcis, Camille. *The Law of Kinship: Anthropology, Psychoanalysis, and the Family in France.* Cornell University Press, 2013.

——. "Liberté, Égalité, Hétérosexualité: Race and Reproduction in the French Gay Marriage Debates." *Constellations* 22, no. 3 (September 1, 2015): 447–61. https://doi.org/10.1111/1467-8675.12168.

Roberts, Dorothy E. *Killing the Black Body: Race, Reproduction, and the Meaning of Liberty.* Pantheon, 1997.

Rodriguez, Nathian Shae, and Lindsey Blumell. "What a Year! The Framing of Marriage Equality Through Media's Selected Sources in 2013." *Journal of Communication Inquiry* 38, no. 4 (October 1, 2014): 341–59. https://doi.org/10.1177/0196859914551767.

Rosenfeld, Michael J. "Nontraditional Families and Childhood Progress Through School." *Demography* 47, no. 3 (2010): 755–75. https://doi.org/10.1353/dem.0.0112.

——. *The Rainbow After the Storm: Marriage Equality and Social Change in the U.S.* Oxford University Press, 2021.

——. "Reply to Allen et al." *Demography* 50, no. 3 (June 2013): 963–69. https://doi.org/10.1007/s13524-012-0170-4.

Roudinesco, Elisabeth. *La Bataille de Cent Ans: Histoire de la psychanalyse en France, 2.* Seuil, 1986.

Roux, Sébastien. *Sang d'encre: Enquête sur la fin de l'adoption internationale.* Vendémiaire, 2022.

Russo, Nancy Felipe, and Jean E. Denious. "Controlling Birth: Science, Politics, and Public Policy." *Journal of Social Issues* 61, no. 1 (2005): 181–91. https://doi.org/10.1111/j.0022-4537.2005.00400.x.

Saguy, Abigail C. "Puritanism and Promiscuity? Sexual Attitude in France and the United States." *Comparative Social Research* 18 (1999): 227–47.

——. *What Is Sexual Harassment?: From Capitol Hill to the Sorbonne.* University of California Press, 2003.

——. *What's Wrong with Fat?* Oxford University Press, 2013.

Sanders, Joseph. "Expert Witness Ethics." *Fordham Law Review* 76 (2008): 1539.

Sapiro, Gisèle. "Modèles d'intervention politique des intellectuels." *Actes de la recherche en sciences sociales* 176–177, no. 1 (March 6, 2009): 8–31.

Sarewitz, Daniel, and Roger A. Pielke Jr. "The Neglected Heart of Science Policy: Reconciling Supply of and Demand for Science." *Environmental Science and Policy*, Reconciling the Supply of and Demand for Science, with a Focus on Carbon Cycle Research, 10, no. 1 (February 2007): 5–16. https://doi.org/10.1016/j.envsci.2006.10.001.

Schilt, Paige. "Sociologist Judith Stacey: Get Rid of Marital Privilege." The Bilerico Project, March 25, 2017. http://www.bilerico.com/2014/03/unhitching_the_movement_from_marital _privilege.php.

Schmidt, Peter. "Professors' Growing Risk: Harassment for Things They Never Really Said." *The Chronicle of Higher Education*, June 22, 2017. http://www.chronicle.com/article/Professors -Growing-Risk-/240424/.

Schwartz, Mildred A., and Raymond Tatalovich. *The Rise and Fall of Moral Conflicts in the United States and Canada*. University of Toronto Press, 2018.

Scott, Joan Wallach. *Parité!: Sexual Equality and the Crisis of French Universalism*. The University of Chicago Press, 2005.

——, ed. *Women's Studies on the Edge*. Duke University Press, 2008.

Seyman, Ingrid. "Homoparentalité: Dessine-moi tes mamans!" *MarieClaire.Fr*, September 3, 2013. http://www.marieclaire.fr/,homoparentalite-dessine-moi-tes-mamans,697050.asp#?slide=7.

Shapin, Steven. *A Social History of Truth: Civility and Science in Seventeenth-Century England*. Science and Its Conceptual Foundations Series. University of Chicago Press, 1995.

——. "Cordelia's Love: Credibility and the Social Studies of Science." *Perspectives on Science* 3, no. 3 (1995): 255–75.

Sheldrick, Byron. "Law, Representation, and Political Activism: Community-Based Practice and the Mobilization of Legal Resources." *Canadian Journal of Law and Society/Revue Canadienne Droit et Societe* 10, no. 2 (1995): 155–84.

Shwom, Rachael, David Bidwell, Amy Dan, and Thomas Dietz. "Understanding U.S. Public Support for Domestic Climate Change Policies." *Global Environmental Change*, Governance, Complexity and Resilience, 20, no. 3 (August 1, 2010): 472–82. https://doi.org/10.1016/j .gloenvcha.2010.02.003.

Simon, Patrick. "The Choice of Ignorance the Debate on Ethnic and Racial Statistics in France." *French Politics, Culture and Society* 26, no. 1 (April 30, 2008): 7–31. https://doi.org/10.3167/fpcs .2008.260102.

Singly, François de. *Sociologie de la famille contemporaine*. 3rd ed. Armand Colin, 2007.

Slaouti, Omar, and Olivier Le Cour Grandmaison, eds. *Racismes de France*. La Découverte, 2020.

Smirnova, Marianna Y., and Sergey Y. Yachin. "Epistemic Communities and Epistemic Operating Mode." *International Journal of Social Science and Humanity* 5, no. 7 (2015): 646–50.

Smith, Anna Marie. *Welfare Reform and Sexual Regulation*. Cambridge University Press, 2007.

Smith, Miriam. *Political Institutions and Lesbian and Gay Rights in the United States and Canada*. Taylor & Francis, 2008.

Stacey, Judith. "Cruising to Familyland: Gay Hypergamy and Rainbow Kinship." *Current Sociology* 52, no. 2 (March 1, 2004): 181–97. https://doi.org/10.1177/0011392104041807.

——. *Unhitched: Love, Marriage, and Family Values from West Hollywood to Western China*. NYU Press, 2011.

Stacey, Judith, and Timothy J. Biblarz. "(How) Does the Sexual Orientation of Parents Matter?" *American Sociological Review* 66, no. 2 (April 2001): 159–83.

Stambolis-Ruhstorfer, Michael. "Labels of Love: How Migrants Negotiate (or Not) the Culture of Sexual Identity." *American Journal of Cultural Sociology* 1, no. 3 (October 2013): 321–45. https://doi.org/10.1057/ajcs.2013.11.

——. "Lesbian and Gay Families in France: Results from the DEVHOM Study." *International Social Science Journal* 70, no. 235–236 (2020): 7–11. https://doi.org/10.1111/issj.12248.

Stambolis-Ruhstorfer, Michael, and Virginie Descoutures. "Licence Required: French Lesbian Parents Confront the Obligation to Marry in Order to Establish Kinship." *International Social Science Journal* 70, no. 235–236 (2020): 79–97. https://doi.org/10.1111/issj.12241.

Stambolis-Ruhstorfer, Michael, and Martine Gross. "Qui lave le linge sale de la famille?" *Travail, genre et societes* 46, no. 2 (November 10, 2021): 75–95.

Stambolis-Ruhstorfer, Michael, and Josselin Tricou. "Resisting 'Gender Theory' in France: A Fulcrum for Religious Action in a Secular Society." In *Anti-Gender Campaigns in Europe*, edited by Roman Kuhar and David Paternotte, 79–98. Rowman & Littlefield, 2017.

Starr, Paul. *The Social Transformation of American Medicine: The Rise of a Sovereign Profession and the Making of a Vast Industry*. Basic Books, 1982.

Steinbugler, Amy C. *Beyond Loving: Intimate Racework in Lesbian, Gay, and Straight Interracial Relationships*. Oxford University Press, 2012.

Stetson, Dorothy McBride. *Abortion Politics, Women's Movements, and the Democratic State: A Comparative Study of State Feminism*. Oxford University Press, 2001.

Stolberg, Sheryl Gay. "Hillary Clinton Backs Same-Sex Marriage." *New York Times*, March 19, 2013, sec. A.

Stoler, Ann Laura. *Race and the Education of Desire: Foucault's History of Sexuality and the Colonial Order of Things*. Duke University Press, 1995.

Stone, Amy L., and Jane Ward. "From 'Black People Are Not a Homosexual Act' to 'Gay Is the New Black': Mapping White Uses of Blackness in Modern Gay Rights Campaigns in the United States." *Social Identities* 17, no. 5 (September 1, 2011): 605–24. https://doi.org/10.1080/13504630.2011.595204.

Stone, Deborah. *Policy Paradox: The Art of Political Decision Making*. 3rd ed. Norton, 2011.

Stryker, Robin, Danielle Docka-Filipek, and Pamela Wald. "Employment Discrimination Law and Industrial Psychology: Social Science as Social Authority and the Co-Production of Law and Science." *Law and Social Inquiry* 37, no. 4 (2012): 777–814. http://dx.doi.org/10.1111/j.1747-4469.2011.01277.x.

Swartz, David L. *Symbolic Power, Politics, and Intellectuals: The Political Sociology of Pierre Bourdieu*. University of Chicago Press, 2013.

Sweet, Paige L. "Who Knows? Reflexivity in Feminist Standpoint Theory and Bourdieu." *Gender and Society* 34, no. 6 (December 1, 2020): 922–50. https://doi.org/10.1177/0891243220966600.

Tarrow, Sidney. "The Strategy of Paired Comparison: Toward a Theory of Practice." *Comparative Political Studies* 43, no. 2 (2010): 230–59.

Teles, Steven M. *The Rise of the Conservative Legal Movement: The Battle for Control of the Law*. Princeton University Press, 2008.

Théry, Irène. *Couple, filiation et parenté aujourd'hui: le droit face aux mutations de la famille et de la vie privée : Rapport à la Ministre de l'emploi et de la solidarité et au Garde dess Sceaux, Ministre de la justice*. Odile Jacob, 1998.

——. "Expertises de service, de consensus, d'engagement: Essai de typologie de la mission d'expertise en sciences sociales." *Droit et société* 60, no. 2 (June 1, 2005): 311–27.

——. "La filiation doit évoluer." *Le Monde*, February 10, 2013, sec. Débats.

Théry, Irène, Laurence Brunet, Jérôme Courduriès, et al. "Mariage des personnes de même sexe et filiation: Le projet de loi au prisme des sciences sociales." École des Hautes Études en Sciences Sociales-Cerles de Formation, December 16, 2012. www.ehess.fr/mariage.

Théry, Irène, and Anne-Marie Leroyer. *Filiation origines parentalité: Le Droit face aux nouvelles valeurs de responsabilité générationnelle.* Odile Jacob, 2014.

Thornton, Patricia H., William Ocasio, and Michael Lounsbury. *The Institutional Logics Perspective: A New Approach to Culture, Structure, and Process.* Oxford University Press, 2012.

Tilly, Charles, and Sidney G. Tarrow. *Contentious Politics.* Paradigm Publishers, 2007.

Tocqueville, Alexis de. *De la démocratie en Amérique.* Edited by Eduardo Nolla. Revised. Vrin, 1990.

Tremblay, Manon, David Paternotte, and Carol Johnson, eds. *The Lesbian and Gay Movement and the State: Comparative Insights into a Transformative Relationship.* Ashgate, 2011.

UNAF. "Les questions du mariage, de la filiation et de l'autorité parentale pour les couples de même sexe." Union Nationale des Associations Familiales, October 29, 2012. http://www.unaf.fr/IMG/pdf/dossier_d_analyse___mariage_et_filiation_v_finale.pdf.

Vargas-Cooper, Natasha. "Raw Drama of Case Against Proposition 8 Given a Slice of Hollywood A-List Ham." *The Guardian*, March 4, 2012, sec. World news. https://www.theguardian.com/world/2012/mar/04/proposition-8-hollywood-stars-staged-reading.

Vecho, Olivier, and Benoît Schneider. "Attitudes Toward Gay and Lesbian Parents: A Comparison among French and Quebec Psychologists." *Canadian Journal of Behavioural Science* 47, no. 1 (2015): 102–12. https://doi.org/10.1037/a0037607.

——. "Homoparentalité et développement de l'enfant: Bilan de trente ans de publications." *La psychiatrie de l'enfant* 48, no. 1 (March 1, 2005): 271–328. https://doi.org/10.3917/psye.481.0271.

Verjus, Anne, and Marine Boisson. "Quand connaître, c'est reconnaître ? Le rôle de l'expertise familiale dans la production d'un sens commun du parent (homosexuel)." *Droit et société* 60, no. 2 (June 1, 2005): 449–67.

Verloo, Mieke. "Gender Knowledge, and Opposition to the Feminist Project: Extreme-Right Populist Parties in the Netherlands." *Politics and Governance* 6, no. 3 (September 14, 2018): 20–30. https://doi.org/10.17645/pag.v6i3.1456.

Vogler, Stefan. *Sorting Sexualities: Expertise and the Politics of Legal Classification.* University of Chicago Press, 2021.

Wagner, Peter, Carol Hirschon Weiss, Björn Wittrock, and Hellmut Wollmann, eds. *Social Sciences and Modern States: National Experiences and Theoretical Crossroads.* Cambridge University Press, 1991.

Waidzunas, Tom. *The Straight Line: How the Fringe Science of Ex-Gay Therapy Reoriented Sexuality.* University of Minnesota Press, 2015.

Walker, Edward T., and Andrew N. Le. "Poisoning the Well: How Astroturfing Harms Trust in Advocacy Organizations." *Social Currents* 10, no. 2 (April 1, 2023): 184–202. https://doi.org/10.1177/23294965221123808.

Walzer, Lee. *Gay Rights on Trial: A Reference Handbook.* ABC-CLIO's on Trial Series. ABC-CLIO, 2002.

Ward, Jeremy K., and Patrick Peretti-Watel. "Understanding Vaccine Mistrust: From Perception Bias to Controversies." *Revue francaise de sociologie* 61, no. 2 (October 6, 2020): 243–73.

Warner, Michael. "Normal and Normaller: Beyond Gay Marriage." *GLQ: A Journal of Lesbian and Gay Studies* 5, no. 2 (1999): 119–71.

Weber, Lauren, Laurie McGinley, David Ovalle, and Frances Stead Sellers. "Unpacking the Flawed Science Cited in the Texas Abortion Pill Ruling." *Washington Post*, April 13, 2023. https://www.washingtonpost.com/health/2023/04/13/abortion-pill-safety/.

Wiest, Sara L., Leigh Raymond, and Rosalee A. Clawson. "Framing, Partisan Predispositions, and Public Opinion on Climate Change." *Global Environmental Change* 31 (March 1, 2015): 187–98. https://doi.org/10.1016/j.gloenvcha.2014.12.006.

Williams, Juliet A., and Paul Apostolidis. "Introduction: Sex Scandals and Discourses of Power." In *Public Affairs: Politics in the Age of Sex Scandals*, edited by Juliet A. Williams and Paul Apostolidis, 1–38. Duke University Press Books, 2004.

Winter, Jean-Pierre. *Homoparenté*. Albin Michel, 2010.

——. "Ne jouons pas aux apprentis sorciers!" *Le Monde*, October 23, 2010.

Woessner, Matthew, and April Kelly-Woessner. "Reflections on Academic Liberalism and Conservative Criticism." *Society* 52, no. 1 (February 1, 2015): 35–41. https://doi.org/10.1007/s12115-014-9864-0.

Woll, Cornelia. "Lobbying in the European Union: From Sui Generis to a Comparative Perspective." *Journal of European Public Policy* 13, no. 3 (April 1, 2006): 456–69. https://doi.org/10.1080/13501760600560623.

Wuest, Joanna. *Born This Way: Science, Citizenship, and Inequality in the American LGBTQ+ Movement*. University of Chicago Press, 2023.

Yoshino, Kenji. *Speak Now: Marriage Equality on Trial*. Broadway Books, 2015.

Young, Neil J. *Coming Out Republican: A History of the Gay Right*. University of Chicago Press, 2024.

Yvert, Emmanuelle. "Des mobilisations victorieuses sans mouvement social. La construction de la cause de l'homoparentalité et sa traduction législative en France (1986–2013)." PhD Dissertation, Université Paris-Saclay, 2021. https://theses.fr/2021UPASU006.

Zald, Mayer N., and Michael Lounsbury. "The Wizards of Oz: Towards an Institutional Approach to Elites, Expertise and Command Posts." *Organization Studies* 31, no. 7 (July 1, 2010): 963–96. https://doi.org/10.1177/0170840610373201.

Zippel, Kathrin S. *The Politics of Sexual Harassment: A Comparative Study of the United States, The European Union, and Germany*. Cambridge University Press, 2006.

INDEX

Page numbers in *italics* refer to tables or illustrations.

politicized science, 5–6
politics of politics, 211
Price, Joseph, 169
principle of precaution, 91–92
Proposition 2, in Texas, 62
Proposition 8, in California, 41, 68, 100, 107, 109, 111, 114, 165; Morse and, 202
psychoanalysis, 80, 85, 93, 146, 223, 226; on adoption, 88; Berger and, 41–42, 177; on children, 196–97; Delaisi de Parseval and, 120, 123, 175; Eliacheff and, 144; Hefez and, 117, 118, 175, 187; Lacan and, 3; Lepastier and, 86; Lesourd and, 43–44; in media, 43–44; on parenting, 35; in United States, 86–87; Winter and, 1, 34. See also Flavigny, Christian; Lévy-Soussan, Pierre
psychological research, 44–45
public opinion: experts and, 4, 5; in France, 41; media and, 37; on parenting, 25–27; in United States, 41

Quinqueton, Denis, 121

racial minorities, 16
Ramos, Lydia, 66
rapporteurs, 127, 129–31, 133, 187; on scientific experts, 200
Raquin, Jean, 56–57
Reagan, Ronald, 105, 219
Regnerus, Mark, 77, 106, 112, 142, 180; ASA and, 154, 167, 168; gender theory and, 177; NFSS and, 169; Witherspoon Institute and, 192–93
Rekers, George, 209
religion, 5–6, 35; adoption and, 272n3; in California, 69; children and, 210; in courts, 76; decision makers and, 224; expert capital and, 11; in France, 88–89, 128, 226; in legislatures, 69, 88–89; marriage culture in, 27; in media, 36, 49–50, 53–56, 226; Pacs hearings and, 132; scientific experts and, 208–11; in

Texas, 62, 69; in United States, 158, 226; universities of, 143. See also specific religions
remarriage, 124
renown. See elite/celebrity experts
reproductive technologies: in France, 24–25, 86, 91. See also specific types
Republican Party, 39, 141; in California, 67, 69; DOMA and, 71–72; gays in, 164
Respect for Marriage Act (RFMA), 73, 268n114
Robcis, Camille, 264n73
Romero, Jean-Luc, 56
Rosenfeld, Michael, 15–16, 111, 112–13, 142; at DeBoer v. Snyder, 188–89; on elite experts, 189; on scientific consensus on children, 149–50; on scientific experts, 205, 206, 227–28; on social acceptance of gay families, 151
Roudinesco, Elisabeth, 146, 173
Rowse, Jayne, 103, 219
Ruth Institute, 68, 98, 168, 169; scientific experts and, 202

Salvator, 178
same-sex marriage. See specific topics
Sarkozy, Nicolas, 176
School of Advanced Studies in the Social Sciences (École des Hautes Études en Sciences Sociales), 48, 175, 184
Schulz, Marianne, 122
science and technology studies (STS), 12–13
scientific consensus, 63, 77; on children, 111, 136, 149–50, 194, 228; scientific experts and, 228
scientific experts, 136–37; bias and neutrality of, 200–205; on climate change, 229; in courts, 79, 137, 204–5; credibility of, 190, 194–215, 221; decision-makers and, 4, 180, 223–24; democracy and, 227–31; expert capital of, 183, 191; in France, 194–200, 223–24; heterosexual family standard of, 228–29; homosexual disqualification for, 205–8; legal experts and, 164–65; in

GPSR Authorized Representative: Easy Access System Europe, Mustamäe tee 50, 10621 Tallinn, Estonia, gpsr.requests@easproject.com

www.ingramcontent.com/pod-product-compliance
Lightning Source LLC
Chambersburg PA
CBHW022136020426
42334CB00015B/916